AQA A2
PHILOSOPHY

AQA A2
PHILOSOPHY

Daniel Cardinal
Gerald Jones
Jeremy Hayward

HODDER
EDUCATION
AN HACHETTE UK COMPANY

Acknowledgements

The Publishers would like to thank the following for permission to reproduce copyright material.

Text credits: pp.6, 49, 50, 62, 339: Peter Singer: from *Unsanctifying Human Life*, ed. H. Kuhse (John Wiley and Sons, 2002); **pp.25, 26, 27, 28, 29, 35, 48, 58, 181, 182, 281, 338, 343: John Stuart Mill:** from *Utilitarianism*, ed. Mary Warnock (HarperCollins, 1972); **p.54: Press Association:** from 'Blunkett tells of joy at Shipman death' from *The Guardian* (The Guardian, 16th January 2004); **p.62: Peter Singer:** from 'Great apes deserve life, liberty and the prohibition of torture' from *The Guardian* (The Guardian, 27th May 2006); **p.111: Ethan Coen and Joel Coen:** from the film from *Miller's Crossing* (20th Century Fox, 1990); **p.164: Matt McCormick:** from 'Is it wrong to play violent video games?' from *Ethics and Information Technology, Volume 3 Issue 4* (Kluwer Academic Publishers, 2001); **pp.177, 201, 203, 291, 345: A.J. Ayer:** from *Language, Trust and Logic* (Penguin, 1990); **pp.183, 189, 190, 192, 193, 194, 343: George Edward Moore:** from *Principia Ethica* (Forgotten Books, 2015); **pp.207, 208, 210, 346: R.M. Hare:** from *The Language of Morals* (Oxford, 1963); **pp.242, 346, 348: David Chalmers:** from 'Consciousness and its place in nature', as quoted in from *The Blackwell Guide to Philosophy of Mind*, eds. S. Stitch and T. Warfield (John Wiley and Sons, 2003); **pp.247, 278, 349–50: F. Jackson:** from 'Epiphenomenal Qualia' from *The Philosophical Quarterly, Vol. 32, No. 127* (Oxford Journals, April 1982); **pp.329, 335, 336: Paul Churchland:** from 'Eliminative Materialism and the Propositional Attitudes' from *The Journal of Philosophy, Vol. 78, No.2* (Journal of Philosophy, February 1981); **pp.296, 299, 347, 350–1: Gilbert Ryle:** from The *Concept of Mind* (Penguin, 2000); **pp.302, 306, 308, 316, 352–3: J.C. Smart and Hilary Putnam:** as quoted in from *Philosophy of Mind: A Guide and Anthology*, ed. John Heil (Oxford University Press, 2003); **pp.313, 353–4: Ned Block:** 'Trouble with Functionalism', as quoted in 'Perception and Cognition: Issues in the Foundations of Psychology', *Minnesota Studies in the Philosophy of Science*, Vol. IX, edited by C. W. Savage (University of Minnesota Press, 1978).

Every effort has been made to trace all copyright holders, but if any have been inadvertently overlooked, the Publishers will be pleased to make the necessary arrangements at the first opportunity.

Although every effort has been made to ensure that website addresses are correct at time of going to press, Hodder Education cannot be held responsible for the content of any website mentioned in this book. It is sometimes possible to find a relocated web page by typing in the address of the home page for a website in the URL window of your browser.

Hachette UK's policy is to use papers that are natural, renewable and recyclable products and made from wood grown in sustainable forests. The logging and manufacturing processes are expected to conform to the environmental regulations of the country of origin.

Orders: please contact Bookpoint Ltd, 130 Milton Park, Abingdon, Oxon OX14 4SB. Telephone: +44 (0)1235 827720. Fax: +44 (0)1235 400454. Email education@bookpoint. co.uk Lines are open from 9 a.m. to 5 p.m., Monday to Saturday, with a 24-hour message answering service. You can also order through our website: www.hoddereducation.co.uk

© Daniel Cardinal, Gerald Jones, Jeremy Hayward 2015

First published in 2015 by Hodder Education,
An Hachette UK Company
Carmelite House
50 Victoria Embankment
London EC4Y 0DZ

www.hoddereducation.co.uk

Impression number   10   9   8   7   6   5   4

Year   2019   2018   2017

Cover photo © Vectorfactory/iStockphoto.com

Illustrations by Peter Lubach, Barking Dog Art, Tony Randell and Richard Duszczak

Typeset in Chaparral Pro Light 11/13pt by Aptara, Inc.

Printed and bound by CPI Group (UK) Ltd, Croydon, CR0 4YY

A catalogue record for this title is available from the British Library.

ISBN 978 1471 85285 5

Contents

Introduction

For the first part of the A-level, you will have studied *Epistemology* and *Philosophy of Religion*. For the second part our attention turns to two of the biggest philosophical questions: what is the right thing to do? and what is my mind made of? These, and other questions, will be explored in the units of *Ethics* and *Philosophy of Mind*.

Descartes' *Meditations* underpinned many areas of the AS course and it is also a seminal text in the *Philosophy of Mind*. His contribution to the field of ethics is less significant, although Descartes was pivotal in shaping the intellectual climate in which ethics could be discussed from a human, rather than divine, perspective.

Descartes' writing represented an important change in the intellectual history of western society, marking the 'epistemological turn', where questions of method started to take priority over metaphysical assumptions and religious beliefs. The *Meditations* embodies this desire to break from the past and start an enquiry from first principles. Although Descartes articulated this new philosophy, he was not alone; others were also breaking from the past and applying reason to the world. The progress of this new approach was most noticeable in the field of science (or natural philosophy as it was then called). Galileo, who was under house arrest at the time Descartes was writing, had started to explore the universe using a new technology (the telescope) and made many important discoveries. This scientific advance was continued by a range of other thinkers, including Descartes, and took a massive leap forward in the writing of Isaac Newton – whose theories and formulae appeared to unlock the secrets of the universe.

The works of Descartes and Newton are often taken to mark the beginning of the *age of enlightenment*. This was a time of great optimism about the potential for human reason. It was triggered by Descartes' attempt to start the quest for knowledge from a human perspective, and also by Newton showing just what was possible when human reason was applied to the world.

Although Descartes wrote little on ethics, the writings of Kant and the Utilitarians, explored in this book, are perfect examples of enlightenment philosophy. In different ways they both use reason to bring order and meaning to the vast and complex arena of human morality and develop systems of ethics that are grounded in the human condition (rather than religion).

In the philosophy of mind Descartes' ideas are still discussed today. He articulated the theory of Cartesian dualism (*Cartesian* means 'of Descartes'). Dualism separates the world in two: there is the physical world, which has mathematical properties such as size, shape and so on, and there is the immaterial world, the world of the soul/mind, which does not exist in space. Of course, beliefs in the existence of a spiritual realm are not new, they are among the oldest recorded and are still held by billions of religious believes today. Descartes, however, was the first to give a clear account of the distinction between the two worlds. Descartes' dualism also helped to make the developments of science more acceptable to the religious authorities of the day. The physical, material world could be discovered and understood by the human mind, but the immaterial world of the soul/mind was out of the reach of the scientists and so could remain the domain of religion.

This dualist approach was widely accepted in Descartes' day and its legacy continues to influence contemporary philosophy of mind. However, during in the last 100 years, as science has discovered more about the brain, the idea of a mind existing as part of another realm has appeared increasingly hard to defend. But amidst all the progress in neuroscience, the 'hard problem' of consciousness still remains. We feel and experience a wide range of thoughts and sensations which just don't seen to be physical in nature. How is this possible? Why is this necessary? Why aren't our brains just like efficient calculators helping us to survive, but without having any conscious experiences? This hard problem of *consciousness* is very much alive today, and, until consciousness can be satisfactorily explained physically, it seems dualism will still be taken seriously.

Using the book

This book is divided in two sections, matching the two units of the A2 specification. We have tried to follow the specification as closely as possible in setting out the different sections of the book. The A-level course is accompanied by a number of key texts, many of which are available online. To aid your understanding we engage with these texts frequently through the book and also provide an anthology section which contains important passages. Scattered throughout the book are activities and more involved 'Experimenting with ideas' sections. These are designed to help stimulate thought and provide an opportunity to apply the ideas to a range of case studies/scenarios. It is through this process of application and reflection that philosophy becomes not just something you read about, but something you live and feel. We hope you enjoy the book.

Key to features

Activity

A practical task to help you to understand the arguments or concepts under investigation.

Experimenting with ideas

Plays around with some of the concepts discussed; looks at them from different angles.

Criticism

Criticism

Highlights and evaluates the issues raised by an argument or a concept.

Quotation

A direct quotation from a key thinker.

Learn More

Learn more

Introduces related ideas or arguments that aren't required by the A-Level specification, but which provides useful additional material.

anthology
0.00

Anthology extracts

When you see the Anthology icon in the margin of the book then you should refer to the relevant extract in the Anthology extracts section at the end of the book.

Glossary

Words or phrases that appear in **bold** are key terms and ideas that are explained in the Glossary at the end of the book.

Section 1: Ethics

1.1 Ethical theories: How do we decide what it is morally right to do?

Introduction

We *all* want to do the **right** thing, surely? Don't we? Well, maybe you do, maybe you don't. The problem is, though, what *is* the right thing to do? *Don't steal, don't lie, eat your greens, don't speak back, be honest, clean behind your ears* and so on. There is no shortage of advice for what the right thing might be from parents, friends, teachers, preachers, politicians and celebrities (among others).

Ethics is the branch of philosophy that explores what the right thing to do might be and this section will explore several ethical systems that attempt this project. In ordinary language, and in many textbooks, the word *morality* is sometimes used instead of *ethics*. Indeed, in the world of philosophy, *ethics* is sometimes called *moral philosophy*. The distinction between morality and ethics is not very clear, nor is it very important. The term *morality* tends to be associated more with an individual's beliefs about right and wrong, whereas *ethics* is more associated with systems that articulate right and wrong. However, this distinction is not universally held and often the two terms are used synonymously. We will also use the terms interchangeably.

As a topic to study, ethics is not just of 'philosophical' relevance; it also has a clear, practical application. There are times in everyone's life when they face big ethical **dilemmas**: should you put your ageing mother in a care home? Should you lend a large sum of money to a friend in need? Other ethical dilemmas may be encountered on a more regular basis: should I buy free range eggs? Should I recycle? It can be argued that ethical dilemmas surround us at every moment, although we may not be consciously aware of them. Should I study a bit harder? Should I speak to Zach after what he said? Should I look at this picture of a semi-naked person? What should I do with my life? Studying ethics should shine some light on these and other questions. At the very least it should help to clarify your thinking.

Ethics and the self: The scope of morality

Experimenting with ideas: The wipe-out

Imagine humanity has succumbed to a deadly virus and you are the only person left in the world. You survived because you were alone on a remote desert island at the time, as part of a soul-searching retreat. Does this new situation change the ethical world you inhabit? You might still face lots of dilemmas in your life: should I sleep in a cave, or on the beach tonight? Should I keep myself fit? Should I have one more coconut before bedtime? Tough choices! However, would these count as *moral* dilemmas?

Imagine you are the last person on earth.

Would you have any clear cut ethical dilemmas?

Would there be anything morally wrong with just following your desires all the time?

Could you do anything morally wrong?

Is morality a human invention?

Do the terms good and bad only have meaning in a society?

There are monkeys on the island. Would you kill and eat them?

It is not easy to answer these questions without already having an account of what an ethical action is. Maybe it *is* possible to do wrong as the last surviving human: perhaps self-harm? Blaspheming? Having nasty thoughts? Hurting the animals? Some would argue that you still face the key decision about how you *ought* to live your life. Yes, you want to eat nice food and stay alive, but what would you ultimately aim for? Pleasure? Self-improvement? Trying to help the animals? and so on. Morality in the widest sense includes this big question of what you should pursue in life. If this fundamental decision is a moral one, this, in turn, makes most actions morally relevant.

Ethics and others

Experimenting with ideas: The wipe-out revisited

Imagine that after two years of living alone on the island, with no one but Ruffles your faithful parrot to talk to, a large boat arrives carrying four people. These people were at sea when the virus struck and have survived all this time on the ship's resources. They are severely malnourished and are pleased to be on dry land. They are also insistent that you have to kill all the birds on the island, as they can spread the deadly virus.

Would you welcome these people?

Would you have any ethical dilemmas going forward?

Would there be anything morally wrong with just following your desires all the time now?

Could you do anything morally wrong?

Would you be willing to kill Ruffles, your parrot?

Most people would suggest that with the arrival of more people, your ethical universe expanded. This is to be expected as ethics, in the narrower sense, can be seen as how we *should* interact with others. These new people on the island have desires too and these may conflict with yours. You may have to modify your behaviour.

Character and virtue

After two years alone, your behaviour would no doubt be different from how it was before the virus struck. Your table manners may have lapsed a bit. You may not take much pride in your physical appearance. Your conversation may be very limited. Growing up in civilisation, through training, education and habit, you would have acquired certain ways of behaving. Some of these might be **good** (**virtues**), some might be less good (vices). However, it is likely that many of these habits have changed since you have been alone. Another feature of the strangers arriving on the island is that you may have to redevelop some characteristics (or acquire them if you never had them to begin with) in order to interact well. You may have to make yourself polite or a better listener leadership skills on consideration for others. Now that the strangers are here, being a 'good person' on the island may involve developing, or redeveloping some important virtues.

Three levels of ethical discussion

Some of the questions we asked above probe different aspects of ethics. Traditionally these are divided into three areas. One area explores what makes for morally good and bad behaviour in general. What are the underlying reasons why we might call an action a good one? This area is known as **normative ethics**. A second area applies the answers from the first area to very specific **moral dilemmas**. This area is known as **applied ethics**. A third area takes a step back from the discussions above and, instead, focuses the attention on moral discussion itself, asking questions such as: *is morality a human construction*? *Do moral words have meanings*? This area is known as **meta-ethics**.

Figure 1.1 The three levels of ethics
(A) Meta-ethics asks questions about morality itself.
(B) Normative ethics seeks to answer questions about good and bad in general. (C) Applied ethics works out how to apply the answer from (B) to the specific cases.

▶ **ACTIVITY**

Revisit the questions in the 'wipe-out' scenarios on page 2.

Which questions belong to the area of normative ethics, which to applied ethics and which to meta-ethics?

This section explores all three areas of ethical thought. The first chapters examine some of the big normative theories of ethics – **utilitarianism**, **Kantian ethics** and **virtue ethics**. The last part of each of these chapters applies these theories to a series of specific topics and dilemmas (applied ethics). The final part explores some of the key questions of meta-ethics.

Normative ethics – different approaches

The bulk of this section is devoted to examining three key ethical theories. These theories differ in several ways, but a key distinction is that they focus on different aspects of what might make an action a *moral* one. Some actions in life clearly belong in the moral arena (*stealing* or *lying, etc.*), whereas others don't appear to have any moral relevance (*scratching your ear* or *staring at the extra full stop at the end of this sentence*).. So what makes an action a moral one (good *or* bad), as opposed to a morally neutral one (neither good nor bad)?

Experimenting with ideas

For each of the ten scenarios below:

    a) Decide if it is morally relevant (good or bad), or morally neutral.
    b) For those that are morally relevant, decide what makes the scenario a moral one.
    c) For those that are morally neutral, decide what makes it neutral.

1 A deer is caught in a forest fire caused by a freak lightning strike and is burnt to death.

2 A killer whale toys with a seal that it has half killed – batting it into the air with its tail and catching it with its teeth. It takes 20 minutes before the seal finally dies. The whale leaves it to rot on the ocean floor.

3 You deliberately step on someone's toe in a lift but pretend it was an accident.

4 You accidentally poison your neighbour's dog.

5 You beat your friend in an ant-killing competition (with a winning combination of bleach and boiling water).

6 You persistently bullied a classmate at school.

7 You successfully pass the ball to members of your team 15 times in a 1–1 draw at a friendly local hockey match.

8 An orphanage is set up to help victims in a war-torn country.

9 You stop to help a blind man cross the road but fail to notice the unstoppable juggernaut that injures you both.

10 An evil scientist releases a new bio-chemical into the water supply of a large city intending to kill millions. However, this agent, when diluted, turns out to be a harmless cure for cancer and countless lives are saved.

Many would label scenarios 1 and 2 as morally neutral, as neither event was caused by a moral **agent** – a being with sufficient awareness to carry out moral actions. In this way we do not hold very young children, or those with severe brain damage, morally responsible for their actions – as they are not moral agents. Scenarios 3 and 4 explore the idea of intentions. Not only do you need an agent, but most would claim that to make an act a moral one, the agent must have intended to do the act. Situations 5 and 6 seem to have agents with intentions, but the question of morality may hinge on what you classify as a moral patient (that is, a thing capable of being at the end of moral actions). For some, this would not include ants. Scenarios 7 and 8 involve intentional agents and patients, but explore the idea that the consequences of an action may dictate whether it is moral or not. Scenario 8 involves helping the suffering, whereas scenario 7 doesn't seem to have any morally relevant consequences. Finally, scenarios 9 and 10 involve intentional agents, patients and relevant consequences but explore the idea that the motive (the nature of the intention) is the key factor.

Overall, the key features that seem to make an action a *moral* one are:

- Agency
- Intentions/motives
- Consequences
- Moral patients

Each of the three theories of normative ethics examined in this chapter puts a different emphasis on these features:

- Utilitarianism claims that the consequence of an action is the important element. Only the consequences determine the moral worth of an action (i.e. whether it was good or bad).
- For Kant, motive is the key. Only actions carried out for the right motive have moral worth; the consequences are irrelevant.
- For virtue ethics, it is the agent and their character that is key. As we briefly explored in the virus scenario, having new people come to the island may require you to (re)develop virtues in order to be a good person. For virtue ethics, the character of the person/ agent is the key, not specific actions.

Intuitions

Each of the theories we explore will tell us what is good or bad, however you will already have your own thoughts on these issues. We all have moral intuitions. The status of these intuitions is itself an area of philosophical discussion (which we will not go into) and these intuitions will play an important part in the examination of the theories that follow. We should not expect an ethical theory to match your intuitions *exactly*, but if a theory claims that certain actions are good, whereas you completely disagree, then this presents a problem. Do you ditch your intuitions and go with the theory? Or should you try to modify the theory to better match your intuitions? A theory that strays too far from intuitions will never have appeal, but a theory that resembles them too closely can be seen as supporting the status quo, rather than aiming for a better world. Probably the most significant ethical philosopher alive today is the Australian, Peter Singer. His claims frequently challenge people's intuitions, but he makes no apology for this:

> If we have a soundly based moral theory we ought to be prepared to accept its implications even if they force us to change our moral view on major issues. Once this point is forgotten, moral philosophy loses its capacity to generate radical criticism of prevailing moral standards, and serves only to preserve the status quo.[1]
>
> Singer

Moral dilemmas

Before exploring any of the three ethical theories, read the scenarios in the Activities below and make a note of what your intuitions tell you. Note, we will return to these scenarios after exploring each theory and you can compare the results to your intuitions. Maybe your ideas will change as a result, or maybe you will reject each theory as not matching up to your own moral ideals.

Crime and punishment

Ethics has a close association with crime and punishment. The morality of a society is often reflected in what is classed as a criminal offence, and the law slowly changes to reflect the evolving moral climate (often lagging behind). For example, homosexual sex was punishable by death in the UK 150 years ago, but now has the same legal status as heterosexual sex. However, the symmetry between morality and law is not perfect, in part because:

- Not everything considered immoral is illegal (e.g. *having an affair*).
- Some things may be considered immoral only *because* they are illegal (e.g. *smoking marijuana*, which some people may not think of as immoral in itself).
- Individual morality may clash with the law (e.g. *conscientious objectors*) and some are prepared to break the law to change it (e.g. *the suffragettes*).

The lack of perfect symmetry between law and morality raises the possibility of unjust laws and also the question of whether it is ever morally right to break the law. However, criminal laws alone would achieve very little if they were not accompanied by some sort of punishment. Punishment involves doing something that the person being punished doesn't want; something they find physically or emotionally painful. How can we justify doing hurtful things to people in this way?

Theories of justification are traditionally divided into those that look *backwards* in their reasoning (most closely associated with the idea of punishment as retribution or 'pay back'), and those that look *forward*. Justifications based around making the future better include:

- deterrence (it stops the person repeating, or others committing the crime)
- prevention (preventing crime by keeping someone locked up)
- restoration (giving money back to the victim)
- reform (to prevent that person repeating again).

The ultimate punishment is the death penalty, which many feel is immoral. **Arguments** for the death penalty can be constructed using most of the justificatory principles above (apart from reform!), but is it ever morally right to kill a person in the name of the law?

▶ ACTIVITY

Test your moral intuitions on these two fictional scenarios.

CP1 During a ten-year period, Jon Mason killed over 26 children while working as a nurse in a hospital. He concealed his crimes well and his motive seems to have been delight in seeing the suffering of the parents. His crimes shocked the nation, and a hastily called referendum on the re-introduction of the death penalty resulted in a change in law. The death penalty can now be used in exceptional cases on the instruction of the home secretary. You are the home secretary. *Do you use the death penalty on Jon Mason?*

CP2 (This example is adapted from Lawrence Kohlberg's famous Heinz dilemma.[2]) Your partner has liver cancer. The chances of survival are 50 per cent at best. For the last few months your partner has been on a new medication, Tastaphon, which seemed to be helping. Last week the NHS decided to stop using Tastaphon as the results are inconclusive, and, at £30,000 a year per patient, it is deemed too expensive. Since ending the medication, your partner has deteriorated. You cannot afford to buy the drug privately. This evening a friend, who works on the cancer wing of the hospital is staying over at your house to help. You notice that their hospital pass and keys are on the table. You know the hospital well, and where the drugs are kept. There is a very good chance that you could get hold of lots of Tastaphon this evening, while the cancer wing is quiet. *Should you steal the drug?*

War

War raises many moral questions. Outside of war, the thought of thousands of people killing each other with weapons would be morally unthinkable. Yet in a war this is 'normal'. So is any war ever moral? Is all killing wrong? Is it wrong to kill civilians in a war? Can *any* methods be used in warfare? The ethics of war can be separated into three areas:

1 **Is war ever just?** The idea of a just/fair war is often discussed using the Latin term *jus ad bellum* meaning 'right to war'. This area of thought explores the conditions that might make warfare morally acceptable. Self-defence is a widely accepted reason in most philosophies (except pacifism). Other morally 'legitimate' reasons cited in recent years to justify a particular war include:

■ The defence of another nation (*First Iraq war, 1990–91*)
■ Reasserting previous territorial rights that were taken in war (*Falklands war, 1982*)
■ Defence of widespread human rights abuses by a government (*intervention over Kosovo, 1998–99*)
■ National interest (*Vietnam war, 1955–75*)
■ Asserting liberal values/regime change (*Afghanistan, 2001–14*)
■ If a state breaks the conditions of peace (*Second Iraq war, 2003–11*, though no weapons of mass destruction were found).

2 **Is there a morally right way to wage war**? *Jus in bello*. This area explores whether (once a country is at war) some ways of waging war are morally better or worse than others. Ideas of morally legitimate warfare include:
■ The minimal use of necessary force
■ The proportionate use of force
■ The discriminatory use of force. This means that civilians should not be targeted
■ Upholding fundamental human rights, including for prisoners of war
■ Declaring war appropriately
■ Ending appropriately, i.e. rules for surrender.

3 ***Jus post bellum*** **('Justice after war')**. This area focuses on the morally right way to end wars and the subsequent behaviour, for example, the pursuit of war crimes, fair terms of settlement, securing long-term peace.

When discussing the ethics of war, writers often use the analogy of the '*state as a* **person**', drawing parallels between the two. So, in the same way as an individual may legitimately (morally and legally) use proportionate force in self-defence or to defend others, so a state can use proportionate force in self-defence. In this way, states can be seen as individuals with **rights** and so on. This approach raises harder questions in cases of civil war (who then is the legitimate state/person?) and terrorism, where the acts of terror are not committed by a state. In these instances, do the acts of violence become a purely criminal issue or should they be treated in relation to the rules and morality of war?

▶ **ACTIVITY**

Test your moral intuitions on these two fictional scenarios.

W1 (This dilemma has been adapted from one suggested by Chris Horner, lecturer at William Morris Sixth Form.) Your country has been drawn into helping another country defend itself from invasion by a hostile neighbour. The war is raging. You are an officer in charge of a small offensive unit. Your intelligence suggests the enemy are planning to use a biological bomb on a major city in the next 48 hours, which is likely to have horrific and far-reaching consequences. Just today your men have captured a senior officer in the enemy's army, together with his son. It is likely that both of them know about the biological attack. The officer is refusing to speak and is resisting all accepted means of ordinary interrogation but you know that the officer would break if you used 'enhanced interrogation techniques' on his son. *Should you use torture to extract information from the prisoners?*

W2 Sumitania (a fictional country) is undergoing a civil war. The north of the country is loyal to the president, whereas the people of the south have been calling for elections and a greater share of the wealth. There are rumours of atrocities along the line separating the north from the south. Recently there has been an increase in civilian casualties on both sides. Last week the conflict changed dramatically. The north started to use chemical weapons on cities in the south, leading to thousands of casualties. The UN Security Council condemns this, but any possible action is being vetoed by one of the permanent members. There are now reports of whole villages being massacred by troops from the north. Britain has warships and aircraft carriers nearby. *As the British Prime Minister should you order the military to intervene? Could an intervention like this be justified as part of a 'just war'?*

Simulated killing (within computer games, plays, films)

Violence in films, in plays and on television has become a common source of public outrage. Since the 1980s the outrage has been increasingly focused on video games, particularly those that place the ability to violently kill in the hands of the player. No one is being hurt when playing these games and no rights seem to be infringed, yet the games have produced moral outrage. Some feel that gaining pleasure in this way is morally dubious; others believe that the games may have negative effects on the player, and, in turn, on society. Both video games and violent films have been blamed in a large number of killings and massacres, for example the Columbine High School massacre (1999) was linked to the killers' obsession with the game *Doom*, also the film *A Clockwork Orange* (1972) was withdrawn from release in the UK by its director, Stanley Kubrick, after several copycat events of 'ultra-violence'.

But, on the other hand, such moral outrages have been commonplace in history. From the ancient Greeks to today, older generations have a well-documented tendency to look at the pastimes of the youth and believe that the world is getting worse.

▶ **ACTIVITY**

Read the following fictional scenarios and see what your intuitions tell you.

SK1 *Crime Spree 6* involves stealing cars and causing mayhem in a 'free to wander' world, while vaguely engaging with a plot. A team of underground programmers have taken the programme's engine and spent a lot of time releasing an altered version. In this version – called *Psycho-Tick* – you have a limited time and score points for each killing you inflict, with extra points for killing children and the elderly. You only have a baseball bat and a screwdriver as your weapons. *Is it morally wrong to play* Psycho-Tick?

SK2 The latest use of technology at the Théatre Nationale has seen the introduction of 'Feelies' (predicted by Aldous Huxley in *Brave New World*). Audiences sit in rows of special chairs, wearing hooded suits and visors that are networked into the actors on stage. Everything the actors see, feel and touch, the audiences also see, feel and touch. The Théatre Nationale has decided to launch this technology with a new performance of *Oedipus-X* by the late playwright Susan Cain. This revival has been the most successful play in the history of the theatre. Audiences have queued round the block to witness this contemporary Greek tragedy – thrilled to experience for themselves the blood-soaked suicide of the Queen, the horrific self-blinding of Oedipus and the murderous slaughter of the King. The production's tag-line says it all: 'Ever wondered what it's like to kill someone … well now you'll know.' *Is it morally wrong to enjoy watching and experiencing a dramatised murder?*

The treatment of animals

The moral status of animals has long been a source of philosophical controversy. In the UK around 4 million people are vegetarian, with the numbers in the 16–14 age bracket being particularly high (up to 20 per cent in some surveys). Many of these people are vegetarian for moral reasons. Many meat eaters also find the treatment of animals in factory farms shocking and repulsive, though not necessarily wrong. But even non-vegetarians would find the deliberate and slow torture of a dog, or horse, to be morally wrong. So, what moral status should we accord to animals? You may have well-rehearsed moral views on these issues already.

▶ **ACTIVITY**

Test your moral beliefs against the scenarios below.

A1 Every day millions of chickens are kept in darkness. They have been selectively bred to the point where many grow so quickly that they cannot stand. The conditions are so cramped that many cannot move. After 40 days of this existence (chickens normally live for seven years) the chicken is killed for its meat. *Is it wrong to eat chickens that are reared this way?*

A2 Globally, around 80,000 non-human primates (including chimpanzees) are used in medical experiments each year. The research includes testing the effectiveness and toxicity of drugs. *Is it morally right to use non-human primates for medical research that benefits humans?*

Deception and the telling of lies

This sentence tells at least one lie.

Well … does it? … Not sure? On the face of it, it doesn't seem to tell any lies. But if it doesn't tell a lie and it says that it does, then surely *that* is the lie! So it does tell a lie after all! But if it does tell a lie, and it says it tells a lie, then it appears to be telling the truth, there is no lie after all. But this would mean that there is a lie, as the sentence claims there is one ...

Still here? To free you from your thoughts, the sentence is a paradox: a **proposition** whose truth implies its falsity and whose falsity implies its truth. There is no easy way out of this one.

What's the point of putting it in the book? Well, it's here (a) to keep you concentrating, (b) to warn you that lying doesn't just get you into ordinary trouble, it can get you into logical trouble too, and (c) the section on lying doesn't really need an introduction. After all, we've all been there! In fact, thinking about your day so far, have you lied to anyone? Have you deceived anyone? Be honest!

But what would you do in these two scenarios?

▶ **ACTIVITY**

Read the following fictional scenarios and see what your intuitions tell you.

DTL1 Shelly has been married to Jacob for 25 years. They have three children and live a supposedly good life. But Jacob has been an absent husband – he has worked away from home for most of his career, and for much of the year he plays golf at the weekend. He is nice enough, but has done very little to help around the house, or raise the children, or show much love or affection to Shelly. Their children have long since grown up and moved away and Shelly is desperately lonely. Recently, Shelly has fallen in love with a neighbour who has shown her genuine kindness and taken an interest in her concerns and her hopes – they have talked about getting married. Jacob has noticed Shelly is anxious and suggests that she has a weekend away with a friend, as a treat. Shelly has asked the neighbour to join her, and when Jacob asked who she was going with, Shelly lied and said it was with one of her old school friends. *Is it wrong for Shelly to explore this new relationship? Was it wrong for Shelly not to tell the truth?*

DTL2 You answer the door to your friend Bob. He takes off his muddy boots outside, rushes into the kitchen and slams the door shouting 'Don't tell anyone I'm here'. A few minutes later there is another knock at the door. It's a man with an axe in his hand explaining that he's knocking on all the doors in the street looking for someone. He is sweating and panting and looking very agitated. As he swings his axe from one hand to the other he explains that he's very keen to find this man and that he just has a couple of questions to ask him. He asks you if a man wearing muddy boots has just come into your house. Bob wasn't wearing his boots when he came into your house, so you say 'No'. *Have you told a lie? Should you now tell the truth about where Bob is? (Why? Why not?)*

We revisit each of these dilemmas (CP1, CP2; W1, W2; SK1, SK2; A1, A2; DTL1, DTL2) when we apply three normative ethical theories to these situations: utilitarianism (pages 51–65), Kantian ethics (pages 97–110) and Aristotelian ethics (pages 158–70). Let us now turn to utilitarianism.

1.1.1 Utilitarianism

Introduction

In the previous part of this section (page 2) we asked you to imagine you were alone on a desert island. How would you behave? Could you be immoral? Many people would try to look after their basic welfare needs – food, shelter, warmth and so on. But after these had been established, what would you do? Perhaps you would try to enjoy yourself: go swimming, train a parrot, work on some new coconut recipes. In other words, you would try to seek pleasure or happiness. Of course, things will get more complicated when more survivors join you on the island and they too seek happiness. Sometimes compromises will be needed. Utilitarianism is an ethical theory based around the idea that trying to maximise happiness is the right thing to do.

Utility

The word utilitarianism is derived from the idea of **utility** or usefulness. In general, any object or action is useful only in so much as it helps us achieve a specific goal (or goals). Is a stone useful? Does it have utility? The only way in which it might be is if you can think of a goal or purpose that it could be used for (such as breaking a window). A bottle opener is only useful because we sometimes want to open bottles. If we never wanted to open a bottle, or bottles had never been invented, then a bottle opener would not have much usefulness or utility.

I might invent a unicorn whistle – which attracts only unicorns. But this has little use/utility as there are no unicorns. However, if the whistle also attracted horses then it might have a use. The same is true with actions. If a bath plug becomes wedged, I might try to empty the bath water out using a sieve. But, however well intentioned, given my goal, the action would have little utility.

So an object, or an action, has utility if it helps to bring about something we want/are aiming for. Note that for objects and actions to have utility we must have goals and desires in the first place. But how many different goals do we really have in life? Consider this example.

Example 1: The purpose of walking

The other day I found myself walking down the street. What was the purpose of this? Did my walk have any use/utility? It could be that I enjoy walking as an end in itself and so this was the purpose/use, but on this occasion I was walking to get to a shop. My walk had utility in as much as it got me to the shop. But why stop our analysis here? What was the purpose of going to the shop? Well, I went to the shop to buy a razor. So my walk really only had utility in as much as it helped me to get a razor. But why did I want to buy a razor? I wanted to buy a razor because I wanted to shave. But why did I want to shave? It could have been because I wanted to 'look smart' or impress someone, but in truth it was because my beard had become very itchy and I just couldn't stand it anymore. But why did I want to stop myself itching? It could be that our explanation ends here – wanting to stop an irritation or pain is an end itself, rather than just a stage or means to reaching a further aim or end.

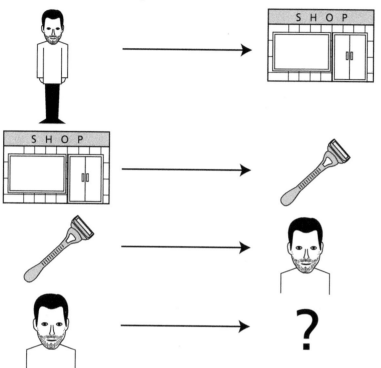

Figure 1.2 The ultimate aim of our actions

What is the ultimate aim of this walk? This analysis of a simple action suggests that the goals of reaching a shop and of buying a razor were not the ultimate ends or purpose of my action (walking). The ultimate purpose was to stop an itch. The walking and the buying of a razor, however well intentioned, had no utility unless they did help me to stop the itch. If the shop had been shut, I would have been wasting my time. Luckily the shop was open and the plan worked, so my action of walking had utility.

Can all actions be analysed like this? And, if so, what are the ultimate ends of our actions?

 Experimenting with ideas: What are your ultimate goals?

For each of the activities below, attempt to work out the ultimate end for the action. To do this, take one of the initial actions from below and on page 14 (X) and insert it into one of the following formulae.

I did X in order to Y

or

I did X so that I could Y

Then use Y as the new X and repeat using one of the formulae. Repeat this until you reach a circle/or a clear goal that is an end in itself and not just a means to some other end.

I got out of bed ...

I ate my breakfast ...

I read this philosophy book …

I cleaned my teeth …

I bought my friend/family member a present …

I gave money to Greenpeace/Save the Children …

Did you find that some of the ends were the same? Perhaps to gain knowledge or to make someone else feel good or for your own pleasure? For classic utilitarians, such as Jeremy Bentham (see page 15) and John Stuart Mill (see page 25), the ultimate aim of our action is pleasure (which they equate to happiness). The idea that pleasure is the ultimate goal is at the heart of three different, but related theories:

1 *Psychological hedonism.* This is not a moral theory, but a **descriptive** theory of human motivation. It claims that the individual's potential pleasure and the avoidance of pain are the sole aims of the individual's action ('**hedonism**' comes from the Greek work *hedone*, which means 'pleasure').

2 *Hedonism.* This is a moral theory which claims that for each individual, pursuing pleasure and avoiding pain is the right thing to do. One *ought* to seek pleasure. This theory has its roots in ancient Greek philosophy. Some writers also refer to the *paradox of hedonism*, which is the loose claim that the more a person pursues pleasure, the harder it is to obtain.

3 *Classic (or hedonistic) utilitarianism.* This is a moral theory that claims that a right action is one that increases the general happiness (not just the individual's).

Figure 1.3 Three related theories

The three theories all relate to pleasure/happiness, but in different ways.

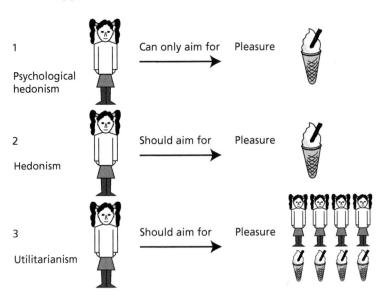

In this section we will be exploring utilitarianism. Some utilitarians, such as Jeremy Bentham also believed in psychological hedonism and used this to justify the theory of utilitarianism. However, it is not clear that psychological hedonism and utilitarianism need to go together.

It may be possible to believe in one without the other. Indeed, believing in both together can generate some philosophical problems. For if you believe that humans *are* motivated solely by their own pleasure and pain (psychological hedonism), then what is the point in telling them that they *ought* to maximise the general happiness (utilitarianism), when they are, in fact, only capable of maximising their own?

Jeremy Bentham

The moral theory of utilitarianism has roots back to the early Greeks, however its first formal articulation was in the work of Jeremy Bentham. Jeremy Bentham (1748–1832) was a member of a group of thinkers known as the British philosophical radicals, who wished to transform the British legal, parliamentary and penal systems. He was a child prodigy (he went to Oxford at the age of 12) and went on to engage in a wide range of political issues and philosophical issues. These included designing a prison (which was never built) and helping to found University College London (UCL) – England's first non-religious university and the first to treat female students equally. After his death, Bentham's body was specially preserved and dressed, and can still be seen sitting in a corner of UCL today. He is even wheeled out to attend the occasional meeting!

Jeremy Bentham lived in London at time of rising population and widespread poverty. In the absence of a police force, alleged criminals were often rounded up on the words of informants or victims and sentencing was swift and harsh. Over 200 crimes carried the death penalty – including the chopping down of trees and even the theft of rabbits. With overcrowded prisons, many were sent on prison ships to America or Australia for fairly minor offences. Bentham thought that the criminal justice system was harsh, arbitrary and unjust. He campaigned to reform it. In his seminal utilitarian work *An Introduction to the Principle of Morals and Legislation* (1780), Bentham attempted to provide a rational underpinning to the justice system. To do this, he outlined the theory of utilitarianism, which he then applied to ideas of punishment and sentencing.

His book begins with powerful and poetic claims.

> *Nature has placed mankind under the governance of two sovereign masters, pain and pleasure. It is for them alone to point out what we ought to do, as well as to determine what we shall do. On the one hand the standard of right and wrong, on the other the chain of causes and effects, are fastened to their throne. They govern us in all we do, in all we say, in all we think: every effort we can make to throw off our subjection, will serve but to demonstrate and confirm it.*[1]

Bentham

anthology
1.1

In the first sentence Bentham proposes that pain (avoiding it) and pleasure are our two masters. In the second sentence he puts forward both a descriptive and **prescriptive** theory. He claims that pain and pleasure are the ends of human action (psychological hedonism) and also suggests that pain and pleasure can form the basis of an ethical or prescriptive theory – utilitarianism. This is the theory that suggests that bringing about pleasure and avoiding pain is the right thing to do.

Before we explore utilitarianism in more depth, we will first turn to the theory that pleasure and the avoidance of pain are our sole motivations, such that we are *'fastened to their throne'*. In other words, the theory of psychological hedonism.

Psychological hedonism

The idea that pleasure is the ultimate end of our actions is a fairly simple idea, although some would argue it paints an unpleasant view of the human condition – that of pleasure-seeking animals with brains acting as a sort of computer to work out how to maximise pleasure.

Although simple, psychological hedonism can be a very difficult theory to argue against. You might claim that a particular act is not pleasure seeking, for example staying in and doing your homework rather than going out and having fun. However, Bentham (were he alive today and not merely stuffed) would come back at you by saying that you are either driven to do your homework by fear of punishment (pain) or by the prospect of future pleasure (praise from a teacher/parent, the pleasure of better grades, getting to the right university, or even getting a better job). By staying in and working hard you are sacrificing shorter-term pleasures (going out) for longer-term ones, but pleasure (and the avoidance of pain) are still your goals.

▶ **ACTIVITY: Is pleasure the ultimate end?**

Look back to the Experimenting with ideas box on pages 13–14 (What are your ultimate goals?):

- Is it possible to argue that each of these activities is ultimately aiming at gaining personal pleasure and avoiding pain?
- Can you argue that any/all of the activities are not aimed at gaining pleasure or avoiding pain?

Some religious believers, as well as others that consider themselves very upright and moral, have claimed (and still do) that seeking pleasure is wrong. Instead these people have chosen to live simple lives that avoid pleasure. Some religious sects have even used self-chastisement (whipping oneself) as part of this overall philosophy of avoiding pleasure. This would seem to be a clear counter example to psychological hedonism. However, Bentham claims that even these people are still driven by pleasure and pain. They may be driven by the prospect of pleasure in the next life, or the avoidance of pain through the punishment of God.

Criticisms of psychological hedonism

**Figure 1.4
The pleasure machine**

The machine will give you guaranteed pleasure. But would you enter if you knew that you could never come out?

 Experimenting with ideas: The pleasure machine version 1.0

Imagine that scientists have developed an amazing new pleasure machine (this idea is adapted from Robert Nozick[2]). You enter the wardrobe-like machine, get hooked up with lots of wires, and, hey presto, the machine gives you guaranteed pleasure! These pleasurable sensations will vary in intensity from mild pleasures (akin to sitting next to a fire, warming your feet) to medium pleasures (such as the taste of marshmallows), to more intense pleasures (the equivalent of racing downhill on skis). It can give you *other* intense pleasures too – ones that it wouldn't be appropriate to describe in a textbook. The only downside is that once you have stepped into the pleasure machine you cannot come back out (but then again, you won't want to!). You will live a long and healthy life of guaranteed pleasurable sensations.

1 Given that the pleasure machine is completely safe, with no side effects whatsoever, and no threat to your health, would you plug yourself in for the rest of your life?
2 Why, or why not?

If you are happy to sign up to the machine then this thought experiment seems to prove the truth of psychological hedonism. On the other hand, if you are not ready to sign up, does this mean that psychological hedonism is wrong? Or perhaps there is something missing from the machine? John Stuart Mill (another utilitarian) would claim that this machine focuses only on what he calls lower pleasures – tastes, physical sensations and so on – whereas many humans want different, perhaps less intense pleasures. He calls these higher pleasures, such as the pleasures of reading poetry, or difficult and sad books (for more on this distinction, see page 26). To overcome this potential shortfall, consider this ...

▶ **ACTIVITY: ... The all new improved pleasure machine version 2.0**

Perhaps the new version of the pleasure machine can tempt you. In this version you are plugged into a virtual-reality machine – as real as the world you now inhabit. You are guaranteed to live a pleasurable life – maybe win an Oscar, or become an acclaimed pop star or footballer. You can also read all the difficult, sad books you want to read! Your memory will be tinkered with a little, so that you won't even know that you are in a machine, a bit like being in the film *The Matrix*, though a much, much happier version. Again, once you step in, it will have to be forever.

1 Would you step in to the new improved pleasure machine?
2 Why, or why not?

Again, this could point towards the truth of psychological hedonism, but it might also count against it. If you would *not* step into the machine, is it because you think that the machine would not give the right sort of pleasures? Or is it because you believe that pleasure is not our only goal, or is not even a meaningful goal? The criticisms of psychological hedonism below may articulate some of your concerns.

Criticism 1
It is not pleasure *that we seek, but the specific actions, activities and objects themselves*

Imagine you have been collecting football/Hello Kitty/*Hunger Games* stickers. You only have one missing and have been trying to get it for ages. You *really* want this missing sticker. Bentham would claim that the sticker is just a means to your ultimate aim, which is the pleasure it will give you. However, you may feel strongly that what you actually want is the sticker, not the pleasure it will give. For example, if I offered to give you the equivalent amount of pleasure that you would gain from getting the missing sticker, but from another source (say a Michael McIntyre DVD) then you might be tempted, but would still probably claim that it is the sticker you want, not just a certain quantity of pleasure.

Another utilitarian, Henry Sidwick, claimed that it is the specific activities/objects in life that we desire and not pleasure itself. I might want to play football for the intrinsic qualities of the game, the smell of grass, the crunch of the tackle, and so on – not for any specific sensation called pleasure. If it were just pleasure I wanted, then I might just settle for the Michael McIntyre DVD after all, and not bother getting muddy and tired.

Criticism 2
It is not pleasure *that we seek, but states of affairs in the world – things outside of our heads*

By creating the thought experiment of the pleasure machine (version 2.0) the philosopher Nozick wanted to show that the idea of humans just seeking things inside our heads (i.e. pleasure) may be wrong. What people often want are specific states of affairs in the world. They want their children to be happy, or for people to think well of them, or for there to be more dolphins. People want these states of affairs in the world, and not just for the sensations that might then result in their heads. If it were just the sensations you were after, then surely you would have stepped into the machine (or maybe you *have* stepped into the machine and stopped reading this!). But many would refuse the machine, as what they seek are things in a real world, not sensations and deceptions.

Criticism 3
Pleasure is a way of talking about behaviour
I gain pleasure from lots of things: a cup of tea, watching football, a nice walk, reading Harry Potter books. These are all things I seek to do, but there doesn't seem to be a specific mental sensation linking them all. In seeking pleasure, there isn't a specific thing – like say, eggs – that I am hunting. But if it isn't a specific thing, then what is it? Behaviourists (see page 291) and others would claim that pleasure isn't a specific sensation. Instead they claim it is a way of collectively talking about all of those things that we seek to do. In other words, calling things pleasurable is really just a shorthand way of talking about '*what we seek*'. If this is true then psychological hedonism can be seen as an empty theory. If we can define '*pleasure*' as '*what we seek*' then the sentence '*we seek pleasure*' really means '*we seek what we seek*' which is a **tautology** (i.e. it is true by definition) and tells us nothing new about the world. This is maybe why Bentham thought it was always possible to show that we seek pleasure – because it is true by definition.

What emerges from this discussion is that it is not clear that pleasure is a mental sensation, it may just be a way of talking about activities we *prefer* to do. Because of this, some utilitarians believe that we should focus on satisfying people's preferences rather than maximising their desires. For more on this, see preference utilitarianism on page 36.

So we have seen that psychological hedonism is a simple, intuitive theory, although it is not without criticism. However, it is not necessary for the theory of utilitarianism, although attempts to prove the theory of utilitarianism often rely on it.

Utilitarianism

According to Bentham's reasoning, if psychological hedonism is true, and our actions are aimed at pleasure and avoiding pain, then the only reasonable moral theory is one that seeks to make such actions as consistent and effective as possible. In other words, we must follow a moral system that invokes us to maximise happiness and minimise pain – for both the individual and the sum of individuals in a community. This is the '**utility principle**'.

Earlier we saw that an object is useful (has utility) if it helps to bring about a specific goal. Bentham claims that pleasure (which he also equates with happiness) and the avoidance of pain are the goals we pursue. As such, any action has utility if it helps to bring about pleasure/happiness or the avoidance of pain. When we consider the effects of actions not just on ourselves, but on others too, we can then judge how much utility an action has by seeing how much more happiness than pain it brings into the world. If an action does this, then Bentham says that this is what we mean by a good act.

Bentham states his principle slightly differently throughout his writings, although the same point (more or less) is being made.

> *An action then may be said to be conformable to the principle of utility, or, for shortness sake, to utility, (meaning with respect to the community at large) when the tendency it has to augment the happiness of the community is greater than any it has to diminish it.*[3]
>
> Bentham

> *... it is the greatest happiness of the greatest number that is the measure of right and wrong.*[4]
>
> Bentham

Bentham claims morally good actions are those that bring about happiness and morally bad actions bring about more pain than pleasure. He claims that this principle – which is variously called the *utility principle*, the *greatest happiness principle* or *utilitarianism* – not only is the correct system of ethics, but is also the principle underlying all other systems.

In other words, all other systems of moral rules (including Christianity) are really just striving to bring about general happiness and the avoidance of pain.

The utility calculus

Bentham offers us a guide as to how we are supposed to apply the principle of utility, in other words how we are supposed to measure the amount of pleasure and pain an action brings and so maximise happiness. Bentham termed the method of calculating, measuring and weighing up the pleasure/pain of individual actions the 'hedonic calculus' (also known as the utility calculus).

Bentham's utility calculus

One of the advantages that utilitarians claim for their theory is that by using a universal feature of human life (pleasure and pain) their theory can be applied to all of our day-to-day actions. To apply the utility principle we simply weigh up the amount of pleasure and pain an action might create and then select the action which brings the most amount of pleasure over pain. Easy, really, when you know how! Figure 1.5 shows Bentham's suggested utility calculus, i.e. the steps for measuring the pleasure and pain that result from an action:

Step 1 Determine the amount of pleasure and pain brought to the person most directly affected by your action. To do this, Bentham gives us four things to measure:
    1 The *intensity* of the pleasure/pain
    2 The *duration* of the pleasure/pain
    3 The *certainty* of the pleasure/pain
    4 The *remoteness* of the pleasure/pain

Step 2 Examine the effects of this pleasure or pain, including:
    5 The *fecundity* of the pleasure/pain
    6 The *purity* of the pleasure/pain
By 'fecundity' Bentham is talking about the tendency of that pleasure to produce other pleasures (fecundity means fertility, or tendency to reproduce). By 'purity' Bentham means the tendency of the pleasure to produce *only* pleasure, and the tendency of pain to produce *only* pain.

Step 3 This step comes only when we are considering the effects on other individuals:
    7 The *extent* of the pleasure/pain
In other words, the number of people affected by the action.

Step 4 You then calculate the total utility by using 1–7 to count up the amount of pleasure units an action causes, and the amount of pain units an action brings.

Step 5 If you have a range of actions available to you then you must repeat Steps 1–4 for all these actions, and choose the action which brings the most pleasure over pain.

Figure 1.5 Bentham's utility calculus

Simple! Or maybe not. Bentham's approach is intended more as a guide than a practical tool. Even as a guide it faces some objections.

Criticism 1
Impossible to compare pleasures
Some would claim that we can't compare the pleasure of, say, watching tennis, with that of eating an apple, with that of helping a friend learn to drive. They are such different things that there is no common currency with which we could compare them. This difficulty is just within one person. Comparing the amounts of pleasure between people may be equally meaningless. How can anyone know if you gain more pleasure from eating spaghetti than me? Perhaps we should all have pleasure-ometers attached to our heads, so that we can compare. However, even if this were possible, this would still treat pleasure as an internal sensation, which, as we saw in the example of the pleasure machine (page 17), can be seen as problematic.

Criticism 2
Is quantity the only factor?
Using Bentham's utility calculus, it is the quantity of pleasure that is the key indicator of the utility of action. If two different pleasures are compared, the one that has the highest quantity is the one we should aim for. As we will see on page 26, John Stuart Mill thought that some pleasures, such as those gained from poetry or opera (he called them higher pleasures) were better to pursue – even though they may be less pleasant. Bentham though did not make this distinction – he thought that only the quantity mattered. He once famously wrote that push-pin (a game played in pubs at the time) was as good as poetry, and therefore that both should be treated equally in the utility calculus:

... the game of push-pin is of equal value with the arts and sciences of music and poetry.[5]

Applying utilitarianism

So now that we have the basics of the theory, let's road test a couple of examples.

Example 2: The mugging

Reuben is walking home when he is mugged. The mugger takes Reuben's mobile phone and money.

Let's add up the happiness/pleasure points this act generates. The mugger may enjoy the adrenaline he gets from mugging, so may gain some pleasure points from the act (say 5). He sells the phone and buys some drugs with the money which he then consumes with some friends. In the short term they all gain pleasure (say a total of 20 points). So, the act of mugging has added 25 happiness points to the world. Now consider Reuben. He will suffer immensely. Violent acts, such as muggings, can live in the mind for a lifetime and be a regular source of discomfort. Reuben's family and friends will all be distressed too, as will others as the news spreads. A total of 1,000 pain points may emerge as a result. Overall, the act brings about 1,000 negative points and 25 positive points, giving a total of –975 points. The act introduces more pain than pleasure to the world, and so is a bad act.

Example 3: Pizza!

An uncle gives you restaurant vouchers worth £80 on your birthday. You treat your four closest friends to pizza at a pizza restaurant. The pizza is enjoyed by all; more so because it is free for four of them, and you also enjoy being host. This gives a total of 100 happiness points. One friend gets mild indigestion, yielding one pain point. A grand total of 99 happiness points. Overall, the act introduced happiness into the world and so was a good act.

▶ **ACTIVITY: Calculating pleasure**

I   Make a rough calculation of whether the following acts bring more pleasure or pain into the world.
2   What difficulties did you have in trying to work these out?
3   Do you agree that the acts that bring pleasure are good acts?
   ● Giving money to a charity
   ● Volunteering to visit an old people's home
   ● Playing a hilarious practical joke on a friend
   ● Buying clothes that were made in a 'sweat shop'
   ● Poisoning your neighbour's cat, as it kept soiling your garden
   ● Stealing from the rich to give to the poor

Consequentialism

One of the key difficulties you may have faced is in deciding what the consequences of an action might be and when, if ever, they come to an end. Because utilitarianism claims that something specific (namely pleasure/happiness) is a 'good' then this makes it a consequentialist theory of ethics. A good act is one that brings about the 'good' (pleasure/happiness). So the moral worth of any action lies in the amount of pleasure it brings into the world and to work this out you need to examine the consequences of the actions. **Consequentialist ethics** are also sometimes called **teleologicial** ethics – as they involve working towards a specific end (or *telos* in the Greek). One big problem for all consequentialist ethical theories is that they can feel counter intuitive.

Example 4: Visiting Grandma

   A Simra visits her elderly grandma once a week. She buys a few groceries, tidies up a little, helps Grandma with her post and reads to her. Grandma loves the visits; Samra doesn't particularly enjoy them, but she visits out of a sense of **duty** to the family.
   B Maisie visits her elderly grandma once a week. She buys a few groceries, tidies up a little, helps Grandma with her post and reads to her. Grandma loves the visits, Maisie doesn't particularly enjoy them – she visits to increase the chances of getting lots of money in Grandma's will.

Which of these two, almost identical, acts has the most moral worth? Many would argue that A does. A utilitarian would calculate the pleasure that each of the acts brings – which is roughly the same in both cases. Both acts are equally good. However, this feels counter intuitive. Surely the motive for carrying out the act plays a the part in the moral worth of the act. (This is exactly the position that Immanuel Kant takes – which we explore on page 66.) A utilitarian would disagree. They would claim that the acts have the same moral worth. Utilitarians often argue that we can still use the concepts of blame and praise, as distinct to the moral worth of the action. Consider these two cases (examples 5 and 6).

Example 5: The evil scientist

Evil scientist Jake decides to poison the water supply of a town (to revenge his horrible childhood). However, it transpires that the poison, when diluted, has no harmful effect, and in fact it acts as a mild pain relief for those with arthritis. Good or bad? A utilitarian would say that because of the consequences, the act was good. A good thing happened that day. The utilitarian would argue, however, that we would not want to praise Jake. In fact, he should be morally blamed as he was trying to cause pain.

Example 6: The elderly lady

Jaspreet saw an elderly lady struggling up some steps to get to a shop. She tried to help, but in holding her arm she made the old lady lose her balance and fall, breaking her hip in the process. Good or bad? In this case a utilitarian would say that a bad thing happened – pain was added to the world. The utilitarian would not blame Jaspreet, however, as she was trying to do good and could not reasonably have foreseen the pain caused.

So, although utilitarianism can be criticised for not including the motive in the moral value of the action, this can be mitigated to some extent through the use of the concept of praise and blame.

Bentham on motive and government

For Bentham, as a psychological hedonist, the issue of 'motive' is a red herring as everyone is motivated by pleasure anyway. We all have the same motive. People may have different intentions in terms of how they will achieve pleasure, but their motive is the same. Bentham was writing primarily for governments when he first articulated utilitarianism. After all, why appeal to citizens? If everyone is motivated to maximise their own happiness what is the point of telling them to maximise the general happiness? They won't do it! This is where the government comes in. By making laws and tweaking crime and punishment we can modify people's intentions and align the pursuit of individual happiness with the pursuit of general happiness.

For example, Billy may enjoy drinking a lot and singing loudly on the street in the middle of the night (which his neighbours find very annoying). If a law is introduced which makes this sort of behaviour a criminal offence, then Billy will be less inclined to sing at night, as he wants to avoid the pain of prison. In this way, how he pursues his happiness will be aligned with the general pursuit of happiness.

Criticism
Utilitarianism as social engineering
One criticism of this approach is that the goal of utilitarianism seems to be best achieved by a kind of social engineering. In the seminal novel *A Brave New World*, Aldous Huxley portrayed a society where people are educated and trained in different

ways. The 'Alphas' are trained to rule and to enjoy this, whereas the manual workers – the 'Gammas' – are trained to hate books and enjoy manual work. In addition, everyone takes a drug called *Soma* to keep them even happier. Hey presto, everyone is happy! A perfect utilitarian world. Yet some people think that this would not be an ideal society. Human **autonomy** and freedom seem to be diminished and replaced by a government trying to socially engineer happiness.

John Stuart Mill

John Stuart Mill (1806–73) was not only a moral philosopher; he was also a social reformer, a Member of Parliament and, in his day, a logician of great eminence. As a child he was the subject of a famous experiment in education by his father, James Mill, and Jeremy Bentham. The young Mill was hot-housed in philosophy, the classics, economics and maths and duly became a child prodigy, although at a cost. Throughout his childhood Mill did not spend any time in the company of other children. At the age of 20, Mill suffered a nervous breakdown, feeling that the emotional side of his upbringing had been neglected. Mill recovered with a renewed interest in not just the intellectual but also the emotional side of his life. In 1863 he published *Utilitarianism*, which continued the work carried out by his father and Bentham. He also wrote *On Liberty* in 1859 which has become one of the most influential texts in the history of philosophy.

Mill agrees with Bentham that the '*one fundamental principle ... at the root of all morality*' is the utility principle:

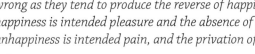

> *Utility, or the Greatest Happiness Principle, holds that actions are right in proportion as they tend to promote happiness, wrong as they tend to produce the reverse of happiness. By happiness is intended pleasure and the absence of pain; by unhappiness is intended pain, and the privation of pleasure.*[6]
>
> Mill

So Mill, like Bentham, proposes happiness as the foundation for his ethical theory.

Mill's 'proof' of utilitarianism

Bentham did not think that the theory of utilitarianism could be 'proved' as such. He thought it was obvious that maximising pleasure is the right thing to do, as this is what everyone tries to do all the time. Mill was also sceptical about whether a formal proof for the theory could be provided, but did attempt to argue from the fact that pleasure is desired to the claim that it is morally desirable.

The only proof capable of being given that an object is visible, is that people actually see it. The only proof that a sound is audible, is that people hear it. ... The sole evidence that it is possible to produce that anything is desirable, is that people do actually desire it. No reason can be given why the general happiness is desirable, except that each person, so far as he believes it to be attainable, desires his own happiness. This, however, being a fact, we have not only all the proof which the case admits of, but all which it is possible to require, that happiness is a good: that each person's happiness is a good to that person, and the general happiness, therefore, a good to the aggregate of all persons.[7]

Mill

This attempted proof has generated much debate. The philosopher Hume, some hundred years earlier, had argued that proving any moral theory is impossible. He claimed that proofs tend to start with claims about what *is* the case in the world, and then suddenly start talking about how we *ought* to behave. But Hume suggests that you cannot argue about what ought to be the case based only on what *is* the case. There will always be an explanatory gap between the *is* and the *ought* which can be reasonably doubted, and so no proof is possible. We discuss some more criticisms of Mill's proof on pages 181–4.

Higher and lower pleasures

Since Bentham introduced the theory, utilitarianism had been widely criticised from various angles and Mill wanted to address these concerns. Some had claimed that utilitarianism involved too little pleasure. The term *utilitarianism*, even today, has connotations of something being plain and functional. Someone might describe a plain, but hard-wearing plate or dress as being *utilitarian*. Mill rightly rejected this criticism as a misunderstanding of the theory. More telling though was the opposite criticism: that utilitarianism is focused too much on pleasure, and, specifically, on bodily pleasures. At the time, the overcrowding in London had led to the poor living very cramped, uncomfortable lives. Many sought comfort in drinking gin, which became very popular. Critics of utilitarianism saw the theory as advocating the pursuit of mindless drinking (and so forth) as a morally good thing to do (as it gave pleasure). Mill sought to defend the theory against this charge. Part of his defence involved introducing a new distinction between 'higher' and 'lower' pleasures.

Previous utilitarian writers had also claimed pleasures of the mind were superior to physical ones, but they did so on the grounds that such pleasures were likely to last longer and so, overall, give more pleasure. Mill, although agreeing with this, also claimed that the 'quantity only' approach is not really necessary.

> It is quite compatible with the principle of utility to recognise the fact, that some kinds of pleasure are more desirable and more valuable than others. It would be absurd that while, in estimating all other things, quality is considered as well as quantity, the estimation of pleasures should be supposed to depend on quantity alone.[8]
>
> Mill

Bentham saw all pleasures as equal, so the pleasures of the body (e.g. having a massage) were of the same value as pleasures of the mind (e.g. reading a book). A good act is one that simply maximises the overall quantity. Mill, however, argued that many humans would prefer the pleasures of the mind over those of the body, *even if* the pleasures of the body were more pleasurable. He called the pleasures of the mind *higher* pleasures. And although not every human would prefer such pleasures, those who have experienced both would choose the higher pleasures over the lower ones – even if they were not as pleasant. Further, being able to experience both kinds is better than only being able to experience the lower kind.

> It is better to be a human being dissatisfied than a pig satisfied; better to be Socrates dissatisfied than a fool satisfied. And if the fool, or the pig, are of a different opinion, it is because they only know their own side of the question. The other party to the comparison knows both sides.[9]
>
> Mill

Experimenting with ideas

Savour the following pleasures and then answer the questions below.

1　Drinking a warm mug of hot chocolate on a cold day.
2　Seeing your favourite film the way the director intended it to be seen.
3　Going clubbing on a Friday night.
4　Reading and understanding a piece of difficult philosophy.
5　Laughing until you can't breathe from watching a comedy on television.
6　Listening to a favourite track on the way back from college.
7　Having a thoughtful discussion with friends about how to change the world.
8　Scratching a hard-to-reach itch between your shoulder blades.
9　Reading a version of the Harry Potter books, in which no one dies, and the tone is much more light-hearted.
10　Reading the real version of the Harry Potter books, which includes the death of several key characters, including **SPOILER ALERT** Dobby.
　　a) Which of the above are the most pleasant?
　　b) Are the ones that are most pleasant the ones that you think are worth pursuing more?
　　c) Which of the above pleasures do you think Mill might call 'higher' and which 'lower'?
　　d) Which of 9 or 10 would bring you more pleasure?

An easy criticism of this approach is that Mill is just thinking of the pleasures that he personally likes and wants to claim that they are somehow superior to the pleasures that some others prefer. However, Mill claims that only those who can appreciate both are in a position to say which is the better. A pig would not be in a position to say that reading Shakespeare is, or isn't, a valuable pleasure. Mill claims this enables him to preserve a degree of objectivity in utilitarianism. We can draw on the pronouncements of 'competent judges', i.e. people who have had experience of both higher and lower pleasures.

Mill believed there would be substantial agreement between these judges, but if there were not then we should stand by a majority decision.

> On a question which is the best worth having of two pleasures, or which of two modes of existence is the most grateful to the feelings ... the judgment of those who are qualified by knowledge of both, or, if they differ, that of the majority among them, must be admitted as final.[10]
>
> Mill

Criticism 1
Is this hedonistic utilitarianism anymore?

The gist of Mill's distinction is that some pleasures are somehow better, even if they give less pleasure. Does this make sense as a hedonistic utilitarian? It would seem that if something could be less *pleasant*, yet *better* then we are no longer seeking to maximise pleasure. Going back to the idea of the pleasure-ometer attached to the head, Activity A may record a lower pleasure score than Activity B, yet somehow be better. If this is so, then surely a utilitarian needs a new type of '-ometer', perhaps one that measures the preferences of competent judges, rather than pleasure. Measuring pleasure seems to be the wrong thing.

In Mill's defence

A Mill does think you can argue that higher pleasures are actually more pleasant than lower, when you take into account the duration (etc.). For example, a good book will give you pleasure for a long time, whereas it seems unlikely that you really remember that lovely cup of tea and muffin you had last September. But Mill thought that utilitarianism does not need to be quantity-only in its approach.

B Mill may be claiming that higher and lower pleasures are simply incommensurable – rather than one being less pleasant than the other. For example, blue is different from red. No amount of blue will be the same as any amount of red; they are simply different. Mill does indeed claim that even for lower pleasures/pains we cannot really compare two side by side, we can only ask someone who has experienced both, which is the better or worse.

> *What means are there of determining which is the acutest of two pains, or the intensest of two pleasurable sensations, except the general suffrage of those who are familiar with both?"*[11]
>
> Mill

So Mill seems to be claiming that we need the competent judges for all pleasures and pains not just for the higher/lower debate.

C Mill did not see happiness just as a question of pleasure. A society of people plugged into pleasure machines would not be a good thing in his view. Humans have capacities to reason, to develop and they enjoy these aspects of life in a different way. These aspects would be overlooked if we were all just busy getting physical pleasures. A competent judge is able to say which pleasure she would prefer precisely because she has developed her capacities. The fact that competent judges do prefer higher pleasures (most of the time) points to the direction we should all be pursuing – and this is to develop our capacities so as to enjoy these higher pleasures. In his earlier work, *On Liberty*, Mill gave a different account of of utility which reflects this broader view of human pleasure.

> *I regard utility as the ultimate appeal on all ethical questions; but it must be utility in the largest sense, grounded on the permanent interests of man as a progressive being.*[12]
>
> Mill

Some have argued that this approach is to move away from hedonistic utilitarianism, however Mill saw it as a more sophisticated development of our account of happiness.

What this criticism (and defence) points to is that there may be something a bit odd about comparing pleasures. In part this may be because (as was suggested above, page 18) pleasures are not simply experiences in the brain that can be placed side by side and compared. Furthermore, if we are reliant on competent judges to say which of two options they *prefer*, then perhaps we should be aiming to maximise people's *preferences*, rather than guess what will give them pleasure. We explore preference utilitarianism on page 36.

Criticism 2
Utilitarianism loses its simplicity

Mill, in trying to make Bentham's utilitarianism more sophisticated and acceptable to the critics, has created enormous problems for himself. What makes utilitarianism so appealing is its simplicity and practicality: it tells us that we can calculate what actions we should take by weighing up the quantity of pleasure (and pain) that different acts produce. However, once Mill introduces the notion of quality into the discussion then some of the simplicity disappears. For example, imagine a council is trying to decide whether to build a gym or a library. Under Bentham's system, the council only has to think about the overall quantity of happiness either would bring (which is hard enough!). Under Mill's regime they now have to compare not only the quantity, but also the quality. It may be that most competent judges would prefer the pleasure a library would bring, but how are we to factor this into the equation? Does it make the library infinitely better than the gym? Does one library = 100 gyms? Is it only up to the competent judges to decide what the right thing is? What if 75 per cent of the local residents would prefer a gym?

The quality distinction seems to make the application of the hedonistic calculus even harder still. Again we might be tempted to conclude that what the council should do is find out what people would prefer and try to maximise the preferences.

Criticism 3
Cultural snobbery
Should the BBC spend public money on buying a 'trashy' new Australian soap opera, or should it spend money on a series addressing the problems of philosophy? The philosophy series would only attract a tenth of the viewers of the soap, but would bring about much higher quality pleasure though less quantity. (Unless, of course, you are the sort of person who gets as much pleasure per minute from reading this book, as from, say, eating a cream cake).

But even where it seems obvious which is the higher and which is the lower pleasure, the question remains: what should we do, as good utilitarians, when the lower pleasure is felt by millions of people and the higher pleasure by only a select few? We are left wondering whether 'higher pleasures' really just means 'the things that Mill and his friends like to do'.

Act utilitarianism

Bentham's version of utilitarianism is a form of 'act' utilitarianism. Although Bentham was writing primarily for law makers, others took his theory to be an ethics that can be used by all. In other words, we should all appeal directly to the 'principle of utility' in order to judge what is right in any particular situation. We must calculate the effects of each potential action, or 'act', on its own merits. However, this form of act utilitarianism is susceptible to a certain number of problems, which we shall now look at.

Criticism 1
Act utilitarianism has counter-intuitive implications
A major criticism of act utilitarianism is that the goodness or badness of an act is based solely on the consequences. The nature of the act is not important. In this way, the ends can justify the means, as long as the end result is happiness. However, this goes against our intuition that the nature of the act itself (the means) is also important in the moral calculation. In this way, act utilitarianism can sometimes feel very counter-intuitive.

Experimenting with ideas: Testing utilitarianism against your intuitions

Consider the decisions made in the following situations and answer the questions below:

The Colosseum

In ancient Rome the impressive Colosseum was built mainly for the purposes of enjoying blood sports. The crowd of 20,000 people regularly derived a huge amount of enjoyment from watching the spectacle of gladiators fighting, or slaves being killed or even Christians being eaten by lions. Most of the time, only a few people would die, and thousands would gain pleasure.

Women drivers

One hundred years ago in America nearly everyone (men and women alike) found it offensive for women to drive cars. As a result, in the state of North Dakota the federal government passed a law that forbade women from driving cars.

The DVD

You borrow a DVD player from a rich friend, promising to give it back. A few months later she has forgotten she even lent it to you, yet you use it all the time, so you decide that you'll keep it.

The scapegoat

A serial killer is on the loose. Thousands of citizens are in a state of panic and fear, and they march on the Town Hall demanding that the killer be brought to justice. This mob is getting out of control, but local police and magistrates have no idea who the killer is. Eventually the Mayor selects someone at random from the mob, a man with a known criminal record who is widely disliked. This man is quickly tried and found guilty, and the mob disperses, feeling happy and secure again.

Bodily organs

A surgeon is desperate to receive some organs (1 × heart, 1 × lung, 2 × kidney, 1 × liver) to save the lives of five well-loved patients. He asks his assistant to find a healthy man with no family or friends, kills him painlessly, and take his organs so that the five can be saved.

Nude pictures

A couple split up. A year later the ex-boyfriend puts various nude pictures of his ex-girlfriend on the internet. She doesn't discover this. The pictures bring pleasure to others.

For each situation or policy:

a) Do you think that the utility principle can be used to justify the situation?
b) Does the situation go against your own moral intuitions?
c) If so, explain why you believe the utilitarian decision is the wrong one.

One key difficulty with act utilitarianism is that it appears to recommend courses of action that go against our moral intuitions. Take the example of the innocent scapegoat. If we could demonstrate that in order to prevent massive harm (perhaps further rioting or a civil war) we must execute an innocent person, then it seems as if Bentham thinks we should kill that person. But this seems fundamentally unjust, and Bentham, as we have seen, is keen to ensure that there is justice in the penal system. It goes against all our intuitions to say that it is morally good to kill, torture or deprive people of their freedom, even if it does lead to beneficial consequences for the majority.

Bentham might argue that we must consider not only the immediate pleasure brought to the majority but also the pain brought by the fear that we too might one day be arrested and tried for a crime we didn't commit, simply to placate the mob. But it is possible to adjust the example so that the crowd wouldn't know that an innocent person had been executed – say, if the police and judicial system were able to orchestrate a perfect cover-up – and therefore that there would be no risk of generating any fear of future injustices.

Criticism 2
Impossible to follow
This criticism claims that act utilitarianism is impossible to use in practice:

A   It is often impossible to work out how much happiness each action might bring (more on this below).
B   Even if this were possible it would take too long to work out for some actions.
C   Sometimes happiness involves being spontaneous, not working out what would maximise general happiness.

For these reasons many utilitarians suggest that for most/all actions, we follow basic rules that will, in general, maximise happiness. Act utilitarianism may be the right way to judge whether an action is a good one or not, but is not really fit for purpose as a method of deliberation.

Rule utilitarianism

Imagine that traffic lights did not exist. At busy crossroads it would be up to each driver to decide whether to go or not. Naturally people would try to maximise their own happiness and go as soon as they could. Chaos and gridlock would ensue. Imagine instead that everyone behaved as a good act utilitarian and tried to maximise the general happiness. What would this involve? Each driver would have to consider whether staying or going would generate the most happiness/avoid the most pain. Obviously crashes would be avoided. If there were more cars queuing one way than another it would make sense to let the longer queue work down a bit. But what about the people inside the cars? Some may be in a real rush. One could be a doctor trying to get to the hospital – surely she should get priority? How on earth would you know this? It would be impossible to work out the exact implications of pulling out or not.

What is needed is a set of rules – in this case traffic lights – that we can all follow. There may be one or two occasions when it would be better to ignore these (as happens when ambulances approach), however it will raise happiness overall if we all follow the rules.

Rule utilitarianism suggests just this. Ethical rules and norms such as *'Don't lie'* and *'Keep your promises'* act as moral traffic lights. If followed by all, they will generally provide the best result.

Mill specifically introduces the idea of 'secondary principles' for this purpose. These secondary principles, or rules, are ones which experience has shown tend to produce the greatest happiness, and they should be adhered to, even though in particular cases breaking the rule might have better consequences. In another of his great works, *On Liberty* (1859), Mill lists some of these rules: for example, we shouldn't encroach on the rights of others, we shouldn't lie or deceive or cause injury to others. By applying the greatest happiness principle to general rules rather than individual actions, Mill avoids many of the problems of act utilitarianism.

In this way, rule utilitarianism also becomes a useable moral theory for individuals; there is no need to make complex calculations in order to take a moral decision, you can simply follow a moral rule. Rule utilitarianism can also be defended on utilitarian grounds by saying that it is only by our acting for the most part according to rules, rather than attempting always to evaluate situations on their own merits, that the greatest good is served.

Rule utilitarianism and rights

One key advantage of rule utilitarianism over act is in its ability to justify the adoption of human rights (and rights in general) as moral rules. In the 'bodily organs' example on page 31, an act utilitarian could argue that killing one man to save five would maximise happiness – and so be the right thing to do. However, for many people, this seems intuitively wrong. A rule utilitarian though would claim that having a moral rule about 'not killing', perhaps in the form of a right to life, would be a rule that, if followed by all, would maximise general happiness. It would be wrong therefore to break the rule. Even if on this one occasion it may seem as if more happiness could be brought about through the killing, people generally feel much safer and happier going about their business knowing the rule/right to life will not be broken in this way.

▶ **ACTIVITY: Rights and rules**

Revisit the scenarios in the Experimenting with ideas task on page 31.

a) In each case, what rule/right could be put in place to prevent the situation/act from occurring?

b) Are these rules that would maximise happiness if everyone followed them?

c) Is rule utilitarianism more in tune with your ethical intuition than act utilitarianism?

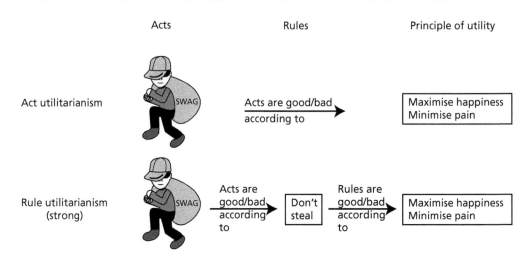

Figure 1.6 Act and rule utilitarianism

For rule utilitarianism, it is following a rule that makes an act good or bad.

Strong and weak rule utilitarianism

Rule utilitarianism offers a two-level account of right and wrong. An action is right if it is in accordance with a moral rule, and a moral rule is right if, overall, it maximises utility (see Figure 1.6).

However, if utility is the ultimate judge of whether rules are morally right, shouldn't we use this as our guide for action, rather than following a rule – particularly when following a rule may seem wrong? Consider this example:

Example 7: The axeman

A friend, Thierry, has asked if he can stay with you for a few days. On the first night a deranged-looking man with an axe knocks at the door and asks if Thierry is staying with you. Do you lie or tell the truth?

Most rule utilitarians would say that '*Don't lie*' is a rule that would maximise general happiness. However, here it would seem that breaking the rule would produce greater happiness. So it seems perverse, given that the rule is itself set up in terms of the principle of utility, not to break it on this occasion. This way of thinking leads from a 'strong' version of rule utilitarianism to a 'weak' version.

A strong rule utilitarian claims that we ought to keep to a rule no matter what the consequences may be of breaking it in a particular circumstance. It is *following the rule* that gives an act its moral value, so in the example above, telling the truth would be the right thing to do. In contrast, a weak utilitarian allows that there may be exceptions to the rule and sometimes the rule needs to be broken to maximise happiness. For a weak utilitarian, it is the *principle of utility* that gives an act its moral value, and so lying would be the right thing to do.

Both versions though have their problems. Strong utilitarianism is a bit like **divine command ethics** – you must always follow the rule, not matter what. This, as in the example above, can lead to counter-intuitive examples. Also, it can involve claiming that some acts were the right thing to do (as they followed the rule) even though they may do more harm than good – which goes against the principle of utility.

Weak utilitarianism claims that you should make exceptions to rules, to maximise utility. However, in taking this approach, critics argue that you have a duty to check each time you apply a rule to see whether the application would maximise happiness or whether you should make an exception. But, of course, this is (more or less) to revert to act utilitarianism – which is not really fit for purpose as a method of deliberation. Also, what is the status of moral rules if the principle of utility is the ultimate judge of whether an act is right or wrong?

Although these are presented as criticisms of rule utilitarianism, Mill (a weak utilitarian) also sees them as a strength. The dilemma of 'lying' can also be seen as a clash of different rules – or secondary principles, as Mill called them. There is a rule that says lying is wrong, but there is also a general rule to prevent harm to others. When these secondary principles clash then we should appeal to the primary principle – the principle of utility. One of the strengths of the theory of utilitarianism is that there *is* a primary principle to appeal to. Without this, what could people appeal to when moral rules or commandments clash?

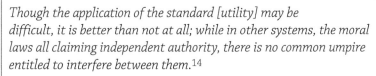

> We must remember that only in these cases of conflict between secondary principles is it requisite that first principles should be appealed to.[13]
>
> Though the application of the standard [utility] may be difficult, it is better than not at all; while in other systems, the moral laws all claiming independent authority, there is no common umpire entitled to interfere between them.[14]
>
> Mill

Criticism
Does rule utilitarianism collapse into act?
Continuing from the example above, a rule utilitarian might argue that *'Don't lie'* is still a good rule, but that it needs refining. The rule should be something like *'Don't lie, unless it is to a potential murderer'*. This looks promising, but the difficulties with this approach are that:

a) The process of refining could go further still. We could always imagine other scenarios where the best outcome is to lie, and we could always refine the rule further, e.g. *don't lie unless to potential murderers, or to partners when they ask if their haircuts are nice.* Every time there is a set of cases where lying may produce more happiness, then we could make an amendment to the rule. However, this process, taken to its logical conclusion, would effectively end up with a version of act utilitarianism, but with rules that apply to very, very specific sets of circumstances. Some have argued that it would in fact become act utilitarianism.

b) The advantage of rule utilitarianism is that the rules are simple and easy to follow. If refinements to each rule are needed to better maximise utility, then the theory loses its usefulness and appeal.

Two-tier utilitarianism

The English philosopher Richard Hare outlined a two-tier version of utilitarianism. Act utilitarianism is the judge, and rule utilitarianism is the principle of deliberation for humans (most of the time). In other words, the moral value of each act is still decided by the amount of happiness it brings/pain it avoids, but for humans we should follow moral rules most of the time, as this will result in maximising happiness. However, there will be times in all of our lives when we need to question a rule, or think harder about a specific dilemma. In these instances we should revert to act utilitarianism and try to work out the best action based on the likely outcomes.

▶ **ACTIVITY: Two-tier view**

Draw a diagram representing this two-tier view of utilitarianism.

Preference utilitarianism

As well as articulating two-tier utilitarianism, Richard Hare also developed a new version of the theory, known as preference utilitarianism.

Earlier we outlined several criticisms concerning the idea of 'pleasure':

- The thought experiment of the pleasure machine suggests that often what people desire are specific states of affairs in the world, not just sensations in their heads (page 18).
- Mill's idea of higher and lower pleasures also raises questions about whether we should just maximise the quantity of pleasure, or rather provide the specific pleasures that people (or competent judges) would choose (page 29).
- We also explored the idea that pleasure is not a singular thing, but rather a way of collectively describing those things that we desire or prefer (page 19).

Preference utilitarianism acknowledges these issues with the concept of pleasure, and puts the emphasis on our preferences instead. It suggests an action should be judged by the extent to which it conforms to the preferences of all those affected by the action (and its consequences). In other words, the morally good thing to do is whatever maximises the satisfaction of the preferences of all involved. So, for example, when considering whether to turn off the life support machine of someone terminally ill, rather that aiming to maximise happiness, you should find out what all the relevant parties would prefer. Furthermore, in line with classic utilitarianism, you are required to think of the general good – so you should count your preferences in the same way as those of other people – no more, no less.

As we saw, it can be argued that act utilitarianism might lead to a world where giving everyone wonder drugs and forcing them to watch Michael McIntyre DVDs was the right thing to do. Pleasurable as it might be, most people would not specifically desire this. It would not be their preference. As a preference utilitarian, it would be wrong to do this. By focusing on what people actually want, rather than on someone else's (say a government's) idea of what makes people happy, preference utilitarianism also avoids the criticism that utilitarianism can lead to social engineering (see page 24).

Preference utilitarianism also has an advantage in that preferences are easier to find out – you can ask people. We don't need to have a hedonistic calculus or pleasure-ometer. Although some system of ranking preferences is still needed, as not all preferences are equally strong.

Differences between classic and preference utilitarianism

Many moral decisions will be the same whichever form of utilitarianism you choose, but the reasons for the decisions may be different. Classic utilitarianism sees lying as wrong as it often leads to *unhappiness*. For a preference utilitarian, lying is also often wrong, but this is because it goes against the *preference* we have to know the truth.

▶ **ACTIVITY: Birthday time**

It's your birthday! But what are you going to get? When people buy you presents they generally try to maximise your happiness (within their budget); however, there are different deliberation processes that might be involved. A buyer might:

a) think about what makes them happy, and buy you the same thing
b) think about what makes people happy in general, and buy accordingly
c) think about what might make you happy, and buy that
d) think about what you might want, and buy accordingly
e) ask you what you want, and buy that.

Which is the best strategy?

What do you prefer on your birthday?

A classic utilitarian might use any of these strategies. A preference utilitarian would use (d) and (e). Strategies (a) to (c) may involve buying you something you have never thought about, which could turn out to be the best way to make you happy (although you might end up with a lot of Michael McInytyre DVDs!). However, over time, it can be argued that it would be better to use (d) and (e) to get you what you would prefer, as this will avoid lots of unwanted and unused gifts.

Please note that this thought example is not a perfect case study, as often people *prefer* to be surprised by gifts, and also, young children might have silly preferences (*I want a baby elephant!*). So strategies (a) to (c) may be preferable or in the best interest of the birthday boy/girl. However, the thought experiment shows how preference utilitarianism (options (d) and (e)) puts the emphasis on your preference – your conception of the good life, rather than options (a) to (c) which involve someone else's idea of your happiness.

The focus on preferences can also be seen as solving some counter-intuitive utilitarian puzzles. From the perspective of act utilitarianism, a husband that cheats on his wife can be seen as doing a good thing – as long as the wife doesn't find out. Likewise with borrowing a friend's precious coat without asking, or reading someone's secret diary. However, in each of these cases, a person's preference would be thwarted – as the wife would prefer the husband to be faithful, a friend would prefer you not to borrow their coat or read their diary.

Peter Singer

Preference utilitarianism is most commonly associated with the Australian philosopher Peter Singer (who was a student of Richard Hare). For Singer, happiness and the avoidance of pain are still at the core of the theory, but these should be gained/avoided by thinking about people's preferences. Singer applies his version of preference utilitarianism to a range of ethical issues, most famously to the treatment of animals.

Bentham, some 150 year earlier, had raised the issue of whether animals' suffering should count in a utilitarian's thinking.

> *The day may come when the rest of animal creation may acquire those rights which never could have been withholden from them but by the hand of tyranny …. The question is not, Can they reason? nor Can they talk? but, Can they suffer?*[15]
>
> Bentham

Singer has developed this line of thinking much further. He argues that the basis for moral equality among humans cannot be derived from any specific talents, such as a certain level of IQ or sporting prowess, as not all humans share these. The basis for our moral equality is our sentience, our ability to feel pain and pleasure – which we all share. Singer argues that as animals are also sentient, we should also take their interests into account when making decisions. To not take into account their ability to suffer would be an example of speciesism (treating species differently for no good reason).

It is therefore wrong to cause suffering to animals. Singer argues that most methods of intensive farming do cause considerable suffering to animals so it is wrong to eat meat from this source. However, eating meat is not always wrong. Animals are limited in their rationality and (as far as we know) do not hold specific hopes and thoughts about the future (with the possible exception of great apes). As such, animals do not have conscious preferences, which Singer claims does make a difference to how we might treat them morally.

What makes killing humans morally wrong is not specifically the potential loss of pleasure, but that the killing goes against the preference of the victim (and the preferences of the victim's family and friends). Staying alive is (generally) the strongest preference that anyone has, and this is what makes murder so bad.

However, animals do not have a conscious preference to stay alive, so the painless killing of an animal does not go against its preference, and so is not morally wrong on this account. However, if someone killed your family pet then this would go against the preferences of the family and so it would be a wrong act.

Controversially Singer extends this line of thinking to young (and unborn) babies. They do not have conscious preferences, so ending their lives does not go against their preference (though again, it is more than likely to go against the preferences of the family).

anthology
1.3

Criticism 1
Bad and crazy preferences
Preference utilitarianism claims that it is good to maximise/satisfy people's preferences. But is this always the case? Consider the following examples.

- **A** Tas wants to drink the wine in her glass (she does not know it is poisoned).
- **B** Little Johnny, aged four, is having a meltdown because he wants a fourth lollipop.
- **C** David has become increasingly psychotic and wants to punch strangers.
- **D** Sim is quite depressed and wants to self-harm.

In these cases it would seem wrong to try and satisfy their preferences.

However, the preference utilitarian has some defences they can mount. In example A, if Tas knew about the poison, she would not want to drink the wine. In these cases we can try to imagine what Tas would prefer from an 'ideal viewpoint' position – in other words, if she knew the wine was poisoned. In which case, she clearly would not drink it. Preference utilitarianism sometimes makes the distinction between a person's manifest preference (to drink the wine) and their true or idealised preference (to not drink the wine, if they knew it were poisoned). In such cases we should seek to fulfil their true preference.

In example B, Little Johnny clearly is capable of preferences, and may even be aware that sugar is bad for his teeth, so has some knowledge base.

However, preference utilitarians may argue that young people, or people with severe mental restrictions, will lack sufficient understanding of the world to reach their true or idealised preference. As such, adults should sometimes seek to act in their interest, rather than satisfying their every preference.

In example C, the preference utilitarian has three lines of defence:

C1 Other people's preference not to be punched would be much stronger than David's desire to punch, so it would be wrong for David to punch others, or for us to help him.

C2 Because David's mental health is becoming a problem, we should not seek to satisfy his preferences, but rather what his preferences might be after a suitable course of therapy. Again, this would be to argue that his manifest desire to punch others is not his true or ideal desire.

C3 As with the classic version, there is rule preference utilitarianism – which claims that we should follow the rules which, overall, will satisfy people's preferences. In this case, 'Don't punch people' would clearly be a rule.

In example D, as with C2 above, it could be argued that this is not Sim's true or idealised desire and that a course of therapy would change the desire. However, if this were not the case, then a preference utilitarian would say that it is right that Sim satisfies her preference.

Criticism 2
Preferences from a distance
Consider the following preferences:

A James is now dead. He told his son (Bobby) to scatter his ashes on his favourite football club's pitch. The club charge £10,000 for this.

B Sammy would prefer that indigenous Amazonian tribes stay in the rainforest and avoid modern life.

Should a preference utilitarian take account of these preferences when making decisions?

In example A, an act utilitarian would say that Bobby could probably spend the money maximising happiness in better ways. After all, James is no longer alive to experience happiness. A rule utilitarian might say that Bobby should keep his promise (if he made one) as keeping promises, in general, will maximise happiness. A preference utilitarian may say that we should still try to fulfil the preference, even if James is not alive, as fulfilling preferences is the right thing to do. This may (or may not) seem counter-intuitive.

In example B, Sammy may have a strong preference about this, but he never intends to visit the Amazon basin, it is just a preference about how he wants the world to be. Should Sammy's preference be a factor in any individual's or government's decisions? How should we weigh this against the preferences of the Amazonian tribes people themselves? It seems a bit odd that we should take into account someone's preferences about things when they have no direct causal connection to the people involved.

Criticism 3
Weighing up of preferences
Bentham's hedonistic calculus was an attempt to quantify different pleasures and pains to help facilitate moral decision-making. Preference utilitarianism needs something equivalent to this. If people have different preferences – for example if some are for, and some against, building a proposed airport, then how are we to know the morally right thing to do? Is it a question of numbers, or does strength of preference make a difference? Also, what about the preferences of people that are not directly affected by the airport, or even expressed preferences of those who have died – should these all count? In the gladiatorial arena, thousands of baying Romans want to see a Christian die at the claws of a lion. The Christian though, would prefer to live. Does this one person's preference override the thousands? These are not insurmountable problems for the preference utilitarian. Act utilitarianism also faced these problems, and rule utilitarianism, for example in the form of a right to life, can be seen as a good solution. Likewise, rule preference utilitarianism can find solutions, although the question of weighing preferences still remains.

Strengths of utilitarianism

So far we have seen that utilitarianism is based on a very simple idea: *that happiness is the good*. Thinking this simple idea through has led to a number of variations of the theory – but the core remains. This gives the theory a number of strengths. Basing the theory on something tangible(ish) allows reason to compare and contrast different actions and provides a common moral 'currency' that is flexible, universal, non-religious and transcends culture.

Bentham initially intended his theory to apply to governments, as a way of measuring which laws/policies were good ones (those that raised happiness). This approach has been adopted by governments throughout the world. When considering any policy or potential spending, governments will frequently undertake some form of cost–benefit analysis. This is essentially a utilitarian method of deliberation. Will building a new road in town A or B add more to the general happiness? When deciding whether a new, expensive cancer treatment should be available on the NHS, the government has to think how the money could be otherwise spent and whether this new treatment is a cost-effective way of reducing suffering. These are difficult decisions, but without utilitarianism how could we even go about thinking them through?

So, utilitarianism has been hugely influential, but the quantitative and consequentialist approach it takes to morality raises some serious questions; and it is to these that we now turn.

Issues with utilitarianism

Individual liberty and rights

Earlier (pages 30–2) we saw that act utilitarianism could lead to some counter-intuitive moral **judgements**, for example, sacrificing scapegoats to please the masses or killing one person to use their organs for five.

Rule utilitarianism can potentially avoid these problems by arguing that following moral rules makes an act right or wrong, and these rules would include having rights – such as the right to life, liberty and freedom of speech.

Using this approach, utilitarians would argue that rights/values such as liberty and right to life have no moral worth in themselves, but are useful devices only because they are a means to bringing about overall happiness. However, some people object to this approach. They claim that ideals and rights such as liberty, honour and justice have value as ends in themselves and not just as side effects of the quest for pleasure. Such ideals have their own moral worth.

Consider these examples.

Example 8: Flatmates

A Zach lives with four housemates (while studying philosophy at university). All of the housemates hate cleaning and tidying, but Zach does not mind it as much as the others. As utilitarians, they work out that Zach should do all of the cleaning and tidying as this would maximise utility. Zach agrees but has a nagging doubt that this is not fair.

Example 9: Slavery

B A family kidnap an orphan boy from a very poor country and keep him as their slave. He is prevented from ever leaving the house. The boy is well fed, not beaten and the work he is made to do greatly increases the happiness of the family.

These situations can be seen as maximising utility, but are they fair? Rule utilitarians might argue that they are wrong as they breach moral rules that in general would maximise happiness. But critics would claim that these cases are wrong – not that they breach a rule which overall would maximise happiness, but because case A is not fair and case B denies someone their liberty. And both liberty and fairness (justice) are worth pursuing as ends in themselves – independently of whether or not they maximise happiness. Such ideals/rights have moral worth in themselves. They are morally primitive and do not derive their moral worth from their ability to maximise happiness.

People have undergone great hardships including sacrificing their own lives in the name of liberty, democracy and justice. It *could* be argued that these people were just trying to maximise happiness – but do people really sacrifice their lives for the ideal of maximising happiness? Many socialists would claim that a society where wealth is more evenly distributed is better than a society that is overall richer and *happier* but more unequal. What is important is not the happiness, but the *fairness*.

Mill on liberty

The case of liberty is an interesting one. If you were reluctant to step into the pleasure machine (page 17) it could be because you didn't like the idea of being trapped inside. Perhaps you valued your liberty more than your happiness. John Stuart Mill was a passionate advocate for liberty. He was concerned that utilitarianism (and democracy) can see the desires of minorities crushed under the weight of the majority. For example, the UK is a democracy, so if there were a majority vote at a referendum to ban homosexual sex, should we do so? Mill was concerned about this and argued that governments and other individuals should only interfere in your life to prevent you causing harm to others. Individuals should be left to pursue their own lives in the way they see fit. His account of liberty has been hugely influential. Mill claimed it is consistent with the principle of utility – i.e. adopting a 'hands off' approach will lead to more happiness in the long run. However, many dispute whether this is the case and would claim that *liberty* is an end in its own right.

Some problems with calculating utility

This next set of criticisms involve difficulties, both theoretical and practical, with assessing how much happiness/avoidance of pain an action may bring about.

It is impossible to compare pleasures

Bentham thoughtfully provided an ingenious utility calculus to aid our moral thinking (see page 21), but he did not explain how we're supposed to go about measuring things like the 'intensity' or 'remoteness' of the pleasure or pain. Should we issue a questionnaire to the people involved? ('On a scale of 1–10 how would you rate the pain of exam revision?') As outlined earlier (page 21) it is hard enough to compare and rate two of your own pleasures in your own head, let alone compare the value of pleasure between people.

Average happiness versus total happiness

▶ **ACTIVITY: Two worlds**

Imagine two worlds:

- World A has 10 billion people who are not particularly happy, but not sad either. Let's say they have a net happiness worth of 1 point each. This gives a world with a total of 10 billion happiness points, at an average of 1 point per person.
- World B has 1 billion people, but they are much happier – say, an average of 9 happiness points each. This gives a total of 9 billion happiness points at an average of 9 points per person.

Which is the better world?

World A has a higher happiness total, but world B has a higher average. When we aim to maximise utility, is it average utility or total that we should aim for? This is a difficult (and real) question for utilitarians and also for governments. Is it better to have large populations who are less happy (perhaps because of overcrowding and limited resources) or smaller populations who may be happier per person, but with a lower total happiness? The answer makes a moral difference. If you are trying to maximise the total, then providing free contraception would be morally wrong (as it stops children being born, who would add to the total happiness), whereas if you were maximising the average, then providing free contraception may be the right thing to do.

Both approaches have their problems. Going for the total may end up with an overcrowded world of barely happy people; going for the average could involve killing anyone less than averagely happy (as this would raise the average). Though taken to its logical conclusion, this would end up with a world with just one person in it – who is fantastically happy!

Strict versus progressive accounts of utilitarianism

This problem isn't really one of calculation, but rather a problem as to what to describe as a good action in relation to the calculation.

The pizza example (page 22) involved you treating friends to a meal. We imagined that this added happiness to the world (a notional 99 points) and so was a morally good act. However, you *could* have used that money differently; perhaps by giving it to a charity you could have treated 100 starving people to a decent, hot meal. This, surely, would have provided more than 99 happiness points. If this is the case, was treating your friends to pizza a good, or right thing to do?

A strict utilitarian would claim that a good action is one that *maximises* general happiness. So treating friends to pizza would not be good, as there are many better options in terms of bringing about happiness. Our moral duty is to maximise happiness with our actions.

A progressive utilitarian would say that treating friends to pizza was a good act as it *increased* general happiness. Though other acts would be better as they would have increased general happiness more. Our moral duty is to increase general happiness (though it would be good to maximise it).

Both versions have problems. The strict version would mean that a non-wealthy single mother who gives away half of her income to charity is still not doing the right thing. It is not a good act, as she could have given even more. This seems too strict. The progressive version would mean that any act that adds happiness is morally good – even telling a joke. Or perhaps a sadistic surgeon[16] who fixes broken bones, but does so deliberately in a way that makes the recovery more painful. He is still performing good acts, as over time his acts relieve more pain than they cause. But to call his actions good seems too lenient. Some argue for a compromise version.

Distribution of happiness

All our happiness should be equally weighted when making decisions. We all count for one. Nevertheless most actions only affect some people; they have no impact on the vast majority. This raises some difficult questions in our deliberation. Is it better to make one person 100 points happier or ten people 10 points happier? The total happiness is the same in both cases.

Left-leaning thinkers argue that a wider, more even distribution is the ideal to aim at. The wealth of the richest few could be better used to raise happiness for all. Right-leaning thinkers disagree; they argue that we are all better off with a liberal, capitalist system that encourages wealth and protects individual property. Yes, some people will be richer than others, but overall this system will make us all happier.

Even within your own life, the question of the distribution of happiness is a dilemma. Is it better to have lots of highs and lows, or a quieter life with less fluctuation (but with the same total of happiness)? Is it better to have a life that starts with less happiness and gets better, or a life that starts with lots of happiness that gets worse? (Again, the total is the same.) Which would you prefer?

Where do consequences end? Example 10: Young Hitler

You are walking alongside an Austrian river in January 1900, as the new century is beginning. You see a young boy, about 11 years old, fall into the river and you wade out and rescue him from drowning. This boy is called Adolf Hitler and he goes on to cause the deaths of millions of innocent people.

From a utilitarian perspective this would initially look like a good act, as the young Hitler and his family would be very happy. In the end it turned out to be a very bad act, as millions went on to suffer and die. So the act would be classed as a bad act. The problem is that if the moral worth of an act is based on its consequences, then the moral worth of the act has to be constantly revised and there is no final moral value that can be assigned. If this is the case, can we ever say whether an act is definitely good or bad?

Please note that this is not a problem for deliberation, e.g. *Should I save the boy or not?* Saving the boy would always be a praiseworthy act, as you could not reasonably foresee the longer-term consequences. And it is good to follow the rule 'Save life when you can'. The problem lies in deciding the moral worth of an act.

The value of motives and of the character

As a consequentialist theory, utilitarianism bases the moral worth of an action on its consequences alone. This has advantages in as much as consequences are more transparent than motives. For example, a government may introduce a new policy to win favour with voters, or for reasons of personal ambition, or to annoy the opposition.

The true motives may never be known. In contrast, what *can* be seen is whether the policy has utility – whether it maximises happiness. It is on this basis alone, according to utilitarians, that we should judge the policy as good or bad.

We have already seen that this approach can appear counter-intuitive (see page 23). In the next section we explore the moral philosophy of Immanuel Kant, who, in contrast, claimed that it is entirely the motive that gives actions their moral worth; the consequences are irrelevant.

Is the character important?

For Bentham, no person's pleasure should be more important than another's. The Queen's happiness counts for no more than yours or mine or a murderer's. All humans are weighted equally in the utility calculus which means that the value of an action is completely independent of any virtues of the people involved. So each unit of suffering that a prisoner may experience from losing their freedom counts equally with each unit of suffering that the victim of the crime experienced. All suffering is bad; it does not matter whose it is – only the quantity counts (and the victim is likely to have more). Likewise with happiness, the happiness gained from bad means, say from bullying, is just as good as that from hard-earned toil. The act of bullying, of course would not be good as it no doubt produces more suffering than pleasure. But when doing the calculation, the pleasure gained from bullying counts equally with any form of pleasure. This can feel counter-intuitive.

Earlier (page 22) we analysed a mugging and concluded that it was a bad act. Now consider these examples.

Example 11: Robin Hood 1

A close associate of Mr Amveryrich (the billionaire owner of Madchester football club), through some clever accounting, steals £10 million from Mr Amveryrich's account (who never finds out). He uses the money to fund an orphanage in Lithuania.

Is this a good act? Some moral systems (often based on commandments) claim that it is not the motive nor the consequence that counts; it is the very act itself that is the source of moral value. Some acts, like stealing, are just wrong. Clearly a utilitarian rejects this view. An act utilitarian is likely to say this was a good act. A rule utilitarian may say that the rule of stealing was broken and so it was a bad act – as this rule, in general, will maximise happiness.

Example 12: Robin Hood 2

A close associate of Mr Amveryrich (the billionaire owner of Madchester football club), through some clever accounting, steals £10 million from Mr Amveryrich's account (who never finds out). He uses the money to fund a group of his criminal, heroin-addict friends. Now they can all live a safe and comfortable life in a big mansion (in a country with no extradition treaties) and can now have as much heroin as they want.

Is this a good act?

Again, an act utilitarian is likely to say that it is (as long as they are convinced that heroin makes you happy in the longer term). However, our intuitions tell us that there is a significant difference between the two scenarios. In the first scenario we may be inclined to think that the motive is somehow better (but why? the thief is raising happiness in both cases). Also, we may not want to count the happiness of the criminals in the same way that we count the happiness of the orphans.

Utilitarianism requires us to drop these moral intuitions and treat all human pleasure equally. The moral value of an act is solely related to the amount of pleasure it brings. The 'moral' character of the person carrying out the act, and of those gaining the happiness, is irrelevant. For some critics, this is counter-intuitive and so is a problem.

Utilitarianism and personal integrity

Bernard Williams argues that ethical systems such as utilitarianism (and Kantian ethics) may require us to do things that go against our intuitions, and this challenges our sense of personal integrity. The following example illustrates a difficult choice.

Example 13: Jim in the outback

A botanist, Jim, is working in a South American country that is fairly lawless. Jim ends up in a small town, where the local warlord treats him as a guest of honour. The warlord has recently captured 20 rebels from local tribes and says that if Jim personally kills one of them, he will release the others as a sign of good will. If Jim does not do this, he will kill them all.

What should Jim do?

An act utilitarian would say there is no dilemma here. You kill the one to save the 19. However, Jim does not want to kill anyone. It goes against his principles. What should he do? Utilitarianism, as a consequentialist ethic, would have us do anything in the name of maximising happiness. There is no act so bad that we cannot invent a scenario where this is the right thing to do. Furthermore a utilitarian would say that if Jim did kill the one man, he should not have any guilt or regret, as it was the right thing to do.

The problem is that consequentialist ethics never allow you to draw a line in the sand and say 'I won't do that'. Yet, Williams argues, for many people, their personal integrity demands that there are such lines in the sand. In this way, utilitarianism undermines our personal integrity. The character of the person committing the act may not reckon in the moral value of the act, but it does matter to the person committing the act.

▶ **ACTIVITY: Should you feel guilty?**

Example 14: The ocean liner

Another example from Williams involves an ocean liner that starts to sink. You jump into a lifeboat which is already at capacity. As the lifeboat drifts away, dozens more people swim towards it and try to climb in. The lifeboat cannot take any more weight and is starting to sink. Utilitarianism demands that you grab the oar and start smashing the hands of those trying to get into the boat, so they cannot climb in. These actions haunt you forever. Yet a utilitarian would say that you are foolish; after all, you did the right thing so there is nothing to worry about.

● Would you pick up the oar and keep the others off the boat?
● Would this haunt you?
● Would you feel guilty?
● According to utilitarianism should it haunt you?
● Does it matter if your conscience or personal integrity run counter to utilitarianism?

These are difficult questions! In Section 1.1.3 on virtue ethics we explore a different approach to ethics entirely. This approach, deriving from ancient times, focuses moral worth not on consequences, nor on the motive, but on the people that carry out the actions themselves. What is important is to be a good person, as this is the key source of moral value.

The value of relationships

As a reformer, Bentham was passionate about equality, especially complete equality for women. The utilitarian morality sees everyone as equally important: '*every individual in the country tells for one; no individual for more than one*'[17] (This is often misquoted as '*each to count for one and none for more than one*').

So a good utilitarian should treat people as moral equals – however, this also involves not favouring yourself, or those close to you, when making moral decisions. In Mill's words:

> [T]he happiness which forms the utilitarian standard of what is right in conduct, is not the agent's own happiness, but that of all concerned. As between his own happiness and that of others, utilitarianism requires him to be as strictly impartial as a disinterested and benevolent spectator.[18]
>
> Mill

This view, taken from a strict utilitarian stance, would seem to make our moral duties far reaching. Given that there are people in the world who are starving and in need of shelter, it would seem to be that I should give nearly all of my money to help these people – and I should do this every time I get money. This is the view adopted by a young Peter Singer. Writing about a humanitarian crisis in Bengal he argued that people:

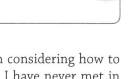

... ought to give as much as possible, that is, at least up to the point at which by giving more one would begin to cause serious suffering for oneself and one's dependents.[19]

Singer

But is it right to treat everyone equally? When considering how to act morally, am I really obliged to treat people I have never met in Bengal equally with my family and friends? Consider the following example.

Example 15: Burning house

Your house is burning. You bravely rush inside to help. Breaking down a door, you find two people lying unconscious. You can only carry one out. One is a young and brilliant scientist who is working on a cure for cancer, the other person is your son. Who should you save?

An act utilitarian would say that saving the scientist would be the most likely way of maximising general happiness; however, most people would save their own son. This, they would argue, was the right thing to do, because we have moral obligations to our family and friends.

How could a utilitarian respond to this difference between what their theory says is the right thing and many/most people's intuitions?

There are two elements to this:

The judgment about what it the right thing to do (J) (save the scientist) and

The intuition about what it the right thing to do (I) (save the son).

- **J is right, I is wrong.** A utilitarian could maintain that saving the scientist is the right thing to do (J) and explain that it is understandable to want to save your son (I), but wrong. They may add that the instincts we have to look after family are driven by evolution, but that they are morally wrong.
- **J is right, I is right.** A rule, or two-tier utilitarian might try to claim that saving your son is the right thing to do, as the rule of looking after family is a good one (as it ensures that everyone is looked after and this will maximise happiness). However, in this instance, saving the scientist would have maximised happiness. So the judgement is that saving the scientist is better, but the rule – the method of deliberation – says that saving the son is better.

Singer later argues for this point of view.

> *It is from an agent-neutral point of view that we determine whether an action was right; but it is a mistake to focus always on the rightness of individual actions, rather than on the habit or intuitive ways of thinking that can be expected, over a lifetime, to do the most good.*[20]
>
> Singer

Whether a utilitarian can maintain this seemingly contradictory position is debatable.

▪ **J is wrong, I is right.** Critics may argue that it is right to save your son, on every level. It is right because we have special moral obligations to our family. This could be because we have duties of care and/or because relationships have moral worth, and not, as a rule utilitarian may argue, because looking after families is just a useful way of maximising happiness. Looking after families is an end in itself, not a side effect of maximising happiness.

Utilitarianism gives moral worth to strange things

Learn More

The focus on pleasure at the core of utilitarianism can be seen to give moral value to counter-intuitive acts. The gruesome killings in the Colosseum entertained thousands – yet most would say they were not a good thing. Although a rule utilitarian can explain how this is wrong, other odd cases still emerge. Stand-up comedians bring pleasure to thousands, yet few would want to claim that their work has the same moral value as the hard toil of doctors and nurses volunteering in a war zone.

For some utilitarians (so-called 'negative utilitarians' because they aim to reduce pain) this emphasis is misplaced. Negative utilitarians argue that rather than strive to achieve the best balance of happiness over pain, we should be concerned with minimising extremes of pain. This modification to the theory is better able to deal with the example of the Romans' enjoyment outweighing the Christians' pain. Such 'entertainments' do not seem to be good in a moral sense, and the negative utilitarian, unlike their counterpart, is not committed to saying they are good.

Preference utilitarianism also gives more attention to suffering and less to pleasure, as most people will always prefer to have pain reduced rather than gain pleasure. In this way, preference utilitarians argue that our moral priorities should be to relieve pain and suffering in the world.

Summary of utilitarianism

Despite the many problems with Bentham's and Mill's versions of utilitarianism, the theory captures a powerful intuition: that morality is not just about following rigid rules and principles irrespective of the consequences (as Kantian deontology tells us). For many policy-makers, utilitarianism is the only moral theory in town: it doesn't depend on any metaphysical system (such as the belief in God); it is flexible (unlike Kantian ethics); and it seems to describe much of what we do mean by a morally good act (one that increases the amount of happiness and decreases the amount of pain in the world). It is a firmly humanistic and practical system, even if it isn't the whizz-bang moral-calculating machine that its originators first thought.

Because of its power, utilitarianism has become influential in policy-making around the world. When economists and politicians try to determine policy they will, in general, perform a cost–benefit analysis on the different courses of action available to them. In other words, they weigh up the costs and the benefits, to help them to decide what policy or decision will maximise the benefits.

Utilitarianism: Applied ethics

In this section we will apply the theory of utilitarianism to five specific areas:

- Crime and punishment
- War
- Simulated killing
- The treatment of animals
- Deception and the telling of lies.

In each section we refer back to the ethical dilemmas presented in the introduction (pages 6–11).

Crime and punishment

For a utilitarian, laws are only justified if they maximise utility; that is their sole purpose.

> *The general object which all laws have, or ought to have, in common, is to augment the total happiness of the community; and therefore, in the first place, to exclude, as far as may be, every thing that tends to subtract from that happiness: in other words, to exclude mischief.*[21]
>
> Bentham

But if a law is only morally right if it maximises utility, does this mean that we should break the law if, on a particular occasion, it looks like breaking it would maximise utility?

Of course, most people who break the law do it for personal gain, at the expense of others. Overall pain is caused, so this is bad. Even when there is no obvious victim, this can still cause harm. For example, I might park in an empty disabled bay when there are plenty of spaces free. This saves me a lot of hassle, which seems to be maximising utility. However, seeing an apparently able person walking away from a disabled bay makes other people furious, so this would make the act morally wrong. Because of the strong disapproval of law breaking, the default position of an act utilitarian is that law breaking is morally wrong.

However, some people may break the law not for personal gain, but for the general good. Recall the case of Robin Hood (page 46). This would seem to be an example of good law breaking. This for some is counter-intuitive. Consider these two cases:

A The Robin Hood case 1 (page 46), where the theft is never discovered.

B The Robin Hood case, where the theft is discovered.

An act utilitarian would say that in the case of A the act was a good act (because of the consequences). Whereas in the case of B, the act was a bad act, as both the victim and the criminal will suffer. The guilty criminal's suffering actually makes the act bad in this case! However, this seems odd as the actual act is the same in both cases. For many people, what makes illegal acts bad is committing the act itself, not the consequences. It's just bad to break the law.

This is exactly the position of strong rule utilitarianism: it is always wrong to break a rule/law (as long as the law is one that overall maximises happiness) as the moral value of an act comes from its observance of the rule. Because many laws *are* moral rules (Don't kill, steal, drive dangerously, etc.) the law *is*, in effect, rule utilitarianism.

For a strong rule utilitarian, the only time it is right to break the law is if you felt the law is unjust. For example, in 1930 Mahatma Gandhi encouraged thousands to march with him in India and extract salt directly from the sea, without paying the salt tax to the British, which he thought unjust. (Also see the case of Clive Ponting, page 100.)

For a weak rule utilitarian, you should follow just laws, but on those few occasions when happiness will clearly be gained by breaking the law, then it is morally right to break it (though not legally right). For example, driving through a red light on a deserted road at night, when your wife is about to give birth may be the morally right thing to do.

A rule utilitarian, however, would *also* argue that utility is best achieved by us all following the law and not making exceptions, which would be to set a meta-rule about rule-following itself. So the utilitarian would not only have to feel that breaking the individual law would maximise happiness, but also take into account the general way that this undermines laws and so makes us less happy. This makes the act of law-breaking even harder to justify.

▶ ACTIVITY

Read CP2 on page 7. What would a utilitarian say?

A utilitarian should not place the value of his wife's happiness above that of anyone else (which, again, some feel is counter-intuitive; see pages 48–50). It would only be right to steal the drug for his wife if it is also right to steal it for a stranger he has never met. The NHS has analysed the situation and obviously feels that the money the drug costs could be used more efficiently to make people happy. This is the rule that has been set. From an act utilitarian perspective it would seem wrong to use the drug as the money could be better used elsewhere (presuming the NHS would get the money back from the drug company for the left-over drugs). Also, drug companies need to sell their drugs to fund research into new drugs. Stealing drugs means reducing this research, which in the long term may result in less reduction of suffering.

From a rule utilitarian perspective the rule has been set by the NHS on the basis of maximising utility. This would seem to be a just rule and so it would be wrong to break it.

Punishment

For a utilitarian, punishment, because it brings about displeasure, is a bad thing. The pain of a prisoner counts for no less than the pain of anyone else, including the victim. (Some find this idea very counter-intuitive.) Because all pain is bad, its use has to be carefully justified. Bentham thought that it can only be justified if it prevents future harm.

> ... all punishment is mischief: all punishment in itself is evil. Upon the principle of utility, if it ought at all to be admitted, it ought only to be admitted in as far as it promises to exclude some greater evil.[22]
>
> Bentham

Bentham's work on punishment has been very influential and his was one of the first attempts to outline a system of punishment that had a rational basis (the principle of utility). He argued that as punishment is bad it should only be justified if it prevents more bad and so cannot be administered in the name of 'retribution', as this is just to add more pain into the world. Punishment must be forward looking and the best way to reduce harm is to affect the ongoing motivation of the individual and others.

Punishments should be weighted so as to change people's motivations. To do this, all punishments should 'cost' more in pain than you could gain from the crime, otherwise there is no motivation to avoid the crime. Punishment should also be graded according to offence, so the less harm from the offence, the less pain in the punishment; as otherwise there is no motivation to commit a smaller crime rather than a larger one (e.g. to steal five apples instead of ten).

Utilitarianism has no clear line on the death penalty. Bentham and Singer argue against it, but not Mill. For a utilitarian, there is no intrinsic 'right to life'; all rights serve to maximise happiness, so we can only justify the idea of right on the basis of utility and it may be the case that 'you have a right to life, unless you kill others' is the rule that best does this. In the UK in 2014, only 45 per cent favoured the death penalty. In many countries, however, the death penalty is very popular. This, itself, can be used as an argument for having the death penalty.

The strongest utilitarian arguments though would be evidence-based ones (empirical ones). Does having a death penalty reduce the likelihood of murder? The evidence for this is not strong.

▶ **ACTIVITY**

Read CP1 on page 7. What would a utilitarian say?

CP1 raises some familiar issues for the utilitarian (see the scapegoat example on page 31). The public are so angry that it may not even matter if the man is guilty or not; it may still be the right thing to do, as people want to be avenged. This is a general criticism of utilitarianism: that the theory makes happiness override justice, and this feels intuitively wrong.

A rule utilitarian would argue that making the severity of punishment correspond to the strength of feeling would be a bad rule and not in the best interest of utility. For example, a man may have built up years of incredible rage over his neighbour, Jim, parking slightly too close to his drive. Should Jim be killed on the day he finally parks too close and illegally blocks the drive? Strength of feeling is too subjective to be the basis for punishment and would not enable a proper system of deterrent punishment to be in place. So it would be wrong to be swayed on the strength of feeling alone. However, if it can be argued that the death penalty would serve as a deterrent to prevent similar crimes in the future, then it could be justified.

In 2000 a doctor, Harold Shipman, was found guilty of killing 15 elderly patients (it is thought the true number of victims could have been 250). He was sentenced to life imprisonment. In 2004, he killed himself. Many of the victims' families felt cheated. The home secretary of the day, David Blunkett, recalled:

> You wake up and you receive a call telling you Shipman has topped himself and you think, is it too early to open a bottle? And then you discover that everybody's very upset that he's done it.[23]

This singular case shows that death itself can be seen as preferable to life imprisonment by some criminals, and also that the death of the criminal is not always preferable in the eyes of those affected.

War

In general, war is likely to be a bad thing, as it will lead to suffering. In Bentham's words:

> War is mischief upon the largest scale.[24]

For an act utilitarian, a just war is one that is likely to lead to more overall happiness than if it were not fought. This may even include starting wars for the purpose of regime change, for example to end malevolent dictatorships and put in place liberal governments. The utilitarian grounds for a just war go well beyond self-defence; in fact, any war is justified, as long as it leads to more happiness than not fighting it. An act utilitarian cannot easily use the justification of 'national interest', however, as it is *general* happiness rather than *nation-specific* happiness that should be maximised.

Although some of the issues relating to war can seem simple from a utilitarian perspective, the big issue is that it's very hard to sensibly discuss what the long-term consequences of going to war will be. War will inevitably lead to a great deal of pain, and the repercussions can last for hundreds of years. Because of this, some claim that discussing a just war on utilitarian grounds, in practice, becomes an exercise in advocacy (justifying a specific outcome) rather than in reason. For example, is the world happier after the second Iraq war (2003–11) than it would have been without the war? Who can possibly say?

A rule utilitarian may argue that countries should collectively work out rules for when a war is just (on the grounds of utilitarianism), then any subsequent decision to go to war should be based on these rules. There would be no need to revisit the idea of utility for each specific war. Again, as with crime, this leads to a two-tier approach. A just war is one that is engaged in for reasons agreed by the rules, and the rules are just if they maximise utility.

Some argue this is a close approximation to what happens in practice. The United Nations (UN) defines legitimate war as being restricted to *legitimate defence* and *measures taken by the Security Council to maintain peace*, and many countries will abide by these rules. (Note that the UN did not specifically agree these rules on utilitarian grounds.)

In terms of fair warfare (*jus in bello*), an act utilitarian cannot view any method as being intrinsically immoral, so no act of war is ruled out absolutely. This means that *any* act can be justified (e.g. torture, the use of chemical weapons), as long as it maximises happiness. For an act utilitarian, the end (happiness) justifies the means. It would be morally wrong to play by the 'fair rules' if this was likely to significantly lengthen the war and cause more suffering in the long term. An act utilitarian would argue that it is better to bring a war to a speedy conclusion, by what ever means necessary ('All is fair in love and war!'). But decisions to 'fight dirty' should not be taken lightly as this has long-lasting implications in terms of revenge, bad will, and repeated wars. So an act utilitarian could equally argue that winning a longer war by methods that are viewed to be 'fair' will prove better in the long term. Again, there is much crystal-ball gazing with act utilitarianism.

A strong rule utilitarian would again take the two-tier approach. Principles of conduct should be decided beforehand (using the principle of utility). Actions in any specific war are then right or wrong, in accordance with the rules (and not the principle of utility).

A weak utilitarian would argue that rules should be followed but in clear-cut cases the rules should be broken, as the principle of utility is the judge of right and wrong, not the rules. Cases in war bring out this dilemma clearly.

▶ **ACTIVITY**

Read W1 and W2 (pages 8–9). What would a utilitarian say?

Regarding W1, a weak rule utilitarian and an act utilitarian may argue for the use of torture, as its use may avert a specific incident which will cause much suffering. Arguments against can also be constructed: the torture may be ineffective and just result in the pain of the individual (remember all pain is bad). It may also result in revenge/torture being used more widely. A strong rule utilitarian would abide by the rules of 'just' war and not use torture.

In W2, an act (and maybe weak rule) utilitarian would be likely to argue for intervention as a humanitarian crisis looks imminent. During the Rwandan genocide (1994), the international community was widely criticised for not acting to stop the massacres. This was a case of internal conflict where the existing rules of just war are much harder to apply (and still are today). However, it was clear that the principle of utility would have demanded an intervention. So in W2 an act utilitarian would intervene. A weak rule utilitarian may too; remember that cases of breaking rules for a weak rule utilitarian have to be clear as there is the longer term damage caused by weakening the rules. A strong rule utilitarian would abide by the pre-established rules on just war. Unfortunately these are not clear in the cases of civil war, where a case-by-case examination is needed. A strong rule utilitarian may argue that a mandate from the UN security council is needed for military intervention, as these are the rules governing war. As this hasn't happened, military intervention would be wrong.

Simulated killing

▶ **ACTIVITY**

Read SK1 and SK2 on pages 9–10. What would a utilitarian say?

For a utilitarian, there is something paradoxical in the 'pleasure' gained from watching people being killed. On the one hand there is the pleasure, and on the other the portrayal of pain and death. Presumably people would think very differently if real death were involved (although public executions were always well attended historically).

This links to Nozick's analysis of the pleasure machine – what we want in life (and want to avoid in this case) are real events in the world, not just sensations in our head. The physical sensations of watching a fake or real death may be almost identical for the viewer; the difference is knowing that one is real and the other is not.

All pleasures are equal for the utilitarian (not quite for Mill though, as we shall see). The pleasure of watching a fake killing is of the same worth as that gained from listening to opera or that gained from watching a real killing. The pleasure counts for the same in each case; what determines whether it is a good or bad thing overall, is whether the sum total of pleasure outweighs the pain, or whether pleasure is maximised (this depends on your interpretation of utilitarianism; see page 44).

So, does watching deaths on stage, screen or in a video game, overall produce more happiness than it does harm? Could alternatives be produced that are more pleasurable, with less harm caused? Would the world be happier without simulated death, or with it?

These are the key questions for the utilitarian. There is no question of such entertainments being intrinsically wrong, as wrong is defined entirely by ends (pain or less happiness), not the means.

On the positive side (happiness) are the following considerations:

- These entertainments produce a lot of pleasure. They are very popular.
- There are often secondary pleasures gained from engaging with a part of a specific culture – chatting with friends about games, conventions, etc.
- They are also part of successful industries that supply jobs, create wealth and also advance technology.
- Video games can have beneficial effects in terms of motor skills.

And on the negative/harm side:

- Violent video films, and in particular video games, have been linked to increased anti-social behaviour in the short and longer terms (however, there is also evidence that shows there is very little link).
- Too much time spent on video games can have harmful effects on health (in terms of sedentary lifestyle).
- People disapprove of these activities and this causes some sadness.

Simulated killing is hugely popular. An immense amount of pleasure is being caused every second by these sources. In the last 20 years violent crime has decreased in the UK and in other western countries too, and this is at the same time that violent video games and films have boomed. This, on the face of it, suggests any causal link between video games and violence cannot be strong.

It would be very hard to argue that such entertainments cause more harm than good. Rock climbing, horse riding and even football cause far more average harm per hour to the player. And football is also associated with a level of violence in and around stadiums (though less so in recent years).

Higher/lower distinction

For Mill, the sorts of pleasure produced by violent films and video games may well be the wrong sorts of pleasure (see page 26). These entertainments may be classed as lower pleasures, which, though still good, are of lower worth. A 'competent judge' may prefer other sorts of higher pleasures and Mill thought that we should prioritise these. Mill wanted utility not just to be about physical pleasure but:

> utility in the largest sense, grounded on the permanent interests of man as a progressive being.[25]

Mill may argue that the pleasures gained from simulated killing appeal to our baser, animal side and not to our progressive, intellectual side. Although they are pleasurable, maximising such pleasures is not as morally good as enjoying the less 'pleasant' higher pleasures of, say, reading Tolstoy, or even this book!

Holding a higher/lower qualitative distinction may alter the result of the utilitarian calculus on simulated killing entertainments. By how much is not clear: do we halve the pleasure total on the 'gained' column? The fact that there is no easy answer to this question is a criticism of having such a distinction in the first place. Also, it is questionable as to whether such entertainments are, in fact, lower pleasures. They are cultural, engage the brain and so are not just the equivalent of, say, drinking gin.

The question of the competent judge is an interesting one too. Mill never played video games; he may have taken to *Grand Theft Auto* like a duck to water. There are many competent judges that can appreciate both video games and Tolstoy, and prefer the former. So the higher/lower distinction (itself questionable), does not necessarily downgrade the status of the pleasure gained from these entertainments, as they are not clearly lower pleasures.

Liberty

Many people are offended by the existence of violent video games. Should their displeasure (or their preferences) be taken into account in the utility calculation? Also, could it not be argued that the same amount of pleasure could be gained by alternative methods of entertainment that offer less offence/harm? If so, it could be argued that playing violent games may not be so good (like the sadist surgeon on page 44).

The problem with taking into account the offence of others is that this approach places too much power in the moral sentiments of the majority. Perhaps all things that the majority find displeasurable or offensive should be considered immoral? Mill argued passionately that the secondary principle (or rule) of liberty should play a central role in utilitarianism. We should all be free to pursue our own pleasures, as long as we do not harm others (the extent to which offence counts as harm has to be fairly minimal). A society committed to liberty, to freedom of expression and the pursuit of different goals will be happier in the long run. And this is a society that doesn't allow the moral sentiments of some to dictate the non-harmful pursuits of others. So, for Mill, allowing people to play video games is a good thing, as this follows the rule of liberty, which is the rule that will enable utility to be best maximised. Exceptions to the principle of Liberty are made in the cases of children. Parents and the state are permitted to restrict freedom, and freedom of access, for children, for their own benefit.

In summary, for a utilitarian simulated killing is morally good as long as the pleasure outweighs the harm. The distinction between higher and lower pleasures is ambiguous, both in general, and in its specific application to the case in question. Mill would also claim that pursuing pleasures that are not harmful to others is, in general, a good thing. Simulated killing is a clear source of happiness for millions; for a utilitarian, such things are morally good.

The treatment of animals

The moral value of an action is determined by the happiness or pain caused, or, in the case of strong rule utilitarianism, by the adherence to rules that in turn will maximise happiness or minimise pain. If happiness and pain are the guiding principles, then why should this be restricted to human happiness and pain? As we have seen (page 38) Bentham raised this very question and Singer has provided some strong arguments to suggest that we should (morally) take into account animals' suffering and happiness in our actions.

Singer's key argument is based on a consideration of the equality of moral interests among humans (this is known as the argument from *marginal cases*). He argues that this cannot be based on intelligence or sporting prowess and so on, as these are not shared by *all* humans – and we want to give *all* humans moral consideration. He claims that the equality of moral interest can only be based on sentience, which is also shared with animals. Formally, his argument looks like this:

- **Premise 1:** If only humans have full and equal moral status, there must be some special quality that all humans share that enables this.
- **Premise 2:** All human-specific candidates for such a quality, will be a quality that some human beings lack.
- **Premise 3:** The only possible candidates will be qualities that other animals have too.
- **Conclusion:** Therefore, we cannot argue that only human beings deserve moral status.

It may be contended that humans do have some unique qualities that grant us special moral status, for example our DNA, and therefore we should be treated differently. However, this can be countered by the following consideration: (a) not all humans have the same DNA; (b) what about intelligent, sentient aliens with different DNA, should they have moral status?; and (c) selecting DNA as the quality seems arbitrary and not morally relevant.

Singer presents another argument for the equality of moral consideration, using the analogy of racism. Racists (say, white supremacists) claim that, because of a particular factor, say, greater intelligence, white people are morally superior to non-white. Their pain counts for more, their lives are worth more, they have greater moral importance and so on. Now it is simply not true that all white people are more intelligent than all non-white people, so a factual mistake is being made here. But another fundamental mistake is also being made. Even if it were true that all white people were more intelligent than all non-white people, it would still be wrong to assign different moral value on the basis of intelligence. For example, we could ask everyone to take an IQ test and divide the world into those with a score above 100 and those with a score below. Should those with a score below be treated differently? This would be wrong. We should not assign moral worth on the basis of intelligence.

This type of argument works for all qualities that admit of degree, such as intelligence and sporting prowess. It does not work so well for other qualities, such as DNA or having a soul. But in the case of DNA, the moral relevance must also be shown, and the arguments about souls have their own weaknesses.

Using this argument, as well as other similarities in human behaviour, Singer sees our treatment of animals as akin to racism – calling it *speciesism*.

Singer, though, does not argue that animals should have all of the same rights as humans, e.g. the right to vote, etc. In the same way that men do not have the right to an abortion – as it is irrelevant because of their bodies – animals should not have rights such as the right to vote or freedom of speech, as this would be irrelevant. What *is* morally required is that we take their interests/welfare equally into account when making decisions.

So, for a utilitarian, all pleasure/pain is equally worth counting, whether it is a victim's, a criminal's or an animal's.

▶ **ACTIVITY**

Read A1 and A2 on page 10. What would a utilitarian say?

In the case of A1, Singer claims that causing such suffering would be wrong if we could gain our food in other ways (which we can). Singer is not against the eating of animals per se (see page 38 for more on this), however he is against the needless suffering of animals. Singer argues that most forms of intensive food farming cause suffering and eating from these sources is morally wrong, as food can be gained in other ways.

Regarding dilemma A2, in his seminal work, *Animal Liberation*, Singer outlines various experiments that seem needlessly cruel. Many of these would be too distressing for this book (surely by reprinting these we would be adding to the misery in the word and this would be a bad thing to do). We include one example featuring dogs.

anthology 1.4

In 1953 R. Solomon, L. Kamin, and L. Wynne, experimenters at Harvard University, placed forty dogs in a device called a 'shuttlebox,' which consists of a box divided into two compartments, separated by a barrier. Initially the barrier was set at the height of the dog's back. Hundreds of intense electric shocks were delivered to the dogs' feet through a grid floor. At first the dogs could escape the shock if they learnt to jump the barrier into the other compartment. In an attempt to 'discourage' one dog from jumping, the experimenters forced the dog to jump one hundred times onto a grid floor in the other compartment that also delivered a shock to the dog's feet. They said that as the dog jumped he gave a 'sharp anticipatory yip which turned into a yelp when he landed on the electrified grid.' They then blocked the passage between the compartments with a piece of plate glass and tested the dog again. The dog 'jumped forward and smashed his head against the glass.' The dogs began by showing symptoms such as 'defecation, urination, yelping and shrieking, trembling, attacking the apparatus, and so on; but after ten or twelve days of trials dogs who were prevented from escaping shock ceased to resist. The experimenters reported themselves 'impressed' by this, and concluded that a combination of the plate glass barrier and foot shock was 'very effective' in eliminating jumping by dogs.[26]

Singer

▶ **ACTIVITY: Animal experimentation**

- Is this experiment immoral?
- Would *you* be able to carry out such an experiment?
- Do you think carrying out such experiments would make you more or less empathetic to the suffering of humans?
- Would it be morally different if the experiments were being carried out on primates?

To answer the first question a utilitarian would need to do a calculation. Is the experiment likely to cause more overall happiness than suffering? If the answer is yes then the experiment is the right thing to do. A stricter utilitarian would need to ask the additional question: can the same information be gained in an alternative way that causes less or no suffering? If the answer is yes, then the experiment is wrong, and the alternative should be used. Singer is not an absolutist about animal experimentation; for a utilitarian, the end *can* justify the means, however he is very sceptical about whether the ends ever *do* justify the means. It is very hard to imagine in the case above that the experiment is adding to the sum of happiness in the world.

Singer notes that people arguing *for* animal experimentation often put forward hypothetical questions such as, '*What if one experiment on an animal could save a thousand lives?*' His reply is to pose another hypothetical question back.

> *Would the experimenter be prepared to perform his experiment on an orphaned human infant [baby], if that were the only way to save many lives?... If the experimenter is not prepared to use an orphaned human infant then his readiness to use non-humans is simple discrimination, since adult apes, cats, mice and other mammals are more aware of what is happening to them, more self-directing and, so far as we can tell, as least as sensitive to pain as any human infant.*[27]
>
> Singer

If experimenters were to ask themselves this question in all earnestness, how many animal experiments would actually be carried out?

The question of whether the experiment on page 61 would be different with primates is an interesting one. For Singer, the principle of equality of moral interest does not mean the equal treatment of all animals (no need for voting rights, etc.). All animals suffer, but not always in the same way. Most animals will not have 'interests' in the way that most humans have specific projects they want to complete, for self improvement and so on. The pleasures a sheep may gain in life would be replicable with another sheep. As long as the same number of sheep exist, the same amount of sheep pleasure will be generated. The same is not true of humans with specific goals. Most humans will have specific interests they are trying to achieve, and these are not replicable in another person.

Apes and primates, Singer argues, also have 'interests' that other animals may not have. (Though it is all a matter of degree.)

> *The great apes are intelligent beings with strong emotions that in many ways resemble our own. Chimpanzees, bonobos and gorillas have long-term relationships, not only between mothers and children, but also between unrelated apes. When a loved one dies they grieve for a long time. They can solve complex puzzles that stump most two-year-old humans. They can learn hundreds of signs and put them together in sentences that obey grammatical rules. They display a sense of justice, resenting others who do not reciprocate a favour.*[28]
>
> Singer

This means taking primates' interests into account will be different from taking into account the interests of, say, a snake. It also means that primates will suffer in different ways, which is relevant. So, for

Singer, the experiment with the dogs is wrong, as no obvious pleasure results. It might also be morally worse if primates were used, as their suffering would be different. A primate's suffering may even be worse than an orphaned infant's. (Singer uses the example of an orphan, as otherwise the parents' interests would be relevant.) A young orphaned infant, in the early stages of life, may have less 'interests' than a primate.

Deception and the telling of lies

As should be familiar by now, for an act utilitarian, the end justifies the means. So lying is completely morally acceptable if it maximises happiness/minimises harm. In fact, in such instances not only would lying be morally acceptable, but it is the right thing to do – we *ought* to lie. (Remember though that it is general happiness that is to be maximised, and not just your own.) For some, this seems an odd conclusion. Consider this example:

Example 16: American tourists

Two American tourists stop you in London. They have just got into town, have never been to London before and ask you for the quickest way to get to St Paul's Cathedral. You do a very hasty utilitarian calculation and instead of telling them the quickest way, tell them the most scenic route, which is to walk across Waterloo Bridge (see the Waterloo sunset), hop along the South Bank and then cross the Millennium Bridge to St Paul's. Though a good ten minutes longer than the quickest route, it is the easiest to describe and you strongly believe they will gain more pleasure this way. They ask you again if you are sure this is the quickest way. You lie and say yes.

Is this right? Surely you should just come clean, but if you do they will take the trafficky, stressful, ugly, quickest route, rather than stroll along the beautiful South Bank.

Some criticise utilitarianism for this approach, claiming that telling the truth (as well as keeping promises) comes with its own moral obligation, regardless of the consequence. A utilitarian would naturally disagree, but would note that lying and breaking promises are highly likely to cause upset in many/most cases, as, in general:

- people don't like being lied to
- people don't like being accused of lying
- people want to be trusted and lying undermines this
- lying frequently causes hurt when discovered
- lying often causes stress to the liar (having to remember lies and the thought of being discovered, etc.)
- lying weakens people's general faith in humanity, and so lowers happiness.

For these reasons alone, lying comes with an inbuilt negative outcome, so the benefits of the lie clearly need to outweigh this too. Because of this, everything being equal, it is generally wrong to lie and break promises. It is also hard to predict what the outcome of a lie may be.

The American tourists above may have a particular need to get to St Paul's in a rush, and the delay may lead to a lot of stress. Also, the positive benefits of the lie often rely on the lie not being uncovered, and it can be very hard to know if this will happen or not. Again, this uncertainty makes the default position of truth-telling much stronger. So, although an act utilitarian would deny that truth-telling (and promises) come with an inherent moral obligation, they would acknowledge that truth-telling, in general, should be the default position.

To test your intuitions about the inherent wrongness of lying, consider the example of a lie that would never be discovered – a lie that has no positive or negative consequences either way. Imagine someone who you will never meet again (and never do meet again), in passing, asks how old you are. You lie, by one year.

Is this wrong? Or is it morally neutral? Some would say the former, some the latter; it all depends on your moral intuition about whether lying is inherently wrong, or only wrong if it has consequences.

Rule utilitarianism

Above we saw the argument that lying has a default position of being wrong. This way of thinking leads naturally into rule utilitarianism. We can conclude from these considerations that, in general, lying will cause more harm than good. The rule *'Tell the truth'* is one that will maximise utility. So, for a strong rule utilitarian, it is always wrong to tell a lie (as the moral value of the act depends on whether it is in accordance with the rule). A weak rule utilitarian would, in general, tell the truth but occasionally lie if it was clear that lying would maximise happiness.

For many people, weak rule utilitarianism is the position that best describes their intuitions. Few would argue that telling the truth is *always* the right thing to do (as in DTL2, page 11).

A final mention should go to preference utilitarianism. Rather than focusing on whether a lie would bring more happiness, the theory suggests we should focus on whether a lie would satisfy more preferences. This is significant as most people have a preference to be told the truth, which further justifies the default position of truth-telling. However, there are times (*Does this suit look nice? Did my speech go well?*) when the questioner would prefer to be lied to, in which case, lying is the right thing to do. The position of the preference utilitarian is also different as someone's preference to be told the truth is frustrated when a lie is told, and this does not rely on whether the person finds out they are being lied to or not. Whereas for plain old utilitarianism, some lies may only become wrong when the lie is discovered, as this is when the upset is caused. See the example of the new friend, page 84.

▶ **ACTIVITY**

Read DTL1 and DTL2 on page 11. What would a utilitarian say?

In DTL1, an act utilitarian may argue that the affair should be pursued. It certainly seems as if pleasure would be gained in the short term. The longer term is harder to gauge; guilt, mistrust and disillusionment may result if it does not work out. The pleasures they are pursuing are fleeting and high risk, the key risk being whether the husband will find out. It is a difficult decision to make using reason alone (you suspect the decision to lie may not have been fuelled by reason alone). This is why act utilitarianism is not a good method of deliberation, as there are too many unknowns. Rule utilitarians may have different answers to this, depending on the different rules that they think would generally maximise happiness. Would the world be a happier place if no affairs ever occurred? Or is it happier for having affairs? A preference utilitarian may have a slightly different take on this too, as the husband may well have a preference for his wife being faithful. In which case, the affair goes against this preference and so this needs to be added into the equation from the start. From a traditional utilitarian perspective, if the affair is not discovered and pleasure is gained then the act is a good thing. The displeasure of the husband is only relevant to the moral value of the act if he finds out. From a preference utilitarian perspective, it is relevant to the moral value whether or not he finds out, as his preference is not being satisfied from the outset.

DTL2 is much easier for a utilitarian – you lie! No sensible rule utilitarian would have a rule that says 'Never lie', as following this would not maximise happiness. In this scenario, the utilitarian approach seems to work well, as the consequences seem obvious. However, if it turned out that Bob were saved by your lie, but himself became a serial killer, then your act would have been a bad one. You would not be blameworthy though, as you could not reasonably have foreseen this. Your decision to lie would be praiseworthy and be the right one based on the circumstances.

1.1.2 Kantian deontological ethics

Background

Immanuel Kant (1724–1804) is one of the most important philosophers of all time – but unfortunately he is also one of the most difficult to understand.

Kant was born and lived nearly all his life in the town of Königsberg (then part of Germany/Prussia, now part of Russia). He was an academic and wrote on a wide range of subjects, including geology, mathematics, science, religion, aesthetics and philosophy. It is his work on philosophy and ethics for which he is most famous.

Kant was writing during a period of intense intellectual activity in Europe, a period that became known as the Enlightenment. Thinkers of this 'age of reason' were beginning to liberate themselves from the restrictive ties to the Church that had characterised most of the Middle Ages, and which had still been felt by the father of modern philosophy, René Descartes (1591–1650). There was a confidence in human reason, boosted by the growing successes of 'natural philosophy' (what we now call science) in explaining the physical laws of the universe. Religious authority could no longer determine what people ought to think about the nature of the universe nor about what is right or wrong. Human beings, it appeared to many, had come of age and were sufficiently 'enlightened' to realise that they had to discover their values for themselves rather than expect them to be delivered by a higher power.

Kant though was sceptical of the optimistic claims made by some '**rationalist**' philosophers about the extent to which human reason alone could grasp truths about the universe. Kant thought that our knowledge is pretty much limited to that which we can experience. However, he also thought that by analysing the nature of human thought and morality, we could unravel their inner structures or forms. This would reveal an important kind of knowledge – knowledge that did not derive from any specific experience of the world, but that would apply to all experiences. In this way, much of Kant's philosophy is concerned with discovering the hidden rules and laws that govern how our mind understands the world, and how morality functions.

> *Two things fill the mind with ever new and increasing admiration and awe, the oftener and more steadily we reflect on them: the starry heavens above and the moral law within.*[1]
>
> Kant

Kant was a Christian, but he did not believe that ethics could be founded on the commands of God. He believed that morality was independent of God's and everyone else's will. The moral law is something that each of us can discover within us, through the use of reason, rather than being instructed from another source. Kant outlines his ethical theory in two important works, *Groundwork of the Metaphysics of Morals* (1785) and the longer *Critique of Practical Reason* (1788).

Introduction

The philosophy of Kant is particularly difficult to understand. There are several reasons for this:

- Philosophy can be quite difficult. After all, it tackles the problems that have not been solved yet.
- Kant's approach in philosophy is very abstract, and he always wants to go back to first principles when exploring any issue.
- Kant developed a complete philosophy that fits together as a whole. This often makes looking at a part of it complicated, as it wasn't meant to stand in isolation.
- Kant invented a lot of new terminology – much of which has remained in philosophy – but it can make his writing hard to follow.

That said, all of what follows comes down to a fairly simple idea, which is that when we perform a particular moral action, we must be able to consistently assert that everyone should act in that way too. In other words, we must be able to assert that this is the right thing for anyone to do, not just me.

Kant presents his philosophy as part of a series of arguments that fit together into a whole. At times it can feel a bit empty or circular, but, like a good jigsaw, the pieces do fit together and make sense in the end. In Figure 1.7 on page 68 we have represented the key steps that Kant makes and we will refer back to this diagram as we proceed. Please note that this is not supposed to make sense at the moment.

As Figure 1.7 shows, Kant is going to argue for something called the **categorical imperative**, which we have a duty to follow. This categorical imperative will enable us to work out how we should and shouldn't act. In prose form, Kant's approach is roughly this:

> *Doing something for the right reason makes it a moral action. The right reason is making sure you only act in a way that you could consistently will that all other people do too. This rule (known as the categorical imperative) acts as a test for the different rules we follow in life. By applying the test we can work out which rules we should follow and which we should not.*

So we have seen the diagram and the five-line explanation (above), now we have to explore the detail.

Good will is the source of moral worth

> *It is impossible to conceive anything at all in the world, or even out of it, which can be taken as good without qualification, except a good will.*[4]
>
> Kant

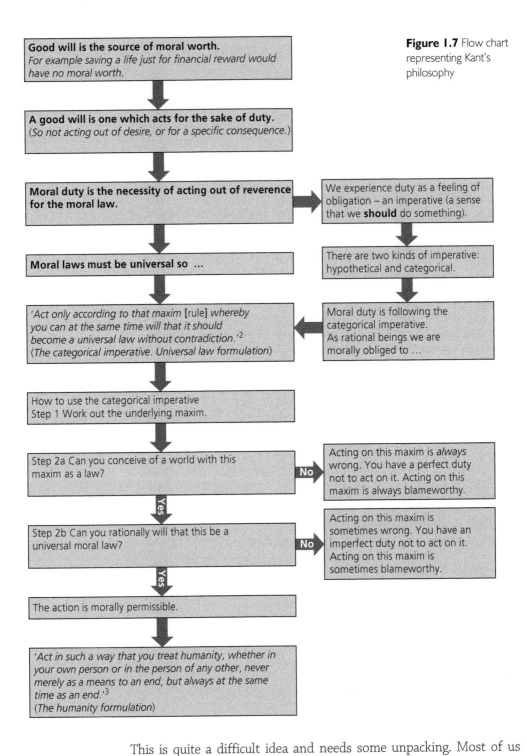

Figure 1.7 Flow chart representing Kant's philosophy

Good will is the source of moral worth.
For example saving a life just for financial reward would have no moral worth.

A good will is one which acts for the sake of duty.
(So not acting out of desire, or for a specific consequence.)

Moral duty is the necessity of acting out of reverence for the moral law.

We experience duty as a feeling of obligation – an imperative (a sense that we **should** do something).

Moral laws must be universal so ...

There are two kinds of imperative: hypothetical and categorical.

'Act only according to that maxim [rule] whereby you can at the same time will that it should become a universal law without contradiction.'[2]
(The categorical imperative. Universal law formulation)

Moral duty is following the categorical imperative. As rational beings we are morally obliged to ...

How to use the categorical imperative
Step 1 Work out the underlying maxim.

Step 2a Can you conceive of a world with this maxim as a law?

No Acting on this maxim is *always* wrong. You have a perfect duty not to act on it. Acting on this maxim is always blameworthy.

Yes

Step 2b Can you rationally will that this be a universal moral law?

No Acting on this maxim is sometimes wrong. You have an imperfect duty not to act on it. Acting on this maxim is sometimes blameworthy.

Yes

The action is morally permissible.

'Act in such a way that you treat humanity, whether in your own person or in the person of any other, never merely as a means to an end, but always at the same time as an end.'[3]
(The humanity formulation)

This is quite a difficult idea and needs some unpacking. Most of us pursue ends that we think of as 'good'; this could be the pursuit of happiness, health, intelligence, creativity, money and so on. Kant argues that each of these supposed 'goods' can sometimes be bad – in other words they are not good *'without qualification'*. For example someone may gain happiness from torture, or use intelligence to swindle money from pensioners and we would not call these ends *'good'*. (Bentham however, would still say that the pleasure gained was good.)

anthology
1.4

For Kant, no 'end' that we pursue can be thought of as morally good in itself. Happiness, intelligence, money and so on, can only be considered good if they are accompanied by, or result from, a good will. In this way, a good will is the source of good. This may sound a little empty; surely a *good* will is good by definition? Thankfully, Kant does give an explanation of what he means by 'a good will': **A good will is one which acts for the sake of duty**.

We will explore what is meant by duty later, but for now think of it as 'doing the right thing for the sake of doing the right thing'. Consider the following example.

Example 17: The drowning man

A man is drowning in a river. You could walk on by or you could help. You decide to help, but what is motivating you?

    A You might want to help because you may receive a reward.

    B You might want to help because you will receive praise (and maybe some attention from the press!).

    C You might help because it is the right thing to do, and you feel it is your duty to do the right thing.

Figure 1.8 The drowning man
What is your motive for saving the man?

Kant would argue that although helping to save the man is the right thing to do (it is in accordance with duty), if you saved the man for the motives A or B, then your action would have no moral worth. Likewise, with example 4 (page 23). Visiting your grandma to potentially gain money would have no moral worth, whereas visiting because you believe it is the right thing to do, and you feel you have a duty to do the right thing, *is* morally worthy.

Note how this contrasts with utilitarian ethics. Utilitarians claim that the amount of happiness produced gives acts their moral value. Happiness is a particular 'end' that we seek to bring about, and a right action is one that brings about this end, regardless of how or why. For a utilitarian, motives play no part in the moral value of an action. Kant's view is the complete opposite: morality is not about the particular ends that we seek to bring about. The only acts that have moral worth are ones that are carried out from a sense of duty – a duty to do the right thing. For Kant, it is the motive, not the consequence, that is key. Because of this, Kant's ethics are often labelled as being '**deontological**'. This is the general term for ethics that are based on duty (it derives from the Greek *dei* meaning 'one must').

▶ **ACTIVITY: Good will hunting**

It is hard to know what a person's motive for an action might be. After all, even if you ask someone they might be lying. Which of the following actions, if any, do you suspect might be done from good will alone (and without a self-interested motive)?

1 Josie enjoys spending time with her children and helps them to practise the piano every day.
2 As part of his community service, Colin carefully sets aside four hours every Saturday to work in his local 'Making the World a Better Place' Youth Centre.
3 In the weeks running up to his birthday, Marlon always makes an extra special effort helping out his parents, checking they're okay and whether they need anything, etc.
4 Leonie gives Friends of the Earth £1. She loves watching the coins whirl round and round the hole before falling into the charity box.
5 Samsia notices a large, unaccompanied rucksack by the door of a train, and asks the crowded carriage who the owner of it is.
6 Jane keeps her promise to show off her latest dance moves to her philosophy class, despite just having been promoted to Head of Department.

Criticism

Is a good will always good?

Firstly it can seem a bit circular to say that a good will is good; after all, isn't a good meal always good? Secondly, it is not obvious that a good will *is* always good. Imagine a person, Billy, who is very well meaning and tries to help everyone, as he believes it is the right thing to do. But Billy is very clumsy and keeps accidently hurting people and breaking things as he helps others cross the road or carry their bags. After a while, people might think that Billy's good will is not such a good thing after all.

Humans as imperfectly rational beings

Another way of seeing why it is important to have the right motive is to consider Kant's view that humans are imperfectly rational beings.

Kant believed that, like animals, humans are driven by desires and instincts. However, unlike animals, we can also reason. We are a mixture of reason and desires; this is what he means by being imperfectly rational. As we shall see below, Kant thinks that it is reason that reveals the moral laws that we have a duty to follow. So it is the rational part of us that reveals how we *should* behave morally. On the other hand, our desires and appetites (when mixed with some reason), tell us how we *should* behave non-morally. Our desires give us the goals that we then try to achieve.

Figure 1.9 Humans are imperfectly rational
Humans are imperfectly rational beings. Our desires tell us how we should behave (non-morally). Our reason tells us how to behave morally.

Reason

2 + 2 = 4

Do not lie

Do not break promises

Desires

Acting from desires is to act out of self-interest. Self-interested motives are subjective, particular to the individual and often in conflict (though not always) with the interests of others. Kant believed that moral laws, like scientific laws, are objective and universal, insofar as they apply to all individuals, no matter what differences in personal circumstances, character, wishes, hopes, desires. These laws are revealed by reason.

If we were perfectly rational, we would always do the morally right thing. On the other hand, if we acted on our desires all the time, we would often do the wrong thing. We may sometimes do the right thing (by accident), but it would have no moral value (as we saw in the examples above). Within humans there is often a tension between these two parts of us: reason and desires. The fact that there is a tension creates the possibility of duty. We may want to walk past the drowning man, or may want to save him for money. However, we have a duty to do the right thing, and that is to assist those in need, when we can. Saving the man, *because* it is the right thing to do, is to act for the sake of duty, and this is what is meant by a good will.

Note that God, or any perfectly rational being would not do the right thing for the sake of duty. For such beings would not experience the tension between desire and reason and so not need the 'call of duty'.

Further, Kant believed that it is our ability to reason, our ability to follow moral laws that gives humans their autonomy. An animal that follows its instincts all the time cannot really be said to be free. It is a slave to its passions. In this way, animals lack autonomy; they are not able to reason, to understand rules and apply these to situations.

Not that following laws by itself gives freedom (although it is the sign of reason). After all, a human that unquestioningly follows the rules of others also cannot be said to be free (for example, a slave may do this). Morality is only possible because we have free will (and do not have to follow our passions) and autonomy is only achieved when we use reason to create our *own* moral laws. Following laws that we have worked out ourselves using reason, is to be our own master and to have autonomy.

When duty and self-interest coincide

In example 17 of the drowning man (page 69) we saw that acting on your desires will sometimes coincide with doing the right thing, but that this is not good enough to make it a moral act. This has considerable implications. For example, Jasmin regularly donates to charity – and she may do so simply because it has become a habit, or because she feels like it, or because she hopes that if she's ever in trouble someone will be similarly generous. If she acts from any of these motives then her action is not properly speaking a moral act.

Moreover, according to Kant, someone who, through the use of dispassionate reason, recognises her duty to help others in distress even though she has no compassion for her fellow human beings, is more praiseworthy than someone who would have helped others whether it were his duty or not, because of a compassion for others. For the former must act, as it were, against the grain of her inclinations, while the latter is slavishly led by his emotions. For Kant, the moral person is someone who, among all the noise and demands of our emotions, is able to think through what principles underlie any action, and make sure they act on the right principles. It may help you to imagine a calm, thoughtful person, who always makes sure they do the right thing. (Although there is no specific need to be calm.)

anthology
1.5

Kant himself gives the example of a shopkeeper who doesn't rip customers off because he wants a good reputation. For Kant, his actions are not moral. They are not carried out because they are the right thing to do, but because of the shopkeeper's desire for a good reputation.

Criticism

At times, this requirement for a moral act to be motivated by a duty to do the right thing can seem counter-intuitive.

▶ ACTIVITY: Fatherhood

Example 18: The dutiful father

Consider these two contrasting fathers:

- Father A spends his evenings developing his son's talents (football and music). He does this because he loves his son, enjoys spending time with him and wants him to flourish.
- Father B spends his evenings developing his son's talents too. He doesn't love his son and really doesn't like spending time with children. He does this out of a sense of duty.

Which of the two fathers' dedication is more morally worthy?

Kant would say it is Father B; however, many would have an intuition that it is Father A. It is sometimes held as a criticism of Kant that it would seem to be easier to be moral if you are a bad person, as it is clear that in acting according to duty you are going against your desires. However, most commentators interpret Kant as saying that in these cases the motive of duty is more clearly seen, not that it is preferable. When your duty and interest coincide, the motive of duty is less clear to see, but as long as you are motivated by duty then the act is a good act. Kant's idea of duty as the source of good does seem counter-intuitive at times. It also leads to a very different account of what virtue is (page 92).

Duty as reverence for the law

So far we have interpreted duty as '*doing the right thing for the sake of doing the right thing*'. Although this interpretation is in line with Kant's thinking, his definition appears somewhat different, and this needs some unpacking. For Kant:

> *Duty is the necessity of acting out of reverence for the law.*[5]

To understand this definition, consider the following scenario.

 Experimenting with ideas: The island

You are king of a small island. You make the laws. As a good king, you try to make laws that enable everyone to rub along together and get on with their own lives. Some of your citizens are naughty and break the law, but most abide by them. Let's examine these law-abiding citizens in more details. There are three groups. Group A like the laws and follow them because they think they gain from them. In group B, some like the laws and some don't, but they abide by them as they fear being caught and punished. In group C, some like the laws, some don't, but they follow them anyway out of respect for the law. The people in group C follow the laws, not for what the laws bring, but because they are the laws.

1   As a ruler, do you think group A, B or C are better citizens?
2   Why?
3   In the UK, which group of citizens do you belong to: A, B or C?

The problem with saying that group A are better is that some of these citizens may stop following the law if their circumstances change and the law no longer suits them; or if a new law goes against their interest. Group A are only following the law out of self-interest. Group B are also self-interested. With this group there is always the risk that they may break the law if they are *certain* they can get away with it. The good thing about group C is that they follow the laws out of duty, out of respect for the law. In this way, they are not acting out of self-interest. Group C can be relied on to be good citizens, come what may.

This is only an analogy, based on political laws, but this is the idea of duty that Kant was articulating: duty as reverence for the law.

This additional thought experiment may be useful for the discussion ahead, where we explore Kant's attempt to articulate the moral law. Again, this is only an analogy – though it is very closely related to the actual ideas of Kant.

[Learn More]

Experimenting with ideas: Trouble on the island

A group C citizen, Immanuel, writes a letter to you, his king. Immanuel expresses how he follows the laws out of respect/reverence for the law. However, he disagrees with some of the rules. He also doesn't like having to follow them as it makes him feel like a prisoner on the island. He feels he has lost his autonomy.

How might you address his concerns?

You may be tempted to move to a democracy. This would enable the islanders to agree rules when there are differences of opinion. Nevertheless, this would not satisfy Immanuel. The citizens will propose laws from self-interested perspectives and the subsequent discussion and voting would just be a bonfire of the interests to see which emerges from the flames victorious. If Immanuel did not personally vote for the law, he would still be living under someone else's laws. As the king you come up with an even more radical idea. The islanders are all rational people so you let them work out and follow their own laws – basic laws that will apply to everyone. The temptation though would be for individuals to come up with laws that are in their interest, but clearly such rules won't work for all. In fact, laws based around any specific interest will not work, as not everyone may share this interest. The only rules that will work, for all, are those laws that are drawn from the mere fact that everyone is a rational agent. Anyone coming up with laws that work for all would then feel autonomous as they would be following their own laws. Also, they would feel obliged to follow them, as these would be the rules that all rational agents should follow.

What laws might you come up with?

If we are all rational beings, would we come up with the same rules?

Universal moral laws

Figure 1.10 illustrates what we have seen so far.

Figure 1.10

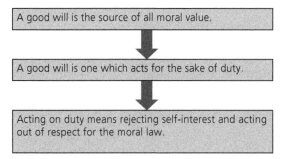

This all seems very abstract; to become more practical we need to discover what these moral laws are. At this stage, you might expect Kant to give a long list of moral laws that we should follow. Unfortunately, he doesn't do this. Instead he shows how there is one general principle/rule that itself can be used to find out what the moral laws are (and are not). Also, if Kant gave a list of rules or commandments, this would run counter to the idea of autonomy outlined above. It is only by using reason to work out and follow our own rules, that we have autonomy.

So, what would a moral law look like? What features would it have? Well, scientific laws are *objective* and *universal* (in that they apply to the whole universe equally). Moral laws, reasons, should have similar features; they should be objective (not based on your specific viewpoint) and universal (apply equally to all people). A scientific law is often in the form of a formula (e.g. $F = ma$) or a principle that you can apply to a specific instance, perhaps to predetermine the outcome. In a similar fashion, a moral law would be in the form of a rule outlining how you should act in a general set of circumstances, which you then apply to your particular circumstance. For example, potential moral laws might include: *'When you are hungry, steal property from others'* (not a good rule!) or *'Help others when they are in need, and no one else can'*.

As suggested, the rules need to be universal, they need to apply everywhere. Now it may be the case that when considering potential moral rules (which Kant calls **maxims**), some of them are impossible to consistently apply in all cases; they *cannot* be rationally **universalised**. In which case, these potential laws are not fit to be a moral law and we should not follow the rule. So, just by considering what a moral law must be like, Kant is able to conclude that:

> *I am never to act otherwise than so that I could also will that my maxim should become a universal law.*[6]

In other words, we should not act on rules which are incapable of becoming universal laws. For example, consider this potential rule *'I will make promises that I cannot keep'*. What would happen if everyone acted on this rule? There would be no institution of promises, and so the rule would undermine what it seeks to do. It is not fit to be a moral law as it cannot be a universal rule.

Hypothetical and categorical imperatives

So, just by considering the nature of a moral law, Kant concludes that we should not act on any rule unless we can universalise it. Kant reaches a similar **conclusion** through a different line of reasoning: by considering the nature, not of *laws*, but of moral *imperatives*.

This is a complex technical point, but so far Kant has just worked out what we mustn't do (act on a maxim that cannot be a universal law); the quotation above is known as the *negative* formulation of the categorical imperative. Kant is now going to explore what we should/must do, and will arrive at the positive formulation of the categorical imperative. To do this, he needs to explore the nature of imperatives in general – which are things that tell us what we *should* do.

Learn More

Kant believed that morality is experienced as a command or 'imperative'; in other words, it tells us what we ought to/should do. An imperative is an inner 'tug' on our will, a compulsion to act in one way rather than another. But there are two different types of imperative, which is to say, two distinct senses of the term *'ought'*: both of which are related to uses of the word *'good'*.

All imperatives command either hypothetically or categorically.[7]

Hypothetical imperatives

One kind of 'ought' is conditional, or (in Kant's terminology) a **hypothetical imperative**. An example of this use might be: 'If you want a cup of tea you should boil the water'. Note that this kind of *ought/should* depends upon your having a certain goal or aim, namely getting a cup of tea. The first part of the statement gives us the condition we aspire to; the second part tells us what to do to meet this condition. In other words, the *ought* is conditional upon the desire – which not everyone will have.

Many of the imperatives we encounter in life are based on this type of self-interested, or prudential, reasoning. Not all of them have the same 'if X then you should Y' formula – sometimes the elements are hidden or implicit. For example: '*You should get your pawns out early in chess*'. This really means '*If you want to win then you should get your pawns out early in chess.*'

Hypothetical imperatives are often linked to the word *good*, as in: '*It's good to get your pawns out early in chess*', or '*It's good to boil the kettle when making tea*'. Although *good* is not used in a moral sense here. This is because hypothetical imperatives are not moral imperatives. After all, consider this example: '*If you want to burgle a house you should wear gloves*' or '*It's good to wear gloves when you burgle a house*'. This is hardly moral!

Imperatives and reason

Kant believed that as rational beings, if you genuinely have the desire, and the imperative is a sound one, then you are rationally committed to follow it. For example, consider the hypothetical imperative: *If you want to lose weight, then you should exercise more and eat less.* Kant believed that if you genuinely do want to lose weight, then your reason commits you to exercise more and eat less. (Kant is sometimes accused of overlooking weakness of the will – when you accept the imperative and want the end, but still don't do it.)

Categorical imperatives

Kant though is not really interested in hypothetical imperatives, as they are not moral imperatives. They lack the universality to be moral imperatives because they rely on desires/ends that not everyone wants (or are not permanent). Not everyone wants a cup of tea, so it's not the case that everyone should boil a kettle. The sorts of imperative Kant thinks are central to morality are ones that are not dependent on any set of conditions or desires. These types of *oughts* are unconditional and absolute, or (in Kant's terminology) categorical. An example might be '*You ought to keep your promises*'. Note that this use is not dependent on any goals or aims you may have – the '*if you want X*' bit of the imperative disappears, leaving only '*you ought to do Y*'. These sorts of imperatives tell us that we have a certain obligation or duty regardless of the consequences. This is what is meant by saying they are unconditional or categorical. And it is this sort of *ought* which Kant regards as the only genuinely moral *ought*. That is to say, any action which we perform because we are trying to achieve some practical or personal end has no moral worth.

▶ **ACTIVITY: You *ought* to sort the imperatives**

Read these commands and answer the questions that follow.

a) I should do more sit-ups.
b) I ought to be more loyal to my friends.
c) I should pay more attention to my charming philosophy teacher.
d) I ought to buy flowers and grapes for my sick aunt.
e) I ought to start revising soon.
f) I ought to give more money to Children in Need.
g) I shouldn't lie as much as I do.
h) I ought not to kick my little brother on the shins.
i) I should get up earlier.
j) I should stop eating tuna fish.

  1 Which commands are hypothetical imperatives? In other words which rely on a hidden '*if*' and a hidden goal/desire?
  2 Which commands are moral commands?
  3 Which commands are unconditional, or categorical imperatives?
  4 What connection, if any, is there between the answers you gave for 2 and 3?

The categorical imperative

So moral imperatives will be categorical ones, but what are they and how can we discover them? Well, as we shall see, there is only one categorical imperative (although Kant gives at least three versions of it). Hypothetical imperatives are based on desires and 'ends'. Categorical imperatives are not, as desires are not universal. Stripped of desires and 'ends', the categorical imperative can only be based on the idea of reason and rationality itself. It is the imperative that I should act in a way that is consistent with rationality, in other words in a way that all rational beings could rationally act. And so I should only act on principles that I can consistently universalise that other rational beings should follow. In Kant's words:

Act only according to that maxim [rule] whereby you can at the same time will that it should become a universal law without contradiction.[8]

Kant

This is the categorical imperative (the universal law formulation). It is an imperative, as a rational being, to be logically consistent. As we shall see, Kant thinks that this imperative can be used as a test – a test we can use to work out how to behave morally.

Another way to conceive of this is to think back to the idea of man as an imperfectly rational being. All hypothetical imperatives relate to our appetites and desires (the animal part of us). Categorical imperatives are the actions that a purely rational person would follow (although a purely rational person would not feel them as a sense of duty, as there would be no other desires to 'tug' against). A purely rational person would only act in a way that it is possible for all purely rational people to act.

Universalising and the golden rule

All of this is very complicated; however, at the core is a simple principle. When any of us say *'we did the right thing'*, what we mean is that anyone in a similar position should act in that way too. In other words, moral rules apply universally. Kant thinks this idea alone is enough to guide moral behaviour, as you should only act in ways that can actually be universalised with consistency.

Sometimes people compare Kant's position to one of the world's oldest moral ideas: the **golden rule**. *'Do unto others as you would have them do unto you'* or *'Treat others as you would have them treat you'*. This, in essence, is a call to act, not just from self-interest, but from a position that you can universalise. The problem with the golden rule is that people like odd things, which other people don't. For example, Lenny might like being punched, so according to the golden rule, it's okay for Lenny to punch people as he, in turn, is happy to be punched. This clearly will not do! To be truly universal, we have to transcend individual desires. Kant's categorical imperative does this. His version of the golden rule would be something like this: *'Do unto others that which you can rationally will that they can do unto anyone'*.

Using the categorical imperative to determine our duties

We have now seen the central idea behind Kant's approach to ethics, namely that in moral terms we are bound by the categorical imperative – this is our moral duty.

Once again, this system still sounds a little empty. As yet, there are no clear rules for action. Kant believes that the categorical imperative can help us determine what these are. It will allow us to distinguish truly moral rules from amoral or immoral ones.

The process is roughly this. Underlying an action there is a rule (which you may or may not be consciously aware of). Kant calls these rules 'maxims'. Strip out the particulars and make this maxim as general as possible, then ask yourself: *Could this be a universal law?* If yes, then the action is morally permissible; if no, then there is a problem and you should not (as a rational being) act on that maxim. For those where there is a problem, the negation of the maxim becomes a duty.

The process is a bit more complex as there are two ways in which a maxim may fail as a universal law:

A Because we cannot conceive of a world in which this was a law – it is inconceivable.

B We can conceive of such a world, however we cannot rationally will such a world.

The two ways in which a maxim may fail are important as it is in *failing* the test that the moral duties arise. We have a duty not to follow maxims that fail the test. Maxims that pass the test are merely morally permissible, they are not duties.

The process is presented as a flow chart in Figure 1.11.

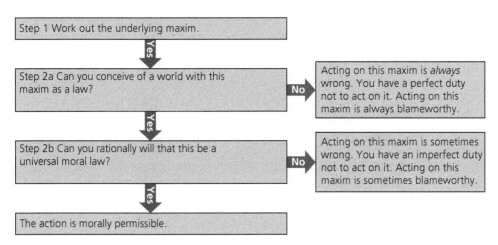

Figure 1.11

Let's test run this process using two of Kant's own examples.

Example 19: The false promise – *A perfect duty to others*

A man needs some money. He intends to get hold of it by promising to pay it back, even though he has no intention of doing this. Is this right?

- **Step 1: Work out the underlying maxim.** A maxim is a sort of rule of action. They normally have the form of an *action* in a *circumstance* with an *end or motive*. We should try to make the maxim as general as possible, in this case the maxim would be something like: *When in need, make promises with no intention of keeping them to gain help.*
- **Step 2a: Can you conceive of a world with this maxim as a law?** What would happen if everyone followed this maxim as a law and made promises that they had no intention of keeping? Presumably, as suggested earlier, no one would trust promises anymore. Kant argues that this maxim cannot be a universal law without contradiction; the maxim relies on the institution of promises, whereas if everyone followed this maxim there would be no institution of promises.

*Should I be able to say to myself, 'Every one may make
a deceitful promise when he finds himself in a difficulty
from which he cannot otherwise extricate himself?' Then I
presently become aware that while I can will the lie, I can by
no means will that lying should be a universal law ... Hence my maxim,
as soon as it should be made a universal law, would necessarily destroy
itself.*[9]

Kant

Following this rule would be wrong. Because the problem happens
at the conceiving stage then the maxim generates a perfect duty – in
this case a perfect duty not to do it. A perfect duty is one that we
are always obliged to follow. We have a perfect duty to keep promises.
Breaking a perfect duty is always wrong and your action would always
be blameworthy.

In this way, Kant believes that the categorical imperative can be used
to work out the moral law. Note that the categorical imperative does
not generate the moral law, nor are laws derived from it; rather, it is
a test that we can apply to any maxim, to see if it could be a universal
moral law. Let's consider another of Kant's examples.

Example 20: Not helping others – *An imperfect duty to others*

Someone who is doing pretty well in life sees that others need help. He
is inclined not to help.

- **Step 1: Work out the underlying maxim.** I will not help those
  in distress, when I easily could, through selfishness.
- **Step 2a: Can you conceive of a world with this maxim as a
  law?** Kant thinks that it is possible to conceive of a world where
  people do not help each other, so the maxim is not ruled out at
  this stage
- **Step 2b: Can you rationally will that this be a universal moral
  law?** Kant says 'no'. Everyone will have been in situations (as a baby,
  for example) when they were unable to help themselves and needed
  the help of others, and we would not want to be in a situation
  where we need assistance and yet no one will help us. Because this
  maxim was conceivable as a universal law, but could not be willed,
  it generates an imperfect duty. In this case, an imperfect duty not
  to not help others, which means that in situations when we can
  easily help, we can't always ignore those who need help. Breaking an
  imperfect duty is not always wrong, and is not always blameworthy.
  So you will not always be blamed if you fail to help others. Quite
  how much of a duty this becomes – how much we should help
  others – is not clear (see pages 95–7 for more on this).

Kant offers two more examples. The ones above concern more than
one person, so Kant labels them as examples of our *duties to others*.

The next two concern just the one person, so are examples of *duties to ourselves*. We will cover these in brief.

Example 21: Suicide – *Perfect duty to ourselves*

Someone miserable is contemplating committing suicide. Kant seems to imply that the maxim underlying this possible action is *'I will end my life if there is more pain than pleasure because of self-love'*. Kant thinks this cannot be a universal law as this fails at the first stage: we cannot conceive of a world with this as a law. As such, we have a perfect duty not to kill ourselves. This is generally considered to be the weakest of Kant's examples and he doesn't go into much detail in his explanation; he seems to assume that to kill yourself from the motive of self-love is contradictory. Sometimes people are tempted to analyse this by saying that if we all acted on the maxim *'Kill yourself'*, then there would be no one left in the world to kill themselves and so the action cannot be rationally willed (stage B). However, Kant does not produce this argument; he also feels it fails at stage A – the conception stage. Kant's argument seems to be that self-love is the motive that keeps us wanting to stay alive, so it cannot also be the motive for killing ourselves. (Kant seems to overlook the fact that many people may kill themselves for self-loathing – which probably wouldn't fail as a rule at the conception stage.)

It is also important to note though that criticism of this example does not mean that Kant's approach is wrong – just that he failed to apply his own ideas correctly to his own example. However, if you think there is something wrong with all of the examples, then it might point to a broader problem with the system.

Example 22: Lazy, but talented – *Imperfect duty to ourselves*

Someone with natural talents lets them go to waste because they are lazy. Kant sees the underlying maxim as something like this: *'I won't develop my talent, when I discover one, so as to remain comfortable'* (laziness). Kant thinks that a world with this as a universal maxim is conceivable, but believes it cannot be rationally willed. So we have an imperfect duty to develop at least some of our talents. It is an imperfect duty, so we can choose to let some of our talents rust. The reasoning being that we have all relied on other people's talents (doctors, teachers, etc.) and so we cannot consistently will that no one has talents.

Using the categorical imperative yourself

To recap, we have seen Kant analyse the concepts of *moral law* and *moral duty* and from these concepts alone he has derived the categorical imperative. This, in turn, can be used to help us work out what the moral law/our moral duties should be; in other words, other moral imperatives. Unlike utilitarianism, which relies on working out the consequence of an action before deciding to act, Kant's approach involves checking your maxims. Before we move on, have a go at using the categorical imperative yourself.

Experimenting with ideas

For each of the examples answer the following questions:

a) What is the maxim? Try to use the formula of action/circumstance/reason or motive.

b) Can you conceive of a world where this is a moral law?

c) Can you rationally will that this should be a moral law?

d) Is the action morally permissible, or is there a duty not to perform it?

The queue

You have been eagerly awaiting the publication date of the new Harry Potter/Hunger Games/A-level philosophy book. You wake up early to head to the book shop before it opens. When you get there, you are dismayed to see that the queue is half a mile long! Many people camped out overnight. As you walk past the queue, you see a friend. She leans over and whispers in your ear – suggesting you pretend you are together. That way, you can join the queue quite near the front. You consider her offer.

Surrender

You are a military commander. Unfortunately your enemy has made significant military gains. There is no point facing them in the battlefield – you will lose. One option is to pretend to surrender, lay down some of your ground weapons, and then, a few days later, launch a deadly counterattack from the air when they are not expecting it. You consider taking this option.

Exams

It is exam time (again). You are really struggling with the maths paper. However, you are clearly able to see the answers on the paper of the person next to you. You consider copying their answers.

Vows

You married very young (18). You said your vows in front of over a hundred people, which involved promising to be together for ever. However, after two years of living together you have (both) realised that you made a mistake. You are considering getting a divorce.

Waiter

You are a waiter in a restaurant. A very wealthy man spends a fortune (£1,600) on a meal for business clients. He is loud, rude and doesn't leave you any tip. However, he miscounts the notes when he hands them to you. He overpays by £100. You believe he will not notice the money is gone (as his wallet was literally stuffed with cash). You are considering keeping the £100 and not pointing out his mistake.

Different formulations of the categorical imperative

Kant argued that there is only one categorical imperative; however, he believed it can be expressed in different forms. He claimed there are three important formulations (he actually uses five different versions in the *Groundwork* – but obviously wasn't counting too carefully!). The version discussed so far is known as the *universal law* formulation. The second formulation is known as the *humanity* formulation; it is one of the famous elements of Kant's philosophy and has a profound legacy in the field of ethics and also in the development of human rights.

The argument for the second formulation

Learn More

This passage briefly summarises Kant's argument for the second formulation. However, it is not crucial to know this, so feel free to skip to the next section.

Kant argues that the categorical imperative (the version we discussed in the previous section) is a theoretical imperative. However, all practical action needs a specific end that is pursued. What end are we pursuing when we use the categorical imperative? Unlike hypothetical imperatives (discussed above), this end must be universal, and it must be contained within the idea of the categorical imperative itself. In this way, the end is achieved simply by using the categorical imperative. It becomes an end in itself (otherwise the ethic would be a consequentialist one). Free will and autonomy arise precisely because of the ability to reason and to use the categorical imperative to generate one's own laws (and so escape acting on desires – see page 74, the island scenario). By considering the first formulation we can see that it would be logically impossible to will that there is no will. As such, we should never act in a way that overlooks another person's (or your own) will/autonomy. Kant argues that it is the idea of an autonomous agent or 'will' that provides the end (as an end in itself) that we pursue when using the categorical imperative.

Another way of seeing this is to think of each human will as its own moral legislator (making its own moral laws). This idea is implicit within the categorical imperative (as the categorical imperative is the means of making one's own moral laws). To treat someone as a means but not as a rational free agent themselves, would be to treat that other human's will as not being its own moral legislator. I cannot make a rule (using my autonomy) that involves others not having autonomy. This is clearly a contradiction, which cannot be universalised. In this way, Kant argues that the autonomy of the human will is the supreme principle of morality.

Jeremy Bentham claims that pleasure is universally pursued, and so this should be the universal end which generates the imperatives that should be followed by all. However, for Kant the seeking of pleasure is an **empirical fact** (which can be disputed) and this is not good enough for the basis of morality. For Kant, the supreme principle of morality (human autonomy) is contained within the idea of morality itself, and so is an **a priori** principle that will apply universally.

The second formulation: The humanity formulation

Having put forward a complex argument, Kant presents his second formulation of the categorical imperative. He claims that there is a categorical duty to:

Act in such a way that you treat humanity, whether in your own person or in the person of any other, never merely as a means to an end, but always at the same time as an end.[10]

Kant

Kant believed that this formulation has the same meaning as the *universal law* formulation, but that it presents the ideas in a way that is more intuitive. Consider the following example.

▶ **ACTIVITY**

Example 23: The new friend

Quite suddenly you acquire a new friend, Sam. Sam goes out of her way to be nice to you, pays you compliments, lets you borrow her fancy camera and even buys you a thoughtful (yet inexpensive) birthday present. However, you find out that in reality Sam doesn't like you at all. She only became friends with you so that she could meet your cousin, who is an up-and-coming journalist. Sam thinks your journalist cousin could help move her career forward.

● How does this make you feel?
● Was Sam's behaviour wrong?

In general, we feel very strongly if we suspect we are being used or deceived in some way. If Sam had been upfront in saying she wanted to meet your cousin, then maybe you would have acted differently towards her. However, she deceived you and in doing so she over-rode your autonomy, using you as a means to an end. For Kant, this is always wrong.

The humanity formulation expresses the idea that it is always wrong to treat you (or any person) in a way that involves you in an action that you do not, in principle, have a chance to consent to.

This does not mean you can never use people as a means. Every time I go to a restaurant, take a taxi or call a plumber, I am using a person to further my ends. However, this person has consented to the arrangement, and they too are using me as a means to an end – to make money. The moral problem arises when you do not have a chance to consent, and so your autonomy/rationality is undermined. When this happens, you are being used *merely* as a means to an end.

Example 24: Fake notes

A man comes round to buy your old bass guitar. He deliberately gives you fake £20 notes, which you do not notice.

This action is wrong because the man is bypassing your autonomy. If he told you the notes were fake, you would not accept them. In keeping it secret he is acting in a way that does not give you a chance to consent. He is treating you merely as a means to get the guitar and not as a person with your own ends.

A

PRIVATE

£1000

GOSSIP

B

£130

**Figure 1.12
The humanity
formulation**
In (A) the
photographer
makes money
by taking photos
without permission.
He uses the couple
merely as a means
to this end. In (B)
the photographer
makes money, but
he takes photos
with the permission
of the couple, who
want the photos
to be taken. In
doing this, he
treats the couple
as people with an
end themselves,
while also pursuing
his end.

So stealing from me, lying, deceiving, drugging, kidnapping, forcing me into slavery or murdering me (and so on) would be to involve me in acts that I have not had the opportunity to consent to. In doing any of these, the person would be using me merely as a means to further their own ends, and not as an autonomous being with my own ends.

Using the humanity formulation

As the humanity formulation of the categorical imperative is (allegedly) the same as the universal formulation, we should expect the same moral duties to emerge when considering the same scenarios. So, in the example of the new friend on page 84 using the universal law formulation Sam would be acting on some sort of maxim like this: *'When I need to I will fake friendships in order to further my cause'*. What would happen to the institution of friendship if everyone acted on this law? Likewise, what would happen if everyone used fake £20 notes? Neither of these actions/maxims would be fit to make a universal law and so we have a duty not to do them. These two cases seem to arrive at the same answer on both formulations of the categorical imperative. In the *Groundwork*, Kant revisits his own examples to see if the humanity formulation yields the same results.

The clearest case is that of borrowing money with a false promise (see page 79). Here you are using the lender merely as a means to further your end. By making a false promise you are denying the lender the right to make an appropriate autonomous decision about lending. As you are using them merely as a means to an end, you have a perfect duty not do this.

The other case of a perfect duty – that of not killing yourself – was not very convincing using the universal law formulation. It is also not very convincing using the humanity formulation (so there is consistency here at least!). Kant argues that in deciding to end your life when it becomes insufferable, you are treating yourself, in the meantime, as a means to an end. Kant also argues that just as killing another person is to treat that person as a means to your end, so is killing yourself. Commentators dispute how convincing this is.

The two cases of imperfect duties (examples 20 and 22) introduce a slightly different interpretation to the humanity formulation. Both cases are permissible, in that not developing your talents and not helping others do not contradict the humanity formulation (you are not treating anyone as merely a means to your end). However, they are not in *harmony* with the formulation. The humanity formulation has the autonomy/rationality of humanity at its heart, as the supreme moral principle. To be in harmony with this would require you not only to respect, but to develop human autonomy/rationality and this would involve furthering your skills and helping others. Failing to do these things (help and develop) does not contradict the humanity formulation, so you do not have a perfect duty to do them. However, failing to do them is not in harmony with the humanity formulation, so you have an imperfect duty to carry them out.

Experimenting with ideas: Testing the humanity formulation

Revisit the Experimenting with ideas examples on page 82. In each case, answer the following questions:

1 Would acting on the maxim contradict the humanity formulation? If so, you have a perfect duty not to act on the maxim.
2 Would acting on the maxim be out of harmony with the humanity formulation? If so, you have an imperfect duty not to act on it (meaning you can act on it sometimes).
3 Are your answers the same as you derived using the universal law formulation?
4 Is the humanity formulation easier to use?

As an extension activity revisit the Experimenting with ideas examples on page 31. Use both the universal law formulation and the humanity formulation and answer the questions above.

The humanity formulation and human dignity

The humanity formulation places a great emphasis on respecting autonomy, which for many people is the key to dignity. Consider again the example of the nude photos (page 31). Utilitarians struggle somewhat with articulating why this is wrong. A strict act utilitarian may even say that it is a good thing; especially if the photos are widely viewed and enjoyed. A rule utilitarian may be able to construct a rule which this act violates; which, if generally followed would maximise happiness. However, this would still treat the rights of the girlfriend as just a side effect of maximising happiness, not as valuable as an end in itself. A preference utilitarian may be able to say that the act would be against the ex-girlfriend's preference; however, the preferences of all the online viewers also need to be factored in. For Kant, though, this represents a violation of the supreme moral principle: human autonomy. The ex-girlfriend is being treated as a means to an end and not as a person with ends herself. She has had no opportunity to consent. The ex-boyfriend has a perfect duty not to act in the way he did. Kant's theory seems to cut right to the core of what is wrong in this situation.

The humanity formulation and human rights

Learn More

The two formulations of the categorical imperative do not look the same on paper; however, Kant's belief is that in committing to the universality of moral law, we are committing to the value of rationality and autonomy in all of us, for it is through the ability to create universal laws that human autonomy exists. This focus on autonomy has been very influential. The development of human rights is closely associated with the belief in the importance of human autonomy, and it was Kant's work that placed autonomy at the heart of ethics.

The relationship between Kantian ethics and human rights can be seen by revisiting the example of the scapegoat (page 31). An act utilitarian would be very tempted to kill the innocent person. A rule utilitarian might claim that having a rule about a right to life, in the long term, would make us all happier (though not on this occasion). For the rule utilitarian, this would not be based on the intrinsic worth of humans, but rather the fact that rights may make us happier. Rights are a sort of side effect in our quest for happiness, a means to an end.

In Kantian ethics, the innocent scapegoat is clearly being used as a means to some other end. This is something he has not had any opportunity to consent to (and wouldn't consent to if he had). Killing the man would undermine his rational autonomy (in quite a serious way!). Slavery, false imprisonment, torture, and so on, are all extreme ways of treating people as a means to some other end and undermining their autonomy; which is an end in itself. The basis of all human rights is to enable individual, rational autonomy, and Kant's philosophy played a significant part in their development.

The third formulation: The kingdom of ends formulation

Learn More

Kant's third formulation is known as the *kingdom of ends* formulation.

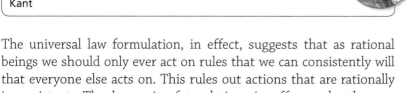

> *So act as if you were through your maxims a law-making member of a kingdom of ends.*[11]
>
> Kant

The universal law formulation, in effect, suggests that as rational beings we should only ever act on rules that we can consistently will that everyone else acts on. This rules out actions that are rationally inconsistent. The humanity formulation, in effect, asks that we respect the fact that others have ends too, and not override this fact. This rules out ignoring the rationality of others.

Humans, as imperfectly rational beings, will all have different ends that we seek – and there is nothing wrong with this. But sometimes our ends will clash (after all, we can't both have the last Rolo/jam doughnut in the shop!). Kant argues that we should act in such a way that we do not just prioritise our own ends, but rather act on principles that could, in effect, be the rules/law that everyone would be willing to follow. This would involve creating laws that enable us all to best achieve our ends. In the 'Trouble on the island' example (pages 73–4), as the king, you suggested a radical idea – that each citizen work out the laws of the land themselves (individually) and act on them. This, in reality, would lead to self-interested chaos! However, if we were perfectly rational, it wouldn't – we would all conclude the same rules and follow them. Kant's third formulation says that we have a duty to act as if we were working towards this idealised end.

Some commentators challenge this version, as it seems a bit strong to ask that I behave in a certain way (e.g. never lie, let people go ahead of me at junctions, care for the environment, and so on) if we know that others won't. In return you could argue that we will never get to this kingdom of ends (which is the perfection of human reason) unless we act as if we can get there; hence we have a duty to act that way.

Strengths of Kant's system

Kant's system of ethics, though complicated, has many strengths. It is rational and universal, and so is not relativistic. It rationally articulates and places a central importance on the worth and dignity of human autonomy. It is not ends based, so avoids some of the criticisms of consequentialism. As there is no singular 'end' that we have to maximise, Kant's system of ethics allows for individuals to pursue their own projects/ends. Despite these strengths, Kant's ethics have also raised many problems, and it is to these criticisms that we now turn.

Issues with Kantian deontological ethics

Consequences

One of the key objections to Kantian ethics is that it places all of the moral worth on the motives of an action. Just as utilitarianism is criticised for placing all of the moral worth of an action on the consequences, so Kant is criticised for placing all of the emphasis on the motive. It seems our moral intuitions want to have it both ways – attach some of the value to the consequence and some to the motive.

▶ **ACTIVITY: To lie or not to lie**

Read the example of the axeman on page 34.

Would Kant say it is wrong to lie?

Here is a clear case in which lying would seem to be the right thing to do. However, in concluding this, it appears we would be thinking about the consequences of the act – and, for Kant, the moral value lies solely in the reason for acting. For Kant, it would be wrong to lie as you cannot consistently conceive of a world in which this is the moral law. Using the second formulation, to lie would be to treat the potential murderer as a means to some other end (saving your friend's life). To lie would be to undermine his autonomy to make decisions himself, and so it would be wrong.

Now, there are various Kantian ways of getting out of this conclusion (see pages 107–10 for more on this), but the fundamental point of the criticism is that telling the truth will have bad consequences – and this is what makes it wrong, not whether you can universalise the maxim underlying the act. On this occasion, the moral value of the act (lying or not) seems to reside in the consequence not the motive.

Kant's larger claim, in essence, is that we all need to focus on our own sphere of control; make sure that *I* do not lie, deceive, etc., and only act on maxims that *I* have worked out to be universal laws. If we all did this, then we would end up in a world where we all had freedom and autonomy (the kingdom of ends). However, in the example above, I might be busy doing the right thing, but the mad axeman sure isn't, and this would have disastrous consequences. This focus on my sphere of control seems to miss the bigger, and consequentialist, picture. It can appear that Kantian ethics are more concerned with being rationally consistent in our actions, than whether a friend is killed. It may well be the case that if we all acted rationally consistently, the world would be a better place. However, we do not live in this ideal world, we live in a world with murderers and cheats. Just focusing on my own sphere of action, as if we are all aiming for an ideal world, would seem to have disastrous consequences in the real, non-ideal world in which we live. Because the world is non-ideal, some argue that we have to look at the consequences of our actions, and override the need to be rationally consistent in our willing.

On a different note, Kantian ethics is also criticised for having consequentialist tendencies (while claiming to be purely motive based). Some suggest that to work out whether a maxim can be consistently willed relies on thinking through the consequences of having this as a law – and so is consequentialist. However, in Kant's defence, the moral value lies in the consistency of the will, and not in whether the world would be 'good' or 'bad' if the maxim were universalised. A harder criticism to defend is that Kant seems to be pointing towards a world where we maximise our mutual autonomy (the kingdom of ends) as the ideal. This is akin to saying there is an end that we should be aiming for, and this end makes actions good. This, of course, would be a consequentialist philosophy, and some argue that we should interpret Kant this way.

Application of the categorical imperative

This series of criticisms relates to difficulties in applying the categorical imperative, mainly to the *universal law* formulation.

Universalising maxims: Oddities

Something odd can happen when we try to universalise maxims that include relative or 'norm'-related positions (comparing ourselves to others). For example, consider the maxim *'When taking an exam,*

I will always try to come in the top half, to push myself'. This seems fair enough, however a world where this is a law is impossible to conceive, as we cannot all, by definition, be in the top half. This would mean we have a perfect duty not to try and come in the top half (and we also would have a perfect duty not to come in the bottom half). I can though universalise the maxim *'When taking an exam, I will always try to gain over half of the marks, to push myself'*, as everyone could get over half the marks. The problem lies in fixing outcomes in relation to other people, in ways that can't be universalised. Perhaps we should never compare ourselves to others. Maybe this is to treat them as a means to an end. Nevertheless, on the face of it, acting on the maxim to try to come in the top half does not seem to be immoral. It is worth noting that these norm-related problems also occur for some forms of utilitarianism (see page 43), so maybe there is something wrong with applying norm-related positions to all people equally.

On a similar note, consider this rule: *'I will always help the poor when I can afford to, to ease their plight'*. It can be argued that this cannot be rationally willed to be a universal law, as if everyone did this, there would be no poor. So we have an imperfect duty to not help the poor! However, this would seem wrong.

The categorical imperative only reveals what we can't do

A criticism commonly levelled at Kant is that many trivial acts, which themselves don't seem to be moral, can be successfully universalised. For example: *'I will chew food 32 times before eating, to aid digestion'*. However, for Kant, those maxims that *can* be universalised are just morally permissible; we have no duty to do them. It is those actions that we *cannot* universalise that generate moral duties (a duty not to perform them or a duty to do the opposite). This though leads to a different criticism – that Kant's ethics only tell us what we can't do (lie, deceive, etc.); it does not give a positive account of what we should be aiming for. On the other hand, this can also be seen as a strength in that it allows for people to pursue their own projects and ends.

Non-moral maxims

The categorical imperative does, though, seem possible to generate trivial duties. Consider the rule *'On trick or treat nights, I will go and collect sweets, but will not provide any at my house, to save money'*. I can conceive of a world where this is the rule (it would be a dull Hallowe'en!), but I cannot rationally will it, as following the maxim would destroy the institution of trick or treat, on which the maxim relies. It would seem that, as a rational being, I have an imperfect duty not to do this. But, although I would agree that I can't universalise just collecting the sweets, this does not seem to be a moral issue – just an issue of cultural practice. (Many of Kant's examples of perfect duties involve acting in a way that would undermine a social/cultural institution that the act also relies on – e.g. promising. In the case above, the institution is 'trick or treat', which does not seem to be a moral one.)

Do we have a duty to offer sweets at Hallowe'en if we also collect them? According to Kant, it might seem so. But if this is not a moral duty, then how can we distinguish moral duties from non-moral duties, unless we have a prior understanding of what morality is – an understanding that is not derived from the ability to universalise maxims?

Imperfect duties

When we apply the categorical imperative we sometimes end up with imperfect duties – such as general duties to help others, or to develop our talents. These are duties that I do not have to do all the time. I am praised if I do them (helping someone), but I am not always blamed if I don't. This seems to leave us with a very vague moral duty. We seem to need more guidance on when I should help people, and how much self-improvement I should undertake, etc. Having an imperfect duty alone doesn't seem to tell us when to perform the imperfect duties. It may well be possible to overcome this issue, but a more elaborate theory of imperfect duty is needed (see pages 95–7 for more on this).

What is a maxim?

Another set of problems involves the specifying of maxims that we test using the categorical imperative. Clearly I can't consistently universalise the maxim '*When in need, make promises with no intention of keeping them to gain help*', but maybe I could universalise the maxim '*When in need on my birthday, make promises with no intention of keeping them*'. After all, people do break promises quite often and the institution of promises does exist, so I could rationally will the occasional breaking of promises. This example can probably be dismissed as the birthday element is not relevant, so I have not tried to seek the *general* maxim underlying my action – as Kant asks us to do. But how about these maxims: '*I will lie to potential murderers in order to save lives*', or '*When asked a question, I will not lie to anyone, except when it is to save a life*'. Here the exception does seem to be morally relevant (it also articulates the rule that many think we should follow). Lying, just on these occasions, certainly seems conceivable; it is also something that I *can* rationally will, as it would not threaten the institution of truth-telling. Specifying the maxim, working out what the rule is, can be seen as a problem for Kantian ethics, as if we specify rules too tightly then almost anything can be universalised. On the other hand, if we specify them too generally, then the theory becomes too strict and misses the complexity of the actual rules and principles that we follow in life.

The value of other motives and commitments

Value in motives

Previously (page 72) we explored the example of two fathers (A and B). A common intuition is that Father A, who helps his son because he wants to is the better dad. Kant, however, argues that only Father B's actions have moral worth, as they are carried out from duty, not desire. This seems counter-intuitive. We seem to want to place value on the motive of Father A too, and more generally also on the motives of people who *want* to help others and devote their life to doing so. For Kant, these actions, though in accordance with duty, are not done for the sake of duty so have no moral value. This seems to be at odds with our intuition that certain emotions have a moral dimension, such as love, compassion, guilt and sympathy, or pride and jealousy. Don't we regard the possession of such emotions itself as morally praise- or blameworthy; as having moral value?

Some also object to Kant's approach claiming it encourages a cold and calculative approach to ethics by demanding that we put aside our feelings for the suffering of others. In Kant's defence, he is not against people *wanting* to do right actions, and positive emotions, but he is clear that acting from desire, not duty, has no moral worth. Happiness is worth pursuing, but for Kant it has no value unless it comes about for the right reasons – from acting dutifully.

Kant's account of duty as the source of moral worth also makes his concept of virtue a little counter-intuitive. For Kant, virtue is *'the moral strength of a human being's will in fulfilling his duty'*.[12] A good will is one that acts out of duty, but this need not be virtuous, as the will might not require much strength to act out of duty. It may come easily to some people. This leaves Kant in an odd position, in that it seems that people who do not want to do the right thing, people who have strong desires to lie and cheat and so on, when they do act out of duty, are more virtuous than those people whose duties and desires coincide. It also means that a perfectly rational being (God) would not be virtuous at all, as there would be no desires to tug against when doing the right thing.

The challenge of care ethics

There is a feminist critique of both utilitarianism and Kantian ethics (from Carol Gilligan[13] and others). The argument is that the emphasis both systems place on reasoning from an abstract, neutral viewpoint, and the adoption of a dispassionate approach in how we assess our concern for different humans, represents 'male' patterns of ethical thought. Females, it claims, often put more attention on the subjectivity of situations and on care and concern for others.

Consider this tale of the hedgehogs and the porcupine (adapted from Carol Gilligan, who adapted it from Aesop[14]).

▶ **ACTIVITY: Moles and the porcupine**

A group of moles live in a system of tunnels and have developed ways of getting along together. One day a porcupine comes to shelter in the tunnels and stays for a few days. This causes a bit of commotion as he is slightly larger, which makes squeezing past him in the tunnels quite difficult. However, he is a jolly fellow, which makes things easier. After a week the moles get together and discuss what to do – specifically whether the porcupine should stay.

1 Is it right that the porcupine stays?
2 If you were a mole, would you let him stay?
3 What sort of things would you consider in making this decision?
4 As a human, would you let a porcupine stay in your house?
5 Is it different for the moles?

During the council of the moles, some start to argue whether justice and duty apply across different species, others debate whether they can universalise the maxim of sending him away, others still look to see if applying their moral rules would maximise utility. In among all this abstract discussion are still more voices. These moles want the porcupine to stay, because they care about him. They care about this specific porcupine. For them this is the most important factor. All of the abstract discussion misses the point. Morality is about individual situations and about care. The problem with Kant and with utilitarianism is that they overlook this very different way of ethically thinking. Nearly everyone would lie to the axeman (page 34) and that is because they care about the person in the house. Only someone that really didn't care, or cared but did not place moral value on care, would tell the truth.

We cannot adopt an impersonal perspective

We may doubt whether it is even possible for us to set aside the interests, concerns and desires that make us individuals, and to think of ourselves, as Kant wants us to, as purely rational autonomous beings engaged in universal lawmaking. Bernard Williams[15] argues that the impartial position that Kant wishes us to adopt may be possible for factual considerations, but not for practical, moral deliberations. For example, if I ask 'I wonder whether strontium is a metal?' it is possible to remove the personal 'I' from this question, and seek an answer that is independent of my own perspective on the world. This kind of deliberation means that it is possible for anyone to take up my question and be given the same answer; there is what Williams calls a 'unity of interest' in the answer. This is because deliberation about facts is not essentially personal, but is an attempt to reach an impersonal position (where we all agree that these are the facts). In contrast, Williams maintains that practical deliberation is essentially personal and it does make a difference whether it is me, or someone else (for example, the madman's mother, his intended victim, the victim's life insurer or the madman himself) asking the question 'Should I lie to this man?' We cannot and should not strive for the same impersonal position as in the factual case. With moral deliberations there is no longer a 'unity of interest', and a different person, with a different set of desires and interests, who is now standing in my shoes, might seek a different answer. The position from which we ask this practical question is a personal position, and the answer will affect us very much. Williams argues that Kant is wrong and that we cannot adopt an impersonal perspective (the perspective of the categorical imperative), because by doing so we lose our place in the world, our interests and any sense of self.

Commitments to family and friends

The difficulty with taking an impersonal perspective is felt most keenly when we think about our ties to family and friends. Is it wrong to lie in order to prevent nasty people hurting my family? Shouldn't I make false promises to keep my children from harm? Focusing the moral value solely on the ability to act in ways that can be universalised, or that treat everyone's humanity with the highest respect, means that I cannot treat my family any differently from strangers (morally). However, critics sometimes argue that personal relationships have moral value in themselves.

Defending Kant

While it is true that Kant's approach to ethics is highly abstract and impersonal, the concept of humanity and dignity takes a centre stage. Often critics focus heavily on the formulation of *universal law*, which is all about abstract universalising; however, it can be argued that the *humanity* formulation is really at the core of Kant's theory, and this is concerned with treating people with appropriate respect. Kant's theory does also have a personal focus, as it is all about the individual working out how to negotiate between the different duties and commitments we have in life. Kant's theory gives us the tools to reason about the rules we adopt and how we treat others in our interactions as all of us go about our lives as self-governing beings.

While Kant's theory does not place specific moral value on friends and family (as moral value is only conferred by a good will), it does allow for us having specific moral duties towards friends and family. Kant did not articulate the entire myriad of perfect and imperfect duties we have towards each other, but it is easy to see that social institutions such as family, friendship and marriage are constructed in ways that mean we do have specific moral duties in their regard. For example, a maxim of 'being mean to friends' can be conceived, but not rationally willed; so we have a duty not to be mean. Likewise, the rule of 'abandoning family members'. It is easy to see that thinking from a universal perspective does not render the personal bonds of friendship and family as meaningless and empty. On the contrary, being part of a family and having friends comes with special moral duties and ways of behaving and Kant's theory can articulate this.

Competing duties

For Kant, we are all creators of our own moral laws. We can use the categorical imperative to work out what is morally permissible and what rules we have a moral duty (perfect or imperfect) to follow. Using this system we can each write our moral duties in our metaphorical book of moral laws. However, what happens when the duties contradict each other? For example, in the axeman scenario (page 34) we might see this as a clash in our duty to tell the truth, and our duty to care for others. Getting into the law book doesn't seem to tell us what order the rules come in, and what weight to attach to each.

For Kant, clashing rules represents a serious problem. His whole moral system involves duties being based on avoiding rules that are rationally inconsistent. Duties arise when rules are rationally inconsistent. We have a duty to not follow such rules, as we have a duty to be rationally consistent. Duties are all about consistency. If it is the case that two duties are rationally inconsistent, then, by definition, they cannot be duties, and his system collapses. In his own words, this is actually inconceivable:

> ... *two rules opposed to each other cannot be necessary at the same time, if it is a duty to act in accordance with one rule, to act in accordance with the opposite rule is not a duty but even contrary to duty; so a collision of duties and obligations is inconceivable.*[16]
>
> Kant

So, for Kant duties cannot clash, by definition. However, we can sometimes be wrong in thinking through our grounds of obligation. If I made a promise to a friend that I would lie for them, then it would seem that I have two conflicting duties: (A) I should keep my promises, and (B) I should never lie. However, it is clear that I am not obliged to keep the promise in this case; we cannot rationally will a maxim whereby we keep promises to lie. It is inconceivable, as a promise. It was wrong to make this promise, in fact we have a duty not to make such promises. In this case, revisiting my grounds of obligation shows that the duties do not in fact clash, as I do not have a moral duty to keep this promise.

Imperfect duties

This approach may work for some 'alleged' clashes of duty – particularly those involving two perfect duties. However, the situation is less clear when imperfect duties are included, such as our imperfect duties to help others, to develop our own talents and so on. These are duties we do not have to follow all of the time. We are praised for following them, but, unlike perfect duties, we are not always blamed for not following them. So I will be praised for helping others, but will not always be blameworthy if I don't. However, knowing which of these duties to prioritise can be difficult.

Utilitarians seem to have an advantage here, as by using the common currency of happiness they can weigh up different actions and see how they compare. Kant's approach is less clear; instead of looking at the consequences, we need to examine our reasons – our grounds of obligation – and see which is stronger. However, it is not easy to do this. But this weakness can also be seen as a strength. Utilitarians can be seen as treating humans as a means to an end, or treating them not as individuals but as numbers of quality-adjusted life years of pleasure, to be weighed and measured when making decisions. This might render decision-making easier, but at a cost. For Kant, human dignity and respect are absolute and so cannot be weighed and calibrated. For Kant, we have a duty to treat everyone as an end in themselves, however this can make decision-making harder.

Jean-Paul Sartre[17] criticises Kant and uses an example from his own experience during the Nazi occupation of France of a young man torn between his duty to his country which impelled him to join the resistance and which would probably lead to his death, and his duty to care for his mother, who had already lost her other sons to the war. He suggests that Kant's ethical theory is of no use in helping him to resolve this conflict between two duties, and that the young man had to go on instinct. The suggestion here is that when our duties clash, we have to use desires and feelings to decide which to choose. Kant, of course, would disagree. He claims that we have to look at the grounds for obligation and assess the strengths.

Consider this case. I come across someone collapsed on the road. Do I help? I know that I have a general duty of care towards others, but if I see that some people are already helping, then there is no blame in me not helping. However, if I come across someone collapsed and there is no one else there, then the rule in question may be different. Do I treat my duty in the same way as before, as a general duty to help? I may even kid myself and say that someone else will come along soon and that other people may help. If I choose to ignore the person, what rule would I be following? The change in circumstance suggests that it may be a different maxim, perhaps *'I will not help someone in need, even though I am the only person that can, because I am in a rush'*. Even though I can conceive of this world I cannot rationally will it. In this case, there seems to be a stronger ground of obligation than before.

This approach is not easy to follow, and Kant does not offer much guidance (although other philosophers have developed elaborate Kantian systems). However, it can be argued that this complexity is just part of the world that we live in. After all, human rights lawyers spend years arguing about the hierarchy of competing rights. Does freedom of speech mean I can say anything? What about when it undermines other people's right to practise religion? Or if I incite hatred, might this undermine people's right to freedom of movement? And so on. On a personal level too, competing obligations can be a minefield. On page 16 we discussed the dilemma of staying in and doing your homework or going out with friends. For Bentham, this would be all about weighing up the pleasure; for Kant, this would be about negotiating obligations. For example, you may have promised friends that you would join them later that evening, and also have homework and know that you have a general duty not to waste your life and develop your talents, but you may also have promised your parents you would tidy up and know that it would be wrong to lie to your parents about completing the homework ... and so on. The world is complicated, and balancing our competing duties is hard. But Kant, at least, presents a theory that helps us think through our duties in a rational way.

A summary of Kant

Kant's approach to ethics requires us to determine what is right and wrong for ourselves by the application of reason, and not expect it to be delivered by any higher authority. Kant argues that a moral action is one which proceeds from the proper motive, namely the 'good will' which is a recognition of *duty*. Moral duties are unconditional (or categorical) demands on our behaviour, for example 'You should give up your seat to the elderly and infirm.' They are unconditional or categorical because they do not depend on any conditions that need to be met; they are imperatives that apply to us all the time, whatever our personal desires and goals. We can work out what duties are determined by the use of reason by considering whether it is possible to universalise the maxim underlying an action. The ultimate duty is always to act in accordance with the categorical imperative, and so act in accordance with a maxim that you will everyone to act by. A second version of the categorical imperative states that we should always treat others as ends in themselves and never as means to our ends. Kant's approach to ethics is quite complex and not without criticism, which we have explored above. However, his approach of giving human autonomy a central role in ethics has been highly influential and underpins the conceptual framework for human rights.

Applying Kantian ethics

In this section we will apply Kant's deontological ethics to five specific areas:

- Crime and punishment
- War
- Simulated killing
- The treatment of animals
- Deception and the telling of lies.

In each section we refer back to the ethical dilemmas presented in the introduction (pages 6–11).

Crime and punishment

So far we have looked at Kant's ethics – this concerns our internal reasons for acting (sometimes called our internal behaviour). The goodness or badness of actions relates entirely to these reasons for acting. In examining some of the cases below we will draw on Kant's politics – his theory of juridical rights (rights relating to law). These concern our external behaviour, so some of the ideas will be a little different, but linking both is the concept of freedom. Freedom is gained *internally*, by being able to follow maxims and use reason, and *externally* (politically) by being able to set and pursue our own ends, without being impeded by the choices of others (as long as my ends don't impede others' too).

Experimenting with ideas: There are no laws

Imagine a world without laws. Imagine today, this very day, this very moment, that all government simultaneously gives up. All police forces/courts/armies are disbanded. All prisons are closed down. There are no more crimes, as there are no laws. What would you do?

- In the first hour?
- In the first week?
- In the longer term?

Some people see laws as inhibiting their freedom (speed restrictions, illegal drugs, etc.) and so we would be freer without them. But would you be freer with no laws?

Kant, in common with other philosophers, calls this idea of a lawless world a '*state of nature*'. In a state of nature we lack external freedom as other people's choices may be imposed on us and there is no way to deal with this – except through violence. Consider possessions. In a state of nature, if I leave my precious flint box in the woods and someone comes across it, then what is to stop them from taking it? What actually makes it 'mine'? Only laws can do this. Living in a state of nature has a kind of wild, anything-is-possible freedom, but it lacks real freedom, the freedom to pursue my ends without other people's choices being imposed on me. We need a civil society for this.

In a civil society I have a means of getting my flint box back. We can settle disputes with reason, not violence. The laws allow us each to have the maximum freedom that can co-exist with everyone else's freedom. Kant calls the idea of a civil society '*a rightful condition*', and rational beings have a duty to enter into it.

In a rightful condition my possessions and freedoms are upheld by the law. When someone acts illegally, it is not just the victims that it affects, but the law/state that is also damaged. The criminal's act pushes us all towards the wild state of nature, and in so doing damages the state.

> *Whoever steals makes the property of everyone else insecure and therefore deprives himself ... of security in any possible property. [In this way, crimes] endanger the commonwealth and not just an individual person.*[18]
>
> Kant

The criminal has damaged the state by using a maxim that (by definition) is incompatible with the rightful condition. So, by turning the maxim back on the individual, the state restores itself to its original position. The reversing of the maxim nulls the offence. As a metaphor, a criminal hurts the state through her actions and by reversing the maxim back on her, the state heals itself and the law is restored.

The government/state has a duty (a categorical imperative) to carry out these punishments, as this is required by the definition of the state. If it did not, there would be no state, so by its own nature the state has a categorical imperative to punish criminals.

So, according to Kant, whatever criminals do, we should do back to them. If they steal property, they should lose property. If they kill, they should be killed. Kant thinks this is justified by a principle of equality: if you are prepared to act on a maxim that breaks the law, you should expect that maxim to be used on yourself.

> *Whatever undeserved evil you inflict upon another within the people, that you inflict upon yourself.*[19]
>
> Kant

Effectively, Kant argues that the ancient system of an eye for an eye is the just system of punishment. He does, however, acknowledge that sometimes the punishment may not be *exactly* the same as the crime (e.g. rape). For Kant, the key purpose of punishment is retribution.

Criticism
Example 25: An eye for an eye
In March 2015 as a result of a court ruling in Iran, a criminal was blinded in one eye by the state and also had his ear removed. The criminal had been found guilty of blinding another man in an acid attack and had also been sentenced to ten years in prison. The carrying out of this sentence caused an outcry by human rights groups. However, it was welcomed by many Iranians who felt that this was proper justice. Along with the human rights groups, many feel that this type of retribution adds to the suffering of the world and demeans the dignity of humanity as a whole. Kant, though, argued that retribution is actually required out of respect for the criminal's autonomy.

Retribution as respect for autonomy

Kant was critical of a utilitarian approach to punishment (and to other things). Writing on Kant, James Rachels outlines how utilitarianism is in breach of the humanity formulation.

> [utilitarianism] has us calculating how to use people as a means to an end and this (he [Kant] says) is morally impermissible. If we imprison the criminal in order to secure the well-being of society we are merely using him for the benefit of others. This violates the fundamental rule that 'one man ought never to be dealt with merely as a means subservient to the purpose of another'.[20]

Rachels

Kant argues that punishing for the purposes of retribution *is* to treat someone as a person, as an end in themselves. This may seem highly counter-intuitive. However, for Kant, you might slap a dog that has been naughty as a means of training them not to do it again, but you would not hold the dog to account for its behaviour as you would a rational being. For humans to use punishment to train people (rehabilitation) is to treat them like animals that are incapable of reason. To punish someone for what they did as retribution, is to treat them as a rational person who is morally responsible for their action. It is to treat them as ends in themselves. So, for Kant, retribution is the only purpose for punishment.

anthology
1.6

▶ **ACTIVITY**

Read CP1 and CP2 (page 7). What would Kant say?

In the case of CP1, the man should be killed. Kant is very explicit on using the death penalty.

In CP2, stealing is morally and legally wrong. Morally, the man borrows his friend's pass without asking, and so treats him as a means to an end. He would also be treating the hospital manager as a means to his end. You cannot rationally will (or maybe even conceive) that people should steal property. Kant is very clear on this. Do not do it. Laws need to be followed.

However, this strict approach for Kant leaves his system in a difficult position when it comes to unjust laws. What if a government passed discriminatory laws. Should these be obeyed? Kant argues that law makers have a duty not to pass such laws, but unjust laws are still a problem, as there is no higher system than the government that can be used to 'settle a dispute' rationally, and not obeying the law is to will us to return to a state of nature, which you cannot rationally do.

Example 26: Clive Ponting

One of the key incidents during the 1982 Falklands war was the sinking of the Argentine warship the *General Belgrano*. There was controversy about whether the ship had been inside or outside the declared 'exclusion zone' at the time it was attacked, which was important in deciding whether it was a legitimate target. In 1984 a senior civil servant at the Ministry of Defence, Clive Ponting, leaked documents which revealed that the ship had been outside the exclusion zone, and travelling further away from it.

Ponting admitted leaking the documents and was charged with a criminal offence under the Official Secrets Act. Ponting's defence in court was that he was acting in the public interest. The judge told the jury that they had a duty to find him guilty, as he had admitted leaking the documents and this was against the law. Also the judge told the jury that the *public interest is what the government of the day says it is*. The jury ignored the judge (and the law) and found him not guilty.

For Kant, the actions of the jury would be morally wrong. They have a duty to apply the law, and determine guilt. For Kant, you cannot rationally will that the law should not function, as this would be to will a return to a state of nature, which itself does not allow for the full expression of the will/autonomy. You would be willing that your will is undermined. However, this leaves a problem about how unjust laws should be changed. There are Kantian ways of overcoming this problem, but it is still an issue. In the Clive Ponting case many people think the jury did the right thing, that laws should not prevent important truths from coming out. However, for Kant, this would be wrong.

War

As with crime, Kant's position on war is related to his political theory, his theory of rights, rather than his ethics. There are, however, close parallels between the two and they are linked by the concept of freedom and human autonomy (outward and inner freedom).

Much as humans have a duty to leave the state of nature and enter a rightful condition, so do states (countries). In a rightful condition, individuals can meaningfully have property and can settle disputes by reason; this is because there is a law-making state that exists independently, 'above' the individuals. The situation with countries/states is a little more complex. When states have dispute, they may go to war and so enter a state of nature (where disputes are settled by force, not reason). What they should do is enter a rightful condition and settle the disputes by reason; with reference to an independent, third agency 'above them'. However, there is no state of states (i.e. a world government) that can act as the law maker and settle the disputes between states.

Kant was writing during the enlightenment – a time of great optimism. He believed that human rationality would lead eventually to a state of perpetual peace with some sort of league of states established (he thought that a single world government would be too unwieldy). Just as humans have a duty to work towards to the kingdom of ends (one of the categorical imperatives), so states have a duty to work towards perpetual peace and the league of states.

Many commentators interpret the United Nations as being this body, although the UN does have its critics too. However, when Kant was writing there was no state of states, so all states technically were in a state of nature and not in a rightful condition; however, they still have a duty to work towards a rightful condition. Kant saw acts of war as moving us further away from this rightful condition. Wars represent the opposite of solving a dispute by reason, which the rightful condition enables. For Kant, the only just war would be acting in self-defence and its purpose would be to return to peace. Much in the way that an individual has a duty to protect his or her life (and so can kill to prevent being killed), so a state has a duty to protect itself.

Kant was very clear about the means of waging war. As the only just purpose of war is to end the war and return to peace, a war has to be waged in a way, that enables the possibility of peace afterwards. In this way, the maxim 'I will fight a just war, in a way that *cannot* lead to peace' would either be inconceivable or could not be rationally willed. Fighting wars in such a way as to lead to deep-seated hate and resentment would be contradictory, as it would make peace much harder, which is the only purpose of a just war. Kant thought we should always wage war *'in accordance with principles that always leave open the possibility of leaving the state of nature among states … and entering a rightful condition'.*[21]

This entails that:

> *No state shall, during war, permit such acts of hostility which would make mutual confidence in the subsequent peace impossible: such are the employment of assassins, poisoners, breach of capitulation, and incitement to treason in the opposing state.*[22]
>
> Kant

▶ ACTIVITY

Read W1 and W2 (pages 8–9). What would Kant say?

In the case of W1, Kant would be completely clear. Torture should not be used. Kant's approach does not depend on the consequences of the action, but whether it can be rationally willed, and you cannot rationally will to fight a just war in such a way as to make peace afterwards harder.

In W2 the situation is fairly complex. Kant was clear that *'No state shall interfere by force in the constitution and government of another state'.*[23] Such interference would undermine the autonomy of a state, which, as it would be with an individual, is wrong. However, whether there is a clear 'state' in a civil war is not always obvious. Sometimes states can divide into two via 'internal rebellion', in which case one of the new states could then be lent assistance to defend itself against the other state.

The position of Kant would not be clear in this case. It would depend on whether there is a legitimate case to say there are two states, which is not obvious. This mirrors recent events (such as the conflict in Syria) where other states are unwilling to get involved directly in a civil war, although sometimes countries do offer assistance.

One seeming advantage of the Kantian approach to war is that it does not rely on consequences in the way that utilitarian approaches do. The utilitarian approach can involve crystal-ball gazing, which is very difficult with wars. Using a Kantian approach, some actions are ruled out on grounds of rational inconsistency, which makes it easier to apply.

Simulated killing

▶ **ACTIVITY**

Read SK1 and SK2 (pages 9–10). What would Kant say?

Kant's morality is based around following rules that we can rationally will everyone to follow, and acting in ways that respect other people's autonomy (for Kant these are the same thing). This usually requires working out if we have a duty to behave in a certain way, which in turn can be equated to whether you or other people have rights. (Having a right, say to free speech, creates a duty in others, in this case to not censor me. Duties are the 'flip side' of rights.) For Kant the moral value (right or wrong) of watching/playing simulated killing is not dependent on the consequences of such activities, but on whether it is possible to consistently will that you should watch them, and whether watching them is consistent with treating others as rational autonomous beings.

Not surprisingly Kant, wrote *literally* nothing about the morality of video games or violent films. So it is up to other commentators to work out what an appropriate Kantian position might be.

When I watch a film, or play a game, on the face of it, I do not seem to be reneging on anyone's rights. The actors were free agents who chose to be in the film/stage. The pixels on the video screen are not real people. Other people may claim to have rights to not be offended by such sights, but as long as such films are not shown in outdoor places, where they cannot be avoided, then those who may be offended are not having their freedom curtailed.

There is a claim that in SK1 the game has been illegally altered and this does affect its moral status. In altering the game, the programmers were not respecting copyright. The original creators of the game did not have the opportunity to agree to this, so their autonomy was undermined and this is wrong. (In terms of the universal law formulation you cannot universalise the maxim to save money by using pirated materials, as there would be no materials to pirate.)

This aside, the watching of simulated killing does not seem to infringe upon the rights of others. However, it may be that I have a duty to myself to not be entertained by simulated killing. An argument along these lines can be constructed from the work of Kant. Kant argues that morally we can treat non-human animals as a mere means to our ends, as animals lack the rationality required to have ends in themselves. However, he does not think this gives us a licence to be cruel to animals.

> *If a man shoots his dog because the animal is no longer capable of service, he does not fail in his duty to the dog, for the dog cannot judge, but his act is inhuman and damages in himself that humanity which it is his duty to show towards mankind. If he is not to stifle his human feelings, he must practise kindness towards animals, for he who is cruel to animals becomes hard also in his dealings with men.*[24]
>
> Kant

Kant believes we have a duty to show our humanity towards mankind. This stems from having a duty to perfect our own moral nature. Our moral nature is our ability to treat others as ends in themselves – to see them as rational, autonomous beings. I cannot will that my ability to do this should diminish, as, when universalised, I would be willing that other people's ability to see me as an autonomous being should diminish. This is inconceivable as the act of willing *is* the act of being autonomous, so we cannot will not to will.

So we have a perfect duty to treat others as ends, and this means we have a perfect duty to encourage our own ability to treat others as ends. For Kant, this involves an imperfect duty to sympathise with the suffering of other creatures and to '*cultivate the compassionate natural (aesthetic) feelings in us*'.[25]

Kant's argument relies on there being an empirical connection which shows that being cruel to animals makes a person less likely to treat others with moral respect. Whether this is true or not is a matter of debate. There is research showing a link between the two; in other words, those who are violent towards animals are more likely to be violent towards humans. Being cruel to animals is widely used as a test for potentially dangerous conditions such as psychopathic personality disorder. However, establishing a link does not show that being cruel to animals *causes* people to be cruel to humans. It could (and probably does) show that there is an underlying condition that causes both the cruelty to animals and to humans.

These arguments can be translated fairly easily to the issue of simulated killing. Kant claims that we have a perfect duty towards moral perfection and an imperfect duty to cultivate compassionate feelings in ourselves. It could be suggested that watching people violently die on films, or killing them violently in video games, makes us less compassionate towards others. Such entertainment may encourage us to see other people as means to an end, as cannon fodder, without ends in themselves. If this were so, then we have a duty not to watch these films or play these games.

Again, this would seem to be an empirical matter and rely on there being a causal connection between simulated death as entertainment and being less compassionate to humans. The evidence does not have to directly suggest that such activities make us more violent, just that it makes us less compassionate (though violence would be an indicator of this).

There is some evidence pointing to this, however there is also evidence pointing against it. There is also the problem that showing a link doesn't always show a causal link. Although society has become less violent in the last 20 years, studies have shown that general empathy levels have decreased during this time. The cause of this is not clear and commentators are keener to suggest that wider societal changes such as capitalism and parenting have had a much greater impact than films/video games.

So Kant's position for both SK1 and SK2 is not fully clear. Engaging in such activities is not treating others as a means to an end (apart from the piracy element). However, it can be argued that it diminishes our ability to treat people as autonomous ends in themselves. If it is shown that this *is* the case then we have an imperfect duty not to do such things, and acting on the maxim of watching video games for pleasure can be blameworthy (but not always). If there is no causal connection between such activities and the diminishing of our compassion, then entertaining ourselves in this way is morally permissible, but not morally good, which utilitarians may claim.

The treatment of animals

▶ **ACTIVITY**

Read A1 and A2 (page 10). What would Kant say?

For Kant, humans are different from other animals. Kant thought that we can escape our animal instincts through reason (see pages 70–1). Humans can use reason to work out what they ought to do – in both senses of ought: what is prudent, given our desires, and also what reason alone demands that we *ought* to do (the moral sort of ought). As we know, reason alone demands that we only act in ways that we can rationally will that others do too. This ability to work out our own moral laws and act on them, gives us freedom and autonomy. Animals lack this ability.

For Kant, this makes a striking difference. The only source of good is a good will. Freedom/autonomy is the supreme moral principle. For Kant, animals lack this autonomy. They are driven by instinct and do not have the ability to reason: to weigh up options and ask themselves what they *should* do. Animals act on the world but they do not 'will'. Because they do not have the ability to conceptualise what they should do, animals do not pursue ends. And because of this, we do not have to treat them as beings with ends themselves – as beings with moral status.

> *The fact that the human being can have the representation 'I' raises him infinitely above all the other beings on earth. By this he is a person ... that is, a being altogether different in rank and dignity from things, such as irrational animals, with which one may deal and dispose at one's discretion.*[26]
>
> Kant

Whereas Bentham, in discussing animals, suggested that '*The question is not, Can they reason? nor Can they talk? but, Can they suffer?*',[27] Kant is firmly suggesting that '*Can they reason?*' is, indeed, the key question.

Criticism

One key difficulty with this position is that it would seem to require us to treat humans that cannot reason, that lack the ability to work out what they *should* do, as having no moral worth. For Kant, we also have no reason to treat them as autonomous beings with ends in themselves.

As we saw above (page 105), Kant believed we have an imperfect duty not to be cruel to animals, because we have a duty towards moral self-perfection. In this way, animals do sort of have rights – a right not to be cruelly treated. However, for Kant, this would be an indirect right, as the right only occurs as a consequence of a duty towards ourselves (humans). His argument, even for this right, relies on there being a causal connection between being cruel to animals and treating humans less morally. As outlined above, there is certainly evidence of a link, but proving a causal connection is harder.

So, for Kant, we should avoid being deliberately cruel to animals. This may rule out some particularly cruel farming methods – but only for the farmer, as it is *his* duty to work towards moral self-perfection that is potentially threatened. It would not be morally wrong for the consumer to eat the meat.

Regarding A2, animal experiments that seem unnecessarily cruel may undermine the morality of the experimenters and so be wrong. For Kant, A2 may be morally wrong – but *only* because it may undermine the experimenters' ability to treat other humans with appropriate respect.

The suffering of the animals is not relevant and not part of the moral calculation. However, some see this as a weakness of Kant's system.

▶ **ACTIVITY**

Read the account of the dog experiment on a page 61.

Do you think the suffering of the dogs is morally relevant in itself?

Or do you agree with Kant that the suffering of the dogs is only morally relevant as it may undermine the experimenters' ability to treat other humans with sufficient respect?

Deception and the telling of lies

▶ **ACTIVITY**

Read DTL1 and DTL2 (page 11). What would Kant say?

As with promises (page 79), it would seem that you cannot universalise a maxim of telling lies. The whole concept of lying relies on the concept of truth-telling. If everyone lied, then lies would not deceive. The wrongness of lying can also be clearly seen using the humanity formulation. Recall the example of the American tourists (page 63). In lying to the tourists you are undermining their ability to pursue their own ends. Although you are not treating them as a means to your end (after all, it is their happiness you were pursuing), you are not treating them as rational people with their own ends, as their end may have been to get to St Paul's as quickly as possible. In telling the truth, we allow people to pursue their own ends, make up their own minds. In lying, we prevent this.

In the case of DTL1, there are several Kantian problems with the idea of the affair. In lying to her husband, Shelly is undermining his autonomy. Maybe he would consent to an affair, maybe he wouldn't, but if Shelly lies, he has no choice. Furthermore, in getting married, Shelly would have made a promise (either explicitly or implicitly) to be faithful – this would break the promise. You also cannot universalise the idea of infidelity, as the institution of marriage would be meaningless.

Kant also found the idea of sex outside of marriage problematic. Although Kant wasn't against the idea of sex per se, he believed that if it was not within a marriage (where you legally 'own' each other's bodies) then you would be treating the other (consenting) person's body as a means to your end.

The case of DTL2 is quite complicated and controversial. Most people's moral intuitions about DTL2 are that you should lie to the axeman. However, it seems as if Kant would be committed to telling the truth. Much has been written about this, in part because Kant himself wrote about a very similar example to this when defending his theory from criticism. Kant claimed that you have a duty to tell the truth in this scenario, which most people find odd. Consequently, many philosophers have revisited this dilemma to try to resolve the difference between our intuitions and what Kant said.

It is important to note that there is no moral requirement for you to speak at all in this scenario. You could simply stay quiet and so avoid lying. This would be an ideal solution for Kant. However, when Kant explored this scenario, he stipulated that you are forced to answer by the axeman (though it is not revealed exactly how). So the scenario is really: *given* that you have to answer, should you lie or tell the truth?

Universal law formulation

Many philosophers suggest that the universal law formulation of the categorical imperative does not require you to tell the truth at all times. It seems perfectly possible to rationally will that everyone should follow maxims such as '*I will always tell the truth, except if in telling the truth I put someone's life at risk*', or '*I will always lie to a would-be murderer*'. These do not seem to lead to any contradictions, as I would be happy to be lied to in these circumstances. Furthermore, we have an imperfect duty to help others, so not only is lying morally permissible, it may also be the right thing to do. So, according to this interpretation, Kant is wrong in applying his own theory, and lying in some circumstances is morally permissible.

Humanity formulation

The situation seems less flexible when we look at the humanity formulation. When we lie to someone, we are overriding that person's ability to make rational choices. We are using them as a means to our end (in this case, saving Bob's life). This is always wrong and so we should tell the truth. This leads to a few potential criticisms. Firstly, that the two formulations cannot mean the same thing (which Kant claimed they did) as they seen to produce different answers to this question. Secondly, if true, this requirement to always tell the truth points to a flaw in Kant's system, as the *consequences* of telling the truth seem to be disastrous in this case. As outlined earlier (pages 88–9), by only focusing on *motive* and making sure our own 'sphere of action' is rationally faultless, we leave ourselves open to the faults in others' reasoning. On the plus side, having a moral system where some acts are *always* wrong means that our personal integrity is never compromised by doing the right thing. Kant's system enables lines to be drawn in the sand that you are required not to cross, whereas utilitarianism might require you to do *anything* to justify the ends (see page 47). The negative side of this is that the system seems inflexible and cannot deal with encountering evil in the real world, as in the case of DTL2.

Telling the truth seems so wrong in this case that some philosophers have tried to find more ways in which Kant's system might allow lying in this case. One approach is to suggest that the moral status of the axeman may be altered because of his intention to kill. The axeman has clearly chosen to leave the rightful condition and enter a state of nature, as, whatever issues he has with Bob, he clearly wants to settle them by force rather than by reason. In a state of nature, we do not have full autonomy as other people, through force, may override our choices. The axeman, in choosing to enter the state of nature, has then given up his entitlement to be treated as a person with full autonomy and so we can lie to him. For Kant, we have a duty to leave the state of nature and enter the rightful condition, so doing this would break that duty and so be wrong. However, something similar happens with war. When a country is attacked, it may defend itself, and in doing so the country enters a state of nature, but does so with the intention of leaving it as soon as it can (in other words, we can fight, but only do so with the aim of getting peace). In war, the country is aiming towards an ideal position but has to resort to violence to get there. In the same way, it is suggested we may lie to the axe murderer, with the intention of getting back to the rightful condition as soon as possible, perhaps by calling the police and getting the state involved at the earliest possible moment (which most people would do in the circumstances).

This seems like a reasonable Kantian way of solving the dilemma and showing that even the humanity formulation can have exceptions. If this solution seems fair enough, then why was Kant so insistent that telling the truth was the right thing to do in the axeman scenario?

Moral and legal lies

Learn More

Several philosophers have suggested that Kant's insistence that telling the truth was right should be interpreted in light of his views about legal rights, not just moral rights. When Kant wrote about this scenario, it was in the context of a discussion about the law.

Kant thought that lying is always morally wrong, but it is not always legally wrong (for example, you might lie to yourself and there is no law against that). Lying to others, though, always runs the risk of leaving the liar (partly) legally responsible for the subsequent events, but telling the truth never does; and it was this point Kant was making when he said that telling the truth is always the right thing to do. It is always legally right. To understand this point, consider some of the following lies.

 Experimenting with ideas

Rank each lie on a scale of 1–10 based on how morally bad you think it is (10 is very bad).

A A friend asks you what the weather will be like today. You know the forecast says it will rain, but you lie and say it will be sunny as a joke.

B You lie about your age on a car insurance form – to get cheaper insurance.

C Two American tourists ask for the shortest way to St Paul's. You lie and tell them the prettiest route instead.

D You borrowed £30 from a friend. The friend can't remember if you paid it back. You didn't. You lie and say you did.

E A school window is broken. You lie to a policeman about where Reuben was the night it was broken.

F The Prime Minister lies, saying he never knew about a critical report before it was published.

Lie A does not seem to be illegal. However, imagine that your friend takes you at your word and goes out in a dinghy at sea. He is caught unprepared in a rain storm, contracts hypothermia and dies. If this were to happen then, it can be argued, you are legally responsible (in part) for your friend's death. In lie C, imagine that the tourists followed your route and in doing so are killed in a terrorist bomb attack. They would not have died if they had taken the quickest route. Would you feel guilty? Probably yes. Would you feel guilty if you had told the truth and they had died on that route too? Probably not. By telling the lie, it is no longer *their* end that they were pursuing; your will altered their end and, in doing so, in part, it becomes your end that they were pursuing. Hence your feeling of guilt. In case B and D your lie denies people what is rightfully and legally theirs (money) and so is illegal from the outset. Case E is also illegal. The state is the means of settling disputes rationally; by lying you are willing that we return to a state of nature – this is legally wrong and morally wrong. Case F is worse still for Kant. Law makers cannot act in this way, as this would be to will us into a state of nature – they have a perfect duty to tell the truth. This is illegal and immoral.

In light of this analysis, some interpret Kant's insistence on telling the truth as making a specific point about law. If you tell the truth, you will never break the law and will never be held legally responsible for any subsequent event. If you lie to others then you are either breaking the law directly, or could be held legally responsible if events turn out badly. For example, you might lie to the axe murderer and say that Bob had gone to the pub. Unknown to you, Bob had heard the murderer at the door and ran immediately to the pub for safety. The axeman goes to the pub and kills him. Kant's point is that telling the truth is always legally right.

Kant did believe that lying is morally wrong, but it is suggested that his strong insistence in the murderer case is making a legal, rather than a moral point. So, what would Kant say about DTL2? Well, you can say nothing. This avoids many issues. But if you were forced to answer, then we know that Kant would say that from a legal perspective, telling the truth will not lead to any legal responsibility for any subsequent events. Kant also seems to say that lying is always morally wrong (not just legally so); however, several 'Kantian' approaches can be constructed to show that it is not necessarily morally wrong to lie on this occasion.

1.1.3 Aristotle's virtue ethics

How is virtue ethics different from other ethical theories?

I'm talkin' about friendship. I'm talkin' about character.

I'm talkin' about – hell, Leo, I ain't embarrassed to use the word – I'm talkin' about ethics.[1]

Miller's Crossing

Character, that's what virtue ethics is all about: character (see page 3). Virtue ethics is the name given to those moral theories that focus on the individual person, rather than an individual course of action. This difference in focus is an important one, and may appear to be at odds with our ordinary understanding of ethics. So, it might help if we consider what utilitarian and Kantian theories share, and then we can see how theories of virtue ethics differ from these.

It may seem as if the two types of normative theories we have already looked at, **deontological** (Kantian ethics) and consequentialist (utilitarian ethics), have very little in common with one another.

Take the example of the potential axe murder who is looking for your friend (page 11). The utilitarian, weighing up the consequences, would recommend that you lie; the Kantian, considering your duties, would recommend that you tell the truth. But when you have a closer look at the differences between these two theories, you notice that they are specifically disagreeing over how to act in this situation. So, what they agree on is that it is the *action* (lying or not lying) that carries the moral weight. Moreover, they also agree that we can specify the method by which we assess whether or not an action is a good or right one. For consequentialists like the utilitarians, the assessment is based on whether this action brings about the best consequences; for deontologists like Kant, the assessment is based on whether performing this action breaks, or adheres to, certain rules.

Despite the flaws in both utilitarian and Kantian ethics, both theories strike a chord with our moral intuition: the intuition that ethics is about working out whether the things we do are good or bad, right or wrong. But in the history of Western moral philosophy, such intuitions are fairly recent, and from the ancient Greeks until the Enlightenment, ethics was centred around a very different intuition: the intuition that ethics is about the kind of character you have, the kind of person you are.

Theories of virtue ethics approach morality by judging the person (the agent) who committed the act, rather than the action itself. Julia Annas describes virtue ethics as 'agent-centred' in contrast to deontological and consequentialist theories, which are 'act-centred'.[2] So, within act-centred ethics, our judgements are made first and foremost of specific acts: we judge them to be right or good. Agent-centred, or virtue, theories make judgements of character: of whether someone is a good or virtuous person. The kinds of questions that a virtue ethicist wishes to address are 'What makes a good person?', 'What sort of life should I be leading?' and 'How should I develop my character?'

▶ **ACTIVITY: What is a virtue anyway?**

1 Write down a list of characteristics (or personality traits) that people might say were 'virtues'.
2 Next to that list, write down another list of characteristics that people might call 'vices'.
3 Is there anything that the characteristics you have called 'virtues' have in common?
4 Is there any obvious way in which they differ from the 'vices'?

We look further into the Greek concept of virtue (*arete*) on page 126 but one simple way of thinking about what virtue is, is to think of it as a **disposition** or character trait possessed by good people, i.e. by people we admire, value or praise. In contrast, a vice is a disposition or characteristic possessed by bad or 'vicious' people, i.e. by people we condemn. What we mean when we are talking about a characteristic or a disposition or a trait is a *tendency to behave in a particular way*, so, for example, we say someone is kind (has a kind disposition) when they tend to be thoughtful and generous to others. The key idea here is that a disposition is not a one-off act (which utilitarians and Kantians seemed happy to pass judgement on) but a description of how someone has acted in the past, and how they will probably act in the future. So, virtue ethicists take a more holistic approach when making moral judgements; they consider not just the present action, but the past and the future actions of the agent. As we shall see, this means that virtue ethicists find it difficult to offer simple rules or guidelines about how we should live.

Virtue ethics has had its supporters throughout the centuries (notably Plato, Aristotle, Aquinas and Hume), but it is only in the last 50 years that it has been revived as a credible alternative to utilitarian and Kantian ethics. We shall now look at the moral philosophy of one of the founding fathers of virtue ethics, namely Aristotle.

Background to Aristotle's *Ethics*

Aristotle (384–322 BC) was one of the greatest thinkers that the world has known; he was a genuine polymath – an expert in many different fields of knowledge. He held a teleological view of the universe, the belief that everything in the universe has a purpose or function, and that the natural state of things is to move towards that final goal (*telos* in ancient Greek). This view governed his philosophical and scientific analysis of the world. Aristotle's writings are extensive, consisting of around 30 different treatises, but these represent only a fraction of what he originally produced. The surviving works appear to be lecture notes for his students rather than finished works for general consumption and consequently, compared to Plato's dialogues, they are rather prosaic. This is unfortunate as Aristotle was known in the ancient world for the beauty of his prose and the missing works, including many dialogues, represent one of the great losses to the philosophical canon. Aristotle wrote on a huge variety of subjects, from zoology and biology to logic and metaphysics, with detours via history, astronomy and psychology. In contrast to Plato's writings, Aristotle's are ordered and schematic, so the Roman editors who packaged his treatises together into books found it possible to divide his ideas up into chapters and sections.

Aristotle's exploration of virtue can be found in one of his most important works, the *Nicomachean Ethics*, or the *Ethics* as it is also known. It is worth noting some possible sources of misunderstanding that may arise when reading the *Ethics*. First, Aristotle's scientific leanings may have informed his **empirical** approach in the *Ethics*, as he presents this book as an investigation which must take into account our observations of people's behaviour and nature. Secondly, we also need to acknowledge that Aristotle had views on women and slaves that we no longer recognise as morally acceptable; nor are they generally considered relevant to his overall ethical theory; and so where Aristotle refers to 'men' we have applied his ideas to all humans (not just men). Thirdly, the Greek words used by Aristotle have a traditional translation, but throughout our analysis we will suggest alternative translations if we feel they are helpful. Finally, the *Ethics*, as we noted above, is best thought of as a series of Aristotle's lecture notes, to be used at his philosophy school (the Lyceum) rather than as a polished piece of literature. It is divided into ten books which explore several interconnected themes. However, it does contain a coherent ethical theory which we shall now investigate, and Figure 1.13 (see page 114) should help us navigate through Aristotle's arguments in the *Ethics* (at least those highlighted by the AQA specification). As you can see from the diagram, Aristotle's thoughts about the significance of virtue (*arete*) emerge from a much larger project, namely an investigation into the highest good for humans. So Aristotle's theory of virtue needs to be understood in this wider context: how virtue can help us in our pursuit of a life that is the best kind of life.

Figure 1.13 Flow chart summarising some of Aristotle's arguments in the *Ethics*

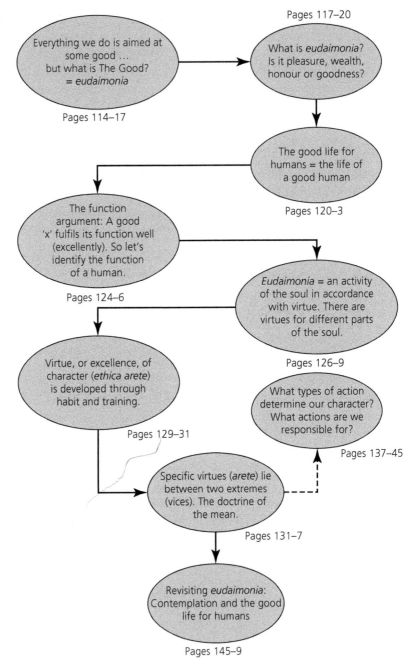

Pages 117–20

Everything we do is aimed at some good … but what is The Good? = *eudaimonia*

What is *eudaimonia*? Is it pleasure, wealth, honour or goodness?

Pages 114–17

The good life for humans = the life of a good human

Pages 120–3

The function argument: A good 'x' fulfils its function well (excellently). So let's identify the function of a human.

Eudaimonia = an activity of the soul in accordance with virtue. There are virtues for different parts of the soul.

Pages 124–6

Pages 126–9

Virtue, or excellence, of character (*ethica arete*) is developed through habit and training.

What types of action determine our character? What actions are we responsible for?

Pages 129–31

Pages 137–45

Specific virtues (*arete*) lie between two extremes (vices). The doctrine of the mean.

Pages 131–7

Revisiting *eudaimonia*: Contemplation and the good life for humans

Pages 145–9

The Good: Ends and means

Aristotle opens the *Ethics* with a bold generalisation that sets out his philosophical stall:

> *Every art, every procedure, every action and undertaking aims at some good; and for this reason the good has rightly been declared to be that at which all things aim.*
>
> **Aristotle (1094a1)[3]**

But what does Aristotle mean by 'good' here? As with other concepts that we shall encounter in his *Ethics* (such as 'virtue' and 'happiness'), we must be careful to clarify Aristotle's terms. 'Good' in this sentence does not refer to a utilitarian good (actions that maximise pleasure and minimise pain), or to a Platonic 'good' (which is an ideal existing only in the World of Forms[4]), or to material goods (of the kind sold by shops). Nor does it refer to the functional concept of good that we will look at later on (the 'good can-opener'), although for Aristotle this is important too.

Instead, 'good' in the first part of Aristotle's opening sentence means something like 'our goal'. We can make sense of the word 'good' here because we believe that by achieving our goal we will add value to our lives, make our lives better in some crucial respect. We will return to this idea shortly, but before we do, we should note that 'the good', as it appears in the second part of the sentence refers to something slightly different, closer to the idea of the 'ultimate good' – the thing that all humans are striving to reach. 'The Good' (which philosophers sometimes spell with a capital 'G') is also known by the Latin phrase the **summum bonum**, the 'highest good', which is valued above all other goods. We saw above (page 14) that the utilitarians thought this 'good' was pleasure. But before we look at Aristotle's own account of the good, it is worth exploring our own intuitions as to what a good life (the best life) would consist of for us.

 Experimenting with ideas: The Ideal Life Show

This is your opportunity to imagine your ideal life. Let your imagination run riot as you sketch the features that would make up your ideal life.

1 Under each of the categories in the table below write down several things that would be an essential part of your Ideal Life. What material objects (including money) would you have? What would you be like physically (health and appearance)? What mental, emotional or psychological characteristics would you have? What relationships would you like to have? What would you like to do or achieve in your Ideal Life? And finally what would the world around you be like?

I Material objects	2. Physical attributes	3. Mental attributes
✓ –	✓ –	✓ –
✓ –	✓ –	✓ –
✓ –	✓ –	✓ –
✓ –	✓-	✓ –
4. Relationships	**5. Achievements**	**6. Environment**
✓ –	✓ –	✓ –
✓ –	✓ –	✓ –
✓ –	✓ –	✓ –
✓ –	✓ –	✓ –

2 Now compare your Ideal Life with that of your friends or class mates. What features did they all have in common?
3 Do you think, as Aristotle and other philosophers suggest, that there is a unifying 'Good' or a single goal that we are all striving for in our lives? What kind of thing might this be?

Let us now return to Aristotle's opening line in the *Ethics*: that everything we do is aimed at some good. His claim here is that everything we do has a purpose or an end, and that *this* end is itself also aimed at some further purpose or goal. Aristotle backs up his claim with various examples from everyday Athenian life. For example, a saddler makes bridles with the aim of controlling a horse; the aim of controlling horses is to improve military horsemanship; the aim of improving horsemanship is to develop the art of warfare (military science). Aristotle might extend this to say that improving our military science leads to a safer Athens (or Macedonia or Sparta). But is this claim true: is *everything* you do aimed at some meaningful goal; moreover, is that goal then aimed at some other further or higher goal?

▶ **ACTIVITY**

Revisit the activity in the utilitarian section (page 13). Can you think of any examples of actions that don't have an 'end'?

Aristotle is drawing our attention to an important philosophical distinction between means and ends. Some things that we do, we do for their own sake (you may have reached this point at stage 3 in the Ideal Life Show), other things we do to bring about some end beyond the activity. Philosophers call those activities that are done for their own sake 'ends in themselves'. Those actions done for the sake of other things are simply the *means* to other ends, although, as was noted above, they are still aimed at some end (good). We can find out whether an activity is done (a) for its own sake or (b) for the sake of something else by asking 'Why did you do that?'. And if there is no further answer than 'I did it for its own sake', then we have found an end in itself. Let's look at an example of this.

Why read this philosophy book?	→	In order to do well at A-level.
Why do well at A-level?	→	In order to go to university.
Why go to university?	→	In order to get a job.
Why get a job?	→	In order to earn some money.
Why earn some money?	→	In order to holiday in the Caribbean.
Why holiday in the Caribbean?	→	In order to feel the warm sun on my skin and the breeze on my face as I look out over a crystal blue sea.

For many of us it wouldn't make sense to ask 'Why do you want to feel these sensations?' I just do. Therefore we could conclude that this must be a final end. So, in this example, the final end (the good) of reading this philosophy book is to have the pleasures of being on a tropical beach, and that is an end in itself. However, although we may think that pleasurable goals like these may be *a* good, we shall see that Aristotle does not agree with the utilitarians that they could be the Good.

► **ACTIVITY**

1   Go back to the Ideal Life Show opposite and identify each of your items as a means or an end.
2   For each item that is a 'means', use the method (page 115) to work out what it is a means to.
3   Is there a single good which all your items, or those of your classmates, are directed towards?

So Aristotle has plausibly shown that every activity aims at a good, an end. But at the end of this opening section (1094a19) he goes further by reiterating that there is one end that we all aim at. We saw on page 115 that he refers to this final end as the 'the Good', the *summum bonum*.

Some philosophers have argued that Aristotle is not offering a proof that everything is aimed at some end,[5] and that alternative translations of this passage reveal that he is merely offering a definition: namely that 'goodness' is what anything aims at. The 'bridle-making' passage suggests that Aristotle believes there is a hierarchy of goals, with each end in itself contributing to a goal that is more valuable (as the goal of keeping a country safe has more value than bridle-making). So Aristotle, in keeping with his teleological view of the universe, believes that by ranking goals we eventually arrive at a goal that is the highest: the supreme Good.

But how are we to know when we have found an answer, when we have discovered something that really is the supreme Good, the final end that we are looking for? Aristotle outlines the following criteria for that supreme Good (1097a15–1097b21):

- It must be an **end**: '*we always choose it for itself, and never for any other reason.*' (1097b2)
- It must be the **final end**: '*that for the sake of which everything else is done.*' (1097a17)
- It must be **self-sufficient**, and it needs nothing more to complete it: '*which by itself makes life desirable.*' (1097b17)
- It must be a life that we all want: '*the most **desirable** of all things.*' (1097b18)
- Finally it must be something that is related to us as **human beings**, which we shall see when we come to the function argument below.

The rest of the *Ethics* constitutes an examination of this supreme Good, and Aristotle is really searching for an answer to the question: What is the good life? Aristotle gives both a short answer and a much longer answer to this question. First let us turn to the short answer.

Eudaimonia #1 – The short answer

What is the highest of all practical goods? Well ... there is pretty general agreement. 'It is happiness' say both ordinary and cultured people.

Aristotle (1095a17)

We are in agreement, so Aristotle says, that the good life, the life we are all striving for, is **eudaimonia** – normally translated as 'happiness'. Even after two thousand years this seems to ring true; but once again we need to be careful about how we understand this translation, as our understanding of 'happiness' is not the same as the Greek concept of *eudaimonia*. The suffix *eu* (as in 'euthanasia', a good death) means 'good', and *daimon* refers to a spirit, so *eudaimonia* suggests a good spirit who could guide us through life.[6] This etymology, although not made explicit by Aristotle, points towards the ancient Greek conception of *eudaimonia* being different from our modern concept of happiness. Aristotle explains that *eudaimonia* is identified with living well and doing well in life (1095a18), in the way that we would fare well if a benevolent spirit really did guide each of us through it. Even though 'happiness' remains the conventional translation when writing about Aristotelian *eudaimonia,* a better translation might be 'flourishing', and we return to this when we examine the function argument, below.

We are now armed with the short answer to the question 'What is the Good life', namely 'it is *eudaimonia*', the sort of life that we all desire; a life that needs nothing added to it to make it more complete, one that is the final end of all we do. But that tells us very little, as what we really want to know is how in practical terms we reach *eudaimonia*, and what the Good life actually consists of? This will give us the longer, fuller answer which will in turn help us to understand how Aristotle thinks we should live our lives.

It is worth noting that in the *Ethics* Aristotle's empirical and descriptive approach (what do people think the Good life is?) sometimes takes a more prescriptive approach (what *should* people do to reach the Good life?), particularly in Book Ten. But, in these early chapters, Aristotle describes some populist answers to this question, the kinds of answers that he might have heard had he stopped people in the Athenian market place and asked them 'So, what do you think is the Good life?' Although Aristotle was writing over two thousand years ago, the answers he considers aren't so different from answers we might hear today and which you may have encountered in the activity above, namely:

- Pleasure
- Wealth
- Honour
- Goodness
- Contemplation.

These are all plausible candidates for the Good life, and we shall now look at Aristotle's assessment of each of these ways of life.

Learn More ## Possible candidates for the Good

Pleasure

The masses 'ask for nothing better than a life of enjoyment' (1095b15). The claim that *pleasure* is what we are all striving for in life is something that the utilitarians took for granted, and built their ethical theory upon (you may have come across it as 'psychological hedonism', see page 14). And perhaps when you think of 'happiness' you are thinking of the many pleasures that life can be filled with and that make life worth living. But early on in the *Ethics*, Aristotle dismisses the common claim that the Good, or happiness (in the sense of *eudaimonia*), is a life of pleasure. A life of pleasure and enjoyment is a 'bovine existence', a life fit only for cattle, writes Aristotle (1095b16). However, we shall see below (page 145) that pleasure does have a crucial supporting role to play in a eudaimon life.

Wealth

Aristotle gives short shrift to the 'life of the business man', in other words someone who seeks to acquire wealth. The acquisition of money is simply a means to an end, to buy fancy meals, expensive goods, super yachts, once-in-a-lifetime experiences. Money is not an end in itself. *Eudaimonia*, we have seen, is by definition the final end in itself and so wealth cannot be 'the good we are seeking' (1096a4).

Honour

More refined people, according to Aristotle, claim that it is respect or *honour* that we are all striving for (eminence in public life was highly valued in Athens). But this is also rejected by Aristotle, because honour, or respect, is something that is bestowed on us by other people, and so is largely dependent on other people; *eudaimonia* isn't like that at all – it isn't given to us, but is something we gain ourselves and is not so easily lost as honour. Moreover, Aristotle points out that people seek honour in order to reach some higher good and so honour in itself can't be the final end: people seek to be honoured for their goodness (1095b27).

Goodness

Is, then, a life of *goodness* or virtue the kind of life we should all be striving for? We may be getting closer to the answer here, but for Aristotle, goodness alone cannot be *eudaimonia*. This is partly because we can imagine a situation in which someone who is good or virtuous is experiencing atrocious suffering or misery. Later on in the *Ethics*, Aristotle pushes home this point: 'those who maintain that, provided he is good, a man is happy on the rack ... are talking nonsense' (1153b11). This may seem an obscure point for Aristotle to make, but he may be responding to a central claim made by his teacher, Plato, in the *Gorgias*: that it is better for someone to be tortured on a rack than to do wrong; and that a person who remains good, even though they are made to suffer, is happier than a person who avoids that suffering, but only by becoming a criminal. This is a rather extreme example, but it emphasises Aristotle's point very clearly. *Eudaimonia* is the kind of life we are all striving for, and goodness or virtue cannot by itself guarantee *eudaimonia* (although it may play a part): for our lives to go well, we need to have external goods (like freedom from torture, safety, a home, warmth) as well as goods internal to our selves or our souls, which we look at below.

Contemplation

The final candidate for *eudaimonia* that Aristotle considers is a life of reflection or *contemplation*, but he promises to examine that later, which he does in Book Ten of the *Ethics*, and we return to it below (page 148).

Concluding this part of the investigation, we now know Aristotle's short answer to the question 'What is the supreme Good?' *Eudaimonia* is the final end of all our actions and it cannot be bettered. We also know that neither pleasure, nor wealth, nor honour, nor goodness alone, will enable us to reach *eudaimonia*. But we still don't know what *eudaimonia* is, and Aristotle now sketches a methodology which should help us determine 'the long answer'. As you might guess, the long answer leads to a discussion of virtue, and the passage that bridges Aristotle's discussion of *eudaimonia* with his analysis of virtue is known as 'the function argument'.

The function argument

> *To say happiness is the supreme good seems a platitude, and some more distinctive account of it is still required. This might perhaps be achieved by grasping what is the function of man.[7]*
>
> Aristotle (1097b22)

Aristotle introduces the notion of 'function' (*ergon* in ancient Greek) quite out of the blue. We would probably agree with the first part of his statement that we do need a more distinctive account of *eudaimonia* and we would like a longer answer to the question of what the supreme Good is; but we may well ask what has function got to do with it? Aristotle's assumption is that if we want to know how to be eudaimon we must analyse how we can function well as humans: how we can be Good humans. But what does the Good life have to do with being a Good (well-functioning) human? The connection between something being Good and its fulfilling its function is brought out in the activity below.

▶ **ACTIVITY**

Consider each of the following pairs and answer the questions below.

1	A good can-opener	An ordinary can-opener
2	A good sheepdog	A satisfactory sheepdog
3	A good musician	An okay musician
4	A good video game	A mediocre video game
5	A good person	An average person

a) What are the qualities and attributes that distinguish the good thing from the other, more ordinary, thing?

b) Which is better at fulfilling its function – the good thing or the more ordinary thing?

c) So, overall, what would Aristotle say made something good?

d) Imagine now that you were confronted with an unknown object 'Z' in a box. What method would Aristotle use to determine whether Z was a good object?

Hopefully this activity will have teased out the connection that there is, even in English, between 'goodness' and 'function'. It should also have revealed the connection between 'good', 'well-functioning' and 'having qualities that enable it to be well-functioning'. We refer to something as 'good', in an instrumental or functional sense, first if that thing has a recognised function and secondly if it fulfils its function really well because it has those special qualities that enable it to do so. Thus a good can-opener fulfils its function well because it has the appropriate *arete* (excellence or virtues): it is sharp, safe, easy to handle, etc. (see Figure 1.14).

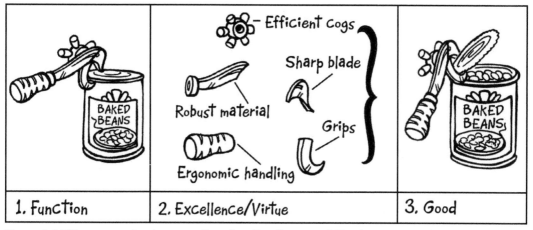

Figure 1.14 The connection between Function, Excellence and Goodness
A good can-opener has all the qualities (virtues) needed to open easily a can of baked beans.

However, now we don't really associate this instrumental sense of goodness with any moral sense of goodness. So why did the ancient Greeks connect good in its broader (moral) sense with the special virtues or qualities (*arete*) that enable something to fulfil its function (*ergon*) well? Why did 'being good at something' mean for the Greeks that you were actually 'good'?

Alasdair MacIntyre, in *A Short History of Ethics*, argued that in Homer's time, centuries before Plato and Aristotle, being a good person was linked to being good at whatever role you played in ancient Greek society.[8]Take the example of a soldier: for MacIntyre you were thought of as a good (in a noble or moral sense) soldier if you had all the qualities that a soldier needs in order to excel in your allotted role (*ergon*) as a soldier. As ancient Greek society developed after Homer, and as social roles became less defined, so the connection between instrumental goodness and moral value became less clear according to MacIntyre. But there remained that lingering association between noble (or moral) goodness, and *ergon* even in fourth century BC when Plato and Aristotle were embarking on their philosophical projects.

It should be clearer now why Aristotle brings in the idea of 'function': to his audience, this might have seemed natural, as goodness in what we understand as its instrumental sense was still connected with goodness in the sense of having moral value. Moreover, you may recall

Learn More

that Aristotle held a strongly teleological view of the universe: that nature and its occupants are directed towards a goal, a purpose, an end. He applied this to his biological studies and his astronomy as well as to his politics and his theories in the *Ethics*. So Aristotle believed that we have a function that goes above and beyond the one prescribed for us through any role we might have in society. This is our function *as human beings*, and Aristotle thought that by understanding our function as human beings we would understand how we could be good, and this was the key to happiness. If we could understand the life of a good human, then we would understand the good life for a human.

Let us turn to Aristotle's argument proper, which has become known as 'the function argument' and which follows from his assertion (at 1097b22) that we might better understand what *eudaimonia* is if we know the function of man. As we mentioned above, the function argument is a critical stepping stone between Aristotle's discussion of *eudaimonia* and his discussion of virtue. Aristotle has three aims in his function argument: first to show that the Good for humans consists in us fulfilling our function (*ergon*) well; secondly to show that humans do actually have a distinct function, and thirdly to say precisely what this function is.

The first aim is crucial to the success of Aristotle's project in the *Ethics*, namely showing us what type of life we should be leading if we want to reach *eudaimonia*. Aristotle draws a clear connection between the instrumental goodness of a human (whether or not we fulfil our function well) with the overall Good for a human (how we can flourish). Aristotle says that if we consider any class of people who have a specific function, for example flute players, sculptors or artists, then the goodness of the flute player, sculptor or artist is determined by their performance of that function. The same,

anthology
1.7

Experimenting with ideas

Let's take a leaf out of Aristotle's botanical work, and focus on plants now rather than humans.

1   In the left-hand box below (or on a blank sheet of paper) draw a eudaimon plant, i.e. a plant that is living a good life (for a plant) and is flourishing.[9]
2   Write down what you think the function of a plant is.
3   Write down a list of those qualities which a well-functioning plant has.
4   Now in the right-hand box below draw the plant you have described, i.e. a Good plant (one that is fulfilling its function well), and on it label the qualities listed in 2.
5   Is there any difference between the two pictures that you have drawn, i.e. between a plant living the Good life and a Good plant?

A: Eudaimon plant   **B: Good plant**

Aristotle says, is true for humans; in other words, our goodness as humans is determined by whether or not we fulfil our function well as humans. The activity (page 122) may help us to clarify the connection Aristotle is making here.

You may have found that your drawings of a good plant and a eudaimon plant weren't that different, they may even have been identical, showing that there is a plausible connection to be made between the life of a good plant and a good life for a plant. Although the example of the plant is our example, we hope you can see how it illustrates Aristotle's direction of thought. If Aristotle can show us that humans have a function, and describe what that function is, then what follows is a route map to *eudaimonia*: we must perform well to become a good human, and in doing so we will be living the good life for a human.[10]

Let us turn now to the second aim: how does Aristotle demonstrate that humans do in fact have a function? Aristotle gives two arguments to support this claim, although they seem more like rhetorical questions than arguments. First, we have seen that people with different occupations (flute players, sculptors, artists) have a function, so is it likely, Aristotle asks, that all these occupations have a function while 'man has none'? Secondly, we can see that the parts of a human body, our eyes, our hands and feet, all have a function, so shouldn't we assume that a human being as a whole has a function?

Criticism

Several criticisms have been levelled at Aristotle's argument in this passage, but we shall look at just two of them. The first criticism is that it appears as if Aristotle is offering a very weak argument from analogy to support his conclusion that humans have a function. You may remember from your investigations into the argument from design[11] that an argument from analogy is at its strongest when the two things being compared are very similar to one another. So a strong analogical argument convinces us that because two things are alike in some respects, they are also alike in a further respect. But if this is indeed an argument from analogy then Aristotle seems to have selected a very small number of random things which have a function (the occupations people have, the parts of the body) and concluded that *like* these things, humans must have a function too. It is not at all clear why a human being should be compared to the occupations we have or to the parts of our body. The analogy would have been strengthened, perhaps, if Aristotle had listed a huge range of things (all living creatures, all human endeavours, all natural processes), shown that they had a purpose, and then asked 'Is it likely that human beings are functionless?' But he didn't do this, and so the purported analogy doesn't ring true.

A second criticism is that Aristotle may be guilty here of the **fallacy** of composition (which you may remember from your study of the cosmological argument): just because the parts of something share a common feature does not mean that the whole has that common feature. Just because the parts of our body have a function does not mean that the whole body (the human) has a function.

The best defence of Aristotle against both these criticisms is to say that he isn't providing an argument here at all, but he is simply articulating his teleological assumptions, namely that everything is directed towards some purpose. The parts that make up a whole (the parts of a body, the different occupations within human life) can only be seen to have a meaningful function if the whole to which they contribute (the body, or human life) itself has a purpose. Aristotelian teleology is no longer widely held, but you will be familiar with religious teleology: people who believe that God created the world, generally believe that the world has a purpose and that humans also have a purpose.

But if we reject Aristotle's teleological view (which most scientists and philosophers now do) then his argument still fails. Not because the argument commits the fallacy of composition or is a weak analogy, but because scientists no longer need teleological explanations to account for the processes of the natural world, and philosophers have long since lost their optimism that there is any external purpose to human existence! Without this purposive view of the world, we think very differently about function: something only has a function if it is specifically assigned a function (a can-opener, a sheep dog, a member of parliament), and unless you believe in God then it's hard to see how humans could have an assigned function.

In Alasdair MacIntyre's modern revival of virtue ethics, he retains certain aspects of Aristotle's teleology.[12] MacIntyre argues that we should understand moral goods in terms of how they are embodied in many different 'social practices', such as teaching, nursing, farming, football, musicianship. Each of these practices has its own sets of virtues, its own goals, its own telos, and these goods are realised through our attempts to reach that standard of excellence (virtue) that is established by those practices. For MacIntyre, then, our human 'function' is identified through our engagement in a plurality of social practices, but it is not identified with any one single activity.

An alternative way of proceeding with Aristotle's project, however, is by understanding ergon not in the sense of 'function' but in the sense of 'work' or 'characteristic activity'. Humans may, in this sense, have a characteristic activity which distinguishes them from other living creatures. So on this view it does make sense for Aristotle to ask: What is our specific ergon? What is the distinguishing characteristic(s) of a human being? What makes us unique as a species?

▶ **ACTIVITY**

1 Write a list of all the things that distinguish us from other species.
2 Now exclude from the list all those features that are shared by other species, to create a shortlist.
3 From your shortlist, which do you think is the single most significant distinguishing characteristic?

Aristotle's argument continues to his third aim as follows. The characteristic that distinguishes humans from other things cannot be mere nutrition or growth, because that is shared with plants; so even though a life of nutrition and growth is important to our survival, it isn't distinct to us and so cannot be our function. Nor can our function be sentience or perception, as that characteristic is also shared, namely with other animals. And so Aristotle comes to the following conclusion: 'There remains, then, a practical life of the rational part ... [a] life determined by activity' (1097a3–7). Aristotle is often misquoted as saying that 'man is a rational animal', a simple and memorable phrase which unfortunately doesn't appear in any of his surviving works. However, the misquoted phrase does capture the gist of this part of the argument, as Aristotle believed that it is our reason (*logos*) which distinguishes us from plants and animals. In short, our function as human beings is to reason:

> *The function of man is an activity of the soul which follows or implies a rational principle.*
>
> Aristotle (1098a8)

But why the soul? Our function, according to the ancient Greeks, is determined by the kind of thing we are. So if we are a dog, then we have a doggy function, and our goals in life are very different from humans': to chase after balls, sleep a lot, guard our cave, eat as much as we can and have loads of offspring (actually they're not that different!). But what kind of thing is a human? For both Plato and Aristotle, we are creatures with a soul (in Greek *psyche*, which is where we get our word 'psychology' from), as this is what makes us human. Our function as human beings is determined by the make-up of our souls. So, if we want to understand our function, we need to understand our soul. Famously, in *The Republic*, Plato argued that our soul consists of three parts: reason, spirit/drive and desires, and it is the job of our reason to control the powerful impulses of our desires and our headstrong drive. Aristotle, however, had developed a more sophisticated, psychological view of the soul. When Aristotle talks about the 'soul' he is definitely not talking about a separate, spiritual, side of our self, or something that lives on after we die. For Aristotle, the soul was a kind of 'blueprint' or 'form' for a living being – the instructions for how it could develop over the course of its life. So our function, our characteristic activity, is determined by the kind of soul that we have. Humans have a rational soul and so our function is to exercise the rational parts of our soul. We shall see below (page 129), in further detail, how Aristotle views the different parts of the human soul.

Let us now try to reconstruct the main steps in Aristotle's function argument (1097b22–1098a15) in the table overleaf. We have already covered premises 1–7, and we look at premises 8, 9 and Aristotle's conclusion in the next section. You can follow for yourself how Aristotle moves through the final part of the argument in the Anthology extract 1.7: ('Function, soul and *eudaimonia*').

Assumption	Premise 1	The good life for a human is determined by the life of a good human.
(Teleological assumption)	P2	Everything has a function (ergon).
Mini-conclusion	P3	Therefore humans must also have a function (ergon).
Clarification	P4	Our function (ergon) is our characteristic activity, determined by our soul.
	P5	We share nutrition/growth with plants (so that cannot be our function). We share perception with animals (so that cannot be our function). But only humans have a rational soul.
	P6	Our characteristic activity (function) lies in the rational aspects of our soul.
Intermediate conclusion (from P4 and P6)	P7	Therefore the function of a human is to exercise the rational aspects of our soul.
	P8	To be a good X requires X fulfilling its function well through the exercise of the appropriate virtue/excellence (arete).
(from P7 and P8)	P9	Therefore to be a good human requires exercising those virtues through the rational aspects of the soul.
Conclusion (from P1 and P9)	C	Therefore the good life for a human is determined by exercising those virtues through the rational aspects of the soul.

anthology
1.7

Eudaimonia #2 – A longer answer: virtues and the soul

At the end of the function argument Aristotle gives his clearest definition yet of the good life for humans. It is:

> ... an **activity** of the **soul** in accordance with **virtue** (or if there are more than one kinds of virtue, in accordance with the best and most perfect kind).
>
> Aristotle (1098a15)

At last we see the word 'virtue' appear but once again we need to understand what Aristotle means by virtue. Above (page 121) we encountered the idea that for something to be good, and function well, it needed certain special qualities, *arete*, which philosophers usually translate as 'virtue'. Unfortunately 'virtue' (derived from *virtu*, which was the Latin translation of *arete*) now has particular connotations in ordinary language: it suggests a sort of Victorian prudishness, a goody two-shoes or perhaps, even more narrowly, a kind of sexual purity. When thinking about virtue ethics it is important that we throw out these connections as they have nothing to do with 'virtue' in the philosophical sense. Remember that virtue has other more relevant cousins: 'virtuosity' and 'virtuoso', in other words being brilliant or excelling in a particular area of life. In fact, *arete* is better translated as 'excellence', and we shall use both 'virtue' and 'excellence' when talking about *arete*.

▶ **ACTIVITY**

Refer to the activity on page 120, and list the virtues (excellences) of the following things:

- A good can-opener
- A good sheepdog
- A good musician
- A good human

You may have noticed that the 'good' things had attributes or qualities that the 'ordinary' versions lacked, which meant they were better able to fulfil their function – we can think of these qualities as virtues. So it is clear how virtue (in the sense of virtuosity) is connected to function and goodness for Aristotle: in order to be good you need to fulfil your function well; but in order to fulfil your function well you need to excel in the right ways – you need to possess virtues. And in order to be a good human, you need to excel in the characteristic activity of a human, which is determined by the rational parts of our soul.

The good life for humans, *eudaimonia*, is therefore achieved through virtue (*arete*): excelling in the rational parts of the soul.

▶ **ACTIVITY**

Look back at the list you wrote in the activity above (page 124) – do you agree with Aristotle that humans are primarily distinguished from other things by our capacity to reason? Why/why not?

Aristotle goes on to assess how closely his view of *eudaimonia* fits in with our commonly held ideas, and in doing so he expands on his own understanding of what it means to flourish, to live the good life.

- Happiness, or flourishing, is something that we work towards over our whole lifetime, it is not something that a single event can bring about – as Aristotle puts it 'One swallow does not make a summer' (1098a20).
- Happiness, or flourishing, is reached in part through the exercise of reason, but it is something that needs external goods as well. It is much easier for people to flourish if they live in a comfortable, safe society (as Aristotle did) than if they live in a state of fear, or war, or hunger, or poverty. These external goods may be down to good luck, but without exercising our reason we will not flourish even if we do have an abundance of external goods.

■ Happiness, or flourishing, isn't something we are born with, but is something we strive to achieve through habituation and training, which we look at below (page 129).

Learn More

By the end of Book One of the *Ethics* we can see where Aristotle's investigation in the *Ethics* is heading. Aristotle has used the first Book simply to introduce the idea of happiness, and to prove that it is achieved by excelling at our function. We have seen that our function is closely related to our *soul* or psyche (the form of a human being) and so if we really wish to understand how to be a Good human then we must understand how we can excel in the different parts of the soul. Aristotle views the soul as divided into a rational and a non-rational part, each of which is then subdivided (1102b10-b30). Aristotle clearly identifies two non-rational sub-sections: first the section related to our body and governing growth and nutrition; and secondly the section related to our character and governing our desires and emotions. Crucially, as we shall see, this second section can be shaped by reason. Then there is the rational part: including practical, day-to-day reasoning (which also shapes our character) and abstract, theoretical reasoning (examined right at the end of the *Ethics*). We have seen that happiness is reached by excelling as a human being, which means exercising virtue, or excellence, in each of the parts of the soul particularly its rational aspects.

▶ ACTIVITY

Read through the last four paragraphs of Book One of the *Ethics*. Create your own diagram that will help you to understand Aristotle's division of the soul, and how the virtues relate to this division.

The remainder of the *Ethics* (apart from some important chapters on friendship) is primarily concerned with the detail of how we can excel in the different parts of our soul, and in so doing how we reach *eudaimonia*. We have represented Aristotle's view of the soul in Figure 1.15 as divided into four parts and have given some examples of the associated excellences for each of its parts. However, you may choose to picture the division in a different way. In Figure 1.15 we have deliberately aligned excellence of practical reasoning close to excellence of character: like Plato, Aristotle believed that we could only be happy if the rational part of our soul were in control and our practical reasoning skills helped to shape our character to ensure our emotions and desires didn't lead us astray. We shall now turn to the part of the soul that governs our desires and emotions, and the virtues or excellences that apply to this part.

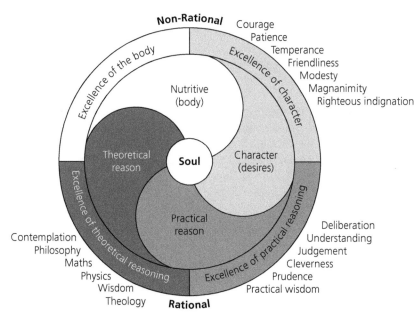

Figure 1.15
Aristotle's division
of the soul

1.1.3 Aristotle's virtue ethics

In figure: Non-Rational, Courage, Patience, Temperance, Friendliness, Modesty, Magnanimity, Righteous indignation, Excellence of the body, Excellence of character, Nutritive (body), Theoretical reason, Soul, Character (desires), Practical reason, Excellence of theoretical reasoning, Contemplation, Philosophy, Maths, Physics, Wisdom, Theology, Rational, Excellence of practical reasoning, Deliberation, Understanding, Judgement, Cleverness, Prudence, Practical wisdom

The role of education and habituation in developing a moral character

Book Two of the *Ethics* analyses what Aristotle refers to as *ethica arete*. We know that *arete* refers to 'excellence' or virtue (in the sense of virtuosity), but what about *ethica*? One common translation of *ethica* is 'moral', which then renders *ethica arete* as 'moral virtue'. Perhaps a better translation of *ethica* though, is 'character', as this captures the idea that we are honing and refining our responses to situations, controlling and shaping our desires and emotional reactions, and generally developing the character traits that will enable us to flourish. The name of Aristotle's work should now become clearer: *On Character* may have been a better title than *Ethics*, and would certainly distinguish it from the act-centred ethics of Kant or Mill. Depending on our translation, *ethica arete* becomes either 'moral virtue' or 'excellence of character', but it isn't concerned with only one virtue, instead it describes a person who, because they react in the right way to the world, demonstrates a number of different traits: courage, honesty, patience, temperance, friendliness, etc.

▶ ACTIVITY

At the start of this chapter we discussed the idea that a virtue is a disposition to behave in a certain way that attracts praise (and a vice is a disposition that is disapproved of). So what dispositions do you have? To find out, think about the actions you would take in the following situations:

1 At the end of your philosophy class your teacher asks you to give a ten-minute presentation next week on some aspect of Aristotle.

2 After the class you have arranged to meet a friend at a café. It's a nice café, even if they do sometimes overcharge. To get there you walk down a quiet street, and as you do so, you see a man lying face down on the pavement, his nose pressed into the concrete.

3 Your friend is late as usual and you have time to nip to the toilet. On the floor of an empty cubicle you see a wallet.

4 At the café your friend asks whether their lateness bothers you. They had a good excuse, but they are late every single time you arrange to meet. What do you say?

5 When you are given the bill it looks as if once again you have been overcharged by about 20 pence, but you can't remember exactly how much everything cost.

   a) What would be your response in each situation?

   b) For each of your responses, what character trait do you think it reveals?

   c) Have you always had this type of character, or are there dispositions that you remember deliberately trying to develop?

You may remember a time when you lacked confidence, but now you have it; or a time when you had a degree of control over your desires, but now you have very little control (chocolate may be a particular issue). You may have been patient as far back as you can remember, or you may have always had a short fuse and angered easily. So how do we acquire dispositions like these, and how can we develop excellence of character – is it through nature or nurture? Aristotle's answer is that:

> *The moral virtues are engendered in us neither by nor contrary to nature; we are constituted by nature to receive them, but their full development in us is due to habit.*
>
> Aristotle (1103a23)

So nature has a role to play insofar as we are born with certain pre-dispositions or potential. But this potential only becomes actual through exercise, practice, action and habit. In other words, our character is not determined merely by having some predestined 'personality' gene, or natural gift for courage or friendliness. Excellence of character has to be developed by practice and training, rather like learning an instrument, until it becomes a habit.

'Habit' isn't quite the right word, as it suggests a passive, perhaps mindless, response to our situation. Picking your nose is a habit; being courageous isn't a habit in the same way – like all the virtues it requires mental effort. But 'habituation', a type of education we undergo through repetition, is certainly where the process of developing a virtue begins. As Aristotle says: 'For the things we have to learn before we can do them, we learn by doing them' (1103a33). This may sound paradoxical, but we learn to play *Grand Theft Auto XV* not by sitting and watching someone else, but firstly by copying someone else, then by playing it and learning from our mistakes. When developing a particular character trait, for example kindness, we may start slowly, perhaps even unwillingly: most of us as children had to be constantly reminded to consider the needs of others. But we can learn to become kind by repeatedly acting in a kind way; in Aristotle's words: 'like actions produce like dispositions' (1103b22). Through the process of educating our emotions we become inclined to kindness, we even start to get pleasure from being virtuous and for Aristotle this habituation is how we start to develop *ethica arete*.

However, mere habituation isn't enough to create the genuine dispositions that we need to develop if we are to be *ethica arete*. Aristotle makes it clear that to be good and have *ethica arete* you must not just act in a good way, but you must also act *as good people act*. To be *ethica arete*, then, it is not enough to do good acts, you must do them in a certain way, with a certain attitude, and having a certain history of similar acts behind you. Someone who has *ethica arete* has not merely done one, or a few, virtuous acts; they have learnt by habituation to do virtuous acts, they enjoy doing virtuous acts (they naturally want to do them) and they have a disposition (a firm character) to always act virtuously. They also know what they're doing, and choose to act virtuously (1105a32).

The doctrine of the mean and Aristotle's account of vices and virtues

Virtue, then, is a state of character concerned with choice, lying in a mean.

Aristotle (1106b36)

We now arrive at the most famous part of the *Ethics*, and one of the most famous, if misunderstood, moral principles in the history of western philosophy. This principle is known as Aristotle's doctrine of the mean and although Aristotle didn't use the phrase himself, it is a term that usefully summarises how Aristotle thinks we can attain excellence of character.

Aristotle introduces his own doctrine of the mean by proposing that it is in the nature of some things to be destroyed by 'excess and deficiency', for example, the physical qualities of health and strength. If we eat too much or too little then our health is destroyed, and if we exercise too much or too little then our strength is destroyed. But both health and strength are preserved and increased by finding the right quantity of food and exercise respectively. We avoid excess or deficiency by aiming at the intermediate, i.e. the mean that lies in between both excess and deficiency, and this rule ('aim at the mean') applies as much to our character as to our body (see Figure 1.15 on page 129).In the same way:

temperance and courage are destroyed by excess and deficiency and are preserved by the mean.

Aristotle (1104a21)

The examples here of temperance and courage are used as archetypal cases to illustrate Aristotle's doctrine of the mean. For both Plato and Aristotle, temperance is an important indication of someone who is virtuous and eudaimon. If we overindulge in physical pleasures then we are likely to damage our soul, and very probably our body. For Plato, self-restraint, or temperance, meant that our reason was in control of (was tempering) our desires, which was an essential part of a balanced and healthy soul. For Aristotle, the control of our desires is also important, and this control should guide us away from excessive or deficient indulgence in our desires and towards the mean, i.e. towards some intermediate point between these two extremes. So, for Aristotle, there are three types of dispositions associated with the indulgence in our desires. The first is the hedonistic person who overindulges, and who is *licentious*; the second is the ascetic person who turns their back on all pleasures and who is *insensible*; and the third is someone able to avoid excess and deficiency of pleasure, and who is *temperate*. Temperance is thus the virtue that lies between the excess of licentiousness and the deficiency of insensibility.

The doctrine of the mean also seems easily applicable to the virtue of courage. Courage means striking the balance between fear and confidence in the face of danger or threat: if you tend to feel and respond with too much fear then you are cowardly; if you tend to feel and respond with too much confidence then you are rash or foolhardy. But if you get the balance right, and are able to overcome your fear, while not doing anything stupid through overconfidence, then you are courageous (see Figure 1.16). Aristotle considers both rashness and cowardice to be a *kakia*, translated as 'vice'; but once again this translation lends itself to some unhelpful associations. The term *kakia* is better thought of as a type of deficiency, a flaw or a defect, rather than as a vice.

Figure 1.16
Courage is midway between rashness and cowardice

Rashness   Courage   Cowardice

Figure 1.16 shows courage as falling on a line somewhere between cowardice and rashness, a sort of point of moderation. Aristotle himself says 'we have a bad disposition ... if our tendency is too strong or too weak, and a good one if our tendency is moderate' (1105b26). Thus Aristotle's doctrine of the mean has been readily interpreted as a doctrine of *moderation*, sometimes recommended as the principle of 'moderation in all things' (which was how the Confucians applied their own version of the doctrine). Interpreting the principle in this way suggests that Aristotle is giving us practical advice on how we should *act* in any situation. This would bring Aristotle's virtue ethics in line with the other moral theories we have looked at, giving us a prescriptive guide to action:

- Mill's utilitarian ethics: *act in a way that maximises happiness and minimises pain.*
- Kant's deontological ethics: *act in a way that conforms with the categorical imperative.*
- Aristotle's virtue ethics: *act in a way that finds the middle ground between over-reaction and under-reaction.*

On this account, the doctrine recommends that in any situation we should act in a way that avoids the extremes and instead displays a moderate amount of feeling, a moderate amount of indulgence, a moderate amount of pride, etc. We shall now assess whether Aristotle's doctrine of the mean should be interpreted in this way.

Experimenting with ideas

Consider the following four situations and answer the questions below.

1   In 1993 a *resident* in an American town discovered that for decades her local power station had been pumping the waste products of its cooling system into nearby ponds. From the ponds, these waste products had found their way into the town's drinking water, which explained the very high rates of cancer in her town.

2   In 1960 *doctors* become concerned about the possible side effects of a new, mild sleeping pill which also reduced morning sickness. Thousands of women who took this pill when pregnant gave birth to children with severe disabilities, and only half of these children survived.

3   In 1992 a well-known tobacco company introduced additional, carcinogenic, chemicals into its cigarettes in order to make them more addictive. When a *researcher* working for this company challenged this practice he was sacked and forced to sign a confidentiality agreement forbidding him from discussing this.

4   On your birthday in 2015 *you* were given an album by your favourite band on CD, even though CDs are only listened to by old people and you don't even have a CD player, so that was a waste of money, wasn't it?

For each of the people in *italics*:

a) What would be an excessive response in each situation?

b) What would be a deficient response in each situation?

c) What would be the moderate thing to do in each situation?

d) Do you think that the moderate response in each situation is the right response?

Criticism

The question is this: should the doctrine of the mean be interpreted as a doctrine of moderation? Is Aristotle claiming that, in a very British stiff-upper-lip kind of way, we should display only a moderate amount of emotion, or desire, as we navigate our way through our lives? One of the emotions that could link the scenarios on page 133 is the anger felt by the people affected by them. The anger of the people affected by the contaminated water, or by the untested sleeping pill, or by the unfair dismissal, or, in fairness, by the uselessness of older technologies. If the doctrine of the mean is a recommendation for moderation then should all these people show the same degree of anger? Is Aristotle claiming that they should all avoid an excess, or a deficiency, of anger and should display only a moderate amount of anger?

This seems absurd, almost irrational, particularly when we recall that excellence of character is shaped by reason. Moreover, sometimes a moderate response simply isn't an appropriate response. It is more reasonable to expect that there will be different displays of anger according to the situation. We expect people whose lives are destroyed by an unsafe drug to be outraged; and people who can't listen to a particular music format to be mildly put-out (and people whose ethical doctrine is misunderstood to be pretty cross). By applying the doctrine of moderation to even a few simple cases we can see that 'act moderately' isn't what Aristotle had in mind when talking about the mean.

Virtue discovers the mean and chooses it ... virtue is a mean; but in respect of what is right and best, it is an extreme.

Aristotle (1107a07)

Aristotle's words above direct us away from interpreting the mean as moderation by highlighting two important features of the concept of the mean and how it relates to virtue. The first part of the quote makes it clear that there is a certain skill to excellence of character, the skill in discovering what the mean is and how this will vary from situation to situation; on these grounds, we can reject the interpretation of the mean as blanket 'moderation'. In the second part of the quote (which is echoed at 1107a22), Aristotle is telling us that the mean is also an *extreme*. This is a further indication that Aristotle is not thinking of the mean as the 'average' or the 'moderate', i.e. as the middle point on a line between two extremes (as in figure 1.16 on page 132). So instead of thinking of the mean as lying on a straight line it may be more helpful for us to picture it as one corner of a triangle. Figure 1.17 shows this alternative view – our emotions of fear and confidence are expressed in different amounts: rashness = too much confidence, not enough fear; cowardice = too much fear, not enough confidence; courage = lots of confidence helps us to overcome the fear, but our fear prevents us from being rash.

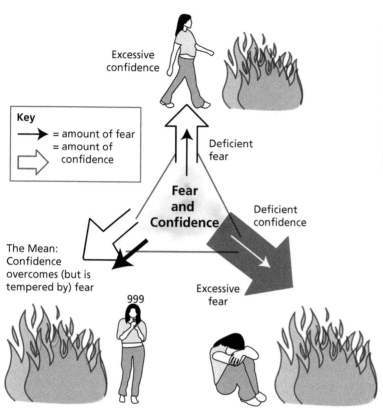

Figure 1.17
Three different reactions to a house fire, showing three types of disposition
The courageous person overcomes her fear to call 999, the coward cowers and the rash person marches into the burning house.

Already we can see there is far more complexity to grasping the doctrine of the mean than seeing it simply as a principle of moderation that can be applied as a moral rule to individual acts.

Aristotle gives an even clearer account of what he understands by the mean in Book Two, chapter 6 of the *Ethics*. Yes, it is the 'intermediate between excess and deficiency', i.e. between two extremes, but that can be understood in two ways. First, the mean could be calculated in an objective sense, giving us a mean which is equidistant between two fixed extremes (e.g. the mean lying between 2 and 10 is 6). Secondly, it could be the mean relative to us, and in this sense the mean is something that is neither too much nor too little *for us*. Aristotle emphasises this last point by using the example of a coach considering how much protein two of his athletes should eat per day. Ten pounds is too much for most athletes, and two pounds is too little, but it doesn't follow that the trainer should give each athlete six pounds (i.e. the trainer shouldn't follow the first, objective, interpretation of the 'mean'). An athlete who is just beginning their career may need just three pounds, but Milo of Croton, who was a legendary Greek wrestler, allegedly needed a hefty 20 pounds of protein a day. So the expert, the person with excellence of character, is able to determine the mean relative to the situation – whatever is appropriate – and sometimes that results in a mean that is itself an extreme.

anthology 1.8

In one of the most important passages in the *Ethics* (see the quote below), Aristotle describes what he believes to be the true mark of virtue, the brilliance of someone with *ethica arete*. We know that they are guided by their likes and dislikes (pleasures and pains) to do the right thing. We have seen that this is brought about by habituation, so that someone who has a kind, or courageous, or temperate character actually enjoys being kind, courageous and temperate. In this way, they are drawn towards the right and appropriate thing to do in any situation. For Aristotle, what characterises someone as virtuous is that they are able to:

> *feel or act towards the right person to the right extent at the right time for the right reason in the right way – that is not easy and it is not everyone that can do it. Hence to do these things well is a rare, laudable and fine achievement.*

Aristotle (1109a26)

anthology
1.9

This is indeed difficult and we need to develop excellence of practical reasoning to assist us. Practical wisdom and *ethica arete* combine to give us skills with which we can flourish. *Ethica arete* gives us the desires, the emotions and the goals; while practical wisdom uses these to drive our action towards exactly the right action and

▶ ACTIVITY

Books Three, Four and Five of the *Ethics* look in detail at a wide variety of virtues, some of which are listed in the table below. Read through the list and (avoiding the mistake of interpreting the doctrine of the mean as 'moderation') for each *arete* add in the appropriate excess and deficiency:

Sphere of action/feeling	Excess (kakia)	Mean (arete)	Deficiency (kakia)
Fear and confidence		Courage	
Pleasure and pain (likes and dislikes)		Temperance	
Giving and receiving		Generosity/ liberality	
Self-expression		Truthfulness	
Honour and dishonour		Proper ambition	
Social conduct		Friendliness	
Getting and spending		Magnificence	
Indignation		Righteous indignation	
Anger		Patience	

Now check your answers by looking in the *Nicomachean Ethics* or the *Eudemian Ethics* or by researching on the internet, to find out what Aristotle thought were the excess and deficiency for each *arete*.

appropriate expression of that emotion. That is someone who really does have excellence of character. So the doctrine of the mean is best understood as a description of people who, by making the most appropriate decision in each situation, nurture the right kind of dispositions to equip them for future situations, and in doing so avoid inappropriate excessive or deficient responses. At 1106b36 Aristotle sums up his position, describing *ethica arete* as 'a settled state of choice, in a mean relative to us, this being determined by reason, as the wise man determines it'. People who are able to shape their character in this manner are well on their way to flourishing.

Criticism

There are problems that emerge from Aristotle's efforts to apply the doctrine of the mean to the messy and complex subject of human emotions. Aristotle talks about the doctrine applying to a particular sphere, or field, of emotions, for example the sphere of 'fear and confidence' (see Figure 1.17 on page 135). We have seen that in this sphere, our emotions can be expressed with an excess or deficiency, leading to rashness or cowardice; or expressed in the appropriate amount, leading to courage. Aristotle makes every effort to identify a wide range of emotions but at times his efforts to find the excess and deficiency of a connecting emotion seems artificial. For example, righteous indignation is analysed in this way (1108b1):

- The righteously indignant man is upset at the undeserved good fortune of others.
- The jealous man (who has the feeling in excess) is upset by the deserved fortune of others.
- The malicious man (who is deficient in this feeling) is pleased at the bad fortune of others.

Therefore what the three men are upset or pleased by is different in each case – and this undermines Aristotle's claim that the excellences and flaws are displays of the same feeling. Aristotle also admits that there is no word for some excellences or deficiencies, such as proper ambition; 'they have no name' he writes, which suggests that they may not exist as common character traits. Finally, Aristotle points out that some emotions (spite, anger) and some actions (murder, theft) are always wrong. He says that there cannot be a mean to what is permanently in excess or deficiency (spite, anger, murder, theft); but this admission also chips away at the universality of the doctrine of the mean. Taken together, these problems undermine the empirical nature of the doctrine. It seems as if Aristotle is searching for some character traits that don't exist, in order to fit his theory.

The strength of Aristotle's theory is the recognition that, if we want to be happy, we must develop our emotional skill set. We must get better at reading the situation we're in, at recognising the impulsive pressure of our emotions, and at acting in a way that is appropriate to our emotion and the situation. In modern psychology this is known as 'emotional intelligence' and it is generally recognised as one of the most important skills you can develop.[13]

Voluntary actions and moral responsibility

The question Aristotle now addresses is which of our actions should we be held responsible for? In Book Three of the *Ethics*, Aristotle provides the first attempt at a comprehensive account of human action and how it relates to responsibility, choice and judgement. We make judgements about people all the time: informally we praise or blame people for their actions, and more formally our legal system makes judgements about who to punish and who to release, while our honours system judges who to reward. But if we are to be successful in making judgements about people's characters, including our own, then we need to identify those actions that are relevant to determining our character and those that are irrelevant.

▶ ACTIVITY

Can you think of examples of actions that are irrelevant to our judgement of whether someone has a good or bad character? Why are they irrelevant?

Aristotle asserts that people are praised or blamed for voluntary (intended acts) but not for acts done contrary to intention. Therefore it is only in intended acts that excellences, and vices, are to be found. What we *intended* to do in any situation reveals our dispositions and desires, and thus our moral character; things that we accidentally did, or which we did against our wishes, do not reveal our character. For example, while surfing in rough seas we noticed the Duchess of Cambridge was in danger of drowning and we deliberately swam to save her. This act of courage was intended and is an indication that we are courageous. If we intentionally stayed away from her because we were scared of drowning, this would indicate cowardliness. But if we were forced to stay away from her *against our intention* (perhaps an evil Bond villain threatened to kill us if we tried to save her), then this would not provide any evidence that we were cowardly. Similarly, if we only saved her by accident (swept under a wave we *unintentionally* let go of our surfboard which she then managed to grab hold of), then this again tells us nothing about whether we are actually cowardly or courageous.

Aristotle identifies and analyses two main types of action: 'voluntary' and 'involuntary', while also exploring a third type of 'non-voluntary' action. Unfortunately, these traditional translations are confusing, and it is once again more helpful to use alternative translations of these three types of action: namely acts that are 'intended', 'contrary to intention' and 'unintended'.

It is by our intended actions that we can be properly judged, and therefore praised or blamed, as only they are representative of our dispositions. When we deliberately do something, we are striving to bring about a goal, or an end, that we desire and in doing so we reveal our current dispositions, as well as shaping our future dispositions. What makes an action intended? We shall see that Aristotle believes an action cannot be 'intended' when its cause lies outside us, or when we are acting in ignorance. For Aristotle, an action is intended when its origin lies in us, in other words there is a clear line we can trace between our internal decision processes (our initial beliefs and desires, the assessment of options and the selection of a choice) and our physical processes (the movement of our body) and the action itself in the world. Because of this clear connection between the action and our choice we are responsible for our intended actions. Moreover, because our dispositions are the result of numerous actions (we become kind by doing kind things, cruel by doing cruel things), we are responsible for the development of our character through our intentional acts.

However, we shall now see that this clear connection between our actions and our responsibility for these actions becomes more complex, as Aristotle starts to dissect the different types of actions that we carry out.

Involuntary actions: Compulsion and responsibility

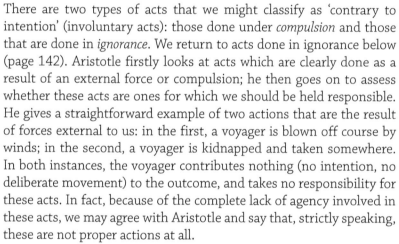

Actions are regarded as involuntary when they are performed under compulsion or through ignorance.

Aristotle (1109a1)

There are two types of acts that we might classify as 'contrary to intention' (involuntary acts): those done under *compulsion* and those that are done in *ignorance*. We return to acts done in ignorance below (page 142). Aristotle firstly looks at acts which are clearly done as a result of an external force or compulsion; he then goes on to assess whether these acts are ones for which we should be held responsible. He gives a straightforward example of two actions that are the result of forces external to us: in the first, a voyager is blown off course by winds; in the second, a voyager is kidnapped and taken somewhere. In both instances, the voyager contributes nothing (no intention, no deliberate movement) to the outcome, and takes no responsibility for these acts. In fact, because of the complete lack of agency involved in these acts, we may agree with Aristotle and say that, strictly speaking, these are not proper actions at all.

However, there are actions done under compulsion which are more problematic, because they are acts which are partly contrary to our intentions and partly intended. Aristotle gives two examples of these 'mixed' acts: dumping your cargo overboard in a storm, or committing a robbery under the threat of blackmail. In this first case, the angry Athenian merchants who paid you to safely transfer their cargo across the Adriatic Sea might ask: 'Did you intend to throw the cargo overboard?' Well, when you set out across the calm turquoise waters you didn't have any intention of losing the cargo as transporting it safely meant you would get paid. So, in the long-term sense, your answer is 'no', losing the cargo was against your intention. But this won't wash with the angry merchants who are now throttling you: Did you, or did you not, throw the cargo overboard during the storm?

> *In cases like the above the agent acts voluntarily [intentionally]; because the movement of the limbs that are the instruments of action has its origin in the agent.*
>
> Aristotle (110a16)

Aristotle argues that, strictly speaking, in the short term, yes, you did intend to lose the cargo. The origin of the action lies within you – you are the agent – you had control of your thoughts, you made a decision about priorities (cargo or survival) and you had control of the limbs that chucked the cargo overboard. This is very different from your colleague, the voyager, who was kidnapped and had no choice at all and no power over where she was heading. But, it is also true that you *felt* that you had no choice, and most people, including a jury and hopefully the angry merchants, would be sympathetic to your claim that you had no choice because you wanted to live. So Aristotle calls such actions mixed as they are both intended (in the short term) and contrary to intention (in the long term).

Experimenting with ideas

It's time for the captains of these three ships to face the music as the Athenian judge wants to know what happened to the merchants' gold. Read through each of the excuses (all of them true) that the captains give (in Figure 1.18) to the judge and answer the questions below.

'I was kidnapped by pirates and forced to sail the gold to Sparta.'

'I threw all the gold overboard – it was either that or be drowned along with all the crew.'

'I spent all the gold – Aristotle was making a one-off appearance at the Lyceum and I had to see it.'

Figure 1.18 The captains' excuses for losing the gold

Now, for each captain:

1 Identify whether their action leading to the loss of the gold was voluntary or involuntary (through compulsion) or involuntary (mixed).
2 Do you think they are responsible for their action?
3 Do you think they should be punished or pardoned for the loss of the gold?

Acts done under compulsion, including mixed acts, share the feature of being involuntary acts (done contrary to our intention) because they contain strong elements of force which direct the actions away from what we intend. But what are the differences in the judgements we make between acts done under full compulsion, and mixed acts? With the first type, Aristotle argues that we are not held responsible (and so should neither be praised nor blamed) because there is no choice. But with the second type, Aristotle believes that, despite the compelling circumstances, there is an element of choice: we are responsible for these actions and so can be judged, praised or blamed for them. After all, it was we who performed the action, and we were free to do otherwise – we could have let the blackmailer post those photos on the internet, but we chose not to, preferring instead to rob the bank. What is important is that such mixed acts demand understanding and perhaps pardoning by those around us, or by a judge or jury. Aristotle notes, however, that there are some things that are unpardonable even if we feel forced into doing them (for example, matricide). So where there is no agency, there is no responsibility; and where there is agency, and the origins of the action lie within you, then there is responsibility, but you may be exonerated if the action is 'mixed' (unless it's matricide). Furthermore, where there is agency and an act is voluntary, then this helps us identify a person as having a particular virtue (for example, justice); where there is no agency in an act, then this act, tells us nothing about whether the person is a just or unjust person.

anthology
1.10

Experimenting with ideas

A You have been investigating the assassination of a politician, and have found that the assassin was systematically brainwashed by a mysterious organisation called the Parallax Corporation. This brainwashing was so powerful that whenever the assassin was told the trigger word 'Manchuria' he would kill the next politician he saw.

I Do you think that the assassin had agency in the moments leading up to the murder?

2 Is his act of assassination a 'mixed' act, or one done from compulsion?

3 Do you think the assassin is responsible for his actions?

4 Should the assassin be punished?

B A colleague is conducting the investigation with you, but starts to put on weight, eating more and more junk food (particularly an American cake called a Twinkle Bar). Finally, he is so large that he cannot get into his car or into your small office, and he loses his job. Eventually he sues the manufacturers of Twinkles, arguing that he was forced by his desire for sweet things to eat their product, and that the manufacturers are thus responsible for his dismissal from his job.

I Do you think your colleague had agency when eating Twinkle Bars?

2 Do you agree that your colleague is compelled to eat Twinkles? Why/why not?

3 Do you agree that your colleague is not responsible for his actions?

4 Should the manufacturers be punished?

---

anthology
1.11

Aristotle does not deal with examples of brainwashing or hypnotism, which we may now acknowledge as causes powerful enough to qualify as examples of full compulsion, rather than as 'mixed' actions, even though the origin of the action lay in the agent. However, he does dismiss the claim that some people may make (in order to avoid taking responsibility) that they were 'forced' by their desires to act in a particular way. For Aristotle, being 'forced' by your desires is exactly what an intended action is all about: we act in a particular way because we want something. So your colleague is completely responsible for eating all those Twinkles. Moreover, Aristotle notes rather cynically that people who offer this defence ('I was forced by my desire, so it's not my responsibility') only offer that excuse for the bad things they've done; we never hear them say 'I was forced by my desire to do something good, so I should not be rewarded or praised for this good act'.

Learn More

Non-voluntary actions: Ignorance and responsibility

Aristotle introduces a further degree of subtlety into his analysis of involuntary action by looking at another class of acts that are not intended. These are acts done from ignorance. Translators usually refer to these acts done from ignorance as 'non-voluntary', but it might be more helpful to think of them as 'unintended' acts. There are aspects of all our actions which we are ignorant of; after all, we are not omnipotent and so wouldn't know the details of every situation in which we have to make a decision. What Aristotle is focusing on is those material aspects of a situation, upon which our decision is based, and which we may think we know but which it transpires we were mistaken about. There are all sorts of ways in which we can be materially ignorant: lack of knowledge, mistaken identity, misinterpretation, errors of judgement, or misunderstanding of a situation (1111a2ff.). What these examples share is this: our description of the situation at the time of the action is different from the description we would give of that same situation once we were made aware of certain other features.

One example of an unintended act can be found in the tragedy of Oedipus, who intended to 'kill the angry posh bloke in the chariot, and marry the Queen of Thebes'. He did not intend to 'kill his father and marry his mother' but that is exactly what happened (Figure 1.19). It was through his ignorance that this tragic event occurred; Oedipus was not aware who his real father and mother were (the angry posh bloke and Queen of Thebes, it turns out). So should Oedipus have taken responsibility for this awful outcome? He certainly felt he should, as when he discovered what he had done he blinded himself with the pin from his mother's brooch. If he had studied Book Three of the *Ethics*, he might have been a little more forgiving. Although Aristotle doesn't discuss Oedipus, the young man was clearly acting in ignorance and his actions were non-voluntary acts. The question remains: when, if ever, should we be held responsible for non-voluntary, unintended acts?

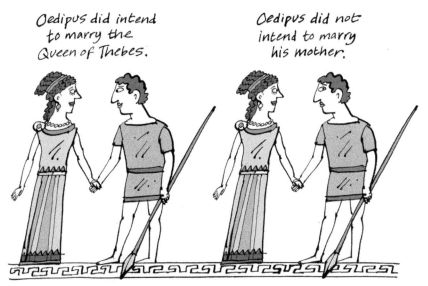

Oedipus did intend to marry the Queen of Thebes.

Oedipus did not intend to marry his mother.

Figure 1.19 Oedipus' non-voluntary marriage

Every act done through ignorance is non-voluntary, but is involuntary only when it causes the agent subsequent pain and repentance.

Aristotle (1110b17)

For Aristotle, whether we are responsible for our non-voluntary acts depends on whether the act was actually one that was contrary to our intention. And we can discover whether it was against our intentions by asking the question: 'Do you regret doing that, and would you have acted differently if you had been in full possession of the facts?' If the answers are 'yes' then we would say that your act was *contrary to your intention*, not merely unintended.

An act done in ignorance can be unintended because it had unforeseen consequences or because we were not aware of all the facts (like Oedipus) but this does not remove our responsibility. After all, it was our action – we were the agent. What may lessen our responsibility is whether it *was* contrary to our intention to, say, marry our mother. This does not imply that we can repent and will receive guaranteed forgiveness, for remorse and repentance cannot change an action that has already been performed. What Aristotle means is this: at the time of the action we were ignorant of certain things, and whether that ignorance is relevant or not depends on whether we would have acted otherwise if we had known all the facts. If we would have acted otherwise then we will reveal regret for our action ('If only I'd known') and our act will be shown to have been contrary to our intention. So remorse and regret are a very strong indication that a non-voluntary (unintended) act is actually involuntary (against our intention), and hence that we should be considered for pardon.

The flow chart (Figure 1.20) summarises Aristotle's analysis of action and responsibility. He has identified two types of action in which our responsibility for an act (and the praise or blame bestowed on it) may be repudiated or lessened: namely, mixed acts done with some compulsion, and acts done from ignorance of a particular fact. He has also identified those actions for which we have no responsibility at all,

Figure 1.20 Flow chart summarising Aristotle's thoughts on responsibility and action

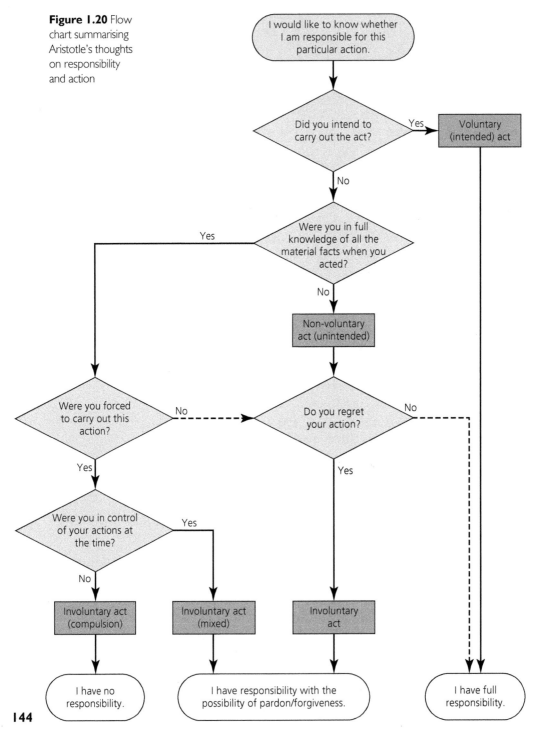

namely acts that are done under compulsion. The actions that we are fully responsible for are our intended actions, and it is in these that our character, and virtue if we possess it, is displayed.

Pleasure and the Good

The role that pleasure has to play in the good life is something that Aristotle addresses throughout the *Ethics*. Alasdair MacIntyre has proposed[14] that Aristotle is arguing against two kinds of opponent. Aristotle disputes the view taken by Plato and his followers that pleasure was not part of the good life in any way and even damaged the good; but he also wanted to avoid the claim made by other ancient Greek philosophers (such as Eudoxus) that pleasure was the supreme good. Aristotle, if you like, is threading his theory between these two extremes by finding the mean: acknowledging the importance of pleasure but not giving it the rarefied status afforded it by hedonists, and later by utilitarians.

> *One school maintains that pleasure is the good; another, on the contrary, that it is wholly bad.*
>
> Aristotle (1172a26)

Let us remind ourselves about what we already know of Aristotle's thoughts on pleasure, and we will see a balanced view emerging. On the one hand we saw above (page 119) that Aristotle's investigation into the good for humans ruled pleasure out as the supreme good. It is a plausible candidate for the good, as people do seek pleasure as an end, and nearly everyone seeks pleasure of one kind of other. However, you will remember Aristotle thought that seeking pleasure as the sole end is only a life fit for cattle, but not for humans who have rational souls and who must excel in all parts of their soul if they wish to flourish. Moreover, one of the identifying features of the good life is that it needs nothing further to complete it (page 117), but there are many goods that we can add to a life of pleasure that would improve it, so pleasure can't be the Good. What are we then to make of this quote:

> *Happiness is the best, the finest, the most pleasurable thing of all.*
>
> Aristotle (1099a27)

There is a vast difference between happiness in the Aristotelian sense of *eudaimonia* and happiness as a hedonist might conceive of it. The difference can be brought out through an anecdote about the 1960s footballing genius George Best. He loved to tell the tale of how, in the early 1970s, a room-service waiter came into his hotel room one morning. The footballer was in bed with one of the most beautiful women in the world, surrounded by thousands of pounds in cash that he'd won at the races, drinking champagne from the bottle. The waiter looked at him, shook his head and said 'So, George ... where did it all go wrong?' And it's true, something had gone wrong. From being hailed as the best footballer in the world, George Best had turned into an alcoholic playboy – he failed to fulfil his real potential. In a hedonistic sense he was happy, but in Aristotelian terms he was not happy – he wasn't eudaimon, he was no longer flourishing. We saw earlier (page 119) that Aristotle specifically ruled out indulgence in pleasure as part of the good life. Like Plato, he saw the restraint of our desires as a virtue, namely temperance, and an excessive indulgence in our desires as a vice (licentiousness). So, for Aristotle, Eudoxus is wrong: pleasure is not the good life, and indulgence in our desires is not a part of the good life.

But, on the other hand, we also know that Aristotle believed pleasure to be an important feature in the development of virtue. You may remember that excellences or virtues are developed through habituation – the training of our dispositions (page 130). Pleasure has a crucial role here in the nurturing of *ethica arete*, by being part of a positive feedback loop. As we start out trying to develop excellent dispositions, it is difficult and we have to force ourselves to be kind, just, courageous, generous, etc. ... Over time, we find that we begin to enjoy these actions, and get pleasure from acting kindly, generously, justly, etc. This pleasure makes us more inclined to do those types of actions in the future, and so we become disposed to kindness, justice, courage and the like. Moreover, although Aristotle rules out indulging in physical pleasures, he also rules out as a vice (*kakia*) the avoidance of all bodily pleasures. Aristotle advocates that some sensual pleasures (enjoying sport, or art or music) should be actively encouraged, while acknowledging that other pleasures (food, sex, drink) are natural and necessary so long as any indulgence is avoided (1147b25). In which case, Plato and his followers are wrong, and pleasure is a critical part of *ethica arete* and the good life.

The middle way between the view that pleasure *is* the good, and the view that pleasure has no part to play in the good, is the route taken by Aristotle. For Aristotle, the good life cannot ignore pleasure, but nor is the good life a life of pure pleasure. So, what is pleasure for Aristotle? When Aristotle investigates this question in Book Ten of the *Ethics* he concludes that it is not any *one* thing at all – it is not a single qualia (or quale, see page 242) for example. Nor is pleasure an end at all, rather it is something that arises from the activity itself. I aim to do an activity and if it goes well then I get pleasure from the activity, and there are as many possible pleasures as there are possible activities. Thus the hedonist is not actually saying anything concrete when they say we aim at pleasure, because 'pleasure' is too vague a term, and is dependent on the activity being done. For Aristotle, pleasure supervenes on activities, it does not exist separately from any activity. However, and this is an important point, Aristotle, like Mill, believed that some activities are superior to others and hence some pleasures are superior to others.

You won't be surprised to find out what activities Aristotle thinks of as the most superior.

At the end of the *Ethics* Aristotle reveals his true colours as a philosopher. Prior to that, the picture of the good life that he has painted during the previous nine books of the *Ethics* is a complex, varied and persuasive one. It requires us to develop skills in practical wisdom, and at the same time to develop our character so that we can make the right decision in any given situation; it requires us to enjoy what we do, and take pleasures in the sensual world; it requires luck and good fortune and external goods; it requires love and friendship and participation in our community. Just as we saw that the good life for a plant was the life of a good plant, so Aristotle has shown that the good life for humans is the life of a good human (Figure 1.21). Aristotelian *eudaimonia* is a life of well-being, flourishing and happiness for us as individuals.

Figure 1.21 The Good life for plants is the life of a good plant; and the Good life for humans is the life of a good human

Striving for *eudaimonia* and developing our character and intellectual virtues is good for us, it is in our self-interest, and on the surface at least this seems to have nothing to do with morality (in the modern sense, as understood by Kant and the utilitarians). But it turns out that it has everything to do with morality after all. Through the development of our practical wisdom we become considerate, fair and reasonable people. Through the development of *ethica arete* we also develop friendliness, courage, truthfulness, justice and a host of other virtues that, while benefiting our journey to *eudaimonia*, also benefit those people around us and contribute to the well-being of our whole community. For Aristotle, humans really are social animals, and our eudaimonia is bound up in that of the other individuals among whom we live. Right at the very start of the *Ethics* Aristotle argues that the good of the community is a higher good than the good of the individual (1094b8) and so our virtuous behaviour ultimately contributes to this higher good. My well-being also contributes to the well-being of my community. And yet ... Aristotle, in the final book of the *Ethics*, seems to take a step away from this rich and complex account of *eudaimonia* and offers another, much more self-centred, thesis.

Eudaimonia #3 – Contemplation and the Good

Criticism

It seems unfair to include part of Aristotle's positive thesis as a criticism of the rest of his theory. But the proposal made by Aristotle in Book Ten does seem to undermine much of what has gone before in the *Ethics*. You may remember that Aristotle set aside a question right at the beginning of Book One (page 120), saying he would return to it later. The question was whether contemplation (*theoria*) is the good life, and in Book Ten Aristotle's answer is a resounding 'yes'.

> If happiness is activity in accordance with virtue, it is reasonable that it should be in accordance with the highest virtue; and this will be that of the best thing in us.
>
> Aristotle (1177a11)

Contemplation ticks all the right boxes as the ultimate candidate for the highest good:

✓ Contemplation is the supreme exercise of reason.
✓ Contemplation is done for its own sake (1177b1).
✓ Contemplation is self-sufficient, it needs nothing to complete it and there is no end to it – it can go on for ever.
✓ Contemplation brings happiness in a real long-lasting sense.

Moreover:

✓ Contemplation is greater than practical wisdom because the objects of Contemplation are the highest objects of knowledge.
✓ Contemplation is of the highest objects because contemplation is Contemplation of God (i.e. pure-reason) and any activity that strives to do this will bring happiness greater than any mortal pursuit (1177b31).

And so the good life is the life of contemplation, a position held by many philosophers from both Eastern and Western traditions. But Aristotle had seemed to be different from all those other philosophers who claim that philosophy is the ultimate human activity: he seemed to be offering a view of the good life with which we could all agree and would all find persuasive, as outlined in Figure 1.21 on page 147. The previous nine Books have been talking about what it is like to live in this world, not in some abstract world of ideas, yet in Book Ten we are told that, after all, the good life is philosophy. But that is hardly something that contributes to the well-being of our community, nor is it something that would help most of us flourish, nor is it something that would persuade non-philosophers that Aristotle is taking the right approach.

Further issues

We have encountered difficulties with Aristotle's arguments and ideas throughout our discussion of his theory of virtue ethics. We shall now turn to further criticisms of Aristotle's theory, all of them arising from the particular approach that virtue ethicists take, which is an holistic approach. Virtue ethics does not claim to have the precision of utilitarian or Kantian ethics, which attempt to be clear in their prescriptive rules. But virtue ethicists would reject Kantian and utilitarian ethics precisely because of this attempt at precision – the world is complex, moral dilemmas are messy, and ethical decisions are rarely straightforward. Over the last 50 years, philosophers like Elizabeth Anscombe, Peter Geach and Alasdair MacIntyre have revived our interest in the virtue ethics of Aristotle, Aquinas and Hume precisely because it is only a virtue approach that seemed to accommodate the complexity of our moral lives.[15] However, this lack of precision does leave virtue ethics open to criticism, as we shall see in the three issues raised below. The first issue emerges because (unlike utilitarian ethics) there is no rule to determine how to rank virtues in order of priority or importance in any situation; the second and third issues emerge because Aristotle doesn't seem to provide any clear prescriptive rules for action.

Can Aristotle's virtue ethics deal with clashing or competing virtues?

The robustness of any ethical theory is tested through its application to 'hard cases' or moral dilemmas, in other words, situations in which there is no clear right course of action that can be recommended by the theory; and virtue ethics is no different from consequentialist or deontological theories in its vulnerability to moral dilemmas. Utilitarian dilemmas may emerge if we have to decide whether to maximise happiness or minimise pain in a situation, but we can't do both. This can be resolved for utilitarians by deciding in advance which of these two outcomes are more important (leading to the distinction between positive and negative utilitarianism). Kantian dilemmas can emerge if there are situations which lead to conflicting duties, and these can be resolved by determining, in advance, which duties take priority.

Dilemmas for virtue ethicists seem to be less clear-cut than they are for utilitarians or Kantians. For any situation, there are many different responses that we could have, a range of virtues that we could display, a number of vices (excessive or deficient responses) that we might fall into. So, potentially, every situation could be one which is a dilemma for an Aristotelian virtue ethicist, as there is always more than one virtuous response available to us, which we could take. Only by developing skills in practical wisdom can we navigate our way successfully through life, making the optimum decision in each situation.

However, occasionally we will encounter situations not just where there is more than virtue 'on the table', but where one possible response obviously conflicts with another possible response. Virtue ethics deals very well with that classic dilemma of Plato's and Kant's:

the mad axe murderer (see DTL 2, page 11).[16] Imagine your neighbour has lent you their axe so that you can chop a tree down. They knock at your door one night, looking and sounding as though they are going to murder someone, and the question is: what do you do? On the one hand, you are an honest person, and have demonstrated the virtue of truthfulness throughout your life. On the other hand, you are a kind person, and hate to think of other people being injured (for example by mad axe murderers). So, should you be honest here, and give back the axe, or should you be kind here and lie about not having the axe? It's pretty clear that Aristotle can deal with this potential conflict of virtues by saying that the right thing to do (the most appropriate thing to do) would be to lie. There is, in fact, no conflict at all. This is because, as Aristotle says, sometimes the mean (i.e. what is appropriate) can itself be an extreme, so a deficiency of honesty here would be exactly what a virtuous person would do. We return to see how virtue ethics addresses cases of lying and deception on page 170.

What about a harder case, where there is no clear route that can be taken? Michael Haneke's film *Amour* (2012) is about a married couple, Anne and George, both ex-piano teachers in their eighties, living in a flat in Paris. Anne suffers a stroke and undergoes surgery, leaving her paralysed and unable to play the piano. Anne tells George that she doesn't want to go on living. George tries to look after her, but she suffers a second stroke and now has severe dementia and is incapable of speech. Both George, as a carer looking after his dying loved one, and his wife, Anne, are undergoing unbearable suffering. At the end of the film, George tells the non-responsive Anne a story and then kills her by smothering her with a pillow. He then adorns the bed with flowers – his last act of love for her. The issue for a virtue ethicist is: What was the virtuous thing to do here? There are clearly competing virtues: the charitable, loving virtue that leads George to kill his wife; and the virtue of justice which should prevent us from killing anyone.

Aristotle does not provide a hierarchy of virtues, but if he had, then justice would have been placed above charity. After all, Aristotle admits that while some virtues might be in an extreme, like lying to the axe murderer, there are some actions which are always vicious, like theft and murder, acts of intolerable injustice. But is George's act an act of charity – euthanasia – and not a murder at all? If so, then there is a genuine dilemma for the Aristotelian virtue ethicist. George's action seems to display not just charity but kindness and love, and heart-breaking regret; but on the other hand he could have displayed courage and justice by not killing her, and lived with the daily sharing of her suffering. In either case, there would be a residue of pain, what Hursthouse calls a 'moral remainder', which can be experienced as intense guilt or regret by the person making the decision. But, Hursthouse claims, one of the strengths of the virtue ethics approach is that it acknowledges this regret as morally significant, even life-changing (just watch or read *Sophie's Choice*, 1982). The moral significance of the remainder is the result of the impact that clashing virtues, and the resultant tough decision-making, have on the agent. Hursthouse contrasts this nuanced view with utilitarian or Kantian ethics which fail to give any weight to moral remainders.[17]

Can Aristotle's virtue ethics give sufficiently clear guidance about how to act?

One of the features that we expect to see in an effective ethical theory is some guidance on how we should act. Act-centred theories, like utilitarian and Kantian ethics, certainly aim to provide some sort of code or set of concrete rules prescribing how we should act and make judgements. At first sight, it appeared as if Aristotle's doctrine of the mean could provide the equivalent rule for his virtue ethics, and if the mean was interpreted as a doctrine of moderation – 'act moderately in any situation' – then this may have been a clear rule about how to act. But we have seen above (page 134) that Aristotle did not take the mean to be 'moderation'.

Instead, Aristotle's doctrine of the mean provides a complex analysis of virtue. It describes how virtuous acts are in a mean between excessive and deficient response, and that this mean is relative to the situation. It describes how the mean response is the right response, leading to the most appropriate behaviour, which may even sometimes entail an extreme response, for example being furious at the unethical behaviour of a large corporation. So, far from offering clear guidance, the doctrine of the mean suggests that every situation is different and there is no single rule:

> To feel or act towards the right person to the right extent at the right time for the right reason in the right way – that is not easy.
>
> Aristotle (1109a26)

The problem is: 'How do we know what the right behaviour is?', in other words: 'What is a virtuous act in any given situation?' Aristotle's theory is vague on this, and we shall see below (page 154) that attempting to define a virtuous act in terms of a virtuous person does not solve the problem of this vagueness.

Aristotle himself admitted that being virtuous was very difficult, and unfortunately the doctrine of the mean does not provide a hard-and-fast rule that will simplify the decisions we have to take and the moral judgements we have to make. For a modern proponent of virtue ethics, the principles, rules and guidelines of Kantian or utilitarian ethics may be too good to be true, as there is no easy way of calculating right and wrong. For Aristotle, there is always going to be a certain looseness about moral decision-making, because experience tells us that for every rule of thumb we prescribe (for example, it's good to be courageous) we shall find exceptions (for example, occasions when the best thing to do is to run for your life as fast as possible). Life is complex, situations vary in subtle but significant ways, and no formula can accommodate these variations. It is up to us to make the judgement call, to reflect on this call, and to absorb this experience into our character. Aristotle himself admits that his doctrine of the mean is somewhat vague:

> In all the states of character we have mentioned, as in all other matters, there is a mark to which the man who has the rule looks ... and there is a standard which determines the mean states which we say are intermediate between excess and defect .... But such a statement, though true, is by no means clear; ... if a man had only this knowledge he would be none the wiser e.g. we should not know what sort of medicines to apply to our body if someone were to say 'all those which the medical art prescribes, and which agree with the practice of one who possesses the art'.
>
> Aristotle (1138b26)

This passage from Aristotle leads into an analysis of the additional understanding and skills, termed practical wisdom, that we need that will enable us to make the right decision (page 136). This emphasis on practical thinking and decision-making skills was one of the reasons that Aristotelian virtue ethics was revived in the 1950s. The practice and application of these skills, while not giving us easy rules, can certainly help us to clarify how we should act.[18]

In addition to the clarity that practical wisdom provides, there may be other interpretations of Aristotle's theory that reveal the guidance it can offer. We know that Aristotle expected people with practical wisdom to develop roughly the same sorts of disposition: these are the virtues listed in the activity on page 136. Rosalind Hursthouse has argued that through the virtues Aristotle has identified, he does offer guidance on how to act after all. We know that Aristotle tells us that we apply practical wisdom in order to act virtuously and to avoid acting viciously (i.e. in excess or deficiently); we also know that Aristotle gives us specific examples of the virtues that we should strive for, and the *kakias* (vices) we should avoid. Hursthouse says that, taken together, these virtues and vices do offer rules or principles for action, and she calls these 'v-rules'.[19] So virtues carry a positive prescription for action ('do X'), while vices carry a negative prescription ('don't do Y'). For example, the virtue of truthfulness entails the v-rule 'do what is honest', while the vice of meanness entails the v-rule 'don't do what is uncharitable'. According to Hursthouse, these v-rules do, after all, provide clear guidance on action (see also page 158 below).

► **ACTIVITY**

Using the list of virtues and vices identified in the activity above (page 136) and the list below (page 158) generate one v-rule for each virtue, and one v-rule for each vice.

Even if Hursthouse is right, and coherent v-rules can be generated from Aristotle's virtues, we might still reject these rules by arguing that these virtues are culturally specific. In other words, these virtues may well have been valued in ancient Athens but that does not give us any reason to value them today (or give us any reason to be guided by the corresponding v-rules). This criticism is one often aimed at virtue theorists, not just Aristotle. Even when we compare the virtue ethics of Aristotle with that of Aquinas or with David Hume or the Victorians we can see that the list of virtues changes. Doesn't this suggest that the lack of any external criteria (telling us what counts as a virtue) means that virtues are culturally relative? In which case, there are no universal v-rules, no prescriptions in virtue ethics that are equivalent to the maxim of the utilitarians or the categorical imperative of Kant. However, James Rachels argues that there are some virtues which all societies need, in other words, without which stable societies could not be sustained.[20] These foundational virtues include honesty, loyalty, generosity, courage … a very similar list to the one that Aristotle gave in fourth-century Athens.

Is Aristotle's virtue ethics guilty of circularity: Defining virtuous acts and virtuous people in terms of each other?

Let us return to the question raised above (page 151), namely 'What is a virtuous act?' If we can answer this question then we may be able to apply Aristotle's ethics more readily as a guide to moral action. As an answer to this question, Aristotle directs us to virtuous people: it is the 'good man' who sets the standard, they are the people who find the mean and do the right thing, they are the people whose example we should follow. Aristotle clarifies this in Book Three when he is discussing the ends that our actions are aimed at:

> *the object of wish is the good, but for the individual it is what seems to be good to him; so for the man of good character it is the true good … For the man of good character judges every situation rightly … he is a sort of standard for what is right and pleasant.*
>
> Aristotle (1113a25ff)

In other words, for most of us, our actions are aimed at the apparent good, what seems good to us; but the good person, someone with *ethica arete*, chooses the actual good, they set the standard for us to aim at. Perhaps we are now making some headway here in our search to find, in among Aristotle's theory, some guidance on how we should act. We wanted to know what a virtuous act is, and Aristotle directs us to virtuous people: a virtuous act is done by someone virtuous. The question we should now ask is 'Who are these virtuous people?' since if we can identify them then we can follow their example. The problem of circularity immediately arises if our answer to this question is 'Virtuous people are those who choose virtuous actions'. For example, if we want to know what the courageous thing to do is, then we should look towards people we know who have courage. And who are these people with courage? Well, they're the people who always act courageously. If that is Aristotle's answer, then we are left with an unhelpful piece of advice, as what we need is some external criterion or criteria that tell us what virtue is without referring to virtue.

Figure 1.22 Is Aristotle guilty of this type of circular reasoning?

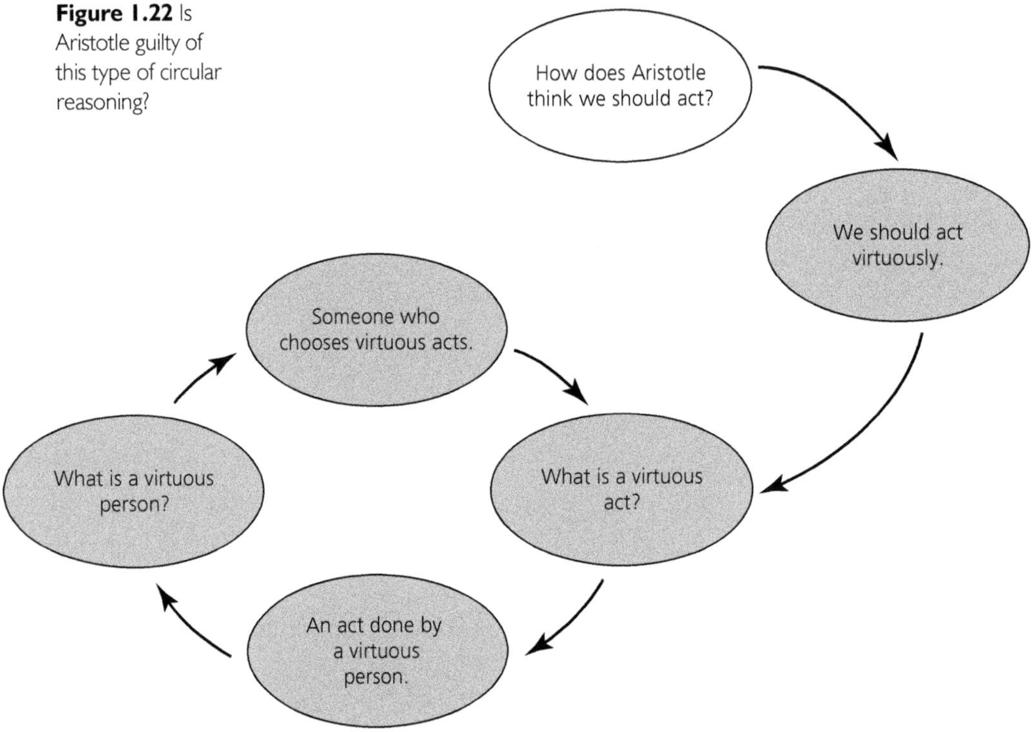

However, Aristotle does have more to say about virtuous people than simply 'They are the ones who act virtuously'. We know at least two other things about virtuous people. First, for Aristotle, virtuous people are those who are *eudaimon*, the men (and they were definitely men) in Aristotle's classes studying philosophy, the wealthy Athenians who formed Aristotle's circle of friends, those people who were comfortably off but had time to devote to contemplation of the good life. Secondly, we should remember (see Figure 1.22 above) that virtuous people are excellent in a number of different ways: they don't just have *ethica arete*, but they are also people with practical wisdom, i.e. those able to make the right choice or wish about the goals they should choose. Practical wisdom (the virtue of practical reasoning) and *ethica arete* (the virtue of character) are bound up with each other, and both of them are needed for us to make the right decisions throughout our life that enable us to flourish.

So, first, can we free Aristotle from the charge of circularity by using the concept of *eudaimonia* to define a virtuous person? J.L. Mackie in *Ethics: Inventing Right and Wrong* argues that Aristotle's account of *eudaimonia* is dependent on his account of virtue and so also leads to circularity.[21] Aristotle's function argument aims to show that the good life for humans (*eudaimonia*) is the life of a good human (i.e. a human who fulfils their function well), in other words someone who excels and is virtuous. So a virtuous person is someone who flourishes, and someone who flourishes is someone virtuous – the circularity remains (Figure 1.23).

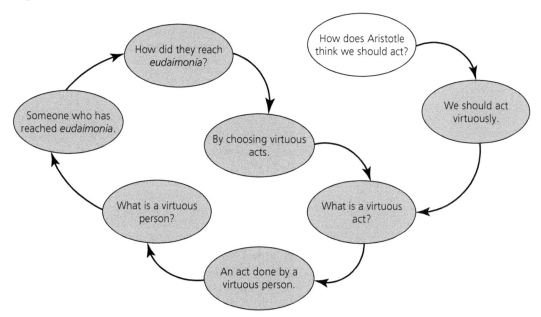

Figure 1.23 Introducing *eudaimonia* does not help Aristotle escape a charge of circularity

Perhaps then we can free Aristotle from the charge of circularity by finding an external criterion in the concept of practical wisdom. Unfortunately this escape route fares just as badly, as St Thomas Aquinas (who revived the work of Aristotle in Western Europe) pointed out nearly 800 years ago.[22] A virtuous person has both excellence of character and practical wisdom: our character provides us with the desire and drive, and our practical wisdom enables us to direct our desires towards the right ends. So how do we identify someone with these excellences? Someone has practical wisdom because they choose the right ends; but to identify the right ends they must have *ethica arete*. But to have *ethica arete* someone must be capable of choosing the right ends, they must have practical wisdom, and again the circularity remains.

Aristotle must himself have been aware of this circularity, but he saw it as a fact about virtue, not a problem with his argument, which meant the two excellences were so co-dependent. The external route that Aristotle would have taken to know who the virtuous people were was to look around him at the good people of Athens. He doesn't need to give a definition of 'virtuous person' which is free from circularity, because it would have been clear to him and his audience who these people were. The virtuous person is someone who has all the qualities that were valued by the middle classes in Athens: people with virtues we would also recognise in a moral sense (they are kind, courageous, just, generous, honest, etc.); but also people with virtues we wouldn't necessarily now value in a moral sense (pride, ambition, wit, righteous indignation, etc.).

So Aristotle may avoid a charge of circularity by pointing to the virtuous people who live all around him. But closely following from this account is the criticism that has been frequently made of the supporters of virtue ethics (including Aristotle, Hume and Aquinas), namely that they are simply describing the values of their social class and age, and their lists of virtues are the preferred characteristics of that class and age. There just don't seem to be any accepted criteria for determining what is a genuine virtue and what isn't. In fact, it seems as if deciding what is a virtue, such as friendliness, or a vice, such as rudeness, is a matter of personal opinion, perhaps a highly informed one (Aristotle was one of the most widely read and travelled intellects of his age) but an opinion nevertheless.

Two thousand years after Aristotle, David Hume put forward his own theory of virtue ethics in his *Enquiry Concerning the Principle of Morals* (1752). In the *Enquiry* Hume argues, like Aristotle, that we have a general agreement about what counts as a virtue and what counts as a vice. However, for Hume, our identification of an action as 'virtuous' or 'vicious' does not pick out some special feature in the behaviour itself; rather we identify something as virtuous because of the feeling of approval that we have for that behaviour. So Hume offers a psychological account of the virtues, and this account does offer an escape route from the charge of circularity. We now have an external criterion to judge something as virtuous or vicious: does it give us a feeling of approval or disapproval? However, this is at the cost of seeing a virtue as a character trait, and as a trait governed by reason (rather than emotion), which are two features of Aristotle's ethics that it's hard to imagine him surrendering. We return to the issue of the meaning of 'virtue' and other moral terms below, page 172.

Summary of Aristotle's virtue ethics

1   Virtue ethics takes an agent-centred approach to morality, in contrast to the act-centred approach adopted by utilitarians (and other consequentialists) and by Kantians (and other deontological theorists). The origins of virtue ethics lie in ancient Greece, most particularly in the philosophy of Plato and Aristotle. But virtue ethics has been revived in recent years as an alternative to consequentialist and deontological theorists.

2 Aristotle's virtue ethics is articulated in his *Nicomachean Ethics* (or simply the *Ethics*) which is an edited collection of his lecture notes for his students at the Lyceum. The *Ethics* begins with an exploration of the *summum bonum* – the Good that we are all striving to reach. Aristotle thinks we all agree on what this is, namely happiness (*eudaimonia*), in other words, living well, doing well and flourishing. But we disagree on how to achieve *eudaimonia* and Aristotle rejects the usual suggestions (a life of pleasure, or wealth, or honour, or goodness). Instead, Aristotle opts for a psychological account of happiness, based on the type of beings we are and on the function or characteristic activity we possess as a species, namely reason. Aristotle argues that this function is determined by the activities of our soul, in particular our capacity to reason. If we excel at reasoning, and thus fulfil our function well (we are 'good humans'), then we will reach *eudaimonia* (living the good life and flourishing). Another term for 'excel' is 'virtue', which is a character trait or disposition, and Aristotle spends most of the *Ethics* investigating those virtues or excellences which we need to possess in order to flourish.

3 Book two of the *Ethics* gives an account of the excellences of character (or 'moral virtues'). Aristotle thinks that we develop these virtues through practice and habituation, but these never become mindless habits. We also learn to take pleasure in acting virtuously. The skill of someone with virtue is to develop responses to situations which are the right responses, and which avoid an excessive or deficient response – in other words, someone with virtue is able to find the mean. For example, someone with the virtue of courage is able to develop her character so that she avoids rash or cowardly behaviour, which are both 'vices'.

4 Our judgements of people's characters and virtues (including our own) are based on particular types of actions, ones which give us a clue as to the person's real character. Aristotle gives a clear account of what types of actions we should be judged on, and which types are irrelevant. Voluntary acts are ones that we intended to do and we must take full responsibility for these. But some actions go against our intention (involuntary acts) and these include acts which we felt compelled to do (which we are partly responsible for) and acts which were beyond our control (which we are not responsible for). There is a further class of unintended acts (non-voluntary) which were the result of us not knowing the full facts of our situation: the key thing is that if we regret these actions once we find out the full facts, then these are treated as involuntary acts.

5   At the end of the *Ethics* Aristotle revisits the Good and suggests that contemplation is the highest goal we can strive for. This seems to contradict the rich and varied life (of skilful and virtuous behaviour, or good fortune and health, of friendship and pleasure) outlined in the rest of the *Ethics*.

Applying Aristotelian ethics

We have seen that both Kantian and utilitarian approaches were able to provide over-arching principles to guide our actions and tell us what we ought to do. However, virtue ethicists like Aristotle do not give us clear rules to follow. In contrast, virtue ethicists urge us to take a more holistic approach, so that we are harnessing all the skills available to us in order to make a correct judgement; this also means balancing a number of different values that pull in different directions. For the virtue ethicist, each situation presents itself to us differently, but over time someone who is virtuous will tend to conform to the sorts of values that deontologists and consequentialists espouse (trying to do good, trying to do what's right and fair, etc.).

Virtue ethics has been accused of vagueness, but philosophers like Rosalind Hursthouse have defended virtue ethics by arguing that it does offer us action guides in the form of v-rules (page 152). These rules are derived from the dispositions that we hold to be virtues and vices, in other words, dispositions that we value and praise, and dispositions that we condemn. Hursthouse lists a wide range of virtues, which include being: compassionate, benevolent, generous, conscientious, fair, responsible, caring, courageous, public-spirited, having good-will, empathy, integrity and self-respect. The list is long, but there is an even longer list of vices, which include being: self-interested, mean, callous, cruel, spiteful, dishonest, thoughtless, unjust, dishonourable, disloyal, lazy, unfair, irresponsible, uncaring, cowardly, materialistic, anti-social, greedy, envious, small-minded, arrogant, lacking integrity, etc.[23] This is a useful list to start with and provides the foundations for virtue ethics (in the way that the categorical imperative is foundational for Kant, and the principle of utility is foundational for Mill). We should note that the list is not necessarily the list that Aristotle would provide, and although there is an overlap, there are significant differences. So, in applying virtue ethics to the dilemmas, we are actually applying an Aristotelian-inspired virtue ethics (such as can be found in Hursthouse or MacIntyre) rather than Aristotle's ethics itself.

▶ **ACTIVITY**

1   What other character traits that are valued and praised would you add to Hursthouse's list?

2   What character traits that are condemned would you add to the list?

So, from the perspective of virtue ethics, what do we actually judge? The questions asked by someone who is taking an Aristotelian virtue ethics approach to a moral dilemma will be:

- What virtues are being demonstrated or reinforced in this situation?
- What vices are being demonstrated or reinforced?
- How can practical wisdom guide us to the right action in this situation?
- How will the various possible actions impact on the character traits and dispositions of the people involved?
- What is the motive for the various courses of action?
- What dispositions (virtuous or vicious ones) does each course of action stem from?

Let us apply this approach to the five issues outlined above (pages 6–11).

Crime and punishment

One of the problems we might have with virtue ethics is that it does not attempt to establish a definitive list of virtues, one which is universal or objective in the way that the foundations of Kantian and utilitarian ethics claim to be universal. We saw above (page 153) that some philosophers have argued that there is a common agreement between many of the virtues, and this is particularly true of modern Western democracies which value freedom of speech, the rule of law, tolerance and plurality. However, even between countries with such a deeply shared set of values there are differences, and none is more divisive than that brought up by a discussion of the death penalty.

▶ ACTIVITY

Read CP1 and CP2 (page 7). What would a virtue ethicist say?

CP1

Capital punishment is the intentional killing of someone by the state, and outside the United States most democracies have rejected the practice. The death penalty is forbidden in member countries of the European Union, but in the United States it is legal in 32 of its states: so what are the virtues (or vices) that could determine whether governments should support the use of capital punishment?

The virtue of justice is, for Aristotle, a pivotal virtue encompassing ideas of fairness, of equality, of law-abidingness, together with the idea that a punishment should be proportional to the crime, 'evil for evil ... good for good' (the *Ethics*, 1131a1). It is this proportional aspect of justice that supporters of capital punishment emphasise when they talk about 'retributive justice': if someone like Jon Mason has committed murder then the punishment should be proportionate, which means to some people that Jon himself should be killed. Aristotle himself does not discuss capital punishment but he does argue that 'proportionality' is not a simple concept. It involves the application of practical wisdom, and an understanding of the motives and the circumstances of the people committing the crime – Aristotle is not advocating a simplistic eye-for-an-eye form of justice. A virtue ethicist might ask of those people who seek capital punishment on the grounds of retributive justice, what their motives are; and if their motives are fuelled by anger, revenge or hatred, then it is not the virtue of justice they are displaying, but an array of vices.

Practical wisdom, itself a virtue, should prompt you as Home Secretary to further research: Is the action, i.e. the death penalty, going to lead to the outcome that you want? Do you want a deterrent, or retribution? Do you want to model (in the sense of 'set an example of') dispositions that you would like to see in your citizens? You may have rejected retribution on the grounds above, but how about introducing capital punishment as a deterrent? Research indicates that countries which have the death penalty do not have lower murder rates (America has far higher murder rates than the democracies that have rejected the death penalty); and within America, states without the death penalty have lower murder rates, although this could be due to other factors. So research shows that there is no conclusive evidence that capital punishment works as a deterrent. Capital punishment is also a brutal, dehumanising and degrading process, as brilliantly conveyed at the ending of Kieslowski's *A Short Film About Killing* which shows the execution of a murderer. The lack of compassion, combined with the multitude of vicious characteristics that fuel the desire for the death penalty (revenge, anger, hatred, brutality) may lead you to continue to reject the death penalty, even in this horrific case.

▶ **ACTIVITY**

How might a utilitarian respond to the virtue ethicist's claim that compassion outweighs a family's and a community's desire for retribution?

CP2

Aristotle's doctrine of the mean proposes that nearly every action, or emotion, can be performed excessively, or deficiently, or appropriately (which is the mean). However, Aristotle goes on to say in the *Ethics* (1107a10) that for some actions, such as murder and theft, there is never an appropriate performance of them. On this original Aristotelian view it is never appropriate to steal, and you should not steal the drug even though your partner may die as a result.

This is not the view taken by modern virtue ethicists, who have been inspired by Aristotle's comments that we should judge the appropriate thing to do on a case-by-case basis, and that sometimes even the mean (i.e. the appropriate) thing to do can be an extreme (see page 135 above). In the case of stealing the Tastraphon, you may be acting out of benevolence: your desire to help people, to reduce the amount of pain in the world and possibly increase the amount of pleasure or happiness. However, a single action isn't enough to judge whether you are benevolent – the virtue ethicist would want to know: Is benevolence a part of your character? Are you habitually benevolent? It is possible that you are only acting benevolently in this case because it is your partner whose life is at risk, but that generally you are a thoughtless or inconsiderate person? Even if your action were a benevolent one, it would at the same time be a dishonest one and it would deprive other patients of the drug who might then go on to suffer. Are you a dishonest or thoughtless person, or is this theft a one-off act of criminality motivated by love, compassion and benevolence? It seems in this case, that the dispositions of honesty and thoughtfulness (consideration of those people who would be affected by your theft of the drug) are competing with your disposition for benevolence and love (of your partner). Partiality, or bias, is a special feature of certain relationships that we have, recognised in virtue ethics;[24] the question is does our partiality towards our immediate loved ones outweigh our consideration of other people in the community? You may have to utilise your practical wisdom to find an alternative, and legitimate, means of getting this drug (a crowd-sourcing website to raise the money, an internet campaign to change NHS rules on this drug, a charitable event held by your friends …?)

▶ ACTIVITY

How might a virtue ethicist go about ranking competing dispositions (e.g. an act of compassion and love for a close family member versus an act of honesty and thoughtfulness towards people we don't know)?

War

We saw above (page 124) that Alasdair MacIntyre's revival of virtue ethics led him to consider the roles that we have in society and to redefine these in Aristotelian terms as 'social practices'. Warfare has been thought of as a distinct practice, and there are associated virtues and responsibilities attached to this practice. A soldier is not only expected to be courageous and truthful (which for MacIntyre are virtues that underpin social practices[25]), but is also expected to develop military virtues including discipline, obedience to superiors, loyalty to comrades and patriotism to their country. But warfare is a dehumanising experience, and soldiers may be tempted or encouraged to develop dispositions that are clearly vicious ('*kakia*' in Aristotle's terminology): to be cruel, to spread fear, to dehumanise their enemy. It is by treating people in this way, as mere obstacles or threats, that soldiers may feel better able to defeat or kill the enemy. However, there is also an expectation in modern armies that their forces respect the Geneva Conventions for the humanitarian treatment of non-combatants, including civilians, wounded enemies and prisoners of war. The responsibility to these humanitarian conventions is an important feature within the application of virtue ethics to the morality of war.

▶ ACTIVITY

Read W1 and W2 (pages 8–9). What would a virtue ethicist say?

W1

The modern soldier is expected to exhibit the virtue of humanitarian care, and as an officer you will feel it is your duty to locate and neutralise the biological weapons in order to prevent the harm these could do. Remember that for a virtue ethicist, Kantians and utilitarians don't have a special claim to the moral values of 'duty' and 'consequences' – these are just two virtues in the vast armoury of virtues available to the virtue ethicist. So there is some moral weight to be attached to making every effort to find out from your prisoners where these biological weapons are being kept – as in doing so you would be acting as a good soldier should act.

However, we saw above that as a soldier you have duties of care to prisoners of war, as well as a responsibility for adhering to the Geneva Conventions which requires you to treat non-combatants humanely. It is now widely acknowledged that 'enhanced interrogation techniques' such as waterboarding, of the kind used in Guantanamo Bay by the CIA and US Armed Forces in the early 2000s, are techniques of torture. Torture is explicitly banned by the Geneva Conventions and is inhumane; your engagement in it would therefore be vicious, both in the sense that it would be horrific, and in the sense that it would be non-virtuous. You may have reasonable motives for considering torturing the prisoner's son – you want to protect the population; but a virtue ethicist might also argue that your character and the characters of your comrades will be damaged by this act. Post-traumatic stress disorder affects a large percentage of soldiers, and if your aim is to flourish in life after the war, then you would need to consider the habits you develop (including habits of treating the enemy inhumanely) during the war that will enable you to emerge as a virtuous person. Moreover, practical wisdom exercised in this situation may lead you to seek a more effective alternative to torture: there is a strong evidence base that torture does not reliably yield useful and true information, and so the information that you extract may be worthless anyway.[26] You also need to consider why you are engaged in the war: if it is to *stop* a vicious regime which resorts to cruelty and torture, then why would you yourself engage in these practices?

▶ **ACTIVITY**

On what grounds could a utilitarian support the virtue ethicist's view that if you want to prevent a cruel regime gaining power that you should not use cruel techniques to stop them?

W2

Let us now turn to dilemma W2, which raises the question of whether a military intervention is ever justified, whether a war can be 'just'. Aristotle does believe that some wars can be just. In Book Ten of the *Ethics* he asserts that we wage war in order to live in peace and this comment is echoed elsewhere in his philosophy.[27] Remember that, for Aristotle, the virtues are a means to reaching *eudaimonia*, and a peaceful society is able to flourish as a whole because people in that society are able to flourish. Some of the specific reasons that Aristotle gives which make war justifiable (for example, the acquisition of barbarians as slaves) we would now find reprehensible, but his teleological belief that war was sometimes a justifiable means to reach a particular end, or good, sparked a discussion which still rages today. So Aristotle might take the view, in relation to scenario W2, that military intervention is justifiable if it secures a better society for Sumitania, and for the people of Sumitania.

A virtue ethics approach must also consider what virtues or vices are being exhibited or ignored and what motives the action stems from. So we need to ask whether the decision maker, in this case the Prime Minister is a belligerent person who has a tendency to declare war on anyone. Or is the Prime Minister a suspicious person who has decided to go to war because of their own paranoia (depressingly, heads of state are not the just, wise and balanced rulers that Plato and Aristotle expected – cf. Alexander the Great). Is the Prime Minister a truthful and honest person who won't deceive us about the possible existence of weapons of mass destruction? Is the motive for going to war one of compassion, which we know is highly valued as a virtue? Deciding to go to war is a formidable, life-changing experience and the motives for it must be the motives of a virtuous person. Difficulties for the modern reader emerge if we try to argue with the Aristotelian motive of 'acquisition' as a legitimate motive. What external grounds do we have for disagreeing with Aristotle (other than that 'acquisition is no longer considered a virtue')?

There is a further issue here about our responsibilities, and the responsibilities of our government, to act within international law. Virtue ethicists do ask us to consider our responsibilities given our role or position, as these require special virtues (as we saw with the soldier above). So the Prime Minister has a particular responsibility towards international law. Intervention in the internal affairs of a sovereign state is not permitted within international law except under very specific conditions, mostly notably intervention on humanitarian grounds. We know the dangers of permitting interventions, such as the programme of 'annexation' of neighbouring countries that Hitler engaged in prior to the start of the Second World War, as well as more recent military interventions including the invasion of Iraq by the United States and its coalition allies in 2003, and the destabilisation of the Crimea and Ukraine by Russia in 2014. In W2, as the UN Security Council has not ratified the intervention, the Prime Minister's unilateral action may not be legal. In which case, the Prime Minister may have to use his practical wisdom to identify other measures that could be taken to protect Sumitania and which all members of the UN Security Council would be persuaded to support. In the final analysis, the Prime Minister may argue that this military intervention is justified solely on humanitarian grounds and proceed. The problem, as we saw in the Iraq war, is the potential for a humanitarian disaster following the end of the war, meaning that the Prime Minister will have to plan for the peace as much as planning for the war.

Simulated killing (within computer games, plays, films)

▶ **ACTIVITY**

Read SK1 and SK2 (page 9). What would a virtue ethicist say?

SK1

In his seminal paper, 'Is it wrong to play violent video games?', Matt McCormick examines the response to this question from a utilitarian, Kantian and virtue ethics perspective. As technology has increased, so has the graphic realism with which violence and murder on screen can be represented, and McCormick points out that the desire for faster-paced games has led not just to killings being more graphic but more numerous as well; that would certainly be true of *Psycho-Tick*. But simulated killings, however graphic, are just that – simulated; no one is actually being hurt, which is why the act of simulated killing poses such a dilemma for most moral theories.

A utilitarian and Kantian approach may emphasise the impact the game has on real people in the real world after the game has finished, but McCormick concludes that, of all moral theories, virtue ethics is best able to articulate why it may be wrong to play violent video games, whatever their impact. He draws this conclusion on the following grounds: first, that our moral intuitions tell us that there is 'something morally objectionable' with people playing a game that graphically mimics the murder of children – even if nobody is affected. Secondly, that neither utilitarianism, nor Kantian ethics, can provide compelling reasons for why playing the game *itself* (not the eventual effect that the act may have on other people) is wrong. Only virtue ethics, according to McCormick, is able to articulate what is objectionable about taking part in the virtual murder of video games: '*engaging in simulated immoral acts erodes one's character and makes it more difficult for one to live a fulfilled eudaimonic life*'.[28]

So virtue ethics, especially of the Aristotelian flavour, does have something to say about virtual murder, even if the action does not affect other people. As you know, virtue ethics is agent-centred and not act-centred, but acts are still important to Aristotelian virtue ethics: actions contribute to habituation, which contributes to our character, which in turn contributes to how we will be inclined to behave in the future. We saw above (page 131) that building a virtuous character does not come easily, but requires careful cultivation. McCormick argues that by indulging in the excessive, indulgent and wrongful acts of games like *Psycho-Tick* we are 'cultivating the wrong sort of character'. This sounds convincing, but there is an important empirical question here that McCormick does not address: whether cruel or callous behaviour in the virtual world of *Psycho-Tick* is actually converted (however unconsciously) into cruel or callous behaviour in the real world, which certainly would be the 'wrong sort of character'.

McCormick may not need this empirical evidence for his argument still to work. After all, actions that don't contribute to habituation of the virtues are an 'opportunity cost' – in other words, time spent doing one thing is a cost against time spent doing something more valuable. Let us imagine that empirical research has conclusively shown that there is no harmful impact on your character as a result of playing video games, thus time spent playing the games is 'morally neutral' time – the habits you're developing, in McCormick's words are 'virtueless'. Even in this case (which may not be true), time spent on reinforcing virtueless dispositions, like gaming skills, is time taken away from developing virtuous dispositions (like volunteering in the community, or developing friendships, or contributing to the daily chores of any household). A virtue ethicist may conclude, and you may agree, that violent gaming at best fails to develop any virtues, and at worst encourages vices, neither of which would help the gamer to flourish or lead a good life.

SK2

'Greek tragedy' is a phrase that has entered our language, and rightly so: the writers of ancient Greece created a body of work to rival any in Western literature, and their stories, characterisation, tragic and dramatic irony, and narrative structures still hold sway over our theatrical and cinematic arts.[29] Aristotle wrote extensively on theatre in his work the *Poetics*, focusing in particular on tragedy. Aristotle's analysis of tragedy is filtered through his interest in how this dramatic form can reflect our efforts to reach the good life, and the effect that tragedy can have on the audience's emotions. The virtue ethicist can usefully employ Aristotle's theory of tragedy to understand the effects on our character of watching murderous acts in film and theatre.

The key elements for Aristotle on tragedy are the journey of the hero, who is a great man (and for Aristotle it usually was a male protagonist), towards some sort of crisis, usually as a result of *hamartia* (an error or a flaw in the hero), which then leads to the denouement, catharsis and the resolution of the crisis. For Aristotle, then, theatre is a form which explores the vulnerability of a good life, even of a near-perfect life, to external factors (see page 127 above): errors, bad luck, other people, the gods, society – all of which mean the hero's life can go dramatically and horribly wrong, sorely testing his character. According to Martha Nussbaum's account of Aristotle, tragedies enable playwrights to explore, in a safe way, the gap between the ideal life and the fragility of our own lives, always vulnerable to disaster.[30] As well as being a crucible in which *eudaimonia* and character can be safely tested, Aristotle argued that the theatre brought emotional benefits to the audience. In the strict narrative trajectory of a tragedy we see the hero's life fall apart (through *hamartia*), which raises feelings of both fear and pity in the audience. As the hero approaches the denouement, or *scène à faire*, the audience's anxieties intensify until the emotion is given a cathartic release and purged as the drama is resolved, the hero dies, or defeats the beast, or finds out that his wife is his mother (page 142), etc. So for Aristotle, theatre, and tragedy in particular, has a purifying effect on the audience – through this cathartic process – enabling them to be better able to cope with tragedy in their own life. Theatre, then, even in its most tragic form, can restore us to psychological health.

▶ **ACTIVITY**

Imagine you are a virtue ethicist interviewing the audience who have just watched *Oedipus-X*. You ask them: about their reasons for attending; about whether they enjoyed it; about their reaction to the murders.

What types of motives, behaviour and responses in the audience would indicate to you that vicious and unhealthy (rather than virtuous and healthy) dispositions were being nurtured by ultra-violent plays like this?

Theatre in the ancient Greek tradition contains no simulated killing, and the horrific violence of Greek tragedies only takes place off-stage, described by the chorus rather than shown to the audience. The experience of modern theatre audiences and cinema goers, who flock to watch simulated killing in Tarantino movies or this new play by Susan Cain, may still be a cathartic experience. Audiences may find relief, and release, in watching simulated violence as Aristotle describes – after all, the negative emotions essential to catharsis (pity and fear) are triggered every day by horrific news stories from around the world. Aristotle believed that without the cathartic effect of theatre we are liable to become 'possessed' by these emotions, damaging the balance in our souls. We are thrilled by fear, but we don't want to be afraid in real life, so watching a play like Susan Cain's enables us to indulge in the thrill of fear and to purge that desire. But the point made by McCormick above could apply here: video games are compulsive, habitual and repetitive which is why a virtue ethicist might be worried about the dispositions being developed. Seeing a one-off play like Susan Cain's should not worry the virtue ethicist too much; but watching the play over and over again, or watching the new strand of torture-based horror movies over and over again raises the point McCormick made, that this habitual indulgence in simulated killing creates the wrong sorts of emotions.

The treatment of animals

When discussing the treatment of non-human animals, many moral philosophers would want to first ask the question: 'What is the moral status of other animals?' They would argue that once we have clarified this question we can then determine whether or not that animal has **rights**, and we have duties to it, or whether its interests and preferences should be included in our utility calculus. But how would a virtue ethicist approach the issue? Aristotle believed that there was a natural hierarchy of living things and, as part of his teleological view, one of the functions of things lower down the hierarchy (e.g. animals) was to serve the needs (e.g. as food) of those beings higher up the hierarchy e.g. animals However, let us look at what a modern virtue ethicist, without Aristotle's teleological baggage, might say about the treatment of animals.

Rosalind Hursthouse has argued that the question of the moral status of animals is not a question that a virtue ethicist needs to answer.[31] This is partly because virtue ethicists have a more holistic approach (and therefore, for Hursthouse, offer a more sophisticated approach); and partly because the 'moral status' issue is highly flawed: there is no familiar set of facts that some animals share but which other animals don't share, that grants them a higher moral status. Instead, there are many different ways in which animals can be grouped (wild animals, working animals, pets, animals in laboratories, free-range animals bred for food, factory-farmed animals), each of which attracts an associated set of responsibilities, duties and other virtues that we have to consider on a case-by-case basis.

▶ ACTIVITY

Read A1 and A2 (page 10). How might a virtue ethicist respond?

A1

What a virtue ethicist asks us is how we respond to the treatment of animals. Factory-farmed animals, like the chickens in the first example, undergo horrific suffering before they are slaughtered and arrive at our supermarkets and fast-food outlets in their millions. Broiler chickens (birds raised for meat) are bred to develop abnormally overweight bodies which cause crippling and painful skeletal deformities. Chickens are social animals, but caged in less than a square foot of cage, they peck and attack each other, leading to the practice of debeaking of chicks after they hatch (their beak is cut off with a hot knife, without anaesthesia). Chickens live short lives of intense stress, pain and disease until they are eventually slaughtered. Not, we would agree, a life of *eudaimonia*.

Hursthouse asks: 'Can we deny that these practices are cruel, or that they are callous?' And the straightforward answer is: 'No, we can't deny that.' Yet it is highly likely that you eat chicken, and it is also highly likely that you don't need to eat chicken (or any factory-farmed meat) in order to survive; you eat it because it is convenient, it's cheap and you like it. In which case, you are failing to exhibit compassion; and you are also failing to be temperate (as Hursthouse points out, temperance requires that we do not pursue pleasure while ignoring the claims of other virtues). It is hard to identify any competing virtues which would recommend that we carry on eating factory-farmed chicken: kindness? generosity? courage? justice? Can you think of a virtue that has a genuine claim on us which competes with compassion in this situation? In which case, virtue ethics recommends that you become more compassionate, that you stop ignoring the disgusting and cruel practices of factory farming, and you change your eating habits accordingly. You might guess that two of the authors of this book are vegetarian (you'll have to ask the other one himself why he isn't!).

A2

Is the virtue ethicist going to make a similar point about animal experimentation? The fact that the subjects in these experiments are primates like us may be a red-herring (!), as we saw above that the moral status and ranking of animals isn't what's at stake. The issue about compassion, as raised above, is important here: to ignore cruelty and callousness is to fail to be compassionate. The virtue of compassion requires that we act to prevent or minimise the cruelty of the act: so are we failing to be compassionate if we fail to act against animal cruelty? The question a virtue ethicist might want to ask then is: 'Are animal experiments cruel?' Moral philosophers, such as Tom Regan,[32] have argued that cruelty occurs both where there is unnecessary pain and where the person inflicting the pain either derives pleasure from that pain or is indifferent to it. For Regan, this means that people who inflict pain but regret it (for example vivisectionists experimenting on animals) are not being cruel. It would follow, from Regan's view, that some experiments are not cruel, and therefore it is possible to still be compassionate even while permitting animal experimentation or at least by not acting against animal experimentation. Hursthouse disagrees, arguing that cruelty is the infliction of any unnecessary pain, independently of how we feel about it, whether we regret it or not. The question for Hursthouse then becomes: 'Is the pain of animal experiments necessary?' (i.e. necessary to secure some good). Hursthouse argues that generally they are not necessary. First, because tests may be done to create new products (e.g. in cosmetics), when old products are just fine; secondly, because there is duplication of experiments on animals across the world; thirdly, because the goods secured by the experiment are disproportionate to the suffering created to bring them about. So in those cases where we know there is cruelty (where the pain caused is unnecessary), we should react compassionately. This may involve avoiding buying products known to be the result of unnecessary animal experimentation; or it may involve actively campaigning against unnecessary animal experimentation. The virtuous person should also hope for, and look forward to, the day when no animal experimentation is carried out.

▶ **ACTIVITY**

Would the virtue ethicist give the same answer if the subject of the experiments was not a chimpanzee but a dog, or a rat, or a crab?

Deception and the telling of lies

The two scenarios on page 11 both focus on the failure of the subject to tell the truth. We will see below how some philosophers draw a fine distinction between lying and deception, but all forms of virtue ethics, especially its Aristotelian form, require us to develop an honest character. It is by being honest together that we as a society will also be able to flourish. Our success depends upon the success of our communication, which itself depends on our trust in the information exchanged, the promises made, the judgements cast, etc. It is by being honest that we as individuals will ultimately flourish, people will trust us, people will look to us for information and advice. Peter Geach argues that the virtue of honesty enables us to develop our practical wisdom; or rather that the vice of dishonesty undermines our practical wisdom.[33] Honesty, like all virtues, is developed through habituation; and dishonesty (even the telling of small lies, or white lies) is also a habit. Dishonesty is a habit that enables us to escape easily from difficult situations: when you haven't done your homework, when you are being interviewed for a job, when your boss asks you awkward questions about data or performance ... a lie can free us from further efforts. But the habit of lying means that we don't work hard to find alternative solutions to those tricky situations, i.e. we don't use our practical wisdom, which means that we are not genuinely equipping ourselves for further tricky situations. Difficult situations don't go away in life, and lying is no permanent solution to them – you simply get a reputation as a liar. But Geach argues that there is a difference between being dishonest by lying, and avoiding being honest by deception. Geach was influenced more by the deeply Christian virtue ethics of Aquinas, than those of Aristotle, and believed that lying is never permitted. But he gives the example of Saint Athanasius who was escaping in a boat from his persecutors when they rowed past in the opposite direction. As they passed, the persecutors asked 'Where is that traitor Athanasius?', to which Athanasius replied 'Not far away.' Geach argues that Athanasius was clever enough to avoid telling the truth (to deceive) without actually lying, and so no damage was done to his honest disposition.

As we have seen throughout this discussion, real moral dilemmas are messy, complex affairs, and virtue ethicists believe their theory is well placed to deal with this complexity as the theory offers no simple answers. It will always consider the range of motives involved, what virtues or vices are potentially being exhibited, and the impact of the action on everyone concerned, in particular the impact on people's characters (as it is this impact that will affect their choices, virtuous or vicious, in the future). Both the first and the second dilemma bring out the importance of two particular virtues: loyalty and honesty.

▶ ACTIVITY

Read DTL1 and DTL2 on page 11. What would a virtue ethicist say?

DTL1

In the first scenario, Shelly is married to Jacob, and generally, with any marriage, various promises and vows are made at the start of the marriage and various expectations are set up, including the expectation that they will be faithful to each other. So Shelly, even though she has been let down by her husband, still has a responsibility to him to be loyal, at least while they are married. Marriages also require a special level of trust in order to work, and dishonesty within a marriage can tear away at that trust with distressing consequences (particularly if there are children in the marriage). It is understandable why Shelly wants to act in this way – but there are special demands made on her by her marriage, demands of loyalty and honesty, that mean she should not lie to her husband. However, the application of practical wisdom (what ultimate outcome does Shelly want to achieve here, and how can she best achieve it?), the virtue of temperance (controlling her desire to be with her neighbour) and emotional intelligence (what would be the impact of this lie on her husband?) may mean that Shelly eventually does begin a successful relationship with her neighbour, but only after an honest conversation with, and separation from, her husband. So a virtue ethicist may conclude that she should not explore the new relationship at this stage, and should start telling the truth to her husband.

DTL2

The case of the axe murderer also involves the virtues of honesty and loyalty, but this time they are pitted against each other. This situation also differs from the first in that you are deceiving rather than lying (a bit like St Athanasius): strictly speaking it's true that nobody with muddy boots came into your house. But that isn't what the axe murderer wanted to know, and you know this yourself, so although you haven't lied, you have deceived and so you are not displaying the key virtue of honesty. For other types of ethical theory, this may present a problem, but an Aristotelian virtue ethicist, one who takes things on a case-by-case basis, may argue that we need to apply the virtues that are the right thing to do in this situation. If you are someone who is generally honest, then deceiving someone in a one-off (life-or-death) situation isn't going to undermine your tendency and inclination to be honest. An axe murderer at your door is just such a situation. We have seen that our relationships with other people can bring with them special demands: our partners, friends and families require loyalty that goes beyond our loyalty to strangers in our community. So you do have a special loyalty to your friend not to betray him, and to keep him safe from harm. This loyalty lays claim on you in a way that easily outweighs the claim that 'being honest to a stranger (with an axe)' has, and so in this case a virtue ethicist may conclude that although you haven't told a lie you are still being dishonest, but that dishonesty is the appropriate response here.

1.2 Ethical language: What is the status of ethical language?

> *Theft in Buna [the factory], punished by civil law, is authorised and encouraged by the SS; theft in the camp, severely repressed by the SS, is considered by the civilians as a normal exchange operation; theft among prisoners is generally punished, but the punishment strikes the thief and the victim with equal gravity. We now invite the reader to contemplate the possible meaning in Auschwitz of the words 'good' and 'evil', 'just' and 'unjust'; let everyone judge ... how much of our ordinary moral world could survive on this side of the barbed wire.[1]*
>
> Primo Levi

Ethics and the philosophy of language

Primo Levi was one of the few people who survived Auschwitz, the largest slave-labour and extermination camp constructed by the Nazis. In this world of 'death and phantoms', Levi describes a process of complete dehumanisation, of bestial degradation. 'It is a man who kills, who creates or suffers injustice; it is no longer a man who, having lost all his restraint, shares his bed with a corpse ... [who] waits for his neighbour to die in order to take his piece of bread.' [2] Levi describes in horrific detail the way of life which emerged among the *Häftling* (prisoners), based on desperate survival from hour to hour. He challenges us to say how our moral concepts have any meaning or application in this hell on Earth. Levi's question demands an answer: What is the meaning of moral judgements like 'good' and 'evil', 'just' and 'unjust'? Are moral judgements discoveries or decisions: discovered, like the unearthing of physical laws about the universe; or decided upon, like the construction of civil laws in most societies?

This question about the meaning of moral judgements is more abstract than the questions we've looked at so far in this section, about how we should live and what we ought to do. We have already needed, on several occasions, to take a more abstract approach – to ask about the meaning of words like 'good' and 'virtue' – in order to assist us in our understanding of normative ethics. Philosophers refer to this more abstract level of enquiry as meta-ethics.[3] Meta-ethics addresses fundamental questions about the status, meaning and origins of ethical terms, which many modern philosophers feel must be answered before the more practical issue of how we should live our lives can be addressed. Meta-ethical questions relating to ethical language include:

- Are there any moral facts?
- What do moral concepts refer to (or mean)?
- Does moral language make statements about reality, i.e. statements which could be true or false?
- Can moral terms (such as 'good') be defined by natural terms (such as 'happiness')?

At the end of our discussion of virtues on page 156, two different views emerged about what 'virtue' referred to, i.e. about what we were judging when we called something a virtue. Aristotle thought of virtues as referring to particular character traits: courage, self-control, practical wisdom, etc. This seems like common sense: if I say that you are virtuous then I am talking about your behaviour, the way you are disposed to act. But Hume disagreed, arguing that our judgement of someone's behaviour as virtuous did not spring from their behaviour, but from *our feelings* about their behaviour. So when I say that you are virtuous I am expressing my feelings of approval about your behaviour; I am not referring to anything intrinsic in your behaviour itself. One way of putting this might be to say that, for Aristotle, our term 'virtue' reflects something 'out there' (in people's behaviour), whereas for Hume, 'virtue' reflects something 'in here' (the feelings of sympathy provoked by people's behaviour).

Figure 1.24
The differences between Aristotle's and Hume's view of what a virtue such as courage means

The question 'What does "virtue" mean?' is a meta-ethical question. This interest in the meaning of moral terms and judgements is a common concern of meta-ethics, and in the last century this concern became central to moral philosophy. In the early twentieth century some Anglo-American philosophers started to reflect on whether, over the centuries, philosophy had actually made any progress in answering philosophical questions. It occurred to some philosophers that perhaps the answers philosophers had proposed, and even the questions they had asked, might not mean anything. So these philosophers turned their attention to refining the most important tool that they had at their disposal, namely language. This change in focus away from substantive philosophical issues towards an investigation of language became known as the 'linguistic turn'. Moral philosophy was no exception to this switch in direction, and for the first half of the last century, moral philosophers focused on the philosophy of language. These moral philosophers no longer made moral judgements, or gave us guidance on how to act; instead, they wished to clarify what moral judgements meant and what moral terms like 'good' and 'right' referred to.

The differences between Hume's and Aristotle's understanding of 'virtue' highlight one of the most important issues in the philosophy of language: do terms refer to something 'real' and 'out there' in the world, or are they something else altogether (for example, expressions of some personal feelings). If they are making claims about something real then we can argue about whether those claims are true or whether they are false. But if moral language does not refer to anything real, then they are not making true or false claims about the world at all. The following activity aims to tease out some of your own intuitions about this issue, about whether a term refers to something real or not.

 Experimenting with ideas

For each of issues 1–8 select the one option that best describes your beliefs. Then answer the additional questions A) and B) below.

1 Where are **rainbows?**
   a) In raindrops in the sky
   b) In cheesy songs
   c) In the minds of people who see them
   d) Nowhere

2 Where does your **soul** reside?
   a) In a spiritual realm which we cannot speak of
   b) 'Only in my music, dude, only in my music'
   c) If what is meant by 'soul' is 'certain brain states' then it resides in your brain
   d) Any answer to this question does not admit of meaningful, i.e. verifiable, truth-conditions and should therefore be dismissed as nonsense

3 An **electron** is:
   a) a tiny little particle that revolves around a neutron.
   b) I don't know – some kind of alien from Planet Electra?
   c) a useful theoretical concept that helps us to understand certain features of the world.
   d) an invention designed to make arty students drop GCSE physics.

4 **Love** is:
   a) a spiritual union of two souls.
   b) an invention to increase the sale of Valentine's cards and perfume.
   c) coming home to find your socks have been ironed and dinner on the table.
   d) caused by a hormonal imbalance in the brain.

5 Are post-boxes actually **red?**
   a) Of course they are
   b) Not round here, because they're all covered in graffiti
   c) No, redness is a property of the mind – a mere perception
   d) *You* might see them as red, but I see them as green.

6 People say that murder is **wrong** because:
  a) it really is wrong to kill.
  b) they are deluded, the slaves of conventional morality.
  c) they have strong feelings of disapproval that need to be expressed.
  d) it's true by definition: what we mean by murder is 'wrongful killing' so of course wrongful killing is wrong.

7 This **book** on moral philosophy is:
  a) a solid object that I can store away on my bookshelf.
  b) about moral philosophy.
  c) just a series of sensations (white, rectangular, etc.) bound together by my mind
  d) full of fancy theories that mean nothing in real life.

8 Beauty is:
  a) a perfect quality that we can all have knowledge of when we see it.
  b) the name of an exclusive new perfume from Paris.
  c) in the eye of the beholder.
  d) an evolutionary indication of health and potential child-rearing/bearing capacity.

Read through your answers again. For each of the words in **bold**:

A Do you think it refers to a property or an object that exists independently of us, out there in the world?

B Do you think it refers to something that is not independent of us, not real, and not 'out there' in the world?

If you answered a) for any of the questions then you are a '**realist**' about the word in bold. Some philosophers might say that you have an '**ontological** commitment' to the existence of the property or object being talked about. In other words, you believe that it actually exists independently of you, out there in the world. If you answered c) for any of the questions then you are an '**anti-realist**' about the word in bold. We might say that you have no ontological commitment to the existence of the property or thing. In other words, you do not believe it exists in the world, and the word refers to something else (for example, some property in our mind). If you generally answered b) then you may need to meet with your lecturer after the next class to have a little chat about your attitude. If you generally answered d) then you are a hardened cynic who needs to lighten up a bit.

An introduction to realism, anti-realism, cognitivism and non-cognitivism

Meta-ethics raises the issue of the status of ethical language, by asking 'What does this term mean?' or 'What does this word refer to?' And there are two pairs of philosophical positions that we need to clarify before we look at the specific theories that philosophers have proposed which answer these questions. The two conceptual pairings emerge from our attempts to understand and define contested terms like 'beauty' or 'good' or 'electron' or even 'red'. (Sometimes in philosophy it seems that every word is a contested term!) The two pairs of positions are:

■ Realism and anti-realism
■ Cognitivism and non-cognitivism

Realism and anti-realism

The first pair of positions (**realism** and **anti-realism**) are broadly concerned with the question of whether the things we are talking about refer to something real, objective, or 'out there' in the world. The second pair (**cognitivism** and **non-cognitivism**) are concerned with whether the sentences, in which we talk about these things, express beliefs that are true or false.

Let us first look at the division between realism, which you would have first encountered when studying epistemology at AS-level, and anti-realism. We saw above that if we believe a term (such as 'beauty') refers to something real and 'out there' in the world, then we are realists about that term. Conversely, if we believe a term (such as 'wrong') doesn't refer to something out there in the world, then we are anti-realists. To illustrate the distinction between realism and anti-realism let us look again at some of the terms given in the activity above. In Figure 1.25 we sketch what a realist and an anti-realist might say about the reference of some terms contested within a particular academic discipline.

Contested term	Academic discipline	Realists might say this term refers to …	Anti-realists might say this term refers to …
Beauty	Aesthetics	Beautiful things out there in the world	Our response to objects that we have been socially conditioned to call 'beautiful'
Red	Epistemology	The property of redness in the world	A mental image or idea of redness
Electron	Philosophy of science	A quantum object which has a negative electrical charge	A term which has a place in a complex theoretical system that usefully explains certain phenomena witnessed in laboratories
Wrong	Moral philosophy	The extent to which an action produces pain and suffering	An expression of our disapproval at certain types of action

Figure 1.25 Table showing what realists and anti-realists might say about contested terms

It's worth noting that realists do not necessarily agree on what the precise thing is that a term refers to. There are differences among anti-realist positions too; there might be many different anti-realist accounts of what a term such as 'beauty' refers to: cultural conventions, an indication of potential child-rearing qualities, an inner feeling of desire, etc. What realists share is their claim that terms refer to something 'out there' in the world, which exists independently of our minds. What anti-realist positions share is their rejection of realism. So how might these two positions be applied to ethical language?

Let us take the statement:

It is wrong to be dishonest.

A moral realist would say that we are making a factual claim about the world, namely that there is a property in the world somewhere, in this case 'wrongness' (or 'badness' or 'lack of goodness'), and dishonesty possesses that property. This claim may turn out to be false, perhaps it isn't always wrong to be dishonest (see page 169 above), but nonetheless a realist believes there are facts which can help us determine the truth or falsity of this claim, and so at least some of our moral statements are true. Later in the chapter we examine two of the main moral realist positions:

- Some realists, such as the utilitarians, argue that there are 'natural' properties that our moral terms pick out, such as the pleasure or pain produced by an action. This position is known as naturalism (pages 181–8).
- Other types of realists, such as G.E. Moore, reject naturalism and argue that there are special, non-natural, features of the world which our moral terms refer to and which can be known through our moral intuitions. A position of this type is known as *non-naturalism* (pages 188–96).

On the other hand, an anti-realist would reject the position that this is a factual claim. In this chapter you will encounter two kinds of anti-realism:

- There are moral anti-realists who argue that when using moral terms like 'wrong' we are not making a claim about the world, because this term doesn't actually refer to any property or fact in the world. This version of anti-realism is known as moral non-cognitivism, and we look at two types:
  - Some anti-realists, known as the *emotivists*, argue that a moral term like 'wrong' is simply an expression of a feeling of disapproval (pages 201–7).
  - Other anti-realists, known as *prescriptivists*, argue that a moral term like 'wrong' is a way of saying to someone 'Don't do that!' (pages 207–11).
- Before we look at non-cognitivism we also examine an anti-realist position which accepts that the moral terms like 'wrong' are part of an attempt to make claims about the world. This form of anti-realism argues that unfortunately these moral claims are systematically false, in other words, they can never be true, and this is because there is no property in the world that the term 'wrong' refers to at all. This version of moral anti-realism is known as *error theory*. This is analogous within the philosophy of religion to the atheist saying '"God is omnipotent" is false, and will always be false whenever we assert it, because there is

nothing in the world that "God" or "omnipotence" refers to at all' (pages 196–9).

So in moral philosophy, realists and anti-realists disagree over whether ethical sentences are making factual claims about the world and over whether ethical terms refer to properties in the world. This debate is closely related to the disagreement between our second pair of positions (cognitivism/non-cognitivism): does ethical language express beliefs that are true or false, or does it have another function entirely?

Cognitivism and non-cognitivism

You may remember that you have already encountered cognitivism and non-cognitivism when looking at religious language.[4] Cognitivists argue that, within a particular area of human thought and discourse, sentences used in that area are ones that express beliefs: they are statements or propositions. Moreover, one of the particular properties about statements, and about the beliefs they reflect, is that they are either true or false – they have a truth-value. The main task for the moral cognitivist is to articulate how ethical statements are true or false. On the other hand, moral non-cognitivists reject this view, arguing that ethical language may still be meaningful, but it certainly doesn't consist of statements or express beliefs capable of being true or false. The main task for the non-cognitivist is to explain what ethical language is talking about if it's not talking about the world. As you will have seen from the activity above, you can be a realist and anti-realist about different aspects of human life and discourse, and the same is true for cognitivism and non-cognitivism. For example, you may be a cognitivist about ethical language, while also being a non-cognitivist about religious language.

You may remember if you have read our AS-level Philosophy book, the example we used when looking at the status of religious language, to illustrate the difference between cognitivism and non-cognitivism:

The philosophy teacher is a brilliant woman with glasses.[5]

A cognitivist would say that you are referring to something in the real world, namely your philosophy teacher; ascribing some properties to this person, that she is brilliant and has glasses; and because of this, your statement is either true or false. Remember that false statements (even the systematically false statements that an atheist may think religious people are making) are still claims about the world and so still fall within a cognitivist account of language.

So what would a non-cognitivist say here about your claim? As you saw in your AS-level, non-cognitivists about religious language argue that religious sentences like 'God is good' are not statements: in Ayer's phrase they are not 'factually significant' and do not express true or false beliefs about God. Non-cognitivism is a common position to take when it comes to aesthetic values, such as describing a piece of art as beautiful, ugly or sublime. You may have had disagreements with friends about whether a particular piece of music, or a film, was any good – and you may have concluded, once the shouting match had stopped, that there is no correct or incorrect answer about the aesthetic worth of the film. A non-cognitivist might resolve your dispute by saying that it's not the case that you are right and your friend is wrong, but that neither of you are making propositional claims: you is simply expressing your likes and dislikes. Referring back to your philosophy teacher, a non-cognitivist may argue that 'brilliant' is a value-laden term (just like beautiful, ugly, sublime), so when you tell Ofsted inspectors 'My teacher is brilliant' you are expressing a general feeling of approval that you have towards her.

Similarly, philosophers who are non-cognitivists about ethical language do not think that sentences like 'It is wrong to be dishonest' are propositions capable of being true or false. We can see how non-cognitivism can emerge from some anti-realist positions. There are moral anti-realists who argue that moral terms don't refer to any property out there in the world, but have a different function, possibly as an expression of approval or disapproval (**emotivism**), or perhaps as recommendations to act in a certain way (**prescriptivism**). Both emotivists and prescriptivists deny that ethical language refers to the world, and following from that they both deny that ethical sentences are true or false statements, so they are both non-cognitivist positions.

Cognitivists about ethical language, however, do think that moral sentences are statements expressing true or false beliefs. It is here that we can see some overlap with moral realism, as outlined above. A moral realist believes that there are moral facts, either natural facts (like the utilitarians) or non-natural facts (as we'll see with the **intuitionists**). Because there are these facts, a moral realist believes that ethical statements refer to these facts, and at least some of these statements are true. But there isn't a straightforward overlap between moral realism and cognitivism. We saw above that there was an anti-realist position, 'error theory', that also considered moral statements in terms of their truth or falsity; and we can now see this as a cognitivist position. Error theorists claim that there are no moral facts and so although moral statements do refer to the world, they are always false (in the way that an atheist may say that claims about God are always false).

Figure 1.26 summarises the cognitivist and non-cognitivist ethical theories that we look at in the rest of this chapter, and how these theories connect to moral realism and anti-realism. The theories differ on whether there are moral facts or not; on what moral statements mean; and on what we're doing when we make moral judgements. These were the concerns of moral philosophy for much of the last century, and this chapter traces the development of meta-ethical thinking over the past two hundred years.

	COGNITIVISM (pages 179–99)			**NON-COGNITIVISM** (pages 200–11)	
Name of the theory	Naturalism	Non-naturalism	Error theory	Emotivism	Prescriptivism
Name of the philosophers associated with the theory	Bentham, Mill	Moore, Pritchard	Mackie	Ayer, Stevenson	Hare
What do ethical terms refer to?	Natural properties	Non-natural properties	No property at all	They are expressions of emotion	They are commands or recommendations
Is ethical language true or false (truth-apt)?	Yes – and mostly true		Yes, but always false	No – neither true nor false	
	Moral realism			Moral anti-realism	

Figure 1.26 Table showing key theories of ethical language related to cognitivism/non-cognitivism and moral realism/anti-realism

Experimenting with ideas

Read through the following judgements and answer the questions below.

1 That new ring tone on your mobile is bad.
2 The morning BBC newsreader looks very fit.
3 Lying to the police is never wrong.
4 Atoms are made up of protons, neutrons and electrons.
5 The chair is bright red.
6 Your philosophy lecturer is tall.
7 It's good to fulfil your potential.
8 Everyone has a soul.
9 It was sad that her mum and dad split up.
10 The creator of the universe is all-loving.

For each judgement:

a) Do you think it is making a factual claim about the world?
b) Do you think it is either true or false, i.e. it has a truth-value (you are taking a cognitivist position on this statement)?
c) Do you think it is neither true nor false, i.e. it has no truth-value, but still expresses something (you are taking a non-cognitivist position on this statement)?

1.2.1 Cognitivism

Cognitivism – moral realism

Since words are only names of things, it would be more convenient for all men to carry about them such things as were necessary to express the particular business they are to discourse on … Another great advantage proposed by this invention was that it would serve as a universal language to be understood in all civilisations, whose goods and utensils are generally of the same kind.[6]

Jonathan Swift, *Gulliver's Travels,* 1726

Gulliver encounters this bizarre proposal on his travels to Lagado, where philosophers and scientists are engaged in all sorts of madcap schemes.[7] Some philosophers in the Academy of Lagado are realists who believe that all words are names of things. Their suggestion is that it would be easier, and put less strain on our lungs, if we were all to carry around large bags of objects and, whenever we wanted to have a conversation with someone, we would simply take the things we needed out of our bag and then point at them in the correct sequence, so that we might be understood. So presumably these enlightened philosophers from Lagado would be able to make moral judgements by taking out of their bags the objects that the words 'good', 'bad' and 'wrong', etc. referred to (whatever those objects might be!).

We have seen that cognitivism in moral philosophy is the view that ethical language makes statements, and expresses beliefs, which can be true or false because they genuinely refer to something (even if there aren't actually Lagadoan moral objects that can be carried around in bags). Philosophers sometimes abbreviate this by saying that in a cognitivist view, moral statements have a 'truth-value' or that they are 'truth-apt'; adding to this, moral statements have a truth-value because they pick out certain features of the world which make them true, or false (i.e. they are not made true by definition) so cognitivists may also say that moral statements are 'fact-stating' or 'factually significant'.

Let us for a moment set aside the cognitivist position held by J.L. Mackie which argues that yes, moral statements make statements about the world, but all these statements are false. We return to Mackie's 'error theory' on page 196 below. But before that we shall examine the cognitivist positions based on moral realism, which are more optimistic about ethical language, arguing that at least some of our moral statements are true. This is because the moral realist believes that ethical terms identify and pick out some feature of the world. The first cognitivist theory we look at is naturalism, which holds that ethical concepts can be understood and defined in non-ethical terms, referring to certain objective features of the world. The second cognitivist theory we assess is non-naturalism, which shares its realist foundations with naturalists, but disagrees with its claim that ethical terms can be reduced to non-ethical properties.

Experimenting with ideas

Read through these summaries of different normative theories then answer the questions that follow.

1 Plato thought that moral goodness (in the form of virtue) was understood and achieved only by grasping the Form of the Good.

2 Aristotle argued that moral goodness (in the form of virtue) could be understood and achieved by analysing human nature – what our purpose was – and then striving to fulfil that purpose.

3 Aquinas believed that moral goodness (in the form of virtue) consisted of understanding the natural law that governed our purpose, as given to us by God and as revealed through reason.

4 Divine command theorists hold that the right moral action is dictated by the commands of God.

5 Hume argued that virtue was a sympathetic recognition of character traits which were either useful or agreeable.

6 Kant argued that moral rightness lay in duty, and that our duties could be discovered through the application of reason.

7 Mill held that moral goodness simply involved ensuring that our actions maximised happiness (the production of pleasure and the reduction of pain).

8 Ethical egoists believe that moral goodness is about doing what is most beneficial for ourselves, such as maximising our own happiness.

For each theory outlined above:

a) Do you think this theory believes that moral judgements refer to certain moral facts that are 'out there' (objective)?

b) Do you think, then, that this theory is a cognitivist one?

c) If you do think this theory is cognitivist, then what features of the world ('out there') is this theory talking about when it uses the terms 'right' or 'good' or 'virtuous'?

d) Are these features of the world 'natural' or in some sense 'supernatural'?

Moral realism: Ethical naturalism

The creed which accepts as the foundation of morals the Greatest Happiness Principle holds that actions are right in proportion as they tend to promote happiness, wrong as they tend to produce the reverse of happiness. By happiness is intended pleasure, and the absence of pain.[8]

Mill

Naturalism looks to the world in search of moral facts and values, hoping to show that moral terms are terms that can be understood and defined by objective, natural properties in the world. For some critics of naturalism (most notably G.E. Moore, as we shall see below), what the naturalist is trying to do is to convert all our talk of morals into talk about something we can understand better, namely natural facts about the world and human beings. In this sense, naturalism is a reductive doctrine. It says that moral values can be reduced to, or explained in terms of, something else. But we shall see later whether Moore is right on this matter.

In the activity above, you might already have identified as naturalistic some of the moral theories we looked at in the previous chapters (such as those put forward by the utilitarians). These naturalistic theories all agree that we can analyse moral terms such as 'good' and explain them in other (naturalistic) terms – but they disagree on the precise explanation of these terms, i.e. there is no consensus as to what the 'natural' properties are that moral terms refer to.

Theories of virtue ethics also generally fall into the category of 'naturalism', as virtues refer to natural facts about the way people behave (or, for Hume, about the way we all feel about the way people behave). For example, according to Aristotle, our virtues are those character traits (which can be described in naturalistic terms) that enable us to flourish (which can also be described in naturalistic terms), and the key to this lies in our capacity to reason (a further naturalistic term). For Aristotle, there is nothing mysterious about ethics: we can work out what we should do on the basis of experience. So a moral judgement such as 'this axe murderer is callous and vicious' is true if he consistently hurts other people in extreme and pointless ways, but false if the anger that led to his wielding the axe was a single moment of madness in an otherwise calm and caring person.

The most commonly identified naturalistic theory is utilitarianism. The hedonistic utilitarian claims that moral judgements are simply judgements about how much pleasure (a natural fact), and for how many people, an action will produce. Mill's quote above makes it clear that he thinks that moral goodness and rightness is located in happiness, pleasure and the absence of pain. These are clearly natural terms and, in Chapter 4 of his book *Utilitarianism*, when Mill addresses the question 'Can utilitarianism be proved?' he provides an argument which seems to build a ladder between the moral concept of 'good' and the natural facts of 'happiness' and 'pleasure'. We shall now examine this ladder in some detail to see how firm the naturalistic foundations of Mill's utilitarianism are.

▶ **ACTIVITY**

a) Read through the extract from Mill in the Anthology extract 1.12, and convert this paragraph into a clear, stepped argument, with numbered premises and conclusions.

anthology
1.12

b) On the basis of this argument, why do you think utilitarianism is thought of as a form of naturalism?

c) What problems and weaknesses can you find in Mill's argument?

The key principle underpinning morality, according to Mill, is that 'happiness is desirable and the only thing desirable, as an end'. Mill's argument aims to show that happiness (or pleasure) is the good that we should be striving to reach, not just for us, but for everyone. In order to clarify this, it may be helpful to identify three important steps in Mill's proof. First, Mill argues that we need only show that people do desire something in order to show that this is desirable. Second, Mill proposes that it is their happiness that people desire and their happiness that is desirable. Third, Mill concludes that each of us desires happiness and that it is the happiness of everyone that is the goal of morality. Philosophers have identified problems with each step of this proof, but what concerns us here is the claim that Mill seems to be firmly grounding his ethical theory in naturalistic terms like 'desirable' and 'happiness'.

Criticism

The first step contains a fallacy that G.E. Moore went on to identify as the 'naturalistic fallacy'. We would all agree that visible does mean 'able to be seen' and audible means 'able to be heard'. But 'desirable' does not mean 'able to be desired', a point which becomes clear when we consider that not everyone's desires are desirable. So the fallacy, or logical error, that Moore thinks he has discovered in Mill's argument is the mistake of identifying 'what is actually desired' (this is a natural fact about humans) with 'what ought to be desired' (this is a moral concept) or, according to Moore, of identifying what's desired (natural) with what's good (moral). We look at Moore's **naturalistic fallacy** in some detail below (page 192).

The second step in the argument gives more detail as to what is desired, and again it refers to a natural property. It is 'happiness' which Mill identifies as the object that is desired and desirable. This is referred to as 'psychological hedonism' (page 14 above) and, as with Bentham's theory, it is fundamental to Mill's utilitarianism. As you know, the concept of happiness has a long tradition within moral philosophy and, among the ancient Greeks, Plato and Aristotle held that happiness (*eudaimonia*) is what we should all be striving for. Aristotle was also explicit that no one would disagree with the claim that happiness is what we are all after. However, for Mill, 'happiness' did not refer to the general 'flourishing' of your life (which is how Aristotle understood happiness) but to the securing of pleasure and the avoidance of pain. It is this that we strive for, and it is this that is the end, or goal, of our actions – what philosophers call the 'Good'.

Criticism

This stage in the argument is vulnerable to Hume's remarks, made a century before Mill, that moral philosophers have a tendency to glide from a discussion of what *is* the case into a discussion of what *ought* to be the case. We look at this criticism in more detail below, when we address 'the **is/ought** question'. The second step is also once again attacked by Moore as an example of the naturalistic fallacy (page 192 below).

In the final step of the proof, Mill moves to the conclusion that there is another, general, good that arises out of the sum of all our individual goods. This general good, Mill thinks, is the good for the 'aggregate' (i.e. sum) of each of us as individuals. Because each of us as individuals desires our own happiness, then the aggregate of all of us desires the general happiness as our ultimate good. So it is not just our individual goods that refer to natural properties (our individual happiness, pleasure and pain) but it is the Good in general that refers to a natural property (the sum total of our happiness, pleasure and pain).

Criticism

Henry Sidgwick (1838–1900), who was a contemporary Mill, made the following criticism of Mill's final conclusion: 'an aggregate of actual desires, each directed towards a different part of the general happiness, does not constitute an actual desire for the general happiness existing in any individual'.[9] The point is the same: we cannot add up individual desires to generate a kind of 'super-desire' that each of us has, in addition to our own desires. To claim this is to commit the fallacy of composition (see page 123). As you may remember, this is the fallacy of thinking that because there is some property common to each of the individuals within a group, this property must apply to the group as a whole. In the same way, it is true that each of us, as an individual, desires our own happiness, but it is a fallacy that the 'aggregate of individuals' desires happiness for that aggregate. So Mill cannot conclude, on the basis that we each think of happiness as our good, that we also think of the general happiness as the good. In which case, he fails in his attempt to give firm, commonsense grounds for understanding 'good' in the natural terms of 'happiness' and 'pleasure'.

Naturalism erodes the autonomy of ethics

If naturalism is correct then there are two important consequences, both of which have enthused or enraged philosophers and have generated their own cottage industry among academics. The first consequence of naturalism is that ethics is not autonomous (Figure 1.27). In other words, morality is not about some unique realm that we can't talk about, or can only discuss in poetic or metaphorical terms. Morality, according to naturalism, is just another aspect of this ordinary world. Naturalism might then be taken to imply that we can make observations about the ordinary world (about the pains or pleasure or amount of happiness that a particular action produces) and then, somehow, draw moral conclusions from these observations. So we can draw an ethical conclusion from factual (naturalistic) **premises**; in short, we can derive an 'ought' from an 'is', prescriptive statements from descriptive ones, and this, as Hume points out below, is a significant problem for the ethical theories that make this move.

A second implication of naturalism concerns the meaning of moral terms. If ethics is not autonomous (if it is not a special, unique or distinct practice) then this suggests that we can define moral words in naturalistic terms. For example, a naturalist might say that 'good' ultimately boils down to 'maximising happiness'. It was this type of reduction that irritated G.E. Moore and led to his claim that naturalism was guilty of a fallacy (the naturalistic fallacy), which we shall return to shortly in the context of non-naturalism when we look at G.E. Moore's intuitionist theory. First let us return to the is/ought question.

A problem for naturalism: The is/ought question

Let us pick up on a criticism made against the second step of Mill's argument, which may reveal a fundamental flaw in naturalism. Many philosophers have insisted that an important distinction needs to be made between *matters of fact* and *matters of value*, between description and evaluation, between 'is' and 'ought'. Such philosophers go on to say that the distinction is such that we cannot argue from one to the other. Hume appears to have been the first philosopher to have made explicit this worry, and his idea has become known as '**Hume's Law**'. There is a small paragraph buried in his *Treatise of Human Nature* that raises this point, and in the twentieth century this controversy fuelled many books and articles. Hume actually wrote the following:

> In every system of morality which I have hitherto met with, ... the author proceeds for some time in the ordinary way of reasoning, and establishes the being of a God, or makes observations concerning human affairs; when of a sudden I am surprised to find, that instead of ... is and is not, I meet with ... ought, or an ought not[. It] seems altogether inconceivable, how this new relation can be a deduction from others, which are entirely different from it.[10]
>
> Hume

What Hume says in this passage is that we cannot infer anything about what *ought* to be the case from any number of facts about what *is* the case. So, for example, the fact that humans can and do frequently eat meat does not entail therefore that they ought to eat meat. But he complained that too many moralists and philosophers ignore this simple principle. So this passage seems to support the **autonomy of ethics**, the view that moral judgements are completely different from other sorts of judgements. Figure 1.27 shows the division between the moral realm and the natural realm.

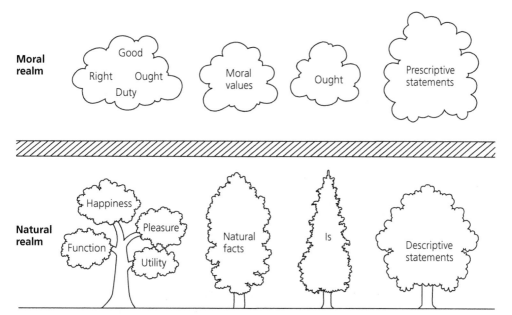

Figure 1.27 The autonomy of ethics suggests that concepts in the moral realm cannot be derived from concepts in the natural realm

In the twentieth century many philosophers took Hume's Law to support their view that there is a fundamental distinction between facts and values, and that moral judgements are essentially different from factual propositions. So naturalism appears to be in big trouble because it *does* seem to draw evaluative conclusions (those in the moral realm) from non-moral premises (taken from the natural realm). Mill's 'proof' of utilitarianism seems to be particularly susceptible to this criticism. Mill is starting out by claiming that people happen to desire happiness, then he moves to say that therefore happiness is desirable and is a good; in other words, that people ought to desire happiness. If Hume is right then Mill cannot so easily take the step from psychological hedonism (the factual, descriptive claim that humans seek happiness) to ethical hedonism (the moral, prescriptive claim that humans ought to seek happiness).

But Hume's Law, at least as stated by Hume, does not support this attack on naturalism. In fact, Hume was himself a naturalist (he thought that our moral judgements were based ultimately on sympathy – a natural emotion). Hume is making a simple logical point. A deductively valid argument cannot slip into its conclusion any information that isn't already in its premises. So no matter how much factual information I provide you with about some state of affairs, you cannot legitimately conclude (on factual grounds alone) anything about what *ought* to be the case. This is because the 'ought', as Hume says, 'expresses some new relation or affirmation'. So Hume's claim is a simple claim about what can and can't legitimately be done when constructing an argument. We might restate Hume's Law as this: *it is invalid to derive an evaluative conclusion (ought) from premises that are purely descriptive (is)*. It's worth noting that this goes for all valid deductive arguments, not just ones in moral philosophy: a conclusion must be based solely on what's in the premises, it can't suddenly smuggle new information in.

Experimenting with ideas

Which of the following arguments do you think break Hume's Law?

(P = premise, C = conclusion)

1 P: Everyone desires happiness.
   C: Therefore happiness is desirable.
2 P: God created us.
   C: Therefore we ought to obey God.
3 P In order to flourish we must fulfil our function well.
   P: Our function is to reason.
   C: Therefore we ought to reason well.
4 P: He is the captain.
   C: Therefore he ought to fulfil his duties as a captain.
5 P: Women are able to have children.
   C: Therefore women ought to have children.

6   P: It is wrong to cause pain.
    P: An abortion causes a foetus pain.
    C: Therefore, it is wrong to have an abortion.
7   P: You promised to pay back that £5.
    C: Therefore you ought to pay back the £5.
8   P: A man murdered his entire family in order to collect their life insurance.
    P: The man was sane and knew exactly what he was doing.
    C: Therefore the man ought to be punished.
9   P: A man murdered his entire family in order to collect their life insurance.
    P: The man was clinically insane.
    P: We ought not to punish the clinically insane for their actions.
    C: Therefore the man ought not to be punished.
10 P: It is bedtime.
    C: Therefore you ought to brush your teeth.

Hume is not saying that we should *never* appeal to matters of fact in order to justify our moral judgements. For example, I may want to argue that abortion is wrong (a moral judgement) by pointing out that a foetus can experience pain (a matter of fact). But, according to Hume's Law, if I wish to propose such an argument I cannot rely on facts alone. If the facts are to support the moral judgement then there must also be supporting premises which refer to some moral standards, in this case, for example, the additional premise that 'It is wrong to cause pain'.

To illustrate this idea, consider the following very simple argument, put forward night after night by tired and irritable parents up and down the country: 'Clean your teeth', 'Why?' 'Because it's bedtime'. We can summarise this argument as follows:

P: It is bedtime.

C: Therefore, you ought to brush your teeth.

Although this is a prudential, not a moral, 'ought' (see page 76 above), the argument as it stands still violates Hume's Law. The *fact* that it is bedtime cannot by itself give parents any reason to conclude that their children ought to brush their teeth. The premise merely states a fact, and so cannot force any value judgement upon you. It may well be bedtime, and yet not a good thing for you to brush your teeth (perhaps you've brushed them ten times already).

Nonetheless, the fact that it is bedtime clearly *could* be an important consideration in drawing a conclusion concerning what you ought to do (if you always go to bed without brushing your teeth, eventually they will fall out). But this, according to Hume, can only be because we are making certain assumptions in the argument which have not been made explicit. In this case, we may be assuming that it is a good thing for children to brush their teeth before sleeping (to avoid losing their teeth). So, to make the argument valid, we need to make this hidden assumption explicit:

P1: It is bedtime.

(P2: At bedtime you ought to brush your teeth.)

C: Therefore, you ought to brush your teeth.

This complete argument is now clearly valid. So Hume's point is not that facts are irrelevant to values and that we can never appeal to facts when drawing moral conclusions. Rather, his point is that we need to make our values explicit when arguing, so that we can be clear about what the argument really is.

Criticism

However, the American philosopher John Searle (1932–) has even questioned the claim that we cannot derive evaluative conclusions from descriptive premises.[11] Searle argued that there are exceptions to the claim that you cannot derive an *ought* from an *is*. Consider the following argument, adapted from the activity on page 187:

P: You promised to pay me back my £5.

C: So you ought to pay up.

Here the premise states a matter of fact: the fact that you made a promise to pay me back my money. And the conclusion makes a value judgement about what you ought to do. But this argument seems perfectly in order. The fact that you have made a promise seems clearly to imply that you ought to keep it, and so suggests that it is possible to bridge the **is/ought gap**. Searle is claiming that there are certain facts about human beings, for example that they have instituted a practice of promise keeping, which have implications for how they ought to act, and so perhaps some form of naturalism could be true after all.

How might Hume react to an example like this in defence of his law? One thing he might try is to find some hidden evaluative premise. Is there a hidden premise here so obvious that it seems not worth stating? In this case, the hidden premise might be that 'we ought to keep our promises'. If we were to add this we would make the argument valid and would not have moved from an *ought* to an *is* (because there was an *ought* buried in one of the premises). Another way of avoiding Searle's conclusion might be to point out that the meaning of 'promise' involves appeal to our moral obligations. So that if we fully explain the meaning of the premise it becomes 'You have made a *moral* undertaking to do something or other' and from this it seems unproblematic to conclude that you *ought* to undertake it. But here we have only moved from *oughts* to *oughts*. So, on this defence, the attempt to bridge the gap simply introduces values in the premises.

Moral realism: Ethical non-naturalism

Naturalism is the position that moral terms like 'good' and 'bad' stand for, or can be identified with, certain natural properties or facts about the world. So we can make moral judgements simply by examining, in each situation, whether those natural facts are present or absent, and thus whether the terms 'good' or 'bad' apply here. But if naturalism is wrong, and if we can't somehow *reduce* moral terms to natural ones, then how do we come to make moral judgements? Perhaps the answer is that we just do. Moral judgements express such basic truths that we don't need to justify or explain them in terms of anything else. This rejection of a reductive position leads to the claim that moral judgements are intuitive or self-evident, and so in no need of being justified by any kind of argument. The theory that moral judgements are known intuitively is called intuitionism. Like naturalism, it takes a realist position, claiming that there are moral truths to be known, and that moral judgements are capable of being true or false. However, unlike naturalism, it thinks that moral predicates do not stand for natural properties but denote special non-natural properties. These non-natural properties are seen as unique (*sui generis* is the technical philosophical term – meaning 'in its own category') and we should recognise them as such. We saw above that naturalism threatens 'the autonomy of ethics' (pages 184–5); non-naturalism reinstates this autonomy, arguing that ethical language contains terms, in particular 'good', that simply can't be reduced to, or defined by, non-ethical terms.

Intuitionism had been around for a number of centuries before the twentieth century, and in a numbers of forms, one of which was the popular 'moral sense' theory of David Hume's time. But in the early twentieth century, two influential forms of intuitionism developed from the reaction against naturalism. These were what we might call consequentialist intuitionism, supported by G.E. Moore, and deontological intuitionism, held by H.A. Prichard and W.D. Ross. First we shall look at Moore's consequentialist version of intuitionism, and then at Prichard's deontological version.

Consequentialist intuitionism – G.E. Moore

> Beg it may be noticed that I am not an 'Intuitionist' in the ordinary sense of the term ... [W]hen I call such propositions 'Intuitions' I mean merely to assert that they are incapable of proof; I imply nothing whatever as to the manner or origin of our cognition of them.[12]

Moore

We noted above that intuitionism has had a long history, and the great debate among the moral philosophers was 'Where do our intuitions come from?' Some, such as Francis Hutcheson (1694–1746), said our moral intuitions stemmed from an internal, god-given, moral sense (analogous to our other five senses) through which we could intuit what was right and wrong. Others, such as Samuel Clarke (1675–1729), said our intuitions stemmed from a rational faculty in our mind that had the power to grasp moral truths, in a way that is analogous to our capacity to grasp mathematical truths. G.E. Moore had no interest in this debate about the origins of our moral intuitions, which is why he said he wasn't an intuitionist in the ordinary sense of the term. Moore's concerns lay elsewhere.

Moore was not a great systems builder, and his influence stems from his analysis of moral concepts and language in *Principia Ethica* (1903). Not that philosophers hadn't analysed ethical concepts before (they had been doing that since Socrates); it's just that no philosopher had done it in quite the same clear and careful way that Moore did. Moore changed the face of moral philosophy, at least in Britain and America, not so much in what he said, but in the questions he asked and the way he asked them. Moore thought it was possible that moral philosophers had been trying to answer questions that simply couldn't be answered. So he drew the attention of Anglo-American philosophers to 'being clear about the question'.

As a consequentialist, Moore believes the moral worth of an action is determined by the good effects it brings. So we need to decide what these effects are. In other words, the question we should be asking is: 'What is Good?'. The answer that Moore has reached by the end of *Principia Ethica* is that 'good' cannot be defined in natural terms (as we see below, page 192), and in fact it cannot be defined at all. Because 'good' is indefinable it cannot be reduced to 'the greatest happiness', or to 'what people desire', or any other such non-moral good. For Moore, what is good is known intuitively, and this is why his approach is known as intuitionism.

anthology
1.13

In order to clarify what he means by indefinable, Moore likens the word 'good' to 'yellow'. If we try to say that 'yellow' means 'light travelling at a particular frequency' then we are simply wrong – 'yellow' refers to what we see when we see yellow objects, not to light-vibrations. So, for Moore, 'yellow' is clearly comprehensible to us, yet we are not able to define it in terms of anything else. The same goes for 'good'. We know what it is when we see it, but we cannot define it in any other terms. But, for Moore, it is important to note that moral properties are unlike natural properties such as 'being yellow', as we do not observe them through our ordinary senses. Moral judgements are evaluative rather than factual and so cannot be justified by purely empirical observation. Moral terms are *self-evident* and can only be known by what Moore calls 'intuition'.

Experimenting with ideas

Imagine that a series of philosophers from across history appeared on a TV quiz show, and were asked the question 'What is good?'. Write down the answers that you think the following philosophers would give to that question.

Moral philosopher	Their answer to the question 'What is good?'
1 Plato	
2 Aristotle	
3 A religious philosopher such as Aquinas	
4 Kant	
5 Hume	
6 Bentham	
7 Mill	
8 A contemporary virtue ethicist, such as MacIntyre or Hursthouse	

The open question argument

The problem as Moore sees it is that most philosophers down the years have been wrong to try to define 'good' in other terms: they have failed to see that 'good' is indefinable. In order to support this view, Moore presents us with a dilemma. When we ask the question 'What is good?' Moore says that we are faced with three possibilities:

Either 1) 'good' is indefinable

Or 2) 'good' is definable

Or 3) 'good' means nothing at all and 'there is no such subject as ethics'.[13]

The last option is given short shrift and rejected almost out of hand, which leaves us with only two options: either good is definable or it is not. In order to show that good cannot be defined, Moore offers an argument which has become known as the 'open question argument'. Consider the argument as follows. Any theory which attempts to define 'good' (for example, naturalism) is saying something equivalent to:

'Good' means X (where X is some fact or set of facts).

But, says Moore, for any such definition it will always make sense to ask:

But is X really good?

So, for example, if a utilitarian says 'Good means maximising pleasure and minimising pain for the majority' it still makes sense to ask 'But is it really good to maximise pleasure and minimise pain for the majority?' In fact (as we saw with some of the examples against utilitarianism), not only does this question make sense, but it is a question we would want to ask when some innocent person is being punished on utilitarian grounds (for example, to placate an angry mob).

Moore goes on. If 'good' can be defined as X, then it shouldn't make any sense to ask 'But is X really good?' We can see this by looking at another definition, such as 'A bachelor is an unmarried man'. It just doesn't make sense then to ask 'But is an unmarried man really a bachelor?' because we would then be asking 'But is a bachelor really a bachelor?' which is an absurd question.[14] However, asking a utilitarian 'But is maximising happiness really good?' *is not* the same as asking 'But is good really good?' Yet if the naturalist were right then the first question would be trivial: it *would* be like asking whether good is good. So the proposed definition must be inadequate. It must mean that 'good' and 'maximising happiness' are not the same. For Moore, we can always meaningfully pose the question 'But is X really good?' for every definition of good, including all naturalistic ones. It remains an open question whether or not it really is good. Moore believes that this open question argument shows that good is not definable, ruling out option 2. This leaves only option 1, namely that good is indefinable.

Criticism

An objection to Moore's open question argument may be that the question only appears to remain open because the meaning of words such as 'good' are unclear in ordinary usage. So when the naturalist provides a definition of 'good' it is not surprising that we don't immediately recognise its accuracy. In other words, the reason we may wonder whether the promotion of pleasure really is good is only because we are still unclear in our minds about the proper signification of the term 'good'. So the naturalist would then argue that strictly speaking it does *not* make sense to ask whether an action that (for example) leads to the general happiness is in fact good.

The naturalistic fallacy

Having established that good is indefinable, Moore goes on to highlight the fallacy that he believes occurs in many arguments given by moral philosophers. The basic form of the fallacy is easy to understand: a term that is indefinable cannot be defined, and any attempt to define the indefinable is clearly fallacious. Armed with this, Moore has a field day in his attack on naturalism, as he sees this fallacy occurring all over the place in such theories. Remember that according to Moore, the concept 'good' is indefinable, and so it is a non-natural concept (it can't be defined in terms of anything natural). But naturalists such as the utilitarian philosopher John Stuart Mill are not only attempting to define 'good' (a fallacy because 'good' is indefinable) but they are trying to do so in naturalistic terms (a fallacy because 'good' is non-natural). What fools, thinks Moore. How could they have failed to see this? So all forms of naturalism are rejected by Moore because they are all guilty of the naturalistic fallacy. It's worth remembering that for Moore the naturalistic fallacy is just a special case of the more general fallacy of defining the indefinable.

Moore was very clear that Mill had committed the naturalistic fallacy (above on page 183). According to Moore's interpretation, Mill attempts to define 'good' as 'desired', and then he goes on to say that it is happiness that we desire. Moore says:

> *the fallacy in this step is so obvious, that it is quite wonderful how Mill failed to see it.*[15]
>
> Moore

It seems clear to Moore that Mill is trying to define, in naturalistic terms, the indefinable (i.e. 'good') – which is the naturalistic fallacy. This attack on Mill's theory is what Moore became most famous for, and many philosophers took this to spell the end for utilitarianism. But is Mill guilty of the naturalistic fallacy? Mary Warnock thinks not. She argues that Mill is not interested in defining what 'good' is, nor is he interested in defining what 'desirable' is. He does not, Warnock says, define 'desirable' or 'good' at all.[16] According to Warnock, Mill's project is primarily an empirical one: he is simply describing for us what sorts of things are, as a matter of fact, considered good. Mill is trying to persuade us of the truth of utilitarianism by informing us that people already consider happiness to be good (and desirable). But that isn't to say (as Moore believes) that Mill therefore considers the 'good' to mean 'happiness' or 'pleasure', etc. If it turned out that people considered something else (say pain) to be fundamentally desirable, then it would be this thing, pain, that was the good.

According to Warnock, Mill was just pointing out that people already pursue happiness as a worthwhile goal, so they already believe it to be good (no further proof is necessary). In which case, Mill is not committing the naturalistic fallacy, and Moore's most famous argument fails to meet its mark.

Moore's argument against naturalism may remind you of Hume's Law, because it is drawing a sharp distinction between the moral realm and the non-moral realm. But Hume's argument is about the logical connection between these realms (you cannot derive an *ought* from an *is*), whereas Moore's argument is about the linguistic or semantic connection between moral and non-moral terms. In a nutshell, Moore is saying that 'any attempt to give a naturalistic account of what it is to do good, still leaves open the question of whether behaving in accordance with that account would be the morally good thing to do'.

Moore's ideals and intuitions

The negative part of Moore's argument is over. He believes that he has established that good cannot be defined, and that any attempt to define it will be fallacious. He also believes that we know what is good, not through analysing it in ordinary, naturalistic terms (such as weighing up pleasure and pain) but through our discriminating intuitive faculty. So what is the positive part of Moore's argument? What does Moore think we should be striving for? In other words, what actually is good according to Moore?

> Goods may all be said to consist in the love of beautiful things or of good persons.[17]

At the end of *Principia Ethica* Moore describes those things he believes to be good (although he obviously doesn't define them because to define them would be to commit the fallacy of defining the indefinable!). This final chapter, entitled 'The Ideal', is a fairly gushing account of the things that Moore believes are intrinsically valuable. Among these goods are, most importantly, the love of friendship and beauty. For Moore, we must strive to bring about these goods, and we must consider our actions in terms of their consequences: of whether they promote these goods or damage them. Alasdair MacIntyre points out that there was a large group of intellectuals, artists and writers (known as 'The Bloomsbury Group') who lapped up this final chapter, even calling it 'the beginning of a renaissance'.[18] Some would question, however, whether Moore was correct to say that love of friendship and beauty are 'by far the most valuable things which we know or can imagine' (section 113 of *Principia Ethica*). If this is as far as our values extend then, as MacIntyre says, Moore has a highly impoverished view of what good is.

Experimenting with ideas

Moore identifies (a) the love of beauty and (b) the love of friendship as two goods that we should be striving for.

What other goods do you think need to be added to this list in order to make it more complete?

For MacIntyre, it was as if Moore had given some theoretical justification for the values that these intellectuals already held dear. But this raises the more important question of who is to judge whose intuitions of the 'good' are the correct intuitions? The hedonistic utilitarians could argue about which action promoted the most happiness, but because Moore believes the good is indefinable we can't really find common ground from which to resolve disagreements. At its most extreme end, we find moral intuitions that are despicable. For example, Rudolf Höss, the commandant of Auschwitz (the Nazi extermination camp where over a million Jews were murdered), wrote in his memoirs after the war that he felt what he had done was 'right'. Mill at least could give reasons against Höss's intuition by pointing to the enormous suffering of the victims of the Holocaust, but Moore could not give reasons against the Nazis beyond saying 'their intuitions clashed with most other people's intuitions'.

So how should we categorise Moore? Is he a moral philosopher, or a philosopher of language? Does he support a utilitarian approach, or is he against it? In the final chapter of *Principia Ethica*, it becomes clear that Moore is not primarily a linguistic philosopher, although it was his attention to language that made him so influential. He had, after all, drawn the attention of moral philosophers to the precise nature of the questions they were trying to answer. But that wasn't all he was doing, as can be seen from that last chapter. Moore, like Bentham and Mill before him, is genuinely concerned with what things are good. Given that this search for what is good is so important to Moore, it is perhaps unfortunate that he is now mainly remembered as the man who accused Mill of the 'naturalistic fallacy'. Despite this rejection of naturalistic utilitarianism, Moore has sympathies with a utilitarian approach. Firstly, he is a realist, like Bentham and Mill, because he believes that 'good' refers to something out there in the world. Secondly, Moore is a consequentialist, because he identifies moral value as lying in the outcome of actions. Thirdly, some philosophers have even called Moore an 'ideal' utilitarian: ideal because he believes that goods we seek to bring about are 'ideal goods', things that are intrinsically good to a high degree. Perhaps most significantly though, Moore is an intuitionist because he believes these values were knowable by intuition. And it was Moore's intuitionism that brought about the attack from the group of philosophers known as the 'emotivists', as we shall see below.

Deontological intuitionism – Prichard

Before we turn to those philosophers who rejected moral realism completely, we should briefly look at another form of intuitionism prevalent in the first part of the last century. Like Moore, these intuitionists believed that we grasp moral principles by intuition; like Moore, they believed that moral judgements refer to the world and can be true or false; and, like Moore, these intuitionists believed there are a number of different values that we have to recognise. However, unlike Moore, they believed that values lie in what is right, rather than what is good, and should be located in the actions themselves rather than in the consequences. So we can think of this type of theory as 'deontological intuitionism', in contrast to the consequentialist form proposed by Moore. There are two key figures in this movement, H.A. Prichard and W.D. Ross.

Prichard's most famous work was his article 'Does moral philosophy rest on a mistake?' published in 1912. In this paper, Prichard presented himself as taking a whole new approach to moral philosophy, bringing to the subject a new clarity and focus. Prichard opens his article by saying that his increasing dissatisfaction with moral philosophy is due to its 'attempt to answer an improper question'. (This is almost exactly what Moore had claimed nine years earlier, but it seems that Prichard, who worked at Oxford University, was not wholly familiar with the philosophy of Moore, who was from Cambridge University, a full 90 miles away!) The mistake that Prichard is referring to is the incorrect belief that reasons can be given as to why something is our duty. Duty, Prichard thinks, is the ultimate moral value, but we cannot ever prove why something is our duty. This is in clear contrast to Kant who believed that reason could determine, through the categorical imperative, what we were obliged to do. However, Prichard believes that obligatoriness (the quality of some action being obligatory and our duty) is only known through intuition, not through reason. He thinks that, as a matter of fact, when we feel obliged to do something this is *not* because we have worked out that it can be universalised, or that it brings about the greatest good. Rather, Prichard claims that our apprehension that something is our duty 'is immediate, in precisely the same sense in which a mathematical apprehension is immediate'.[19]

Criticism

So, just as it is self-evident that $2 + 2 = 4$, Prichard believes that it is also self-evident whether an act is our duty or not. But what happens if we disagree with someone about whether a course of action is a duty or not? For example, if we wish to persuade a Nazi officer that they had a duty to *disobey* an order which would increase the number of people being exterminated in Auschwitz?[20]

W.D. Hudson believes that there is a further problem with Prichard's mathematical analogy. This is that with mathematics we never have to choose between two self-evident, but conflicting principles or axioms.[21] Yet when it comes to obligations, there are moral dilemmas in which we do face such a conflict, where two duties seem to have equal weight and yet point in opposite directions (for example, in our on-going confrontation with the axe murderer: we have a duty to be honest, but also a duty to prevent harm to others). It was W.D. Ross, another deontological intuitionist, who proposed a procedure for dealing with such conflicting duties.

G.J. Warnock argued that the mysterious ideals, goods and duties proposed by the intuitionists were introduced into the analysis of ethical language in a way which avoids really addressing the questions meta-ethics was concerned with, that is: how ethical judgements are justified, what precisely they are, in what way they relate to other kinds of judgements and so forth. Isn't an appeal to intuition a simple expression of bewilderment – a failure to find an answer to the question of how we are able to apply the property of 'goodness' to things? It introduces properties and objects in an *ad hoc* manner but fails to explain anything. This is a criticism similar to Mackie's 'argument from queerness', which we look at below, and G.J. Warnock finds it astonishing that thinkers like Moore and Ross believe that 'there is a vast corpus of moral facts about the world – known, but we cannot say how; related to other features of the world, but we cannot explain in what way; overwhelmingly important for our conduct, but we cannot say why'.[22]

anthology
1.14

Error theory

We turn now to the final cognitivist theory, which is set apart from the others we have looked at because, unlike naturalism and non-naturalism, it is an anti-realist theory which does not believe there are any such things as moral facts, or any referents at all to moral terms.

J.L. Mackie opens his book *Ethics: Inventing Right and Wrong*, with the bold claim that 'There are no objective moral values'. You may remember when studying the philosophy of religion that Mackie was equally provocative about belief in the existence of God.[23] We have just seen that Moore and the intuitionists certainly did believe in objective moral values, and that the property of being good, which certain actions have, is one that we know intuitively. But Mackie argues that *all* moral realists, not just intuitionists but naturalists as well, are committed to the existence of objective moral values. You can probably list them: Kant believed there exists a categorical imperative; Aristotle believed the good lay in *eudaimonia* which was intrinsically desirable; Mill and the utilitarians believed that the good lies in happiness, and the prevention of suffering, which is also intrinsically desirable. Indeed, according to Mackie even in ordinary language we all have a tendency, when making moral judgements, to include a claim to objectivity. This ingrained claim of ethical language to objectivity is a mistake, says Mackie. But he is very clear that this mistake is not a linguistic or conceptual mistake (which is the approach that the non-cognitivists like Ayer and Hare are going to take, below). As Mackie says:

> the denial of objective values will have to be put forward not as the result of an analytic approach, but as an 'error theory', a theory that although most people in making moral judgements implicitly claim ... to be pointing to something objectively prescriptive, these claims are all false.[24]
>
> Mackie

So the mistake is not an analytic mistake about misunderstanding how moral terms work. Instead, says Mackie, our moral judgements make a systematic error based on our belief in things (namely moral properties of the world) that don't literally exist, a belief promoted by moral realism in whatever form it occurs. This 'error theory' account of ethical language places Mackie in the clear camp of moral scepticism.

▶ **ACTIVITY**

Look at the moral dilemmas above on pages 6–11. For each dilemma:

1 Identify and write down each of the moral properties (goodness, badness, rightness, wrongness, etc.) that you find in the dilemma.
2 Now compare what you found with your classmates – did they identify different moral properties?
3 Where you disagreed with your classmates, what features of the dilemmas would help you to resolve who was correct, and who was incorrect?

Mackie offers two main arguments in support of his error theory, the first of which is his 'argument from relativity'. This is the well-known sceptical argument, enthusiastically put forward by first year philosophy and social science undergraduates in cafés across the world, that the moral values which humans hold vary from society to society over place and time; and that your moral values are largely determined by the society in which you grew up. For Mackie, the wide variations in moral codes are more readily explained by reference to the ways of life that they reflect, rather than by reference to our perception (and, in some cases, our distorted perception) of any objective moral values.

Mackie's second, and more important, argument for his moral scepticism is the 'argument from queerness'. Moral realism raises puzzling questions to do with what kinds of things exist in the world (ontological questions); as well as questions to do with knowledge, or how we come to know things (epistemological questions). For what the moral realist does is to posit the existence of some odd things into the world, namely moral facts and moral properties. For example, we saw above that intuitionists like Moore and Prichard must believe in the existence of simple indefinable properties – properties of a peculiar 'non-natural' or 'normative' sort. Perhaps the intuitionists were more open and honest about these very strange properties of the world,[25] but Mackie thinks that all other moral realists, like Kant, Aristotle and Mill, have theories that also commit them to an unusual ontology, namely the existence of these queer, objective moral properties. Moreover, Mackie points out that, in order for us to detect these special moral qualities, we must have special faculties that enable us to detect and gain knowledge of these moral properties – for the intuitionists, this was our moral intuition, but other realists require us to possess a similar sort of 'moral sense'. So moral realists are not only committed to belief in these strange moral entities, but also end up committed to quite an elaborate epistemology.

Mackie argues that one of the essential, and unusual, ingredients of moral values is that they must provide a motivation to action. This is one of the key features that distinguishes a moral property (like goodness) from a non-moral property (like redness): it has an authority which compels us to behave in a certain way and gives us reason and motivation for doing so. These motivations that are attached to moral values are binding, categorical even. Mackie is a strong adherent of this view, which is known as 'moral internalism'. He believes that all moral values, not just Kantian imperatives, have at their core the assumption of a strange, magnetic quality that motivates us to act. He uses Plato's theory of forms as an example of how objective moral values provide motivation[26] as, for Plato, once we know what is good (the form of the Good) we are compelled to pursue it. If Mackie's internalist account is correct then this 'motivational' property of moral values is very strange indeed, as it would mean that something in the world (let's say the moral property of 'good') would generate a motivation for action, independently of any reasons or desires that we might have. We're used to understanding motivation in terms of our needs, desires, reasons – but how can a part of the world (namely a moral property) be intrinsically motivating, which is what Mackie thinks the realists are saying?

Mackie believes that the very queerness, or oddness, of moral objects and properties should make us sceptical about objective values. When you engaged in the activity above you may have found it very difficult to answer the questions, and you may not have been able to say which features of the dilemma would show that you, and

anthology
1.15

not your classmate, were correct. After all, moral properties and entities are unlike any other that we know of – we can't really point at them or count them or measure them or interact with them in any way. For Mackie, they are unlike any other object or property *because they don't actually exist*! Moral values are not out there to be discovered, as the moral realists would claim, but they are invented by us. How then to explain the power that we feel moral values have over us? Mackie believes that we can account for the reaction that we have to moral values (many of us do feel obliged to do things that we think are morally 'good') with a psychological explanation about how we have been brought up and the social institutions within which we exist. This complex social arrangement creates a moral theory which we then project onto the world as if it were true of the world. This, Mackie believes, is where the error arises, because we believe our projections of moral values onto the world are inherent in the world itself.

Mackie was an anti-realist insofar as he rejected the claim that there were moral facts; but he was a cognitivist in that he thought ethical language was directed towards the world and attempting to describe the world. But perhaps when we use moral terms we aren't intending to refer to the world at all, perhaps we are expressing something else, something that picks up on the action-guiding, prescriptive aspect of ethical language. In the next section we look at philosophers who would agree with Mackie that there are no moral facts, but who reject any cognitivist account.

In the meantime, Figure 1.28 sums up a few of the key features of the moral realist theories we have just examined.

	Do moral terms refer to something independent of humans?	Can moral terms be understood in non-naturalistic terms?	Do moral values lie in the consequences of a course of action?	Can moral principles and values be grasped by intuition?
Naturalism	Yes – to natural goods	No	Yes – for hedonistic utilitarians	No
Consequentialist intuitionism	Yes – to non-natural goods	Yes – in terms of intuitions	Yes – for ideal utilitarians	Yes
Deontological intuitionism	Yes – to non-natural obligations	Yes – in terms of intuitions	No	Yes
Error theory	Yes, they try to, but fail	No, but they can't be understood in naturalistic terms either	No, but nor do they lie in categorical imperatives	No – because there is nothing 'out there' to intuit

Figure 1.28 A reminder of some of the main features of the different cognitivist theories

1.2.2 Non-cognitivism

The three cognitivist positions we looked at above differed in what they thought ethical language was about. Naturalists argue that moral terms such as 'good' can be understood in natural terms, such as happiness; non-naturalists argue that moral terms certainly can not be understood in natural terms, and are unique and indefinable but knowable through our intuitions; error theorists argue that moral terms don't refer to anything at all. But what all three cognitivist positions have in common is that they hold that moral judgements, containing words like 'good' and 'bad', are statements expressing beliefs about the world, and they can be true or false.

Non-cognitivism rejects this claim; it rejects moral realism and also rejects Mackie's error theory, because non-cognitivism holds that ethical language is not fact-stating, moral terms do not pick out anything in the world, and so they are not truth-apt. In other words, ethical language does not make moral statements or propositions about the world, but performs some other function entirely. In this part of the chapter we look at the emergence of emotivism and prescriptivism as two important non-cognitivist theories.

Hume's influence on emotivism

Emotivism holds that ethical language does not make statements or assertions about the world; instead, our moral judgements should be seen as expressions of our feelings, possibly with the intent of influencing other people's behaviour.

David Hume (1711–76), like most pre-twentieth century philosophers, was not concerned with the analysis of ethical language, but his emphasis on the emotional aspects of moral judgements sparked an interest among linguistic philosophers who rejected intuitionism. Thus Hume is important to non-cognitivism even though he is thought of as a naturalist, and hence a realist, by many commentators.[27] His naturalist leanings are based on his belief that there are natural facts about morality, namely facts about how we feel about the way people behave, and our moral judgements are based on these natural facts. However, certain comments he made proved to be influential on non-cognitivism and in particular on the theory known as **emotivism**. For example, have a look at this claim in his *Treatise of Human Nature*:

> *Where a passion is neither founded on false suppositions, nor chooses means insufficient for the end, the understanding can neither justify nor condemn it. It is not contrary to reason to prefer the destruction of the whole world to the scratching of my little finger.*[28]
>
> Hume

For Hume, reason cannot provide us with a motive for action. However, this approach need not imply that moral judgements are made on the basis of a simple examination of the facts revealed to us through experience. Hume believes that value judgements cannot depend on sense perception, so we cannot see, hear, smell, etc. good or evil. In his *Treatise*, Hume argues that an empirical examination of a vicious act, of murder for instance, can never reveal to us anything we can term 'vice'. That is, there is nothing about the event itself, no fact which we can observe, which constitutes its being wrong. So where then do ethical judgements come from? Hume argues that all our preferences including our moral ones must be based upon passions, i.e. our basic emotions and desires.

anthology
1.16

> *Vice and virtue, therefore, may be compared to sounds, colours, heat and cold, which, according to modern philosophy, are not qualities in objects, but perceptions in the mind.*[29]
>
> Hume

On this view, ethical judgements are grounded in experience not in reason; that is, they are a matter of our own 'feelings' or 'desires'. While in this sense they are subjective or mind-dependent, Hume nonetheless tries to argue that they are objective insofar as they are rooted in facts about human nature. We do not choose these desires; they are simply given to us by our biological heritage. We are just the kind of creature that has the feelings that we do, and it is these shared feelings which constitute morality. On Hume's account, our ethical nature is characterised by the capacity for *sympathy*, or the ability to feel with (empathise with) others. On such an account, any variations in moral codes must be a consequence of differing social conditions, while ultimately all such codes must express some fundamentals which humanity shares. This appeal to the innate sympathy in human nature makes Hume's theory a broadly naturalistic one (with a touch of moral sense theory thrown in). But philosophers in the twentieth century who rediscovered Hume found that his comments about feelings and passions led them to a different, *anti-realist*, conclusion. What inspired these linguistic philosophers was Hume's account of morality as grounded in our emotions, and this rang true for philosophers searching for an alternative to intuitionism.

Emotivism

> *In every case in which one would commonly be said to be making an ethical judgement, the function of the ethical term is purely emotive. It is used to express feelings about certain objects, but not to make any assertion about them.*[30]
>
> Ayer

Emotivism can be seen as a reaction against intuitionism, and Alasdair MacIntyre thinks it is no coincidence that most of the emotivists studied under intuitionists.[31] Remember that Moore thought that we knew what was 'good' through intuition, for example the love of friendship and beauty. Now, among a certain intellectual elite, Moore's examples of 'goods' seemed obviously correct. But to everyone else, including many of Moore's pupils (such as C.L. Stevenson), what seemed obvious was that what Moore thought of as 'goods' were simply an expression of his own feelings and attitudes, to which he had given an objective spin that simply wasn't justified. So the theory of emotivism could be seen in part as a reaction against Moore's confident pronouncements as to what was and wasn't good.

One of the strongest statements of emotivism as a moral theory came from A.J. Ayer (1910–89). As you may remember from studying religious language, Ayer was a British philosopher who was very much under the influence of a group of Austrian philosophers known as logical positivists. These philosophers were angered by the gibberish that they thought many philosophers, particularly in the nineteenth century, had a tendency to spout. Language, they said, was only meaningful when it referred to the world; if we go beyond this then we venture into nonsense. Ayer was greatly affected by this idea and in 1936 he wrote a book called *Language, Truth and Logic* that popularised logical positivism in Britain and America. The theory of meaning that is now associated with Ayer is the verification principle and it is a kind of test that sentences must pass if they are to be judged genuinely meaningful. The verification principle states that:

anthology
1.17

A sentence is meaningful if and only if

either (a) it is a tautology (i.e. true by definition)

or (b) it is verifiable through sense experience.

What the principle is saying is that in order to say something meaningful we must know what makes our statement true. Ayer believed that if a statement wasn't a tautology (i.e. true by definition), and if there was no empirical way of discovering its truth, then it was meaningless. Like all positivists, Ayer put a lot of faith in science and in our observations of the world. He used the verification principle as a tool to sort out the good from the bad, the philosophical sheep from the metaphysical goats.

Experimenting with ideas

Read through the following sentences and decide for each whether or not it meets A.J. Ayer's verification principle (i.e. whether it is capable of being true or false).

1 Stealing money is wrong.
2 There is life after death.
3 A bachelor is an unmarried man.
4 It is good to give money to charity.

5 It is your duty to tell the truth.
6 There are tiny pixies that live in my fridge who disappear without trace as soon as I open the door.
7 The universe is expanding.
8 Bondi Beach contains more than 1 billion particles of sand.
9 It is wrong to abort a 20-week-old foetus.
10 The sunset over Victoria Falls is the most beautiful sight on Earth.

So what did Ayer have to say about judgements of value, which include such terms as 'right' and 'good'? He agreed with those who claimed that these terms were unanalysable, but that is because he said there is nothing to analyse. 'Good' and 'right' are what Ayer calls 'pseudo-concepts': they don't refer to anything at all. So if they do not refer to any property of the world, then moral judgements are not propositions and are not capable of being true or false. According to Ayer's verification principle, moral judgements are therefore meaningless. Given the frequency of moral judgements in our everyday lives, and their importance to us, what then does Ayer think is behind moral language? He concludes that moral terms are simply expressions or exclamations of our emotions, like going 'Boo!' (at things we don't like) or 'Hooray!' (at things we do like). Although Ayer didn't use this phrase, occasionally emotivism is known, rather disparagingly, as the 'Boo/Hooray' theory. In Ayer's terms, when I say:

anthology 1.18

> *'Stealing money is wrong' I produce a sentence with no factual meaning … It is as if I had written 'Stealing money!!' – where the shape and thickness of the exclamation marks show … that a special sort of moral disapproval is the feeling which is being expressed.*[32]
>
> Ayer

Now this 'emotive' account of moral terms was not new. Ogden and Richards had said almost the same thing 13 years previously in their book *The Meaning of Meaning* (1923), writing that "'good' … serves only as an emotive sign expressing our attitude'.[33] So emotivism claims that moral assertions express attitudes or feelings. By arguing that all ethical statements are simply expressions of emotion, a bit like expletives, Ayer is taking a non-cognitivist stance towards moral terms. 'Good' doesn't refer to anything in the world, but is only an expression reflecting something in me. It is important to emphasise that, unlike Hume's position outlined above, emotivism denies that moral expressions *describe* feelings or emotions any more than they describe other empirical facts. This is what leads Hume back into a naturalist view of ethics. But on an emotivist account, moral terms *express* a feeling, much as does a frown or an angry tone of voice.

The American philosopher C.L. Stevenson went a step further than Ayer in analysing the emotive meaning of moral judgements.

He argued that moral judgements which employed terms like 'good' and 'right' were not simply expressions of a feeling, as Ayer had maintained. More importantly, thought Stevenson, they were also attempts to influence other people, to persuade them to feel as we feel and to have the same attitude that we have. So Stevenson might say that when we claim 'That's a good song' we mean 'I like this song; you should do so as well.' Similarly if we say 'Abortion is wrong' we mean 'I disapprove of abortion and so should you'. So Stevenson is able to give an account of how moral terms motivate or guide action – they do so like someone shouting or urging us to do something, they motivate through the power of the emotion behind the words.

▶ **ACTIVITY**

Revisit sentences 1, 4, 5 and 9 on pages 202–3 and write down the emotive meaning that Stevenson would find in them.

So emotivism opposes intuitionism by not regarding moral propositions as descriptive. They do not ascribe a special property to events. This means that they are not informative. They are not intended simply to indicate facts, but are designed to influence other people's behaviour by conveying approval or disapproval. So emotivism has the advantage of doing away with the mysterious 'non-natural' properties of intuitionism. It also connects moral judgement with conduct in an intelligible way, which, as we have seen, intuitionism cannot (above on page 196).

The disagreement between emotivists and intuitionists turns on their analysis of simple ethical propositions. Consider the following propositions (illustrated in Figure 1.29): Boris is big, and Boris is bad.

Figure 1.29
According to the emotivist, the intuitionist's mistake is to think there must be something in the world corresponding to the expression 'is bad', and so to imagine that there must be a non-natural property – badness – that Boris possesses.

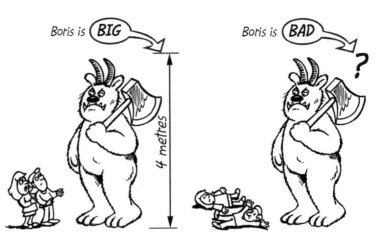

Both these propositions have the same basic grammatical form. They both have a subject term ('Boris') which picks out an individual in the world (Boris himself). And both statements have a predicate term ('is bad' and 'is big') saying something about Boris. The intuitionist claims that what is ascribed to Boris in both these statements is a property which we can discover in the world. Both bigness and badness are real properties of people, albeit natural and non-natural ones respectively. And it is here that the emotivist takes issue with intuitionism. The emotivist claims that, although these two propositions are superficially similar, in reality they are very different. While the first does indeed ascribe a real property to Boris, the second does not. Badness is not really a property of people or actions at all. This means that the second proposition is deceptive as it leads us to look in the world for something corresponding to the word 'bad'. And this is the error of the intuitionist who, having searched around for something corresponding to the word 'bad' and having failed to detect anything in the normal way (being unable to see, or hear, or smell Boris's badness), concludes that badness is a very peculiar or 'non-natural' property. But, in reality, says the emotivist, there is no such thing. For the real meaning of 'Boris is bad' is closer to 'Avoid Boris!' or 'Boris, yuk!'; that is to say, it expresses disapproval and does not ascribe any objective property to him at all.

Some criticisms of emotivism

One conclusion that can be drawn from emotivism is that value judgements are not rational and so no rational agreement is possible on ethical matters and no knowledge can be had of them. Different people feel differently about different things and each has equal right to their opinion: I like strawberry ice-cream, you like chocolate ice-cream; I feel 'ugh!' when I think about capital punishment, but you feel 'hooray!'. If emotivism is correct then there is no point in having a moral discussion, since two people cannot really contradict each other when they appear to be expressing a disagreement over some moral issue.

The immediate difficulty with this conclusion is that it appears to misunderstand the true character of moral judgements. When I claim that 'the abortion of a 20-week-old foetus is wrong' I intend to contradict your claim that 'the abortion of a 20-week-old foetus is permissible'. For when we disagree on a moral issue we argue with reasons and it seems as if we are literally contradicting each other; we are not just expressing conflicting ethical attitudes or feelings. Emotivism appears to make such rational moral argumentation impossible. If moral judgements were purely subjective it would be senseless for me to condemn someone who professed a different moral attitude.

This objection, however, need not be fatal, and an important lesson needs to be drawn from the emotivist's defence. For emotivism can allow for rational dispute over matters of fact (for example, whether or not a 20-week-old foetus can feel pain, or can survive outside of the womb), and over the definition of terms (for example, whether a foetus is a person, or a potential person). So if we are in disagreement over some issue, it may not be irrational to argue so long as our disagreement concerns something objective, such as a factual belief about the world, or concerns the meaning of the terms we are using.

The rational approach, according to the emotivist, is to seek out any shared values that we have and use these as leverage in the argument. In the case of the argument over the abortion of a 20-week-old foetus, we may both share the view that harming innocent human beings is wrong. If I can demonstrate that the foetus is a human being (for example, by showing that a foetus has complex responses, can survive outside of the womb with special care, has all the necessary body parts in place, etc.) and that it can be harmed (because it feels pain), then the other person may come to agree with me on this argument. What has happened here is that the pro-abortionist did not initially realise that their moral position was actually inconsistent, because they were unaware of certain facts.

Despite this defence of emotivism, while particular value judgements may be a matter for rational debate, ultimately, on an emotivist account, the criteria on which we base such judgements boil down to the expression of feelings. And in the final analysis any reasons I may offer for why something is wrong can only reduce to some gut feeling for which no justification can be offered. Thus any sense that there is a rational basis for moral dispute is illusory.

We said above that emotivism explains how moral judgements motivate action. So ethical statements may be instruments for the control and influence of social behaviour, etc. But so are advertisements, political speeches, bribes, blackmail, orders and so forth. In order to influence someone's behaviour, in other words, I may engage in moral exhortation, but I may also threaten, plead with or bribe them. This observation raises the question of what, if anything, is distinctive about purely *moral* discourse, for according to emotivism it would seem that it is 'ethical' to deploy any effective means to persuade someone to adopt a certain kind of behaviour. The consequence is that there can be no way of saying whether a moral argument is good or bad, but only whether or not it has the desired effect (i.e. to motivate a change in other people's behaviour), and thus ethics appears to be on a par with propaganda and rhetoric.

Emotivism is also mistaken in claiming that moral discourse always involves itself in trying to change attitudes or influence action. For it is possible to condemn someone's behaviour, without holding out any hope of influencing it. Moreover, moral discourse can be meaningful without its being any expression of an emotional state. I can express a moral opinion without being emotionally excited, for example when giving someone moral advice. Indeed, often it is regarded as important to be dispassionate in evaluating a moral dilemma, since our emotions when they are not kept in check by reason can cloud our ability to make moral decisions, as Aristotle pointed out (see page 137).

Kantian theorists may turn to the principle of **universalisability** to resist the claims of emotivism. For, following Kant, they may insist on the need for the element of *reason* in moral conduct. In other words, there is a crucial difference between saying that something is right or wrong, and expressing a liking or dislike for it. If I do something because I ought to do it I will be prepared to act the same way if the same circumstances arise. But this is not true of feelings. If I do something because I feel like it, not because I ought to, there is no commitment to acting in a similar way in similar circumstances. Moral judgements, in other words, refer beyond the particular case in a way that feelings or emotions do not. Further, they involve not just how I ought to behave in certain circumstances, but how *anyone* ought to behave in such circumstances. What this means is that to make a moral judgement implies having principles; and while non-rational beings can have feelings and express them, only a rational being can hold universal principles of this kind.

Finally we should return to the historical point that Alasdair MacIntyre drew our attention to at the beginning of this section (page 194). MacIntyre isn't surprised that emotivism arose when it did as a successor to the intuitionist theories that came before. (For example, A.J. Ayer studied at Oxford, where the views of Prichard and Ross prevailed, while C.L. Stevenson studied under Moore at Cambridge.) This is because the intuitionists confidently proclaimed that they could intuit what was 'right' or 'good'. The emotivists then pointed out that all the intuitionists were doing was expressing their own preferences and attitudes; except the emotivists ambitiously went beyond this and claimed that all moral judgements, not just 'moral judgements made by intuitionist philosophers circa 1930', were expressions of feelings (which is a dramatic oversimplification of the uses of moral terms). MacIntyre maintains that the emotivists 'confused moral utterance at Cambridge after 1903 ... with moral utterance as such'.[34] If MacIntyre is right then this undermines the emotivists' claim that their analysis applies to moral judgements everywhere and at all times.

Prescriptivism

All the words discussed [i.e. 'right', 'good' and 'ought'] have it as their distinctive function either to commend or in some other way to guide choices or actions.[35]

Hare

R.M. Hare (1919–2002) was the foremost prescriptivist of the twentieth century, developing his theory over three books and a period of 20 years, and it is his version of prescriptivism that we assess in this section. Like other moral philosophers of his time, Hare focuses almost entirely on meta-ethics and the meaning of ethical terms;[36] it is only later in his life that he turned to more normative questions. Hare's prescriptivism can be seen as a development of emotivism, insofar as it further explores the uses and purposes that moral judgements have in our dialogue with other people. But it views emotivism as too simplistic: value judgements are not expressions of feelings, they have a much more important use, namely to tell other people how they ought to act.[37]

Like emotivism, prescriptivism is a non-cognitivist theory and denies that values are types of facts, and denies that moral discourse is informative or descriptive or that moral judgements state moral facts. Hare uses G.E. Moore's open question argument (page 191) to show that no definition of moral terms such as 'good' can adequately account for the meaning of 'good'. For Hare, naturalists make the mistake of attempting to derive value judgements from 'statements of fact', and by doing so they miss out on one of the essential features of a value judgement, namely that it *expresses* something. But the missing element is not a feeling (as the emotivists would assert) but something more important:

> Value-terms have a special function in language, that of
> commending; and so they plainly cannot be defined in
> terms of other words which themselves do not perform this
> function.[38]
>
> Hare

On Hare's analysis, making a moral judgement like 'Stealing is wrong' comes close to issuing a command, or giving advice, or offering a recommendation, or prescribing. When a doctor gives you a prescription they are recommending a course of action, and similarly our moral judgements are a form of prescription (hence the name 'prescriptivism'). So according to prescriptivism when John Stuart Mill claimed that 'happiness was desirable', what he really meant was not that 'happiness is something we are able to desire' but that 'happiness *ought* to be desired'. In other words, by using the moral language of desirability Mill was commending happiness as something we should strive to reach. Thus, against the emotivist, the prescriptivist argues that ethical propositions are not expressions of the way the speaker feels, but exhortations to action.

Geoffrey Warnock highlights the differences between emotivism and prescriptivism in this way: emotivism sees moral language as an attempt to influence others, so if Theresa tells us 'it is wrong to join terrorist organisations fighting in other countries' then she is trying to affect our attitudes and behaviour so that we don't join a terrorist organisation.[39] But, for the prescriptivist the essence of moral language is not to influence but to guide: Theresa is actually saying 'Do not join terrorist organisation'. The emotivist doesn't think Theresa has much more to add, as for them ethical language is non-rational. However, Hare's prescriptivism accounts for our expectation that Theresa would be able to offer reasons for her instruction, and be able to enter into a discussion with us about these reasons.

A further way to understand the distinction between emotivism and prescriptivism is to distinguish between (a) my telling you what to do and (b) any effects or consequences of my so telling you. The prescriptivist focuses on what I am doing *in* saying 'Terrorism is wrong', that is, recommending a certain course of action ('You ought not to support terrorism'). Whereas the emotivist highlights what I may hope to achieve *by* saying it (namely for my emotive exclamations to prompt you to rethink your decision to support terrorism). If naturalist theories compared value judgements to statements of fact, and emotivist theories compared them to exclamations, then the prescriptivist compares them to commands.

Viewing moral judgements as primarily commands is key to Hare's account of ethical language: all moral judgements ('It is wrong to become a terrorist') entail an imperative ('Do not become a terrorist'). Hare is not saying all imperatives are moral ones, or that moral judgements are identical to imperatives. If Descartes, in his lonely room by the fire, screams 'Shut the door, I can't *think* when it's so cold!' then he is issuing an imperative that applies only to that very specific context. But for Hare, moral judgements are universal imperatives, and they differ from other commands in that they do not simply speak of the obligations of a particular person in a particular situation, but imply that anyone and everyone, in a relevantly similar situation, would be likewise obliged. For the moral judgement that I make in a certain situation must be founded on certain features of that situation; and accordingly I must, in consistency, be prepared to make the same judgement in any situation which shares those features and does not differ in any other relevant respect. What is particular about the imperatives implied by our moral judgements is that these are imperatives that I am willing to apply universally. Thus Hare follows Kant in regarding *universalisability* as essential to the logic of ethical judgements, in addition to their *prescription*.

anthology 1.19

▶ **ACTIVITY**

Revisit sentences 1, 4, 5 and 9 (from the activity on pages 202–3) and write down the meaning that Hare would find in them (bearing in mind the two elements of his theory: prescription and universalisability).

The immediate advantage of such an approach over that of emotivism is that it enables us to avoid the conclusion that moral discourse is fundamentally non-rational. The problem of getting somebody to do something, or of influencing her feelings with that end in view, is simply the problem of employing effective means to that end; and those means need not involve my putting forward reasons. For, as we saw, for a judgement to be 'emotively' effective it is required only that it works to influence behaviour. Yet it seems to be essential to our concept of morality that we can ask for a rational response to practical questions. For Hare, prescriptive discourse is therefore concerned with answering questions about conduct, as contrasted to informative discourse which seeks information about matters of fact. In giving moral advice, or arguing a moral point, what we are engaged in is a rational attempt to show that our position is *consistent* with the logical character of ethical discourse, namely its being prescriptive and universalisable. Thus, for Hare, it is in virtue of the universalisability of moral propositions that rational argument in ethics is possible.

According to such an account we are able to have moral disputes because we can advocate different moral principles. So long as there is consistency in what we prescribe we are speaking the language of morals. In other words, the prescriptivist affirms that any imperative to action which can be universalised and consistently adhered to must count as an ethical principle.

Some criticisms of prescriptivism

Hare's prescriptivism gives a detailed account of what it is to make a moral judgement, and his theory is more plausible than the 'Boo/Hooray' theory of emotivism. But Hare's account still seems to be a narrow one and Warnock asks if it is really plausible to suppose that all moral discourse is primarily and essentially concerned with telling people what to do. Surely, as well as prescribing, we may deploy moral terms in order to undertake, implore, resolve, confess and so forth.[40] In other words, Hare restricts his analysis to those contexts in which one speaker addresses to another a moral judgement upon some course of action.

This objection, however, is perhaps based on a misunderstanding. For what the prescriptivist surely intends is to stress the interconnection between moral discourse and action. Thus, while moral utterances clearly do not always tell someone what to do, it is plausible to hold that the acceptance of a moral proposition consists in acting in a certain way if the appropriate circumstances arise. Nonetheless, while it is clear that there is an interdependence between ethical pronouncements and behaviour, we can raise questions about the prescriptivist explanation of it.

Prescriptivism is vulnerable to claims about the moral content of some prescriptions – if moral judgements are our personal prescriptions as to how we should behave, then what are the standards against which our personal prescriptions should be judged? Because prescriptivism is a non-cognitivist theory it rejects the notion that there are external moral criteria (existing 'out there' in the world) which can be used as a measure of our prescriptions. For Hare, the only criterion seems to be: 'Is your judgement an imperative that you would universalise?' But there are two types of cases in which this criterion becomes inadequate when thinking about morality.

First, there are trivial prescriptions that could be universalised (such as, 'It would be good at Hallowe'en if I started to provide sweets at my house as well as collecting them from other people's'). As we have already seen (above, page 90), although this is a prescription, and is universalisable, it doesn't seem to be a moral imperative. Secondly, and more importantly, let us take the case of prescriptions that emerge from a fanatic culture that we would want to condemn, for example people who promoted and carried out genocides in the twentieth century (including Nazi Germany, Stalinist Russia, the Khmer Rouge in Cambodia – the list goes on[41]). Prescriptivism appears to say that, so long as people are consistent in putting forward horrific judgements such as Höss's claim (above, page 194) that 'the murder of millions of Jews was right'), then their consistency makes the judgement a moral one. To be consistent, Höss would have to say 'and if I were Jewish then I should be murdered too'; and if he accepted that, then his judgement is a universal one and on Hare's account it must be seen as a moral judgement. But what we want to say, what our intuitions scream out to us, is that Höss is *wrong*, no matter how consistently or universally he and other murderers like him, applied their prescriptions.

Both of these cases lead to the further criticism that they undermine Hare's claim that he has shown how prescriptivism retains the rationality of moral discussion. We have seen that emotivism is unable to account for argument and discussion when it comes to ethics, and that this troubles us because we see moral discussion as having worth and purpose. Prescriptivism took us away from a simple 'Boo!' and 'Hooray!'; it invited us to look at the reasons for our judgements, and it raised the question – which is a very useful one in any moral discussion – namely 'Would you apply that same moral judgement to yourself?' But it turns out that universalisability isn't enough to save moral argument, as you might universalise a prescription that I disagree with ('Eating meat is right'), and I might universalise a judgement that you disagree with ('Eating meat is wrong') and we want a successful moral theory to be able to show how we can have this disagreement. Cognitivists, because they think morality describes something in the world, do give us a foundation to argue from; but non-cognitivists, including prescriptivists, find it difficult to give independent grounds that we can both appeal to, and so we may end up 'agreeing to disagree', or drifting towards **relativism**.

	Do moral terms refer to something independent of humans?	Do moral terms have a non-descriptive meaning?	Do moral terms influence action?
Emotivism	No	Yes – an emotive meaning with impact/influence	Yes – through emotional impact
Prescriptivism	No	Yes – a prescriptive meaning, like an imperative	Yes – through commendations

Figure 1.30 A reminder of some of the main features of the different non-cognitivist theories

Summary

1 In the first half of the twentieth century – as part of the 'linguistic turn' – moral philosophy took a distinct step away from discussions of normative ethics and towards meta-

ethics. The study of ethical language which dominated last century forms part of meta-ethics, raising questions about the meaning and nature of moral judgements and of the evaluative terms (good, bad, right, wrong) employed in these judgements.

2 Some philosophers make an ontological commitment to moral properties and objects – they believe that there are things that exist 'out there' in the world to which terms like 'good' and 'right' refer. These philosophers are known as moral realists. Other philosophers don't make such an ontological commitment: they don't believe that 'good' or 'right' refer to anything out there in the world at all. These philosophers are moral anti-realists. Overlapping with the realist/anti-realist debate about the ontological status of moral terms (about whether they refer to anything that exists or not) is a semantic debate about the meaning of moral judgements. On the one hand, cognitivists believe that moral judgements refer to the world; they are propositions that correctly or incorrectly describe the world: in other words, moral judgements can be true or false. On the other hand, non-cognitivists do not believe moral judgements refer to the world, and so they also don't believe that they are capable of being true or false.

3 We looked at three forms of ethical cognitivism:

a) Ethical naturalists, who are moral realists, argue that moral language (such as 'good') should be understood in naturalistic terms. For Aristotle, 'good' could be understood in terms of the successful fulfilment of our function. For the utilitarians, 'good' is understood in terms of the impact an action has on the pleasure, pain or happiness of the population as a whole.

b) Ethical non-naturalists, who are also moral realists, argue that moral language should be understood in non-natural terms. For Moore, our intuitions reveal to us what things are good (and there are a number of goods) and he thought we should strive to bring about these good states of affairs through our actions – he was a 'consequentialist' intuitionist in that respect. For Prichard, our intuitions reveal what is right. These 'deontological' intuitionists believe we have certain obligations (and there are a number of obligations) that we must adhere to.

c) Error theory is an anti-realist theory, proposing that moral language does indeed make claims about the world, but that all these claims are false. This is because moral terms like 'good' don't actually refer to anything in the world at all, but we project our moral values onto the world and then see these values as part of the world (rather than as a projection).

4 Some philosophers believe that ethics is 'autonomous' and this leads them to reject naturalism. They believe that ethics forms a unique and distinct realm which cannot be reduced to or analysed in terms of other things. Hume believed in the *logical autonomy* of ethics, claiming that it was a logical error to derive an 'ought' from an 'is' (i.e. we cannot move from a discussion of facts to a conclusion which is evaluative). Some philosophers believed that naturalism systematically makes this kind of error. Moore believed in the *semantic autonomy* of ethics, claiming that you could not define moral terms in non-moral terms. Specifically, Moore thought that moral terms were indefinable *and* non-natural and that it was a double fallacy (a) to try to define them and (b) to do so in naturalistic terms. So Moore accused naturalists, and in particular the utilitarians, of committing this naturalistic fallacy. However, many philosophers doubt whether in fact the utilitarians are guilty of this fallacy.

5 We looked at two types of ethical non-cognitivism, both of which are anti-realist positions:

a) Emotivism can be seen as a reaction against the objective pronouncements of intuitionists like Moore about what was right or good. It seemed to A.J. Ayer that these pronouncements were really just expressions of personal approval or disapproval. So moral judgements expressed emotions but had no factual content at all (they were neither true nor false). C.L. Stevenson found a further emotive element in moral judgements, namely that they were attempts to persuade other people to feel the same way.

b) Prescriptivism can be seen as a reaction against emotivism. Prescriptivists such as R.M. Hare agreed with the emotivists that moral judgements weren't being used to describe the world, so can't be true or false, and instead have a non-descriptive meaning. But Hare felt that emotivism hadn't captured the real use of moral judgements, which was to issue recommendations, or universal imperatives, about how other people should act. So moral judgements are meant to guide action, and to urge everyone in a similar situation to behave in the same way.

The mind–body problem: What is the relationship between the mental and the physical?

Introduction

This unit is concerned with what is known as the 'mind–body problem'. So that we can get a grasp of the problem, we need first to be clear about what we mean by 'mind' and by 'body'. The idea of the body is fairly straightforward. It is the living physical form that all humans have, that is, our legs, arms, torso, head and so on, including all our bodily organs and, importantly, the brain. In common with other physical things, like toasters or turnips, my body is composed of matter, occupies space and can be seen and touched. It is the part of us that medical science is primarily concerned with. My body is, at the very least, a very important part of what I am. Certainly we all have a special interest in our own bodies and make efforts to keep them in reasonable condition, e.g. by avoiding damaging them and providing them with what they need (food, warmth, etc.) to keep them from malfunctioning or dying.

However, I appear to be more than just a physical thing like a toaster or a turnip. For I have **consciousness**; I have a mind and am aware (in a way that toasters and turnips are not) of myself and of the things around me. What exactly this conscious awareness is, though, is a far trickier question than asking what the body is, and a key piece of the mind–body puzzle is directly concerned with trying to understand its true nature. But before we can get properly to grips with this question, we need to get a clearer idea of what philosophers are talking about when they use the words 'mind' and 'consciousness'. So, to this end, have a go at the activity below.

▶ **ACTIVITY: What is consciousness?**

To get us started with the mind–body problem, try to describe what it is like to be conscious. Make a list of things that you are now aware of in your consciousness; that is, of what you have in your mind. To do this you will need to 'introspect', in other words, you will need to look into your own mind. ('**Introspection**' is a word we will be using a good deal in this chapter. It means literally 'looking inwards' and is used in philosophy of mind to refer to our ability to examine the contents of our own conscious experience.) This obviously doesn't need to be a complete list, but try to include a good range of different sorts of things.

Now try to group the things you're aware of into different categories. Here is a possible list of categories:

1 *Sensations produced by objects around you*, e.g. the hardness you feel from the chair you are sitting on, the smell of stale coffee, the sound of the rustling paper as you turn the pages of a book.
2 *Sensations in your body*, e.g. a sore throat or itchy nose.
3 *Inner feelings*, e.g. emotions such as anger or joy.
4 *Imagination*, e.g. conjuring images of things in your mind such as of a winged horse or of what it feels like to stroke a cat.
5 *Ideas or concepts*, e.g. you can think of all kinds of ideas, such as the ideas of a triangle, snow or fairness. Empiricists argue (as you may know from studying AS-level philosophy) that such concepts ultimately derive from sense experience.
6 *Beliefs*, e.g. the thought that philosophy is hard, or that too much sugar is bad for your health. We might call such thoughts 'items of knowledge'.
7 *Desires*, e.g. the thirst for a fresh cup of coffee, the urge to scratch your nose or to go on holiday to Sri Lanka.

But what then am I? A thing which thinks. What is a thing which thinks? It is a thing which doubts, understands, conceives, affirms, denies, wills, refuses, which also imagines and feels.[1]

Descartes

The mind has traditionally been understood as all that I am conscious of. The mind is also thought to be that which makes me *me*. In other words, it is what constitutes my personal identity; it is the essence of what I am. And it is this view that René Descartes (1596–1650) expresses in the quotation above in the core text for this course, his *Meditations* (1641). So the investigation into the nature of consciousness amounts to asking: What medium do thoughts, feelings, emotions and ideas take place in? How are mental states produced? Is the mind really just the same thing as the brain? Or is it some sort of product of the brain? If so, just 'how and why', as the contemporary philosopher David Chalmers poses the question, 'do physical processes give rise to experience? Why do not these processes take place "in the dark," without any accompanying states of experience? This is the central mystery of consciousness.'[2] Chalmers calls this the 'hard problem' of consciousness. The problem may also be expressed by pointing out that there is an 'explanatory gap' between understanding the nature of the brain processes which underlie conscious experience and the nature of the experience itself.[3] For example, we may know what happens physiologically when someone experiences pain, that

anthology 2.1

is, we may be able to point to certain neurons firing in the brain. But this doesn't seem to answer the question of why pain feels the way it does. We can understand the brain's processes without this appearing to give us any explanation of why these give rise to certain sorts of experience. Because of this explanatory gap, some philosophers deny that the mind is produced by the physical at all, arguing that it is a special spiritual thing, different in kind from our physical self, but somehow attached to it.

So this gives rise to a basic division of views on these issues. On the one hand, **dualism** is the view that there are *two* basic sorts of thing that make up a human being: one is *spiritual* or *mental* (i.e. the mind) and the other *physical* (i.e. the body). Dualists argue that the mind cannot be *reduced* to the physical, which is to say that we cannot ever explain the mind in terms of the body, or any part of the body such as the brain. So dualism is the view that mental states and processes are not states and processes of a purely physical animal, but constitute a distinct kind of **phenomenon** that is essentially non-physical in nature. According to dualism, as it is often put, no **reduction** of the mental to the physical is possible.

By contrast, **monism** is the view that there is just *one* kind of **substance**. By 'substance' here is meant a kind of stuff; something that can exist on its own. Substances are contrasted with properties, which are qualities of substances and which depend for their existence on substances. For example, water may be regarded as a substance as it can exist on its own. But wetness is a **property** of water and depends on water to exist. In other words, wetness cannot exist on its own. Now, what monists argue is that fundamentally there is just one kind of substance. Some monists claim this substance is spiritual (as in George Berkeley's (1685–1753) **idealism** which you may have studied at AS-level), others that it is physical: the view known as **physicalism** or materialism.[4] Today various forms of physicalist theory of mind hold sway. What most physicalists believe is that what we think of as mental can ultimately be explained in terms of, or reduced to, the physical. For example, some physicalists argue that what we call mental events and processes are really nothing more than events and processes of a physical organ, namely the brain. What this means is that the mind can successfully be *reduced* to the brain and its operations.

| Learn More |
Some historical background

Examples of *physicalist* theories: Epicurus and La Mettrie

Physicalist theories of mind are generally allied to a more general physicalist world view which regards the whole universe as composed of matter. Such physicalism has a long history. One well-known physicalist from the ancient world is Epicurus (c.341–270BC). Following the teachings of Democritus (c.460–370BC), Epicurus argued that the universe consists exclusively of indestructible physical atoms moving in empty space. Out of these atoms, their combinations and their movements, all the things and all the events in the universe are to be explained. So everything, including human minds, is ultimately nothing more than matter in motion. For Epicurus, the mind or soul is not made of any special spiritual stuff, but rather of particularly fine material atoms like breath or air, which animate the body and make us alive, but which disperse at death. Death involves the decomposition of both the body and the mind and so there is no after-life. Moreover, there is no transcendent or spiritual dimension to the universe: in other words, no God.

These two denials of an immortal soul and of a transcendent God clearly go against Christian teaching and so physicalism has long been regarded in the West as a threat to religious authority. However, during the Enlightenment period – around the seventeenth and eighteenth centuries – a new optimism in scientific explanations emerged in Europe. To some, it began to seem that everything could be explained in terms of physical laws and so any distinct 'spiritual' realm would become superfluous in a complete account of humankind and of the universe. Descartes argued that animals were purely physical beings, the behaviours of which could, in principle, be explained in terms of physical laws, and some influenced by this approach came to believe the same might also be possible for humans. It was La Mettrie (1709–51) who most famously defended a physicalist vision of humans in his *L'Homme-machine* (*The Human Machine*) of 1748, and went as far as to say that it might be possible to build a talking, sensing and feeling human being.

Example of an *idealist* theory: Berkeley

As you may remember if you have studied AS-level philosophy, Berkeley argued that everything that we can possibly think or experience – all our *ideas*, to use his terminology – must be our *own* thoughts and experiences. We cannot think what is not our own thought, or experience what is not our own experience. Since ideas are clearly *mental* entities, it follows that everything we can ever be acquainted with must be mental. Consequently it is in vain to suppose that there might be something other than the mental since we can never have access to it. Matter, therefore, can be discarded from our account of what there is in the universe. What we think of as physical objects are no more than collections of our perceptions of them. His conclusion was that all that there can be in the universe are minds and their various *ideas*, hence 'idealism'. We won't be looking at idealism in any detail in this chapter, but rather will focus on dualism and physicalism.

Example of *dualist* theory: Plato

While the term 'dualism' covers several quite different theories of mind, as we have seen they are all agreed in regarding the essential nature of consciousness as residing in something *non-physical* and so beyond the understanding of the physical sciences. According to this view, mind and matter are so fundamentally different that no matter how much we know about one, certain aspects of the other will remain unexplained.

One influential dualist theory is that of Plato (427–347BC). Plato believed that the virtuous soul would be rewarded by living a better life after bodily death. In Book X of *The Republic* (c. 380–360BC), in the discussion of 'the Myth of Er', Plato talks of the soul's surviving bodily death and facing the crossroads of judgement. As Er – a man who has miraculously come back from the dead – explains, the scales of justice are presented to individuals after their death and the decision is taken whether to reward or punish them for their earthly existence. This takes the form not of heavenly salvation or hellish damnation but of rebirth in a suitable body. The choice of new life made will depend on the character of one's soul. In the *Phaedo* (c.380–360BC) Plato argues that the philosophical life consists in a preparation for death through the soul's efforts to escape imprisonment in the body. For the acquisition of knowledge, and with it of virtue, involves purifying the soul of its contamination with the body. For this reason, Plato argues, death is not something the philosopher should fear.

Plato's arguments for dualism are not ones we will be examining here. Instead we will begin with those from the modern period that Descartes puts forward in his *Meditations*, which have had a profound influence on modern philosophy of mind. Indeed his version of dualism was so influential in the centuries that followed that Ryle was able to call it the 'official doctrine' in his 1949 work *The Concept of Mind*, which is one of the Anthology texts. Read the Anthology extract for Ryle's outline of the main ideas of the Cartesian view of mind and body.

anthology 2.2

2.1 Dualism: The mind is distinct from the physical

Experimenting with ideas

Suppose one member of your class were to relate a story of how she had an experience last night of leaving her body. She was able to float up, look down upon her motionless body, and rise up through the ceiling, through the attic and out above the roofs and chimney pots. From there she could fly anywhere she pleased; could look around the town and see all the people going about their business and could listen in on their conversations. After a while she flew back into her bedroom, returned to her body and went to sleep.

Experiences of leaving one's body – out-of-body experiences – are not uncommon. But do they provide us with good evidence for the view that mind and body are distinct things (dualism)? Why, or why not?

Now try to imagine yourself without a body, as a disembodied consciousness or pure soul. To do this, you might imagine opening your eyes one morning to find you cannot see your body. Thinking you may be invisible, you try to touch yourself, but find you have no hands to move. Is this possible to imagine? What difficulties do you encounter? Take note of your thoughts.

Part of the attraction of dualism is the sense that I cannot be identified with my physical form. If you lose parts of your body, it seems you don't cease to be the person that you are. I am still completely me, even if my body is diminished. As Descartes has it: 'although the whole mind seems to be united to the whole body, yet if a foot, or an arm, or some other part, is separated from my body, I am aware that nothing has been taken away from my mind'.[5] You can even imagine being consumed by a boa constrictor from the feet up, and as the snake gradually swallows your torso and neck, the person contemplating your fate, would still be you. For as long as you remain conscious you would be entirely the self-same person, despite having lost almost all of your body. But what when the snake consumes your head? Can you imagine remaining conscious without any body at all?

Figure 2.1 As long as you remain conscious, it would still be you whose body had been eaten. This seems to suggest that you are not the same thing as your body.

Descartes conducts a comparable thought experiment in *Meditation 1* (which you will have looked at if you have studied epistemology at AS-level). Descartes supposes that an extremely powerful evil spirit or demon would be capable of feeding his mind with perceptions which

219

appear to represent a physical world to him. He even imagines that his own body could be part of the illusion produced by the demon. But although it is possible that he has no body, he would still remain the self-same consciousness or person that he now is. He would still be able to philosophise, do mathematics and to imagine. He concludes that his true self can be identified with his consciousness or mind; that his essential nature is thought. I, as he says, am a 'thinking thing' and it is conceivable that this thing might exist without a physical body.

> *I find here that thought is an attribute that belongs to me; it alone cannot be separated from me.*[6]
>
> Descartes

The idea that I might exist without my body is given some **empirical** support from reports people give of out-of-body experiences, that is the experience of leaving one's body and very often being able to look down upon it. Such experiences sometimes occur when a person is near to death (near-death experiences), or quite commonly when near to sleep and can be induced by meditative techniques. If it could be established that such experiences genuinely involved the mind leaving the body, then this would present us with some powerful evidence for dualism, since they would show that consciousness can exist outside of the body. However, there are serious difficulties with such evidence, some of which we will be examining in this chapter (see particularly the *Mind without body is not conceivable* section, page 235). You will doubtless have begun to explore some of these in discussion, using the question in the Experimenting with ideas box on page 219 as a starting point, but perhaps the main problem is how to establish that such experiences are not simply hallucinatory. If we cannot prove that such experiences genuinely involve leaving the body, then their force as evidence for dualism is limited.

Substance dualism: The arguments

Direct empirical evidence for dualism seems at best inconclusive (the view that it is meaningless or confused even to talk about immaterial minds is one we will return to below when discussing **analytical behaviourism** – see page 291). But let's now turn to the philosophical arguments that Descartes uses in *Meditation* 6. The first of these draws on a consideration we've already begun to explore, namely the fact that the body can be divided into parts and so separated from me without this seeming to impact on the wholeness of my consciousness or mind.

2.1.1 The indivisibility argument for substance dualism

anthology
2.3

> *For we are not able to conceive of the half of a mind as we can do of the smallest of all bodies; so that we see that not only are their natures different but even in some respects contrary to one another.*[7]
>
> Descartes

In this short comment from the synopsis of the *Meditations*, and again in the longer extract from *Meditation* 6 (see Anthology extract 2.3), Descartes is drawing our attention to the fact that my awareness of myself is of something unitary or indivisible so that whether I am experiencing a pain in the foot, smelling coffee, imagining a sunny day, or considering a philosophical problem it is all the time the same self or mind which is enjoying these conscious experiences. So different aspects of my consciousness, such as willing, understanding, imagining or perceiving, are not like *parts* that could be removed from me, since it is the same mind that **wills**, understands, perceives or imagines. In other words, my self is unitary and indivisible. I am a single centre of consciousness and my consciousness cannot be divided into parts. To see this, try to imagine your consciousness dividing into two separate streams. In doing so, you are capable only of imagining it from the point of view of just one stream so that it appears to be impossible to be conscious in two places at once. It seems to follow that there can only be one me; my consciousness cannot be divided in two. And if I am aware of an experience, it is to me and me alone that the experience is happening.

Contrast this now with the body. Any physical thing, because it is by nature extended in space (that is to say it necessarily has three-dimensions) can always be divided up into parts, at least in principle. This means that you can take an axe to anyone's body, cleave it in two, then into quarters, and continue in this fashion indefinitely (or at least until the police arrive and cart you away). Bodies, in other words, are by their nature *divisible*. Descartes concludes that since minds and bodies differ in this important way, they must be different substances. This is the central claim of the first type of dualism we will be examining, namely **substance dualism** (also called **Cartesian dualism** after Descartes). It says that human beings are composed of two distinct types of stuff or substances. A substance in Descartes' understanding is a thing that can exist on its own and doesn't depend on anything else (except God) for its existence. So substance dualism is saying that both mind and body can exist independently of the other. What this means is that while mind and body are linked together in this life, when the body dies and decomposes, this will not extinguish the mind. In this way, Descartes' argument can 'give men the hope of another life after death'.[8]

It's worth noting that Descartes' argument makes use of a principle known as **Leibniz's Law** (named after Gottfried Leibniz 1646–1716). The law says that if two things share all the same properties, they must be one thing; but that if one has any property that the other lacks, they must be distinct things. Since divisibility is a property of bodies which minds lack, minds must be different from bodies.

Although complex sounding, the principle is intuitively easy to grasp. Consider the following example: At the time of writing, 'David Cameron' and 'the present Prime Minister' are different names for the same person. So anything that is true of David Cameron will also be true of the present Prime Minister and vice versa. For example, if it is true that David Cameron is married to Samantha, then it must also be true that the present Prime Minister is married to Samantha. But if there is one thing true of David Cameron that is not true of the Prime Minister, then we would be able to prove that they are different people. If David Cameron had lost the election in May 2015, but the Prime Minister had not, then David Cameron would not be the Prime Minister.

This same principle is used in courts of law every day. Imagine a murder case in which the accused is called Finbar Good. What the prosecution are trying to prove is that 'the murderer' and 'Finbar Good' refer to the same person. They do this by showing that lots of things that are true of the murderer are also true of Finbar Good. For example:

- The murderer was left handed.
- Finbar Good is left handed.
- The murderer was in Peckham on Friday the 13th.
- Finbar Good was in Peckham on Friday the 13th.

This could even go right down to:

- The murderer has fingerprint xyz.
- Finbar Good has fingerprint xyz.

The defence, on the other hand, are trying to show that they are not the same person, by trying to prove that what is true of the murderer is not true of Finbar Good. For example:

- The murderer was over 6ft tall.
- But Finbar Good is 5' 6".

If these last two claims are both true, then it follows that Finbar cannot be the murderer. So, this application of Leibniz's Law is clearly valid.

We can summarise the indivisibility argument thus:

- **Premise 1:** My mind is indivisible.
- **Premise 2:** My body is divisible.
- **Conclusion:** My mind is not my body.

This argument is clearly valid – the conclusion must follow from the premises. In other words, it is impossible for anything to be divisible and indivisible at the same time, so if mind is indeed indivisible and body is indeed divisible, then, by Leibniz's Law, they cannot be the same thing and dualism would be established. So to evaluate the argument we need to determine whether these premises are actually true.

Premise 2 is hard to question. Our bodies and all the organs that compose them, including our brains, are physical objects and can be divided. But what about the first premise? Is the mind truly indivisible? Well, there certainly does seem be something important about the nature of consciousness that Descartes has hit upon. Our minds do seem to have a unified nature. I am a single conscious entity and all my conscious experiences belong to the one thing that I am. So while we know from **neuroscience** that our brains are composed of millions of individual cells and that our brains are divisible, we do not experience the mind as anything but a singular consciousness. Surely this must mean that the mind cannot be the brain.

Another way of making this point about the mind is to consider that mental things, like beliefs, desires and thoughts, cannot be thought of as having any size or shape. In other words, they do not seem to be the kinds of things we can think of as being extended in space. This means that I cannot say that my belief that it is raining is two inches long, or triangular, or to the right of my desire for a beer. It also means that it makes no sense to talk about dividing a belief into parts. If the contents of my mental life don't seem to be extended in space then they must be indivisible.

Criticism 1: The mental is divisible

However, the apparent unity of consciousness has been questioned by modern neuroscience. The sense I have of being a singular consciousness may be an illusion, meaning that what we perceive when we look into our own minds – when we introspect – need not be an accurate representation of our selves. If, as physicalists argue, the brain is responsible for consciousness and for our sense of self, then cutting the brain up might well literally involve dividing the mind. Experimental evidence that seems to support this idea concerns what happens to people who have the main link between the left and right hemispheres of the brain – the corpus callosum – severed; an operation which has occasionally been performed on patients suffering from severe epilepsy. Patients whose brains had been divided in this way often reported unsettling experiences. While shopping, one such patient described her efforts to pick what she wanted from the shelves. No sooner had her right hand collected the item, and placed it in the basket, than her left hand set about returning it to the shelf, as though part of her had a different idea about what she should be shopping for. Such experiences are most naturally interpreted as showing a divided mind, or two distinct consciousnesses occupying the same skull.

It is known that the two hemispheres of the brain play different roles; the left is responsible for processing visual information from the right side of the visual field, and the right hemisphere from the left. The left hemisphere is also responsible for motor control and tactile information from the right side of the body, while the right hemisphere deals with the left side of the body. If split-brain patients have the two sides of the visual field artificially separated, for example by wearing special contact lenses, then information available to one hemisphere appears not to be available to the other. In one experiment, a patient was asked to press a button when he saw an image flashed on a screen. When the left hemisphere was presented with an image his right hand pressed the button and he was able also to name what he saw. This is what we would expect since the left hemisphere has the main responsibility for speech. But whenever the right hemisphere was shown an image, the patient would report verbally that he could see nothing, and yet his left hand would still press the button, suggesting that the right hemisphere was aware of the image but the left was not. Similar experiments have also shown that the right hemisphere is able to report what it has seen by producing accurate drawings of the image, at the same time as the patient denies verbally that he sees anything.[9]

Figure 2.2 Diagram of split-brain patient Dividing the brain appears to divide the mind into two distinct and mutually unaware centres of consciousness. This raises doubts about Descartes' claim that the mind is indivisible.

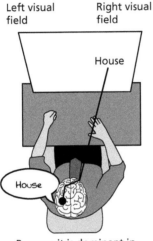

Because it is dominant in language, when the left hemisphere reads the word 'house' it verbally reports what it sees.

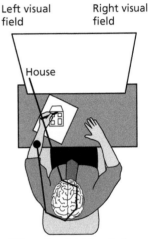

When the right hemisphere reads the word, the patient denies seeing anything, but the right hemisphere is nontheless able to draw a house.

Another important line of attack on Descartes' claim about the unity of consciousness comes from the eighteenth-century Scottish philosopher David Hume (1711–76). As you may recall from the AS-level epistemology module, Hume was an **empiricist** philosopher and so believed that all our concepts come from experience. This means that if I have a concept or idea of my self or mind then I should be able to trace this idea back to some sort of conscious experience. Introspection is the method by which Descartes claims to arrive at the experience of his mind as a unity. In Hume's words, Descartes' claim is that 'we are every moment intimately conscious of what we call our self; that we feel its existence and its continuance in existence'.[10] But Hume claims that when he introspects he finds he is conscious of no such thing.

Experimenting with ideas

Close your eyes and look into your own mind to see if you can find your self or what the word 'I' refers to. Can you find it? Is there an actual experience you can identify which is where you get the idea of 'me' from?

For my part, when I enter most intimately into what I call myself I always stumble on some particular perception or other, heat or cold, light or shade, love or hatred, pain or pleasure. I never can catch myself at any time without a perception, and never can observe anything but the perception.[11]

Hume

According to Hume, all I am ever aware of when introspecting is a series of conscious experiences, but never of any single thing which is having these experiences. In this respect, he agreed with what the Buddha said over two thousand years earlier. According to Buddhists, the self is an illusion. There is no thing that is the singular owner of your experiences; there is just the stream of conscious experiences itself. If Hume is right, then Descartes is misdescribing the way the mind appears to us. We have no immediate consciousness of an indivisible self. There's no denying the awareness of the many and varied experiences that make up mental life, but *I* am nothing over and above these experiences; rather, I simply am the collection of experiences themselves. If this is right, then the mind is not a singular entity at all, but a multiplicity of experiences. And since these many experiences are distinct from each other, the mind appears to be divisible.

But then what of the fact that I cannot imagine my consciousness dividing and remain aware from two perspectives at once? One response is just to say that what our imaginations find impossible to frame need not be a good indication of what is actually possible. Split-brain patients do indeed seem to have two streams of consciousness operating in the same skull. And the fact that I cannot imagine myself as having a divided consciousness doesn't show that two streams of consciousness cannot simultaneously exist. After all, I cannot imagine seeing the world from your point of view and from mine at the same time, but it doesn't follow from this that you and I cannot both have minds.

Criticism 2: Not everything thought of as physical is divisible

A second criticism focuses on the inference from the fact that it is difficult to make sense of the idea of dividing the mind or mental states to concluding that they cannot ultimately be physical. For there would appear to be states humans can be in which it is senseless to talk about dividing, but which are clearly physical, such as being too hot, being soaking wet or running. Perhaps mental states need to be understood as being like such bodily states. Running, like thinking, is not divisible, yet we don't on that account need to suppose that running must be the activity of an indivisible thing. No one would want to argue that because it makes no sense to imagine my temperature divided into two or to say that being wet is triangular, that these must be non-physical states. To take a different example, the solubility of sugar is not something that it makes sense to divide, but it wouldn't follow that solubility is an indivisible non-physical substance somehow connected to the sugar. So, the fact that it makes no sense to talk about splitting the mind doesn't in itself show that it is a special kind of indivisible stuff. It may simply be that the concept of divisibility doesn't apply to the self. We can't talk about dividing beauty or music either, but this doesn't mean they are indestructible substances.

This sort of objection to Descartes' dualism is one we will return to when examining the work of Gilbert Ryle (1900–76). Ryle argues that Descartes' mistake is to presuppose that the mind is a kind of *thing*, and when he sees that it lacks the properties normal physical things have, such as divisibility, to conclude that it must be a strange non-physical thing. Actually, thinks Ryle, the mind only seems strange because Descartes doesn't recognise that it isn't a sort of *thing* or *substance* at all. To escape from the confusion, what we need to do is to pay careful attention to how we use words such as 'mind'. Ryle's own analysis of its use leads him to claim that the word doesn't refer to any mysterious substance, but is really a way of talking about our behaviour. This means there is nothing surprising in the fact that it is senseless to talk of dividing the mind, since we cannot divide other terms which describe our actions and capacities, such as running or being swift. We will explore this idea further below (under Analytical behaviourism, see page 291).

2.1.2 The conceivability argument for substance dualism

> To speak accurately I am not more than a thing which thinks, that is to say a mind or a soul.[12]
>
> Descartes

▶ **ACTIVITY: What is conceivable?**

Some things that you've never experienced in real life are pretty easy to imagine. For example, you can probably imagine winning the lottery jackpot or going to the Moon. Other things never actually happen, but we can still imagine them. For example, you can probably imagine a log fire that gives off no heat or bears that can talk. These things, we might say, are *conceivable*. Then there are other things that are much harder, perhaps impossible to imagine or conceive. Can you imagine a ball that is blue and red all over at the same time? Or a cube with just five sides? Can you conceive of its being Tuesday *and* Sunday today? Or a married bachelor?

Things that are inconceivable in this way are said to be logically impossible. That is they involve a contradiction.

Try to categorise the following into those that are inconceivable and those that are conceivable:

1 A male nun
2 Round pyramids
3 Alcohol-free whisky
4 A flying horse
5 A dry cup of tea
6 Water being H_3O
7 Cold soup
8 Lead that floats
9 Vegetarian haggis
10 Women bishops

Logical possibility, physical possibility and metaphysical possibility

This activity gets you to think about the distinction often drawn by philosophers between what is logically possible and what is physically possible. Philosophers since Hume have standardly argued that things that cannot be conceived without contradiction are logically impossible. One way of understanding what this means is to say that there is no possible world in which they occur. (You may have studied the philosophical idea of possible worlds at AS-level when doing the **ontological** argument.) That is, if we imagine all the possible ways the universe might have been, then none of them would contain logically impossible objects or states of affairs, such as round pyramids. By contrast, if something is conceivable, then it *is* logically possible, meaning that although it may not happen in our world, there are possible worlds in which it does. So while there is no possible world in which the Egyptians built round pyramids, there are possible worlds in which horses fly. Because flying horses are clearly impossible in our world because of the laws of nature that hold here, they are said to be *physically impossible*. But because there are possible worlds in which horses *do* fly, such beasts are often said to be *metaphysically possible*.

anthology 2.4

In the passage quoted in Anthology extract 2.4, Descartes begins by arguing that if he is able 'clearly and distinctly' to conceive of two things separately, then it must be possible, at least in principle, for them to be separated. Descartes makes the point by saying that if they can be conceived of separately, then it would be possible for God, since he is omnipotent, to separate them. Note that Descartes' argument doesn't rely on the existence of God here. Rather, he is using the idea of God as a way of talking about what is logically possible. Since God is all-powerful, he can do anything that it is logically possible to do. However, he cannot do what is not logically possible. Even God can't make round squares. This claim relies on the general principle that whatever is clearly conceivable, in other words, anything that we can think which is not logically contradictory, is possible. For example, there is nothing contradictory in the idea of a horse without a mane. So, according to this principle, it follows that it is possible for a horse to lack a mane. Conversely, anything that is not conceivable would be impossible. For example, a square without four sides is not conceivable (the idea is contradictory) and this shows that a three-sided square is not possible.

Note that the principle doesn't imply that what is conceivable is *physically* possible in the real world. After all, I can conceive of myself as being able to fly by jumping out of the window and flapping my arms. However, this clearly doesn't mean that this is a real physical possibility and I would be reckless to think it did. But while conceivability doesn't entail that something is physically possible, it is often thought to entail that something is *metaphysically* possible. As we have seen, to say that something is metaphysically possible is to say that there is a possible world in which that state of affairs obtains. So while there is no possible world in which squares have three sides (because this is logically impossible), there is a possible world in which the laws of physics are different from this one and in which flapping one's arms will allow one to fly. Descartes might say that it would be possible for God to have created a world in which humans could fly, since God is omnipotent.

Next he returns to a point he began to explore in *Meditation 2*, the idea that introspection reveals the true nature of the self or mind to be thought or 'thinking'. As we have seen, in *Meditation 2* he argued that he can conceive of himself without a body, but that he cannot conceive of himself as not thinking. In other words, thought or consciousness is the only attribute which cannot be taken away from me, without my ceasing to be what I am, and so I must in essence be a 'thinking thing'.

Then he claims to have a clear conception of the essence of his own body and of bodies in general as extended things – that is to say, things which necessarily have three spatial dimensions. Since this conception of body is not part of the idea he has of his self or mind, he can conclude that his mind is really distinct from his body and could exist apart from it. And if they could exist separately, then they must ultimately be distinct things or *substances*. In other words, since his ideas of his mind and of his body reveal the true natures or essences of these things, and because the essences of the two are clearly different, they have to be distinct things even though they may be mixed together in some way in this life. Note that Descartes doesn't appear to be claiming that his mind and body are ever separated from each other, but just that they could be separated if God chose to separate them. It is, in other words, a metaphysical possibility that they be separated. And it is this possibility which he claims implies that they are distinct substances.

We can summarise the conceivability argument like this:

- **Premise 1:** If I can clearly and distinctly conceive of the essential natures of two things separately, it must be possible to separate them.
- **Premise 2:** I clearly and distinctly perceive myself (i.e. my mind) to be essentially a thinking and unextended thing.
- **Premise 2:** I clearly and distinctly perceive my body to be essentially an extended and unthinking thing.
- **Conclusion:** It must be possible for mind and body to be separated in reality, meaning that they are distinct substances.

Criticisms: What is conceivable may not be possible

Descartes invited comments from the scholars of the day on his *Meditations* and an important objection to his conceivability argument was made by Antoine Arnauld (1612–94). The objection focuses on the credibility of Descartes' appeal in the first premise to the principle that whatever is conceivable is metaphysically possible. Arnauld offers a parallel argument to Descartes' which is clearly fallacious which makes use of Pythagoras' theorem that the square of the hypotenuse of a right-angled triangle is equal to the square of the other two sides (Figure 2.3). He points out that someone ignorant of the proof of this theorem might well suppose that they could conceive of a right-angled triangle that lacked this property. But it wouldn't follow from this that it is actually possible for a right-angled triangle to lack the property. Not even God could make a right-angled triangle with the square on its hypotenuse not equal to the squares on the other two sides, so this property is not separable from a right-angled triangle, even in principle, despite it being conceivable that it could be. So in the same way, the fact that Descartes may conceive of the essence of his mind as distinct from his body doesn't show that it is actually possible to separate them. Arnauld concludes that while I may clearly and distinctly recognise my nature as something which thinks, I may be wrong in thinking that nothing else belongs to this nature and it may be that being extended is indeed a part of what I am.[13]

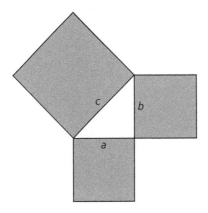

$$a^2 + b^2 = c^2$$

Figure 2.3 Pythagoras' theorem
Pythagoras' theorem shows that the square on the hypotenuse of a right-angled triangle is always equal in area to the sum of the squares on the other two sides. But if you didn't know this, you could think it possible for a right-angled triangle to lack this property

Descartes defends his argument by emphasising that it depends on his perceiving the essential natures of mind and body 'clearly and distinctly'. If indeed he has a clear and distinct conception of both, then his idea of both must reveal their true natures. So Descartes believes that when contemplating the idea of mind and the idea of body, he has a clear and distinct grasp of both and it is only because he truly perceives the essential differences that he can conclude with confidence that they really are different.

And yet Descartes' efforts to discover what an object's essential nature is, are based purely on what he can and cannot conceive, in other words on how those things appear to him. But, we may object, this is not a reliable guide to reality since appearances may be deceptive and it remains the case that there could be aspects to himself of which he is not directly aware. In other words, while it is reasonable to say that consciousness is essential to me, it is a big step to say that consciousness *alone* is essential and that, therefore, I might exist without a body or brain. Thought might still be the product of some material processes in the brain of which we are not directly aware via introspection. So just because there *appear* to be two things here, wouldn't necessarily mean that there really *are* two things.

To see the flaw, consider a parallel argument. I have a clear and distinct perception of heat. My idea here is simple, readily recognisable and I don't perceive anything else to be part of this idea. I also have a clear and distinct idea of motion. Again, I can recognise movement and appear to understand everything which is a part of this idea. Yet, can I conclude from this that heat and motion are totally different? Certainly they appear very different and so, from the subjective point of view, I would have to say that they have different essences. And yet, if science is to be believed, heat turns out to be no more or less than the vibration of molecules and atoms. Heat, in other words, is reducible to motion; despite appearances, they are not in reality different. So even though two things can be conceived of separately, it does not follow that they must be separate in reality. Descartes' error is to suppose that by contemplating the natures of mind and body he is determining their objective or true essences, whereas he is really only describing the way they appear to him.

The masked man fallacy

Learn More

In trying to distinguish objects on the basis of what can or cannot be conceived, Descartes may be accused of committing what is often termed the *masked man* fallacy. To understand this fallacy we need to examine Descartes' use of Leibniz's Law (see page 222).

Descartes puts forward two differences between his self or mind, and his body; namely that he is aware of one as being conscious and unextended, and the other as being extended but not conscious. So we can distinguish two separate arguments:

- **Premise 1:** I have an idea of my mind as a thinking thing.
- **Premise 2:** I have an idea of my body as a non-thinking thing.
- **Conclusion:** Therefore my mind and body are different.
- **Premise 1:** I have an idea of my body as an extended thing.
- **Premise 2:** I have an idea of myself as unextended thing.
- **Conclusion:** Therefore my mind and body are different.

By applying Leibniz's Law here it seems Descartes can prove that the mind and the body are distinct entities and that they do not depend on each other for their existence. However, there is an important exception to Leibniz's Law. In 'intentional' contexts, it does not hold. Intentional contexts are those that involve the mind's thinking *about* or being aware *of* something, such as when it has a belief, a hope, or a desire. Beliefs, hopes and desires are said to be intentional states, in that they are directed at something in the world, or are about something. Now, since here Descartes' argument involves the intentional states of being aware of his body and mind, and having an idea of their properties, he cannot apply Leibniz's Law. This is because Descartes' awareness of his body and mind need not reveal the true nature of either. In other words, while Descartes may have an *idea* of his body as extended and unthinking, and an *idea* of his mind as unextended and thinking, this doesn't guarantee that the two really do possess these properties in themselves.

To understand the point, consider the following argument:

- **Premise 1:** My idea of Batman is of a masked crusader.
- **Premise 2:** My idea of Bruce Wayne is not of a masked crusader.
- **Conclusion:** Therefore Batman is not Bruce Wayne.

This argument is clearly fallacious since Bruce Wayne could well be Batman if, on occasions and unbeknownst to me, he dresses up in a cape and mask to perform heroic deeds. And in the same way, my mind could well be my body, if, unbeknownst to me, the activities of some part of it, say my brain, are able to produce conscious experiences. The fact that I am unaware of my brain doing this, doesn't show that it doesn't, so while my mind and body may appear very different, in reality they could still be the same.

Note, however, that we may have distorted Descartes' arguments somewhat in making this criticism. While he does state the argument in intentional terms, he is careful to say 'I have a *clear and distinct idea* of myself inasmuch as I am only a thinking and unextended thing, and ... I possess a *distinct idea* of body, inasmuch as it is only an extended and unthinking thing'.[14] The fact that his awareness of his body and mind are said to be 'clear and distinct' clearly involves for Descartes the claim that his awareness reveals the true nature of each. As you may remember from AS-level, Descartes' strategy in the *Meditations* involves arguing that anything he understands 'clearly and distinctly' must be true, so he is not simply distinguishing the way mind and body appear to him, but rather talking about their real properties. So perhaps a fairer interpretation of his arguments would be:

- **Premise 1:** The true nature of my mind is a thinking thing.
- **Premise 2:** The true nature of my body is a non-thinking thing.
- **Conclusion:** Therefore my mind and body are different.
- **Premise 1:** The true nature of my body is an extended thing.
- **Premise 2:** The true nature of my mind is an unextended thing.
- **Conclusion:** Therefore my mind and body are different.

In this version, the criticism above does not hold, as the key differences identified are not intentional states but real properties of the objects in question. So if the premises of these arguments are true we must accept the conclusion. However, the problem now is whether we should accept these premises. In other words, can we be sure that Descartes' ideas of his mind and body are accurate? For while it may well be true that Descartes believes himself to have a clear and distinct idea of himself as an unextended thing, this is not quite the same thing as saying he really *is* an unextended thing. Physicalist philosophers will deny the second premises of both arguments and claim that the mind is indeed extended (for example, they may claim it occupies the same space as the brain) and that the body is indeed capable of thought (for example, consciousness may be produced by the electrochemical activity of the brain). So does Descartes really have a clear and distinct idea of his mind as unextended and of his body as non-thinking?

One reason to think not is that it is difficult to see how he could ever be clearly and distinctly aware that his mind and body *lack* any property at all. While he may not be aware of his body being able to think or of his mind being extended, this is not the same as being able positively to say that they couldn't be. In other words, it is not that he is aware that his body and mind lack these qualities, rather it is that he is not aware that they have them. All that Descartes can clearly and distinctly know is that when he examines his idea of his body, he is unaware of its being able to think, and when he examines his mind he is unaware of its being extended. So his arguments should really be of the following form:

- **Premise 1:** I am aware of myself as a thinking thing.
- **Premise 2:** I am not aware of body as a thinking thing.
- **Conclusion:** Therefore my mind and body are different.
- **Premise 1:** I am aware of my body as an extended thing.
- **Premise 2:** I am not aware of myself as an extended thing.
- **Conclusion:** Therefore my mind and body are different.

However, these arguments are fallacious since the fact that he is not aware of his mind and body in either of these ways is not the same as saying that they cannot be such. Not being aware of an aspect of something is not the same as being aware of the absence of that aspect. To see the point, consider the following example. Imagine you are at a masked ball, in which the identity of all the guests is disguised. Someone enters the room wearing an elaborate mask and you try to reason as to the identity of this person along the following lines:

- **Premise 1:** I am aware that my best friend has blue eyes.
- **Premise 2:** I am not aware that the man in the mask has blue eyes.
- **Conclusion:** Therefore the man in the mask is not my best friend.

Here something is true of your friend – that you are aware he has blue eyes – that is not true of the man in the mask. Both premises are true, and so it would seem that, according to Leibniz's Law, the two terms 'best friend' and 'man in the mask' cannot refer to the same person. There must be two people involved. However, this is plainly wrong. The man in the mask could be your best friend, but with a mask on. Leibniz's Law fails in this instance because the two premises of the argument tell us more about your state of mind, than about the colour of the man's eyes. So the fact that you are unaware of the colour of his eyes doesn't tell us anything for sure about whether or not he actually has blue eyes in reality. In other words, not being aware that he has blue eyes, is not the same as being aware that he doesn't have blue eyes, yet it is this premise that is needed for Leibniz's Law to apply.

In the same way, imagine if someone, Kevin, did not follow politics very closely and doesn't know who the Prime Minster is at the moment. After asking Kevin several questions we might be able to put the following argument together.

- **Premise 1:** Kevin is aware that the Prime Minister works in the Houses of Parliament.
- **Premise 2:** Kevin is not aware that David Cameron works in the Houses of Parliament.
- **Conclusion:** Therefore David Cameron is not the Prime Minister.

Again the conclusion is plainly false, even though the premises may be true since they do not reveal any real differences in the objects themselves (the Prime Minister and David Cameron), but merely in the way he is conceived by Kevin. Not knowing that David Cameron works in the Houses of Parliament is not the same as knowing that he doesn't, and this is what would be needed for Leibniz's Law to work here; and likewise with Descartes' argument. Not being aware that his mind is extended is not the same as being aware that it is not. And not being aware of his body as a thinking thing is not the same as being aware that it is not. Putting forward differences between the mind and body on the basis of what he is or is not aware of does not really tell us that minds and bodies are in fact different. Minds may well be extended. And bodies may well be thinking.

▶ ACTIVITY: The masked man fallacy

Which of the following arguments commit the masked man fallacy? Why?

- **Premise 1:** I am aware that I have a cold.
- **Premise 2:** I am not aware that germs exist.
- **Conclusion:** Therefore my cold cannot depend upon the existence of germs and might exist without them.

- **Premise 1:** Harry believes Severus Snape is out to get him.
- **Premise 2:** Harry does not believe the Half-Blood Prince is out to get him.
- **Conclusion:** So Severus Snape is not the Half-Blood Prince.

- **Premise 1:** Derren knows that the Morning Star is the planet Venus.
- **Premise 2:** Derren does not know that the Evening Star is the planet Venus.
- **Conclusion:** Therefore the Morning Star is not the Evening Star.

- **Premise 1:** Abi wants to become famous.
- **Premise 2:** Abi does not want to be hounded by the press and general public.
- **Conclusion:** Therefore becoming famous does not involve being hounded by the press and general public.

- **Premise 1:** I am aware of looking out for my own safety when crossing roads.
- **Premise 2:** I am not aware of a having a guardian angel who looks out for my safety when crossing roads.
- **Conclusion:** Therefore my safety depends only on myself and not on a guardian angel.

What is possible tells us nothing about reality

If we accept that dualism is logically possible, and that God could have created two substances, what can we legitimately infer from this about the actual situation in this world? We've seen that Descartes argues that conceivability entails logical possibility and therefore that there are possible worlds where minds are distinct from bodies. However, such metaphysical possibility doesn't show that it is physically possible in our world. The natural laws governing the behaviour of everything in the universe may prohibit consciousness from appearing without a properly functioning brain to produce it. For, as we have seen, logical possibility doesn't entail physical possibility. We may not now understand just how the brain produces consciousness, but this is a limitation in what we know. And limitations in what we know about the natural world do not tell us anything about how things actually work in nature. So this objection is saying that we cannot use **a priori** reasoning – that is reasoning without any reference to experience – to analyse our concepts of mind and body and thereby to make substantive empirical claims. On this view it may be a **contingent** fact about consciousness that it can only be produced by brains, and whether or not it is is something that can only be determined by empirical investigation.

Mind without body is not conceivable

Descartes' and Plato's claim that the true nature of my self is not physical also seems to go against our common sense understanding of what it is to be a person. In everyday life we recognise people as being the same by their bodies. Your friends and family members are flesh and blood beings, not disembodied souls. And if they were to lose their bodies you would be unable to recognise them. So, for example, you recognise your teacher as the same person who taught you last week because they have the same face. If next week someone turned up to teach you with a different face and different body, doubtless you would conclude that it was a different person. I doubt that you would be persuaded that it was really the same person, no matter what they said. This suggests that wherever someone's body goes, they go, and that their body is an essential component of who they are. Certainly in the ordinary course of things we are unable to detach ourselves from our bodies and take off as disembodied spirits to roam another plane, or to hitch up with a new body. But if dualism were true, there would seem to be no principled reason why we shouldn't do this kind of thing regularly.

 Experimenting with ideas

How can you tell that a student is absent from a particular class?

If a student claimed they were present even though their body was not, should their name be put on the register?

What do your answers suggest about the relationship between someone's body and their self?

The Experimenting with ideas activity on page 219 asked you to try to imagine losing your body. Is this actually conceivable? It may appear so on the face of it. You seem to be able to imagine looking down on your body and floating upwards. But on reflection it seems that such accounts must make implicit reference to embodiment. For example, to talk of *looking down* on your body implies you have eyes to see. Looking in different directions must involve turning one's head or body around. Moreover, how could someone float upwards and through the roof without having some physical body to move through space? Indeed, the very idea of moving around in space implies having some physical position, and yet it seems that without any physical form not only could you not perceive anything, you couldn't actually *be* in any place either.

Another difficulty for out-of-body experiences is the apparent impossibility of verifying them. Because the experiences are essentially private, there can be no independent checks by others that what is experienced genuinely involves leaving one's body. Contrast such experiences with the evidence a scientist uses when conducting experiments. The claims they make must be subject to independent test. They must be repeatable. Logical positivists such as A.J. Ayer (1910–89), whom we studied when examining religious language at AS-level, argue that for an apparently empirical claim to be meaningful, it must be verifiable. But the possibility of establishing the existence of anything non-physical, such as a mind, lies beyond any possible empirical test, and so such entities cannot be considered scientifically respectable. In this case, according to **verificationism**, it is literally nonsense to talk about a non-physical substance or of being outside of one's body.

We can arrive at the same conclusion by following David Hume's argument that we can have no idea of the mind (see page 225). For Hume, genuine concepts have to originate in sense experience. So, if I have the concept of hand or ear, it's because I have seen and felt these things at some point. However, if we reflect on our sense experience we find, claims Hume, that there is no impression of the mind. We are aware of the various experiences we enjoy, such as sensations, emotions, beliefs and so forth, which are the contents of consciousness. But we are never aware of any *thing* which is the owner of these conscious experiences. Moreover, if the mind is, as dualists claim, immaterial and lacking extension, then it could not be a possible object of sense experience. Sense experience, after all, is necessarily of physical things which are extended in space. For this reason, the idea of an immaterial mind as a thing which is not a possible object of experience, must lack any meaning for Hume.

Learn More

Immanuel Kant (1724–1804) argues that for a concept such as 'mind' to be meaningful it must apply to some possible experience. But if we cannot conceive of an experiential situation in which the concept could be used then we don't really have any proper idea what we are talking about. Here a word may seem meaningful, but without any application it would just be an empty sound. And if the concept of immaterial minds has an application to experience there must be criteria we could apply to identify them. But what if each morning I had a new soul? How could we tell that this is not the situation? There are no criteria available to establish this either way, because souls are not the kinds of things that can be individuated. Physical bodies can be because they occupy specific positions in space. But since souls do not, it seems we have no basis for identifying them.

Dualism is saying my mind, rather than my body, is to be identified with the person that I am. This means that the distinction between me and anyone else must be to do with the nature of differences between our minds. However, it is possible to imagine that someone else might have exactly the same thoughts, feelings and so forth as me and yet still be a distinct consciousness. We might imagine such a person as being a kind of mental twin, with their mind having exactly the same content as mine. But now let's ask, in this case: What is it that distinguishes my mind from my twin's? How do we know there are two minds here, rather than just one? The dualist is not able to appeal to anything physical to distinguish the two (such as our bodies), and cannot appeal to anything mental either, since, they are, in this respect, identical. So it seems there can be no way for them to draw the distinction. And so it seems to follow that I must have a body in order to be differentiated in such a case and therefore that a body must be essential to who I am.

Note also that without a body it would seem to be impossible to communicate with other people, for communication involves the use of the sense organs, the eyes, mouth and ears. So if disembodied consciousness is possible, it would appear to be a rather lonely prospect, perhaps a form of torturous solitary confinement; unless we could commune with others through some form of telepathy. And yet there are good reasons to doubt that telepathy is possible. Ordinary experience, for one, suggests we cannot peer into other people's minds to see what they are feeling or thinking. If you want to know someone's secret thoughts, after all, you need to wait for them to tell them to you.

The dependence of mind on brain

Finally it is worth mentioning here a crucial argument we will be returning to and which has had a profound influence on the direction the philosophy of mind has taken since Descartes' day. The argument draws on the evidence provided by modern neuroscience (science of the brain) to suggest that our mental life depends on our brains. Memories are stored in the brain, for example, and stimulation of specific points in the brain can cause a person to recall events from their past. Brain damage can cause memory loss and this suggests that when the brain decomposes, our memories must disappear (if not before). So how can we retain a sense of self without our memories? Sensations also appear to be produced by the activation of specific areas of the brain. Most fundamentally, the evidence is that consciousness itself is the product of a living, functioning brain. Disrupt the operations of the brain with drugs or trauma and consciousness can be radically affected. This dependence of mind on brain suggests that the destruction of the brain must destroy consciousness, so that the person cannot survive independently of the body and that substance dualism must be false.

> *Although the soul is united to the whole body, its principal*
> *functions are, nevertheless, performed in the brain; it is here*
> *that it not only understands and imagines, but also feels; and*
> *this is effected by the intermediation of the nerves, which*
> *extend in the form of delicate threads from the brain to all parts of the*
> *body.*[15]
>
> Descartes

Note, however, that Descartes was not unaware of the importance of the brain to the proper functioning of the mind, as this quotation shows. Indeed, he was one of the first to recognise that the brain is the true location for much of our conscious experience. He based his conclusions on his own researches into anatomy and physiology which showed that the system of nerves by which sensations are communicated from the body to consciousness and by which motor movement is controlled in our limbs, have their ultimate centre in the brain, and he rejected the common opinion of the day that it is in the heart that our feelings of emotion, our 'passions', are located.[16] So while in the *Meditations* he maintains that the mind is a distinct substance, he was nonetheless alive to the fact that consciousness of the body in sensation, our capacity to imagine and perhaps even some of our higher cognitive functions such as memory and even some reasoning are a product of the union of mind and body, and so his dualist view can arguably accommodate some, if not all, of the evidence of modern neuroscience. Nonetheless, if Descartes is right, then the destruction of your brain will not ultimately destroy your consciousness and you will be able to continue to think without it and it is this which many find hard to accept in the face of the neuroscientific evidence.

Evolutionary history

Charles Darwin's (1809–82) theory of evolution is a well-established account of the origins of all living things including human beings.[17] According to the theory, all species derive from a common ancestor and differences between them are the product of random variations between parents and offspring and the pressures of 'natural selection', which mean that those best adapted to their environments are most likely to pass on their genes and survival strategies to their offspring. We need not go into the theory in detail, but assuming it is correct, it implies both that humans are related to all other animals and that our appearance on the planet can be explained in purely physical terms. From the perspective of evolutionary theory, the appearance of a non-physical mind cannot be explained. If humans are the only creatures with minds, as Descartes claimed, then their appearance is a complete anomaly, something that would stand out as unexplained and inexplicable within the theory of evolution. Where did minds come from? Why did they appear? How did they become attached to our brains? And when in our evolution did this miraculous event take place? Such questions cannot be answered by evolutionary theory and this suggests they are misguided questions. So how would evolution explain the appearance of consciousness?

Like many other species we have a nervous system and ours is distinguished from those of other species only in its degree of complexity and power, not in kind. The theory of evolution suggests that the mind evolved in the same way as the capacities and organs of all living things, as a survival strategy emerging from the physical processes of genetic variation. Consciousness is certainly a remarkable evolutionary development and its usefulness is not hard to see. Being aware of one's environment and one's body via sensations will clearly help an organism to find sustenance, avoid being eaten and so on. Advanced cognitive capacities also have an obvious benefit in helping us to solve the problems of survival in hostile environments. Observation of other animals suggests strongly that they too are conscious and that the nature of their mental capacities is related to the structure of their brains. All this points to the conclusion that our minds evolved gradually over millions of years and that mentality is the product of the increasing complexity of our brains, and not something else entirely. We can reach the same conclusion by observation of the development of the individual person from birth, or even before, and through to adulthood. Consciousness is not something which appears all at once and fully formed. Rather it emerges gradually as the baby and its brain grows. When you wake up in the morning too, it seems your consciousness gradually surfaces, suggesting it is a complex phenomenon, not a simple and unitary substance.[18]

Property dualism

The evidence of neuroscience and evolutionary theory is pretty compelling against substance dualism and has led many philosophers to embrace physicalism. But there is an alternative form of dualism, known as **property dualism**, which appears better able to accommodate the scientific evidence. We have seen that a property is a quality of a substance which depends for its existence on the substance. And what property dualism claims is that the brain has a special set of non-physical properties alongside its ordinary physical properties; properties possessed by no other kind of physical object. The properties in question are the ones you would expect, namely mental phenomena such as experiencing sensations, thinking, desiring and so forth. So consciousness is a real phenomenon, but is not *substantial*, that is, it cannot exist alone without a living brain to produce it. Conscious experiences are held to appear or *emerge* when the developing brain reaches a certain level of complexity. In other words, mental properties are *emergent*, that is, they do not appear until ordinary physical matter has managed to organise itself into a sufficiently complex system (e.g. by evolution). Examples of properties that are emergent would be that of being coloured or living. All these require matter to be suitably organised before they appear. But the property dualist is arguing that *mental* properties are a special sort of emergent property in the sense that they are *irreducible* to matter. This means that they are not just organisational features of physical matter. Rather, mental properties are essentially non-physical in the sense that they cannot be *reduced* to physical properties and so cannot be explained by the physical sciences. Because property dualists believe in the irreducibility of mental phenomena they remain dualists even though they claim there is just one kind of substance.

2.1.3 The 'philosophical zombies' argument for property dualism

 Experimenting with ideas

In the eighteenth century Leibniz criticised the view that the mind might be reducible to matter with this argument:

One is obliged to admit that perception and what depends upon it is inexplicable on mechanical principles, that is, by figures and motions. In imagining that there is a machine whose construction would enable it to think, to sense, and to have perception, one could conceive it enlarged while retaining the same proportions, so that one could enter into it, just like into a windmill. Supposing this, one should, when visiting within it, find only parts pushing one another, and never anything by which to explain a perception. Thus it is in the simple substance, and not in the composite or in the machine, that one must look for perception.[19]

Leibniz

In this quotation Leibniz invites us to imagine going inside a thinking, perceiving machine. If physicalists are right we are machines of this sort. So let's turn the thought experiment around and imagine ourselves reduced in size so that we could walk around inside someone's brain. We can imagine being able to watch neurons sending electrical signals across synapses, neurotransmitters sluicing around and so forth. But the question is, would we be able to find inside this brain the person's thoughts, feelings and perceptions?

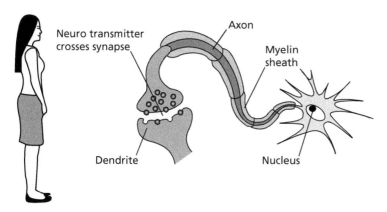

Figure 2.4 If you were shrunk to the size of a cell and could wander around inside someone's brain, would you be able to find their thoughts, sensations or emotions?

A variety of mental phenomena may appear impossible to account for in purely physical terms. Descartes pointed to our ability to use language and to reason, especially about mathematics, as beyond the capacity of any physical system. In the quotation on page 241 Leibniz focuses on thinking, sensing and perceiving, and his argument is that we could know everything that there is to know about a physical mechanism that thinks, senses and perceives, and yet this knowledge would not provide us with an explanation of these conscious states. Physicalism must therefore be an incomplete account of what there is in the world and we need to posit a non-physical mind, what he calls here a 'simple substance', to locate consciousness.

anthology
2.1

Arguments of a similar nature have been put forward by contemporary philosophers, notably David Chalmers in an article given in the Anthology, 'Consciousness and its place in nature'. The problem Chalmers is wrestling with is how to explain subjective experience, or what it is like to be a conscious human being. (See Anthology extract 2.1 for Chalmers' outline of what he means by 'consciousness'.) He has a similar list of what consciousness involves to Leibniz – 'perceptual experience, bodily sensation, mental imagery, emotional experience, occurrent thought, and more.'[20] And he illustrates these: 'There is something it is like to see a vivid green, to feel a sharp pain, to visualize the Eiffel tower, to feel a deep regret, and to think that one is late.'[21] What Chalmers is keen to emphasise here is what he calls the **'phenomenal** character' of these conscious states, that is, what it is like to be in such a state or how they appear in my mind. These properties are known as **qualia** in contemporary philosophy (*quale* in the singular), that is, in Chalmers' words 'those properties that characterize conscious states according to what it is like to have them'. [22] In other words, qualia are the intrinsic qualities that our sensations of pain, smell or colour have: the redness of red, or the peculiar unpleasantness of a pain. They are what we are immediately conscious of when we experience such sensations and it is claimed that we are directly aware of them through introspection.

Now Chalmers asks us to imagine a human that lacks qualia and other mental states; a human with no conscious experiences at all. He calls such a being a **zombie**. But Chalmers' zombie bears little resemblance to the walking dead of horror movies and so is normally called a **philosophical zombie** to mark this distinction. The difference is that it exactly resembles a normally functioning person. It is physically identical to a normal human; even its internal constitution, in particular the functioning of its brain, is indistinguishable from that of the rest of us, and it behaves just like you and me. The only difference is that it has no subjective awareness. When it hears the chink of a spoon on china, sees the colour brown and sips its cup of tea, it enjoys no qualia. And while it will scream when you step on its foot, there is no actual pain going on. There is nothing that it is like to be the zombie.

Figure 2.5
A philosophical zombie is a being which behaves the same as other human beings but which is not conscious. Although it displays the outward signs we associate with beings with minds, in the zombie's case there is nothing going on on the inside

▶ **ACTIVITY**

Is a philosophical zombie conceivable? Is it possible?

If you are in a class, work in pairs and consider whether your partner might be a philosophical zombie. Consider the evidence or reasons you have for thinking they have a mind. Is this evidence conclusive? If not, does this mean it is conceivable that they have no consciousness? If it is conceivable, is it physically possible? Is it metaphysically possible?

Now imagine you are God and you create a world which is exactly like this one right down to the positions and movements of all the elementary particles and the laws which govern their behaviour and including, of course, humans and their complex brains. Having completed this work, you sit back and ask yourself whether there are any finishing touches to be made to your creation. Suppose you would like conscious beings in your universe. Is there anything more that needs to be done to bring them into being?

Comment on the activity

You may have thought the easiest way to find out whether your partner was a zombie would be simply to ask: 'Are you a zombie?' However, obviously the zombie is going to deny it – its behaviour is, after all, indistinguishable from ours. If you ask it to explain its thoughts or describe its qualia, it will be able to do as convincing a job as you or I, even though it has neither thoughts nor qualia. But if your partner was a zombie, what could it have been talking about when it told you it was conscious, that it was enjoying its cup of tea and wondering whether you could enjoy the same mental states as it? Clearly it couldn't have been telling the truth since it has no mental states. So was it lying about its mental states? No. A zombie couldn't lie either since lying presupposes having mental states. But if the zombie's utterances are neither true nor lies, then what is their status? It seems hard to make sense of what is going on when a zombie talks. Considerations such as this might make you wonder whether the zombie idea is really conceivable after all.

We cannot tell, no matter how closely we inspect someone, whether or not they are a zombie. This is because zombies are, by definition, identical to us in every possible physical test we can make. They only differ in a way we cannot physically test. But in this case you can never know that someone else is not a zombie and worse, you cannot even know that everyone else is not a zombie. Perhaps the whole world, apart from you, is made up of mindless machines which merely appear to you to be conscious.

Chalmers accepts this line of thought. He thinks it is conceivable that there exist philosophical zombies – after all, there seems to be nothing contradictory in the idea since we seem to have no difficulty imagining zombies. But he doesn't think they actually exist. Indeed, he thinks it is very likely that they are physically impossible given the laws of nature which operate in this universe. But the fact that we can conceive of such beings shows, he argues, that there are other possible universes – other ways things could have been – in which such beings could exist. So there is a possible world which is physically identical to this world, except that in this parallel world all the human beings are zombies. Zombies are, in other words, metaphysically possible. It follows that consciousness cannot be identical to physical properties and there is more to being conscious than can be captured in a complete physical description of you.

His argument can be outlined as follows:

1 Physicalism claims that consciousness is ultimately physical in nature.
2 It follows that any world which is physically identical to this world must contain consciousness.
3 But we can conceive of a world which is physically identical to this one but in which there is no conscious experience. (In other words, such a world is metaphysically possible.)
4 Therefore physicalism is false.

Criticisms

> But just try to keep hold of this idea in the midst of your ordinary intercourse with others, in the street, say! Say to yourself, for example: 'The children over there are mere **automata;** all their liveliness is mere automatism.' And you will either find these words becoming quite meaningless; or you will produce in yourself some kind of uncanny feeling, or something of the sort.[23]
>
> Wittgenstein

A zombie world is not conceivable

The argument above is clearly valid, so if we are to criticise it we need to examine whether the premises are true. Steps 1 and 2 are fair statements of the physicalists' claims so it is the second premise (step 3) which we need to examine. Now Chalmers defends the conceivability of zombies by pointing out that there is no obvious contradiction involved. But care is needed here because contradictions don't have to be obvious. Daniel Dennett has argued that Chalmers' zombies are not actually conceivable.[24] I may think I can conceive of such a being, but if I examine the idea more carefully I will discover that it contains hidden contradictions. This is because he claims that consciousness is necessarily linked to our various capacities to act, but in ways we may not immediately recognise. We fool ourselves into thinking we can strip consciousness away from a person's ability to converse or react appropriately to perceptual stimuli, but, Dennett urges, having a mind is integral to being able to perform such tasks and he encourages us to appreciate the way such abilities are inextricably linked to such mental states. Is it really conceivable that a zombie would be able to respond intelligibly to you in conversation without having any understanding of what it was talking about? Can we make proper sense of the idea of a human describing their experience of qualia which they don't have? Certainly to many it seems practically impossible to imagine that the person you are talking to has no consciousness – try pricking them with a pin and telling yourself they may be experiencing no pain. In the quotation on page 244, Wittgenstein suggests that reflection on the zombie possibility involves using words in ways that make them lose their sense. We take words which make good sense in everyday contexts, and begin to use them in ways which stretch their applicability to breaking point. The 'uncanny feeling' should make us realise that we have lost any clear grip on what we are talking about. Dennett uses an analogy with health to help make a similar point:

> *Supposing that by an act of stipulative imagination you can remove consciousness while leaving all cognitive systems intact … is like supposing that by an act of stipulative imagination, you can remove health while leaving all bodily functions and powers intact. … Health isn't that sort of thing, and neither is consciousness.*[25]
>
> Dennett

Let's consider again what exactly Chalmers is asking us to conceive. What is clearly not possible is to bring to mind what it is like to be a philosophical zombie, since there is nothing it is like. He sometimes speaks metaphorically of the life of the zombie as empty or dark to suggest the absence of consciousness. But while we can imagine experiencing darkness or emptiness, this is not a literal description of the zombie's inner life since it doesn't just lack light or objects of awareness but any awareness at all. In fact, the zombie's real inner life is non-existent and so is literally unimaginable.

If we cannot imagine life as a zombie, however, then we surely can imagine meeting one, that is, imagine how the zombie appears to me, from the outside, as it were. But according to the hypothesis, from this perspective the zombie is the same as any other person; and it would appear we are being asked simply to imagine a normally functioning human being. So, in sum, it seems that we are being asked either to imagine something that can't be imagined, or something which is very easy to imagine but which doesn't differ from everyday experience. Perhaps, then, the puzzling nature of this thought experiment stems from us mistakenly thinking we can hold these two conceits together: imagining being mindless, a being with a dark empty mind, crossed with imagining an encounter with an ordinary person.

Considerations such as these may lead us to claim that because the zombie hypothesis cannot be distinguished from the world we live in by any empirical test, that it is actually a hypothesis empty of meaning. For if utterances get their meaning from what they tell us about the world, then any which cannot be shown to be true or false by reference to experience would appear not to be telling us anything. So if we are genuinely to make sense of a situation we are being asked to conceive, we have to be able to point to some experience which would differentiate it from the normal situation. Yet in the zombie case, according to the hypothesis, this is not possible; zombies cannot be distinguished from ordinary people. But in this case, we may be led to the conclusion that the zombie hypothesis merely seems to be conceivable, but is actually a nonsensical idea. This is the line verificationists take. Wittgenstein argues in a way that has affinities with verificationism in his 'private language' argument (see page 285). And **behaviourism** is a school of thought in the philosophy of mind which also rejects the zombie hypothesis for similar reasons. We will be exploring these approaches when examining the problem of other minds below (see page 279).

What is conceivable is not possible

A different response is to accept that a zombie world is conceivable, but to deny that this allows us to draw safe conclusions about what is possible. A zombie world may not be logically contradictory, yet zombies may nonetheless not be genuine metaphysical possibilities. Consider whether it is conceivable that water not be H_2O. It certainly seems it is. It's possible to imagine that the water in your glass has a very different molecular structure. We can even imagine a world exactly like ours, with a transparent liquid which behaves just like water but with an alternative chemical composition. However, what are we really imagining in such a scenario? Given that water actually is H_2O, any liquid with a different composition, no matter how similarly it might behave to real water, is not actually water. So it seems that it is not possible in any world for water not to be H_2O. In the same way, it can be argued that philosophical zombies may be conceivable, but are nonetheless not metaphysically possible. Any possible world where the people are physically identical to us would have to be conscious. And if they were to lose their minds, they could not possibly continue to behave as we do.

2.1.4 The knowledge/Mary argument for property dualism

anthology 2.6

I am what is sometimes known as a 'qualia freak'. I think that there are certain features of the bodily sensations especially, but also of certain perceptual experiences, which no amount of purely physical information includes.[26]

Jackson

Another contemporary philosopher, Frank Jackson, introduced a now famous thought experiment into the literature to question the physicalists' claim that the mental can be explained in terms of the physical. The paper appeared in 1982 and was called 'Epiphenomenal Qualia'. (The meaning of the title of the paper will become clearer below when we explore a form of property dualism known as **'epiphenomenalism'**.) Like Chalmers, Jackson argues that the intrinsic nature of certain mental states – qualia – is irreducible. This is an argument for a kind of dualism. However, Jackson, like Chalmers and most contemporary philosophers, accepts that the brain must have some role to play in the production of consciousness. The evidence of neuroscience is in this regard pretty overwhelming, making Cartesian or substance dualism seem untenable. So Jackson supports a version of property dualism whereby the mental is irreducible, but nonetheless a product of the physical brain, a view introduced above.

Jackson introduces his paper by confessing to being what he calls a 'qualia freak'; that is someone for whom it appears obvious that no amount of physical information can capture what it is like to experience qualia. He gives a very simple argument to this effect: 'Nothing you could tell of a physical sort captures the smell of a rose, for instance. Therefore, Physicalism is false.'[27] However, while this argument may be very appealing to other qualia freaks, Jackson thinks he needs to develop the basic intuition behind its premise to persuade the more stubborn physicalist. And so he develops his 'Knowledge Argument'.[28]

The knowledge argument begins with a thought experiment about a brilliant neuroscientist named Mary. Mary, we are asked to suppose, has been confined her whole life to a black and white room and has access to the rest of the world only via a black and white television screen. The point of this is that we must suppose that she has never seen any colours herself. Despite this handicap, she has studied the science of vision and come to know everything there is to know about what happens physically when someone sees and talks about colours. So she knows all about which wavelengths of light produce which effects on the retina, and how this information is translated into certain excitations in the brain's visual system and how this in turn leads people to announce they have had certain colour sensations of red, blue or whatever. Next suppose that one day Mary leaves the confines of the black and white room and is able for the first time to look directly at the sky, the grass and a rose, and so to experience colours.

Does she learn something she didn't know already? Jackson thinks it is clear that she does – she learns what it is like to experience colours. It follows that her knowledge before she left the room must have been incomplete. Since this prior knowledge included everything there is to know physically about colour vision, physicalism leaves something out; specifically it cannot explain qualia. Hence physicalism is not a complete account of reality.

The knowledge argument can be summarised like this:

1 Mary knows everything about the physical processes involved in colour vision.
2 But she learns something new when she experiences colour vision herself.
3 Therefore there is more to know about colour vision than what is given in a complete physical account of it.
4 So physicalism is false.

Criticism 1: Mary gains no new propositional knowledge

An initial defence of physicalism against this argument makes use of a distinction you may be familiar with from studying epistemology at AS-level, namely the distinction between **propositional knowledge** and **acquaintance knowledge**. Propositional knowledge is knowledge of facts and can be expressed in propositions; it is knowledge *that* such and such is the case. This kind of knowledge includes Mary's knowledge of the facts of colour vision. For instance, she would know that the wavelength of red light is between 620 and 750 nanometres on the electromagnetic spectrum. Acquaintance knowledge is the kind you get from encountering something, as when we speak of knowing a person or a place or a type of object. For example, we might say that Mary knows her father, London or spaghetti bolognese, in that she has encountered them and is familiar with them.

Now, to say that Mary knows everything there is to know about colour vision is to say that she knows every physical fact about it. So it concerns her propositional knowledge. Then, when she leaves the room she does indeed learn something new, but it is not new propositional knowledge and so she learns no new facts. Rather, she becomes acquainted with the phenomenal character of colours, that is, with certain qualia.

To see the point, suppose you are a big fan of some celebrity; you follow their career avidly and know all there is to know about their professional and private life. Now suppose that you are introduced to them for the first time. As your eyes meet and you shake hands, do you learn anything new about them? In one sense you need not. You already knew what colour eyes they have, and might even have known what clothes they would be wearing and that they would be meeting you. So you have acquired no new factual knowledge. However, having met the person, you are now *acquainted* with them and so have acquired a different type of knowledge.

So, according to this objection, the plausibility of the knowledge argument rests on an equivocation on the word 'know' (that is it uses the word in two different senses) and if we use it just in the sense of propositional or factual knowledge, the argument fails.

Jackson's response is to deny that what Mary learns on her release is confined to acquaintance knowledge. Certainly she does become acquainted with colours for the first time, but she also acquires some propositional knowledge in the process. For now she is able to know facts about what it is like for human beings to see colours. Before, she knew everything physical about human colour vision, on her release she knows something more about it, so her new knowledge isn't confined to mere acquaintance with colours herself.

Let's suppose she has a companion who shared her black and white prison all her life and she returns to the room after her foray into the outside world. Like Mary, her companion, let's call him Marvin, also knows all the facts about human colour vision; yet we can imagine him being eager to hear about her experiences and we can imagine him questioning her concerning what she has learnt. Doubtless Mary would make efforts to communicate what it was like to see a red rose or the blue of the sky. But Marvin would remain in the dark about what these experiences are like, and so he would appear to lack important factual knowledge that Mary has recently acquired. Marvin may know the physical facts about Mary but still not know about her qualia. (Jackson discusses this objection from Churchland in the Anthology article, 'What Mary didn't know', particularly pages 292–3.)

Others[29] have also argued that Mary doesn't acquire any new propositional knowledge, but rather than it being confined to acquaintance knowledge, focus on her acquisition of ability or practical knowledge. Practical knowledge is the knowledge of how to do something, such as tie shoelaces or ride a bike. On this account, it is also accepted that Mary learns something new on her release, but it is not any fact she didn't already know. Rather, what she acquires are new abilities or skills. By becoming acquainted with colours she acquires the capacity to remember and to imagine the colour of ripe tomatoes, to recognise objects of similar colours by sight, to group objects together according to their common hues, and so on, which she didn't possess before. These new abilities are important in their way, but, the objection runs, they are not knowledge of new facts about what is the case. So the fact that she learns something new doesn't undermine physicalism since it is perfectly possible for her to acquire new abilities without this meaning she didn't have complete factual knowledge of what happens when people view colours.

It shouldn't surprise us that we cannot learn how to do things just from learning all the relevant facts. After all, it's not possible to teach someone how to ride a bike just by teaching them all the facts about the dynamics of cycling. We can imagine Mary also having learnt all there is know about what happens physically when someone rides a bike – the mass distribution and balance, the gyroscopic effects and so on – but not being able to ride herself. If she then learnt to ride, would she learn something new about what happens physically? Surely not. She has simply acquired a new skill. In the same way it may be that Mary learns no new facts about colour vision.

Jackson's response to this objection is to accept that Mary does acquire new abilities, but that she also acquires factual beliefs about the mental life of others. She now knows what others have been experiencing all along when they see ripe tomatoes. To force this point home he asks us to imagine Mary debating with herself over whether other people really do have the same sorts of experiences as she does when they see red tomatoes. The sceptical question here is whether, since I cannot directly access anyone else's subjective experiences, I can truly know that their experiences resemble mine. This is an aspect of the problem of other minds which we will be considering in detail below (see page 279). Jackson's concern here is not with resolving the problem, but merely with pointing out that the problem could worry Mary. But in order to worry about the problem, she has to be asking herself a factual question: 'Is it the case that others have the same experiences as me?' Whatever the answer, her question concerns whether she has sufficient evidence to accept a factual claim, whether, in other words, a belief she only acquires after her release can count as knowledge. If she decides she can know what others' experiences are like, she may be wrong, but this doesn't matter to Jackon's argument for it is still propositional beliefs she is trying to justify in overcoming scepticism. All he needs to show is that she lacks knowledge of others' experiences – what they are like – before her escape, despite having all the physical information, and so some information about other people's experiences escapes a complete physical account.

Criticism 2: All physical knowledge would include knowledge of qualia

> *How can I assess what Mary will know and understand if she knows everything there is to know about the brain? Everything is a lot, and it means, in all likelihood, that Mary has a radically different and deeper understanding of the brain than anything barely conceivable in our wildest flights of fancy.*[30]
>
> Patricia Churchland

Some have resisted the knowledge argument by insisting that if Mary did indeed know all the physical facts about colour vision, then she would be able to work out what colours would look like, and so, even in the black and white room, could imagine what it is like to look at the sky or at a red rose. To persuade us of this, Dennett urges us to recognise just how hard it really is to imagine Mary knowing *absolutely everything* about colour vision. We currently know really very little about how it works, so are not in a position to get a proper imaginative handle on what it would mean to know it all. So, faced with the invitation to imagine Mary's body of knowledge, we must conjure a very vague and general sense of what she would know. But this vague idea is not, says Dennett, a safe basis upon which to make judgements concerning what it would or would not be possible for Mary to understand. We may well be unable to imagine how she could come to know qualia, but this just shows that our imaginations here may be limited. Here we may be guilty of what Dennett calls 'Philosophers' Syndrome: mistaking a failure of imagination for an insight into necessity'.[31] Jackson himself changed his mind about the knowledge argument and came to endorse this objection. For his brief discussion of his change of heart see the Anthology 'Postscript on qualia' (1998). There he argues that it may seem to us that Mary would have to learn something new on first seeing red, but this may just be because we have only a very confused idea of what knowing all the physical information would involve. We acquire information via the senses, which seems to have an intrinsic and unanalysable nature and it is as well that we do, as this allows us to recognise salient features of our environment, such as tastes and colours, very efficiently. But this doesn't mean these experiences really are unanalysable. In reality, qualia may represent complex internal states, so that if Mary genuinely knew everything about such states, she might well be able to work out what colours would look like before seeing them herself. Despite this, in practice, knowing 'everything' physical about colour vision is likely to be beyond us, so that nobody could ever actually have a complete neuroscientific understanding of how colour vision works. So we are likely never to be able to work out what it's like to see red without actually seeing it. But this just shows the limitations of our understanding of neuroscience and so it remains true that *if* Mary knew everything then she wouldn't learn anything new when she first sees red.

Figure 2.6 The blue banana trick Suppose to test Mary upon her release we present her with a trick banana, that is a banana we have surreptitiously coloured blue. Would she be able to recognise that it was the wrong colour? If Jackson's original argument in 'Epiphenomenal qualia' is right, then she would not. However, Dennett, whose example this is, argues this conclusion is based purely on intuitions generated by a bad thought experiment and asks us to imagine Mary's complete knowledge of colour vision enabling her to spot the trick

Criticism 3: There is more than one way of knowing the same physical fact

An alternative strategy that may be taken in defence of physicalism is to deny that Mary does acquire new factual knowledge. Rather, she comes to know the same facts via a different route. After her release she acquires a new set of concepts based on her experience of colours. Possession of these 'phenomenal concepts' now enables her to describe the same facts in a new way. Before her release Mary knew all about the physical facts from the third person point of view; after her release she comes to know them from the subjective, first person, perspective. This subjective access is simply a different way of presenting the same neurophysiological states that Mary already knew under the third person description, and so is not knowledge of a new set of facts. So the fact that I can have access to my brain states via qualia without knowing any neurophysiology just shows that qualia are another way for these brain states to be presented.

Figure 2.7 Mary looking at a red apple Mary doesn't acquire any new factual knowledge. Instead she acquires a new set of concepts derived from her experience of qualia with which to represent the same knowledge

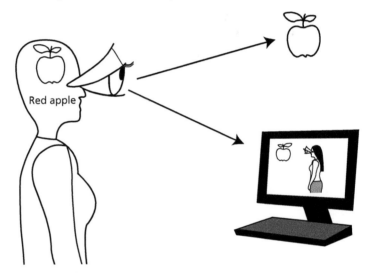

Suppose that Mary goes to a party and meets Bruce Wayne and learns that he is a billionaire. Never having heard of Batman, she could not claim to know that Batman is a billionaire. But suppose that later she meets Batman and learns that he is a billionaire. Would she be learning a new fact? Presumably not, for the fact that Batman is a billionaire and the fact that Bruce Wayne is a billionaire are not two facts, but one. It is the same item of knowledge, but under a different description. So when she meets Batman she acquires a new concept with which to pick out the same individual, but doesn't learn any new facts.

In the same way, Mary may know all the physical facts concerning what goes on in the brain when we see red things. And when she sees red for herself she learns that the experience of seeing red things involves a certain 'red-like' qualitative feel and she acquires a phenomenal concept from this experience. So now she is able to represent the same physical facts going on in her brain under two different descriptions, one involving physical, the other phenomenal terms. But these are just two ways of describing the same fact about seeing red.

Criticism 4: Qualia do not exist and so Mary gains no new propositional knowledge

> *Nothing, it seems, could you know more intimately than your own qualia; let the entire universe be some vast illusion, some mere figment of Descartes' evil demon, and yet what the figment is made of (for you) will be the qualia of your hallucinatory experiences. Descartes claimed to doubt everything that could be doubted, but he never doubted that his conscious experiences had qualia, the properties by which he knew or apprehended them.*[32]
>
> Dennett

We've seen that qualia present physicalism with a problem; for there appears to be an explanatory gap between the physical facts about our neurophysiology and the subjective feel of our phenomenal experiences. But if qualia could be shown not to exist, this would provide the physicalist with a powerful counter to the knowledge argument. For if there are no such things as qualia, then we no longer need to suppose that Mary learns anything new on leaving her black and white room. However, on the face of it, this strategy doesn't look particularly promising. After all, there seems nothing more real than qualia. And, as Dennett points out in the quotation above, we may follow Descartes in doubting the existence of the entire universe beyond our minds, but the qualitative feel of our sense experiences appears an indubitable fact about consciousness. Surely we cannot be mistaken about qualia since we are directly aware of them in our experience!

But despite the initially counter-intuitive nature of the claim that qualia don't exist, both Patricia and Paul Churchland (see Anthology extract 2.17[33]) have been attracted by this route to a defence of physicalism. The central claim they advance is that the whole range of mental-state terms which are part of our common sense picture of the nature of our minds, such as qualia, but also beliefs, desires, emotions and so on, should be *eliminated* from a proper understanding of human mentality. This is because there is nothing in reality that corresponds to terms such as 'qualia', 'beliefs' or 'desires'. So in the future when neuroscience is sufficiently advanced, we will be able to abandon talk of such mental states and speak instead of brain processes. This view is known as **eliminativism**, and we will be examining this theory in more detail below. For now, though, it will be worth examining just how eliminativists think we can eliminate qualia.

anthology
2.17

The eliminativists' argument begins with the claim that our common sense understanding of the mind is really a kind of pre-scientific theory about human behaviour. This theory is called **folk psychology** meaning that it is the theory of mind (psychology) of ordinary people (folk). This theory employs entities such as beliefs, sensations and desires to explain and predict human behaviour and it does so tolerably well. I can, for example, predict that someone will exhibit certain pain behaviours (holding their foot and screaming) if I drop an anvil on their foot; and I can explain why they might subsequently hobble off to A&E on the basis that perceiving the anvil land on their foot and the accompanying sensation of pain has caused them to form the belief that their foot may be broken, and this, coupled with the desire to have the foot restored to health, along with various other beliefs (about the modern medicine, the location of the hospital, etc.), will cause this behaviour.

If folk psychology is indeed an empirical theory of this kind, then it follows that it is open to refutation. If a better theory comes along, one which explains and predicts human behaviour more effectively, then we should abandon folk psychology in favour of the new theory. Now, modern neuroscience is making dramatic advances in its ability to unravel the complex relationships between the brain and behaviour. This research looks much more fruitful than folk psychology as a way to a better, more complete understanding of our behaviour. And as it advances it will eventually, perhaps quite soon, show that folk psychological concepts are redundant. In defence of this prediction, eliminativists point to the weaknesses of folk psychology: the things it singularly fails to explain. These include the nature and purposes of sleep, the causes of mental illnesses, how learning works, how we remember, and so on. In fact, folk psychology hasn't made any significant advances in the last few thousand years and so is, they urge, in need of overhauling. Once we adopt the new science of the mind, we will see that there is no place within it for qualia.

Experimenting with ideas

The language which ordinary folk use to talk about our minds has not remained completely static over the years. Since Sigmund Freud (1856–1939), for example, people have become inclined to accept the idea of unconscious motives, defence mechanisms, projecting their fantasies or of people being 'anal'. Nowadays you may also hear people speak about having a 'caffeine spike', rather than feeling edgy; an endorphin rush as opposed to feeling elated; a serotonin imbalance rather than feeling low and tired; or an adrenaline overload rather than feeling excited. Does this mean that folk psychology is on the way out?

Imagine a world, in the future, where no folk-psychological terms are used; only medical/scientific terms. Would this change the way we think about ourselves? Would the idea of qualia still have a role?

Paul Churchland, in the anthology paper 'Eliminative Materialism and the Propositional Attitudes' offers many examples of entities which were once thought to exist and which were abandoned when a new and superior theory emerged which could explain the phenomena better. One such example comes from cosmology. The ancient Greek astronomer Ptolemy claimed that there were rigid crystal spheres which surrounded the earth like the layers of an onion and these kept the various heavenly bodies, such as the Moon and planets, from crashing down to Earth.

These spheres played an important function in Ptolemaic cosmology, but with the advance of modern physics, the crystal spheres became obsolete and we came to see that they just don't exist.

But, we might ask, surely qualia cannot be compared to theoretical entities of this kind. No one could actually see the spheres, and so they could easily be abandoned once we developed a better way of explaining the movements of the heavenly bodies. But things are not the same with qualia; we are directly aware of them and so it seems implausible to suggest we could ever jettison them completely from our theory of the mind.

However, this response can be resisted. Take a different example from the history of science. 'Caloric' was a theoretical substance thought to be responsible for making things hot. According to the theory, caloric was a very fine gaseous substance that was suffused through objects rather like liquid in a sponge, and which flowed from where it was dense to less dense and so moved from hotter to colder objects. Modern thermodynamics has abandoned caloric and we now no longer suppose there is any substance corresponding to the term. Heat is not a substance, but is produced by the mean kinetic energy of the particles which compose objects. Now suppose that someone were to defend the existence of caloric by pointing out that it must exist because we can directly feel it when we touch hot objects. This proof of the reality of caloric should not convince. The reason this fails is that caloric's reality is being presupposed in the concepts they use to interpret the experience of heat. In the same way, it may be that we are so in thrall to the theoretical framework of folk psychology that we have to interpret the data of introspection in terms of its theoretical entities, such as qualia. When we adopt the new neuroscience of the future, we will have a more sophisticated set of theoretical concepts to operate with and so will no longer need to think in terms of qualia. So what we think we directly perceive is not something which is free of any theoretical framework. If qualia are part of a theory, then when we change the theory we may have no need for the concept of qualia either.

We will be examining eliminativism in more detail below (see page 329) and much of the discussion there will be relevant to whether you think this solution to the knowledge argument is successful. But for now let us return to another contemporary philosopher who denies qualia exist, Daniel Dennett. He does not go so far as to deny that consciousness has certain properties, but rather his point is that qualia cannot have the properties standardly given to them. For example, the standard view says they have an *intrinsic nature* that cannot be broken down into parts. A particular quale, for example the taste of beer, is what it is completely independently of any other qualia. Similarly, pain is thought to be inherently horrible and this horribleness is inextricably bound up with the experience so that it is not something that could be subtracted from the pain. Qualia are also said to be *directly accessible* via introspection so that we cannot be mistaken about what they are like or confuse them with other qualia.

Learn More

So, for example, it is not possible to think you have a headache, when in fact you are experiencing an itchy foot. And they are also supposed to be *private*, meaning that my qualia are only accessible to me. If I am experiencing the pain of child birth, for example, then you cannot peer into my mind to see what this experience is like. Finally, they are *ineffable*, meaning that their essential nature cannot be put into words and so they are impossible to communicate to someone not acquainted with them already. So while it is possible to compare our reactions to our qualia, it is not possible to compare qualia themselves. For example, we may be able to discuss our different reactions to the taste of beer, perhaps you like it while I hate it. But it is not possible to compare the taste of beer to me with the taste as it is to you. And it would be impossible adequately to explain to a person who has never drunk it, what beer is like.

Dennett tries to show that these features of qualia are ultimately incoherent and so that the concept is hopelessly confused. There is nothing that could have the properties given to qualia, so that while their existence may seem intuitively obvious, we are actually subject to a philosophical confusion. He concludes that the judgements we make about our conscious experience are comprehensible in terms of what is publicly observable to anyone and thus are ultimately explicable on physicalist terms.

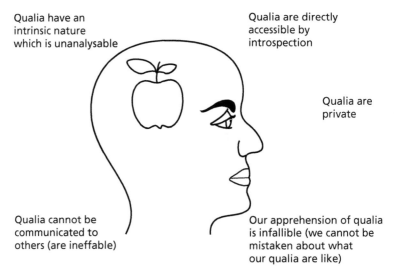

Figure 2.8 The standard picture of qualia according to Dennett

Qualia have an intrinsic nature which is unanalysable

Qualia are directly accessible by introspection

Qualia are private

Qualia cannot be communicated to others (are ineffable)

Our apprehension of qualia is infallible (we cannot be mistaken about what our qualia are like)

To help us out of our confusion, Dennett offers a series of thought experiments and arguments, some of which we will briefly look at here.

One argument focuses on the phenomenon known as 'reactive dissassociation', which can be brought on by the use of morphine to control pain. Some patients report being in pain, but not finding the pain unpleasant. How are we to understand such reports by the lights of the standard picture of qualia? Two options are possible. Either the patient is mistaken about being in pain so that they think they are in pain, but are not. Or we have to say that it is possible to subtract the horribleness from the pain experience. Either way, we violate the standard picture since we are either saying someone can make a mistake about what qualia they are experiencing, which means introspection is not infallible, or we have to say that qualia are not, despite appearances, unanalysable, but may be broken down into parts so that what seemed to be intrinsic to the experience turns out not to be.

 Experimenting with ideas

1   Suppose you hate cauliflower. One day you see me tucking into a plate of cauliflower and get to wondering how it could be that I can enjoy that horrible taste. But, you then consider, perhaps it tastes different to me than it does to you. *Questions for reflection*: Does cauliflower taste the same to someone who likes it as it does to someone who doesn't? Suppose you hated cauliflower as a child and then grew to like it as you got older. Did the taste change? Or did you come to change your mind about the same taste?

2   Imagine someone whose colour vision is inverted so that when they look at the sky they see what you call yellow, and when they look at a banana they see what you call blue. Since this has been their situation since birth, they have learnt to call bananas 'yellow' and the sky 'blue', and as their colour vision is systematically inverted by comparison to yours for all the colours of the rainbow, there seems to be no way they could ever have noticed that their experience of colours is different from anyone else's and they would behave in their use of colour words exactly like me or you. *Questions for reflection*: Would there be any way of detecting the fact that someone has inverted spectrum colour vision? If there is no way of telling, is it still conceivable that their vision is different from yours?[34]

A thought experiment Dennett employs uses the example of acquiring a taste for beer in order to argue that we appear not to be able clearly to identify the supposedly intrinsic nature of qualia. So what happens when you acquire a taste? There are two possible ways of describing the situation. One is to say that the taste itself gradually changes from an unpleasant one, to a pleasant one and this implies that the way beer tastes can change. In this case it seems not to have an intrinsic nature, but one at least partly constituted by one's past experiences of tasting beer. For if one's changing reaction to it has altered the taste itself then its nature cannot be what it is only in virtue of itself alone. On the other hand, we might then suppose that the taste doesn't change, but that it is just your reaction that has changed; in other words, that prolonged exposure teaches you to enjoy a taste you previously thought was horrible. But this way of viewing the situation is also problematic for the traditional view of qualia, since it becomes puzzling how you could come to enjoy a taste if its horribleness is an intrinsic part of the taste. Surely, if tastes have an intrinsic nature, then we cannot experience them differently from how they are. So either way we look at the situation we seem to be saying that the way we experience a taste and the taste itself are not identical which contradicts the idea of qualia having an intrinsic nature.

In fact, Dennett argues that we cannot tell which of the two situations has occurred when we acquire a taste. That is, by introspection, we are unable to determine whether the taste itself has changed, or whether our liking for it has. For while we might try to retrieve the original quale from memory in order to compare it with the taste now, we could never be certain that the memory was accurate or that our current attitude towards the quale wasn't colouring how we now recall it. But if it is not possible neatly to distinguish the part of the quale of beer that has remained the same and the bit that has changed, then this problematises the idea of qualia as intrinsic and directly and indubitably known. If we can't tell whether we have the same qualia or not, then Dennett argues, we should abandon talking about qualia altogether. For if qualia are indeterminate then we cannot claim that they have intrinsic properties and if we cannot unambiguously identify qualia, then we cannot claim that such entities exist.

Consider finally the inverted spectrum case from the Experimenting with ideas activity above (see page 257). If two people behave in exactly the same way when it comes to their use of colour terms, and there is no way of checking whether their qualia are inverted or not because they are private and ineffable, it seems we could never know whether or not this were the case. This has led some philosophers to argue that we imagine such a case is a real possibility, but that if there were genuinely no way of detecting the difference between you and the person with inverted spectrum vision, then there is no real difference between us. Since the hypothesis cannot be refuted or confirmed, it is not a situation we can make genuine sense of, despite appearances. Wittgenstein famously likened the situation to each of us having a beetle in a box that no one else could see.[35] In such a situation, the intrinsic nature of our respective beetles cannot be compared, and without such **intersubjective** comparison, their natures cannot meaningfully be spoken about. Perhaps, then, we are talking nonsense when we speak of the intrinsic nature of qualia, precisely because linguistic meaning must be connected to what is publicly verifiable.

Dennett is clearly influenced by this way of considering the issue. But he goes further in trying to persuade us that there is something incoherent about the very idea of spectrum inversion. Other versions of the spectrum inversion idea have tried to get around the problem that qualia cannot be intersubjectively compared by supposing that you wake up one morning to find your qualia of the colour spectrum have been inverted (perhaps some evil scientist has switched the neural pathways from the colour receptors in your retina to your visual cortex). You wake up to see the sky as yellow and bananas as blue and because you can compare your current qualia with your qualia from the day before and so recognise what has happened, this shows such inversion is a genuine possibility.

However, in this case, it is not clear that the reason you would notice the switch is not because the way you are disposed to react to different colours has not changed. That is, you notice your red–green qualia have been switched because you now have a tendency to pull away from traffic lights when the top light comes on and to stop at the bottom light. Or you are put off your spaghetti bolognaise sauce because it now has a peculiar rotten-looking hue. So the experiment must be modified so that these extrinsic clues as to the switch are eliminated so that we can establish for sure that it is just the intrinsic natures of the qualia that we are able to recognise have changed. But if we somehow were to switch these as well, claims Dennett, it is far from clear that we would indeed be able to tell that the switch had happened. With the full switch, you would regard your qualia of the top light on the traffic signal as exciting and vibrant and it would cause you to apply the brakes. The bottom light would now be calm and cool and would incline you to accelerate away. And if all your reactive dispositions to these different colour experiences were systematically switched, surely you would be none the wiser. In this way, Dennett urges us to accept that we cannot really isolate the intrinsic properties of qualia from our reactions to them and so that the idea that we have an intrinsic awareness of them independently of these reactions is a mistake. In other words, with the complete switch you could never detect it had happened. And if we cannot detect qualia changes, then we should abandon the notion that we have direct and infallible access to their intrinsic natures.

2.1.5 The issues of causal interaction for versions of dualism

Interactionist dualism

The idea that mind and body interact is an article of common sense. After all, if I decide to reach out for my cup of tea then (under normal circumstances) my arm will move and my hand will grasp the handle. Here a mental act of **volition** (my willing my hand to grasp the cup) seems to have caused a physical action to occur in my body (my hand reaching for the cup). And this causal relationship also works in the other direction. If I sip my tea, the contact between the warm liquid and the inside of my mouth causes various tea-like sensations to appear in my consciousness. These sensations may in turn cause me to form various beliefs, such as that this is a nice cup of tea or that it needs another spoon of sugar. Here, physical changes in my body seem directly or indirectly to have caused mental events such as sensations and beliefs. And my beliefs and thinking in turn often lead to speech, such as asking my friend to pass the sugar.

So how does this interaction work? Descartes' dualism gives us one influential account which we need first to examine.

> *I further notice that the mind does not receive the impressions from all parts of the body immediately, but only from the brain, or perhaps even from one of its smallest parts, to wit, from that in which the common sense is said to reside, which, whenever it is disposed in the same particular way, conveys the same thing to the mind.*[36]
>
> Descartes

You will recall that according to Descartes' *substance* dualism (see page 220), the non-physical mind is a distinct substance from the body, but, in this life at least, they are linked together. Part of the relationship involves the kind of causal interaction outlined above: physical changes in the sense organs cause various sensory experiences in the mind. And, conversely, the desires and decisions of the mind cause the body to behave in purposeful ways. Descartes identified the brain as the organ most directly connected to the mind so that it is changes in the brain that cause sensations. Descartes suggested that body and mind communicate with each other via a small organ in the centre of the brain called the pineal gland. This is one of the brain's 'smallest parts' that Descartes conjectures in the quotation above is the seat of the 'common sense', that is, the point where all the sense experiences we enjoy come together in one unified consciousness. This 'common sense' is what enables me to be aware that my foot aches, that I am hungry and that I can see the pie shop, all within the one mind. From the pineal gland, information is communicated via the nervous system to and from all parts of the body by means of what he terms 'animal spirits', a kind of fine air or fluid. Although distinct substances, the mind and body are in an intimate union so that the mind feels itself projected throughout the body. I do not feel myself to be a distinct substance, but rather experience life as an embodied being. So, for example, when the animal spirits communicate information about the state of the body to my brain I experience the sensations of pain, thirst or cold as located in the body rather than in the mind. It is through these sensations that the mind is made aware of the needs of the body and it is via the sensations of colours, sounds, smells, etc., communicated via the sense organs, that my mind becomes aware of my physical surroundings.

Problems facing interactionist dualism

Given that the soul of a human being is only a thinking substance, how can it affect the bodily spirits, in order to bring about voluntary actions?[37]

anthology
2.7

The causal interaction problem for dualism

Experimenting with ideas

Look around you and identify an object, a cup or book, say, which is out of reach. Now try to lift the object up into the air just by the power of thought and wiggle it around.

How did you do? Did you manage it? If not, why do you think you failed?

Now focus on your own body and try to wiggle you ears. Can you do it?

Repeat the experiment with your hand or your foot. Can you wiggle them? Can you lift them into the air?

How did you do? Did you have similar success with all these objects? If not, why exactly is it easier to move some things by the power of thought than others?

One problem for Descartes' **interactionism** is its apparent inability to explain how causal interaction between the mind and body is possible. For, let us recall, the mind, in Descartes' view, is unextended in space, it is immaterial and has no solidity or mass. And it makes no sense to ascribe physical properties (such as size or shape) to minds. By contrast, the body is extended, and it makes no sense to ascribe mental properties (such as thoughts or sensations) to bodies. But, it is plausible to suppose that for two things to causally interact they need to have properties in common. There must be some common medium in which transactions between one and the other can take place. We accept that we cannot move objects just by the power of thought, no matter how hard we try, and yet we are able to move our bodies and this power may appear as miraculous as if we were able to move the objects at a distance, since in both cases it is the immaterial and ghostly mind which is impacting on gross matter.

Princess Elisabeth of Bohemia in her correspondence with Descartes expresses the problem in terms of the need for some contact between the two substances in order for the mind to affect the body. Since the mind has no extended surface, it is unable to touch the body and so cannot causally interact with it.

We can formulate the problem of interaction as a challenge to Descartes' claim to have a clear and distinct idea of the different natures of the mind and body, and so to substance dualism. For if causal interaction requires two substances to come into contact with their surfaces, and mind does interact with body, then mind must have a surface and must be extended. This suggests that the mind must have more in common with physical things than dualism allows; it might even be taken to show that the mind must be physical and so that substance dualism is false.

Another way of approaching the problem of interaction is to consider how a particular mind can be linked to a particular body. For since minds have no spatial characteristics, they can have no location in space. But, in this case, there would seem to be no particular *place* where the mind might come into contact with the body. So the idea of its connecting at the pineal gland is hard to make sense of. And although we may talk of the mind being 'inside' the body, this is only a metaphor since non-spatial minds can't really be anywhere. Yet without being located within the body it's hard to see how the mind could be connected to your physical being. Just how does your mind attach itself to your body as opposed to someone else's?

In his response to Elisabeth, Descartes argues that mind–body union is a basic notion and 'thus can be understood only through itself'.[38] By this he means that we shouldn't try to make sense of it in terms of anything else. Elisabeth's mistake is to think of mind–body causation on the model of the way physical things causally interact. He writes: 'The principle cause of our errors lies in our commonplace attempts to use these notions to explain things that they aren't right for. For example, ... when we try to conceive how the soul moves the body in terms of how a body moves a body.'[39] For while it may be true (and Descartes believed that it was) that physical things can only causally affect each other through contact, it is not the case that we can make no sense of the idea of causation which doesn't involve such contact. After all, he points out, it makes sense to think of a physical object being caused to fall to Earth because of its weight. Here, weight impels the object downward, but we don't need to suppose the weight must come into contact with the object, like a hand pushing it down. In the same way, we are able clearly to conceive of mind–body interaction, claims Descartes, involving no surface to surface contact. So it may be that we need to rid ourselves of a naive view of the nature of causation which sees it in terms of the impact of two objects. Certainly there doesn't appear to be anything contradictory in the idea that two things could act upon each other at a distance, such as when the Earth's gravitational field holds the Moon in its orbit. (Note that Descartes doesn't actually think that weight causes the object to fall in the way described. The point is rather that we have a primitive notion of such causation, one which in fact should only be applied to the mind–body relation.)

> *If the unlikeness of draughts and colds in the head does not prevent one from admitting a causal connexion between the two, why should the unlikeness of volitions and voluntary movements prevent one from holding that they are causally connected?*[40]
>
> Broad

We could also question the assumption that for two things to interact they must have common properties or be similar in some way. C.D. Broad (1887–1971) writing in the 1920s makes the point well, arguing that the dissimilarity between mind and body doesn't warrant us claiming that they cannot be causally related and he uses the example of draughts and colds in the head which we are happy to regard as causally related and yet which are not at all alike.

> *The mind can never possibly find the effect in the supposed cause by the most accurate scrutiny and examination. For the effect is totally different from the cause and can never be discovered in it.* [41]
>
> Hume

We can elaborate on this defence of interactionism by following Hume in arguing that we cannot make any a priori judgements about what can or cannot be causally related. Causal relations, according to Hume, can only be discovered by empirical investigation. To show this, Hume points out that if we encounter an object for the first time we would not be able to work out by reasoning alone what its causal powers are: 'No object ever discovers, by the qualities which appear to the senses, either the cause which produced it, or the effects which will arise from it'.[42] So, if I were to encounter a loaf of bread for the first time, having never observed anything like it before, I would be unable to deduce how it was made or that it could nourish me. In order to know how bread is made, we need experience of the various complex processes from harvesting the wheat to baking the dough which bring it about, and to discover that it is nourishing I would have to experience myself or others actually eating it and note the effects. In other words, the idea of one event has no necessary relation to the idea of its effect and the relation between cause and effect is arbitrary or contingent.[43] But so long as experience provides us with repeated occasions where two events are connected, then we may infer that the two are causally related. Repeated experiences of gaining nourishment from eating bread persuade us that there is a necessary connection between the two. So there can be nothing in principle to prevent us from supposing that mental events cause physical events; so long as we experience a constant conjunction between acts of will and actions, this is the only basis we can have of establishing a causal connection. Indeed, presumably it is by experience that we learn which parts of our body we can cause to move by acts of volition, that is which we are able to move by *intending* or *willing* them to move. If you try to move your ears you may find you can or you may find you can't, but it doesn't seem to be something you could know was possible without making the experiment. In the same way we learn that we have the power to move our arms by experience of acts of will apparently doing just this – I intend my arm to move, and immediately it moves. So since the empirical evidence supports causal interaction, this is all we need and no a priori reasoning to the contrary can carry any weight.

Causal closure of the physical and the law of the conservation of energy

If the a priori argument against mind–body interaction fails, what of empirical arguments? Well, it is often pointed out by critics of dualist interactionism that physical science tells us that everything that happens within the universe is caused to happen by something else within it. All physical occurrences, in other words, are to be explained by reference to some other physical occurrence, meaning that the physical universe is *causally closed*. Now, if it is true that objects are only affected by physical forces then our own bodies cannot act because of the intervention of some force beyond the physical such as the mind. This argument for the impossibility of non-physical interaction with the body begins by appeal to the principle that every physical event can be completely accounted for in terms of physical causes.

In other words, any account of the causes of any physical event need not appeal to anything non-physical; we can give a 'complete' account of the causes of any event without appealing to anything non-physical. Bodily actions, since they are a part of the physical universe, must conform to this principle, and so must be explicable without reference to the non-physical.

We can give further support to this conclusion by appeal to a fundamental law of physics known as the principle of the conservation of energy. The principle states that within a closed system such as the whole universe, the overall amount of energy remains constant; it cannot be created or destroyed. It is because of this principle that perpetual motion machines are impossible – any mechanism in motion will lose some energy to friction and since no energy can be added to it, it will tend to run out of energy. To keep any mechanism moving we need to give it some injection of energy from outside, and this includes ourselves via food. However, if substance dualism is correct, then minds would add energy to the physical universe by acting on our bodies. Every time I choose to raise my arm or run for a bus, my mind exerts some force on my body to impel it this way or that and in so doing the net amount of energy in the physical world would go up, so breaking this law of physics. So if interactionist dualism is at odds with well-established physical laws about the conservation of energy then perhaps we need to reject it.

To see the point, imagine you are driving and you run out of petrol. How are you going to move the car forwards? If there is no force acting on the car, either gravity (because you are on the flat) or by pushing it, then it will not move. Simply sitting in the car and willing it to move will not work. It needs an injection of energy from within the physical universe. But now consider your own body. Suppose you are running a marathon and your body runs out of glycogen, the main fuel your body uses for aerobic exercise. This is known as hitting the wall and involves dizziness, confusion and an inability even to stand unaided. Without an intake of energy you are unlikely to be able to continue. But unlike cars our bodies are able to draw on another source of energy, our fat reserves, and so if these can be accessed, you may be able to continue for a while. However, once all possible sources of energy are depleted, the result is inevitable, total collapse. You will not be able to will your body forward unless there are some physical reserves of energy to deploy. But if interactionist dualism were true, we might expect marathon runners to be able to continue on will power alone, running, as it were, purely on the energy produced by the mind.

This objection can be framed as an argument for physicalism:

1 The physical universe is a closed system.
2 And in any closed system, energy must be conserved.
3 Mind and body causally interact.
4 But causation involves the transfer of energy.
5 Therefore, mind must be physical.

Defending interactionism

Interactionism could be defended by arguing that the overall amount of energy can remain constant since the effects of mind on body and of body on mind cancel each other out. Perhaps whenever I inject energy into my body by getting up to make a cup of tea, energy also escapes from it by some other wormhole, thus keeping the overall energy levels constant. However, to be convincing, such a solution would need some explanation as to why imports and exports of energy should exactly balance each other out. Otherwise, to suppose there is such a mysterious mechanism at play looks like an article of faith simply brought in to save interactionism, but with nothing else to recommend it. It appears, in other words, as an *ad hoc* manoeuvre to save interactionism.

Another strategy is to question the fourth step in the objection argument outlined above: that causation must involve a transfer of energy. Perhaps this is an overly restrictive idea of how causation must work and it may be that it is possible to interact with the physical without actually adding energy to it. On this picture, the mind wouldn't inject new energy into the body via the brain, but could 'steer' the body by redistributing the energy which already exists within the physical world. It would not be possible to move a body depleted of energy by will power alone on this model, but if there were some energy left in my body to use, it would be possible to choose whether to walk a few more steps or sit down and wait for assistance.

However, if the principle of the conservation of energy is properly understood, this redistribution idea seems less plausible. For the principle is saying that any change of trajectory can only be brought about by some expenditure of energy. When driving a car, the petrol is providing the energy for the forward motion, but in order to steer the car left or right, I also need to expend some energy, albeit comparatively little. In the same way, if the mind steers the body in different directions using the physical energy reserves the body contains to perform various actions, this steering process must at the least change the direction of movement of neurons in the brain, and this will take some energy, even if it is very little. So once again, it seems that mind–body interaction breaks this law of physics.

Parallelist theories

Occasionalism

One reaction to the problem of mental causation that substance dualists may pursue is to accept that there is no causal reaction between the two substances, but simply a *correlation* between states of the mind and of the body. A historically interesting version of this strategy comes from a follower of Descartes, Nicolas Malebranche (1638–1715) and his theory is known as **occasionalism**. Malebranche was convinced by the arguments for dualism which appear to show that the mind is a substance and that it is of a totally different nature to matter. But he was also convinced that two substances with such radically different natures could not possibly come into causal interaction. How then could he explain the facts of our everyday experience which seem to show that mental events such as sensations are caused by physical events in the world around us, that these produce further mental events such as beliefs and desires and these in turn cause physical events in our bodies as we move our limbs to satisfy our wants?

His answer is radical. The appearance of interaction is in fact an illusion. Certainly events in the physical body are associated with mental events. When I decide to pick up a hammer, my arm moves and grasps it; and when my arm slips and I hit my thumb I experience a pain. But while these two sets of events, the mental and the physical, occur together, they are not directly causally related. Is it just a *coincidence* that my thumb aches after it has been struck by the hammer? Clearly not, as this would be too fanciful a view even for a philosopher. Rather, argues Malebranche, it is God who organises things such that events in the mental and physical universes coincide in the law-like ways that they do. His argument for this involves the claim that only God can be a genuine causal agent. So a decision to move my arm will generally be followed by my arm moving because when God observes me making this decision, he intervenes and moves my arm. And when he observes the hammer crush my thumb, again he intervenes to place a pain in my mind.

The pre-established harmony

Like Malebranche, Leibniz was also persuaded both by the idea that the mind is a distinct substance from the body and that causal interaction between two substances is impossible. Since no genuine substance, he argued, could have any causal influence on any other, whatever happens within someone's mind must be produced internally. The appearance of causal interaction between minds and the physical world occurs because when God created the universe he created each substance so that it would unfurl under its own internal dynamic in such a way that events in one would correspond with events in others. For example, this means that the pain in my thumb is pre-programmed to occur at a particular time, and the impact of hammer and thumb is similarly pre-programmed. In Leibniz's own analogy, the situation is like someone winding up two clocks so that the movements of the hands of the one are paralleled by those of the other. This produces the appearance that one is causing the other to move, but in reality they are completely causally independent of each other. Leibniz calls this arrangement the '**pre-established harmony**' of substances.

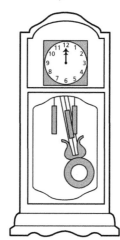

Figure 2.9 Analogy of clocks If you set two clocks to the right time then the movements of the hands will parallel each other. When one strikes 12, so will the other. To the naive observer it may look as though one clock striking is causing the other to strike while in reality they were both pre-programmed to strike at precisely midday. In the same way, because mental states and bodily states are correlated, it appears to us that they are causally related, but in reality they were pre-programmed by God.

We are not here going to attempt to evaluate these theories, but you doubtless will have your own objections. As well as being extremely counter-intuitive, **parallelist** theories rely completely on the existence of God to orchestrate the correspondence between minds and bodies, and that is one of the reasons they are not taken seriously in contemporary philosophy of mind. The neural dependence of the mental which we have discussed, also, makes such solutions appear implausible. And we have already seen that the evidence of modern neuroscience tends to make property dualism a more attractive option for those who are sceptical of the idea that the mental could be reduced to the physical. So if interaction is indeed impossible between distinct substances, rather than abandon interaction altogether, perhaps a more attractive solution to the mind–body problem would be to deny that we are actually dealing with two substances.

Epiphenomenalism

Conscious will is a symptom, not a cause; its roots ... are invisible to it. [44]

Santayana

As we have seen, property dualists accept that the mind depends upon the brain. As a property of it, it is unsurprising that damage to the brain can affect your mind, or that alcohol consumption can affect your ability to do mental arithmetic, for example. Moreover, property dualism fits rather better with the theory of evolution than does substance dualism. Minds don't mysteriously appear fully formed at some arbitrary point in our evolutionary past, but emerge gradually over millions of years as the brain has become increasingly complex. Similarly your own mind wasn't transplanted whole into your body, transforming you from a mindless baby into a fully conscious person, but developed gradually, beginning in the womb and throughout your early life as your brain grew. However, if mental properties are irreducible, but at the same time physical causes alone are needed to explain behaviour, then we are led to the view that the mind is a product of the brain, but one which can have no causal influence on the body and its actions. In other words, if property dualists accept the causal closure of the physical, then mental states may be produced by physical brains, but they cannot have any reciprocal influence on bodies. This is the view known as epiphenomenalism, meaning that mental phenomena sit 'above' the brain but do not causally affect it.

T.H. Huxley (1825–95) was an early advocate of Darwin's theory of evolution and so of a naturalistic account of the nature of human beings which saw them as closely related to the rest of the animal kingdom. In his well-known paper 'On the Hypothesis that Animals are Automata' of 1874[45] he develops a mechanistic account of the body and its actions, inspired by Descartes. Focusing first on animals, he defends Descartes' thesis that we can explain their behaviour in purely physical terms; that is to say, the actions of animals are determined completely by their complex physiologies, in particular their nervous systems, interacting with the environment. Animals, in other words, are in reality complex machines. Descartes had already observed that reflex actions show that we can react to certain stimuli without the intervention of the conscious mind or will. Huxley quotes Descartes' example of when someone 'moves his hand rapidly towards our eyes, as if he were going to strike us'[46] leading us to blink involuntarily even if we know he isn't actually going to hit us. This, according to Descartes, is explained by the nervous system and brain reacting automatically without the mind having to be consulted, and there is no reason to suppose the same sort of process isn't going on when a sheep receives the visual impression of a wolf and reacts by bolting. Further observations concerning how the body can continue to act despite consciousness being absent are explored, such as how victims of spinal injury who may have no feeling in their legs and feet will nonetheless react to being tickled by curling their toes. Experiments with frogs in which the spinal column has been severed but whose legs continue to react to stimuli are also used to argue that the nervous system can produce complex behaviours without the presence of conscious experience. Huxley also discusses the case of a brain-damaged soldier who would perform complex tasks such as singing, or loading a rifle, while appearing to be unconscious, as evidenced by his failure to react to loud noises, having pins stuck into him, or drinking vinegar. The soldier appeared to be acting on 'auto-pilot', so supporting the claim that complex behaviours don't require conscious experiences as their cause.

Now, despite all this evidence, Huxley doesn't follow Descartes in the claim that animals are not conscious. Automata they may be, that is, they may act automatically and without the intervention of conscious experiences, but we nonetheless have good reason to suppose that they have experiences like us. One reason for this is that, with the benefit of evolutionary theory, we now know that we are related to all other animals and so it would be peculiar were we to be very different from them in respect of having conscious experiences correlated with certain types of physiological reactions. But we have no reason to suppose, argues Huxley, that these conscious experiences are involved in the causal process. So while a frog may feel discomfort when acetic acid is placed on its foot, the discomfort doesn't cause it to move its foot; this happens automatically.

> *The consciousness of brutes would appear to be related to the mechanism of their body simply as a collateral product of its working, and to be as completely without any power of modifying that working as the steam-whistle which accompanies the work of a locomotive engine is without influence upon its machinery. Their volition, if they have any, is an emotion indicative of physical changes, not a cause of such changes.*[47]
>
> Huxley

Finally he argues that we have no reason to suppose that humans are any different from other animals in this respect, so that mental states, such as our sensations, beliefs and desires are caused by the various activities of the brain, but they do not have any causal effects in turn on the physical world. This means that mental phenomena are merely incidental, and that the universal conviction that our actions are determined by our

Figure 2.10 Epiphenomenalism Huxley likens conscious experiences to the whistle on a steam train and the body and brain to the train itself. The steam that drives the whistle is produced by the engine which drives the train forward, but the whistle doesn't affect the forward motion, it is just a by-product and the train would move as well without it. The whistle, like consciousness, is a 'collateral product' or 'epiphenomenon', meaning it is produced by underlying processes but has no causal impact on those processes.

beliefs, desires and decisions is false. Our actions are completely causally determined by processes in the brain and body, and while these processes produce conscious experiences of sensations and volitions, these have no causal role to play in our behaviour. So volitions and actions are closely correlated. I have the urge to move my arm and my arm reaches for the cup of tea. But the causal process goes in one direction only. Neither my thirst nor the desire for tea cause me to reach for the cup. And the sensation of heat doesn't cause me to drop the cup. Both are automatic. Both caused by unconscious physiological processes like reflex actions. We are, as Huxley puts it, 'conscious automata'[48], machines whose actions

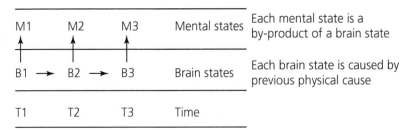

Figure 2.11 The relation of mental states to brain states according to epiphenomenalism If the body requires liquid, signals are sent to the brain and, after some complex neurological processing, these will lead me to reach out and take a sip from my cup of tea. Accompanying this physical process will be a sensation of thirst and a feeling of willing my arm to reach for the tea. But neither of these has any causal role to play in the process.

are physically determined and in whom conscious experiences are a mere by-product. 'Volition' concludes Huxley, 'is an emotion indicative of physical changes, not a cause of such changes'.[49]

Such a view avoids the Cartesian problem of accounting for how a non-material substance can intervene in the normal course of nature. This means that we may be able to produce an account of human behaviour exclusively in terms of physical mechanisms. In this sense, epiphenomenalism is able to respect the desire for a scientific explanation for human behaviour. As a form of property dualism it is also able to accommodate the dependence of conscious life on the brain and the apparent fact that consciousness emerges with the evolutionary development of the brain. It is also consistent with experience. Mental states are caused by changes in the brain and so accompany the impact of physical things on our bodies, as when, for example, damage to your foot causes pain.

 Experimenting with ideas

Despite the advantages of epiphenomenalism outlined above, many philosophers have been very hostile to it, and you may also find it rather implausible. Reflect on the following questions and see if you can turn your answers into possible objections to epiphenomenalism.

- Do you have any good reasons for supposing that your volitions (i.e. acts of will or intentions whereby you choose to do something) really cause your actions?
- Do you have any good reasons for supposing that your sense experiences cause behaviour, e.g. a pain causing you to flinch?
- What of conscious perception? Is there good reason to suppose that your visual awareness of a cup of tea is causally involved in you reaching for it?
- Consider other mental states such as beliefs. In what ways do they seem to be causally related to the physical world? Do you have good reasons to suppose they really are so related?

Issues with epiphenomenalism: The causal redundancy of the mental

> *Our mental conditions are simply the symbols in consciousness of the changes which takes place automatically in the organism; and that, to take an extreme illustration, the feeling we call volition is not the cause of a voluntary act, but the symbol of that state of the brain which is the immediate cause of that act. We are conscious automata.*[50]
>
> Huxley

Criticism 1: The evidence of introspection

Perhaps the most significant objection to epiphenomenalism is that it seems to be an affront against common sense and against what appears to be revealed to us through **introspection**. To start with, epiphenomenalism goes against the common sense opinion that our volition causes our actions. Surely, we may object, when I decide to reach out for a cup of tea, the conscious decision must be what causes me to reach out. To deny this seems to fly in the face of everyday experience. Moreover, introspection seems to show that different mental states are causally related to each other. For example, the smell of melted butter on toast may transport my mind back to reminiscences of my grandmother's kitchen. The belief that it is raining and the desire to stay dry cause me to deliberate over where I might find an umbrella. So our introspective awareness of our minds strongly suggests that they represent a stream of causally linked events.

Huxley is unconcerned about this consequence of the theory and reminds us that the causal closure of the physical requires that we explain all actions in terms of physical causes and so the idea of mental states being causally involved must be given up. And while we may think we have conscious control over our actions there is actually nothing in experience that can establish that we do – after all, if volitions are indeed a 'collateral product' and epiphenomenalism is right, our experience would be no different than if they were causally involved. For all experience reveals is that volitions tend to be conjoined with certain actions, and this is consistent both with them being the cause and with them being a side effect.

Some have seen support for the idea that the sense of volition is a side effect of action in the experiments of Benjamin Libet.[51] Libet asked subjects to watch a clock for a period of time and at a point of their choosing to perform a voluntary action such as raising their hand. They were also asked to identify the time when they became conscious of the urge or intention to raiseing their hand. While they performed this task, Libet monitored their brain activity and found that he could identify the beginnings of the neural process that led to the voluntary action occurring *before* the subjects identified becoming aware of deciding to act. The brain, it appears, is already preparing to perform an action before the person is conscious of any volition. This suggests that at least some conscious decisions are not the initiating causes of actions and therefore that – at least in some cases – it is an illusion to suppose that our feelings of volition cause actions. This at least shows that our common sense assumption that experience demonstrates that decisions or intentions cause our actions can be mistaken and so that it is possible that this is the case for all our actions.

Criticism 2: The role of qualia

But what of our reactions to sensory stimuli, to qualia? Surely, we may be inclined to say, it is the pain I feel when I touch something hot which causes me to withdraw my hand. And surely the intrinsic horribleness of pain must have something to do with why we make efforts to avoid it. After all, it seems that when I hit my thumb with a hammer, it is the pain that causes me to scream out, and if, for some reason, it doesn't hurt, I would not scream. Moreover, if it never hurt when I hit my thumb, I would doubtless take far less care to avoid doing so when hammering nails. These observations seem such obvious articles of common sense as to render the epiphenomenalist position absurd.

However, once again we can point out that pains may occur whenever I exhibit pain behaviour without this proving that they must be the cause of it. The two may be distinct effects of another underlying cause, namely the activation of the brain's pain centres. In Anthology extract 2.8 from Jackson's 'Epiphenomenal Qualia', he likens the situation to watching a punch fly in a cowboy film. The appearance is clearly one of the punch causing the person punched to collapse. But we know in this case that this appearance is an illusion. The conjunction of the two events is produced by the film projector and there is no direct causal link between one frame and the next. So, once again, we cannot conclude from the fact that two events are regularly conjoined that there is a direct causal link. There may be a third factor causing both. In the case of pain and pain behaviour, the third factor is the brain, which, like the projector, causes the pain and the pain behaviour to occur together.

anthology
2.8

Reflex actions also show that the conscious experience is not always necessary for a reaction to occur. It can happen that you touch a hot stove and react by withdrawing your hand before any pain is felt. This at least shows that pain doesn't have to be present for someone to react to damage to the body and so that it is possible that the pain is merely epiphenomenal in ordinary situations too.

Criticism 3: Issues relating to free will and responsibility

But epiphenomenalism also seems to be in conflict with another central aspect of our everyday experience, namely the sense that our actions are free. When I deliberate over whether to go to bed early with a book, or go out to the cinema, I seem to be exercising my free will. If I choose to go out, this decision was reached freely, meaning that I was not forced to go out and I could have chosen to stay in. However, if my actions are determined exclusively by physical processes, and the intention or decision is causally impotent, then it seems I have no choice over my actions. If human actions are determined by physical laws, then the choices I make in any given instant are the result of these laws, meaning that I could not have chosen otherwise than I did. And yet if I could not have chosen otherwise, then it seems I am not free.

Epiphenomenalists may again be unconcerned by this consequence. Free will and the feeling we have that we could have chosen otherwise may be another illusion. This illusion may be the consequence of not having access in our consciousness to the workings of our brains. The human brain is, after all, one of the most complex objects in the known universe: it is said that there are more potential connections between the 100 billion or so neurons in the brain, than there are atoms in the entire universe. And at the neurological level, decision-making must be a very complex process. The urges we are aware of may reflect some of the brain processes going on, but the true complexity is clearly beyond our conscious reach. Since we are in the dark about the processes underlying our decisions, it may appear to us that we are making the decision freely. However, being unaware of the causes of an action is not the same as being aware that there is no determining cause. Our mistake may be to suppose that because we cannot observe how an action comes about that it must have come about by some mysterious indeterminate cause.

However, the denial that our decisions are free faces another difficulty. For freedom of the will seems to be critical to our understanding of moral responsibility. For example, if, for whatever reason, I decide to murder Jones, then we would normally suppose that my action was not inevitable. This is because I could have chosen not to do it. And it is precisely because I did choose to, having freely weighed up the options, that I can be held responsible and punished for my actions. Let's suppose that I argue in court that I didn't intend to kill him; that the gun went off in my hand while I was cleaning it. This would represent a legitimate defence against the murder charge. For in this case, it was a mechanism outside of my control which caused his death, not me. Murder must involve a guilty intention.

But if epiphenomenalism is true, then the intention to kill Jones is not what made me kill him; and if my decision to pull the trigger has no causal role to play in my pulling the trigger, then it seems that I am not responsible for his death. Indeed, I could legitimately defend myself in court by saying, as I did with the gun above, that it wasn't me that did it, but my brain. Could I not reasonably claim that I could have done nothing about it, that the action was caused by processes beyond my conscious control?

This is a hard conclusion to draw. The implications for the criminal justice system would be devastating. So, rather than accept this consequence, it may be urged, we should reject epiphenomenalism.

Proponents of this line of argument may defend interactionist dualism as the only theory which can make sense of the lived experience of free will and our common sense conviction that people are responsible for their actions. Because the mind is non-physical, it is not bound by physical laws and so it is possible to locate the will within it. After all, if you allow your mind to wander it doesn't appear to be bound by any laws. You can imagine or think what you please, suggesting that the mind is by its nature free and unbounded. And when it intervenes in the physical world through acts of will, according to the dualist, it changes the course of nature, meaning that our actions are not determined by causal laws.

However, even if the mind escapes from physical causation this may not provide the interactionist with a full explanation of free will. For suppose I am deliberating over whether to kill Jones. I may weigh up the various slights he has made against me over the years, against my concerns about being caught and spending a lifetime in gaol. And let's suppose I decide to go ahead with my evil plan. Wasn't the decision necessitated by the various considerations I weighed up? In other words, were we able to rewind time and replay the process of deliberation, is there any reason to suppose I would choose anything different? After all, my mind would have exactly the same set of considerations to weigh up, and if it was tipped one way the last time, then surely it would tip the same way every time. If my choices are done for reasons, and the reasons are the same, the choice would be the same. This suggests that the idea that an immaterial mind could act in different ways in the same circumstances is not true and therefore that our actions are determined after all.

But let's suppose it could have acted differently. Would this actually involve my being free? Arguably not, for if my decision not to kill Jones is based on exactly the same reasons as my decision to kill him, then the decision appears to be completely random. But if it is random, a matter of pure chance, then it doesn't seem as though I am responsible for it either. It would be as though the mind made its choices based on the throw of a die. This might mean I could have done otherwise, but it doesn't seem to mean that I chose to do the action freely. So it may be that the interactionist's claim that dualism is needed to make sense of free will fails.

Must we then accept that our common sense notion that our actions are free and the associated concepts of moral responsibility are fundamentally confused? Not necessarily. What is needed, perhaps, is a better analysis of what we are after when we require that human actions be free. We've seen that we don't mean that they are random. And many philosophers have argued that a proper analysis of free actions will show that they are indeed causally determined, but what makes them free is the manner in which they are determined. Huxley was well aware of the free will objection to epiphenomenalism but argued that it is quite possible to allow that our brains determine all our decisions and yet, at the same time, to consider ourselves free. Huxley, in other words, is a **compatibilist** about free will. This means that he believes that actions can be free in the sense that matters for moral responsibility, *and* that they can be determined by physical processes. In this, his view has affinities with Hume's analysis of free will where he argues that an action cannot be completely random if it is to be considered free. Rather what makes it free is that it is appropriately caused. So long as the action is in accordance with your motivations and desires, then it is a free action. In Huxley's hands, my desires may not cause my actions, but so long as the action I perform is one which fulfils the desire, then it can be considered free. 'An agent', he writes, 'is free when there is nothing to prevent him from doing that which he desires to do'.[52]

So the feeling of acting freely, that is, in accordance with our intentions and desires, is distinguishable from being coerced. If, holding a gun to Jones, I order him to hand over his cash, then Jones may rightly say that giving up his money was not a free act. Conversely, if I desire to kill Jones, and there is nothing that prevents me from performing this action, then the action is free. But if an action occurs which is not in accordance with my intentions, then it is not free. So we can distinguish free actions from constrained ones in terms of whether they are accompanied by the epiphenomenal intention or not. This means that free and constrained actions are both equally determined by physical causes. Neither could have happened otherwise than as they did. But it doesn't follow, according to Huxley, that we cannot identify free actions and so attribute moral praise and blame. A consequence of this revision of our concept of free will may well be that we cannot justify punishing people as retribution for the crimes they couldn't help commit. But we may still be able to justify punishment as a way of reforming their behaviour and possibly as a deterrent.

Criticism 4: Evolution

If conscious experiences have no causal role to play in our behaviour, then we may find ourselves puzzled about why we have them at all. The universe and all human behaviour would, it seems, be exactly the same as it is now if there were no mental phenomena at all. In other words, a zombie world would be possible. But if a zombie world is possible, what explains the fact that brains in this world happen to produce minds which are completely causally redundant? This concern can be given additional force if we consider human evolution. If we accept that the process of evolution is driven by natural selection then we are committed to the idea that evolved traits must benefit the species in some way. In other words, evolved characteristics should help us to survive and pass on our genes. But, if mental states have no causal role to play, then they cannot have any survival value and, therefore, we would expect them not to have evolved. If we can operate successfully without minds, why would evolution have favoured beings with them?

anthology
2.9

Jackson considers this objection and rejects it. His argument begins by drawing an analogy with a polar bear's thick coat, which we can say with some confidence evolved to enable the bear to survive in cold conditions. However, the polar bear's coat is also very heavy, and this heaviness is not conducive to the bear's survival. But the fact that a heavy coat is not a survival advantage is not inconsistent with evolutionary theory. This is because evolving a heavy coat is an inevitable by-product of evolving a warm coat. And so long as the benefits of a warm coat outweigh the drawbacks of a heavy one, it will still be an advantage to have one. In the same way, it could be that mental states are a by-product of the complex brain process which our ancestors evolved in order to help them to survive. The abilities to identify ripe fruit may inevitably produce the qualia of red as a collateral product, for reasons we don't understand. Pain may be the epiphenomenal product of a nervous system which guides us to avoid damage to the body. If so, mental states could have evolved even though they have no causal role to play in our behaviour.

Criticism 5: Introspection and self-knowledge

An uncomfortable consequence of epiphenomenalism is that it appears to be incompatible with being able to form beliefs about, or meaningfully to talk about, your own mental states. For if mental states cannot cause anything physical then they cannot cause me to talk about them. So when I say 'I am in pain' this cannot have been caused by my introspective awareness of the mental state of pain, for the pain causes nothing. But if the pain doesn't cause me to say that I'm in pain, what am I talking about when making a complaint about a headache? Surely, the meaning of the term 'headache' must come from the experience itself, and if it doesn't, then the term would appear to have no meaning. Similarly, the possibility of having knowledge of my own mind requires that mental states are causally related to these beliefs. If the introspective awareness of my headache is unconnected with the belief that I have a headache, then the belief seems unjustified. If epiphenomenalism were true, then we wouldn't be able even to talk about our mental states, since to do so, those mental states would have to be causally connected to our utterances about them. So the very act of talking or writing about mental states such as intentions, and qualia, and then denying that they have a causal role to play in human behaviour, is self-refuting. For if qualia and intentions don't affect the physical, then they cannot have anything to do with the appearance of these words on the page.

In response, the epiphenomenalist may argue that the brain could evolve a capacity to employ sensation words without these having any causal connection with sensations themselves. Zombies, after all, may be imagined who can speak our language. All that's needed is that they be caused to speak of certain colours when in the presence of certain objects. The zombie's eyes pick up on certain wavelengths of light and its unconscious brain has been trained to connect the subsequent neural activity with certain vocalisations. And the same process may be going on in us. Our qualia words need not get their meaning from our experience of qualia. All that's needed is for these words to be causally connected to the neural correlates of qualia.

Criticism 6: The other minds objection

How do we know that other people have minds? This is a question we will be tackling in the next section (see page 279), but it is often felt that epiphenomenalism has a particular difficulty in answering it. Standard answers to the question begin by pointing out that we can directly observe other people's behaviour and that we must therefore infer that they have conscious experiences which we cannot directly observe, based on their behaviour. So, for example, if someone steps on a nail and hops around the room holding their foot and screaming, I use this behaviour to infer that they are in pain. The fact that animals behave in similar ways to us is presumably one important reason why we suppose they have conscious experiences like us, while the fact that plants and stones do not is the reason we tend not to ascribe mentality to them. However, if, as epiphenomenalism asserts, someone's behaviour is not the product of their mental states, then on what basis can I make the inference from their behaviour to their mental state? If hopping around the room screaming is not caused by the person's pain, then surely the inference that he is in pain is not justified.

Jackson's response is to point out that we may infer a correlation between behaviour and mental state even though there may be no direct causal link. I know in my case that there is an association between certain mental states and certain behaviours, and so there is an indirect causal inference that can be made. I know in my case that stepping on nails causes pain, and hopping and screaming behaviour. So, I can infer from the behaviour of others back to its cause; the nail in the foot is the likely cause, not just of the pain-behaviour, but also of the experience of pain. As Jackson has it:

> [T]he epiphenomenalist allows that qualia are effects of what goes on in the brain. Qualia cause nothing physical but are caused by something physical. Hence the epiphenomenalist can argue from the behaviour of others to the qualia of others by arguing from the behaviour of others back to its causes in the brains of others and out again to their qualia.[53]
>
> Jackson

2.1.6 The problem of other minds and the threat of solipsism

anthology
2.10

The last section introduced the problem epiphenomenalist dualism has in explaining how we come to have knowledge of other people's mental states. Earlier we also examined how non-reductivists like Chalmers argue that it is conceivable that others may not enjoy mental states at all. This was the zombie world hypothesis (see page 241). If, as dualists hold, the mind is irreducible to the physical, then knowing everything there is to know physically about someone needn't involve knowing the content of their consciousness and so it seems that it is conceivable that others don't have minds at all. In this section we are going to focus on the sceptical worry touched on in these discussions: the sceptical worry known as the *problem of other minds*.

Experimenting with ideas

To get a handle on the issue, consider the following argument. Then discuss how the sceptical conclusion might be avoided.

I have many beliefs about other people's moods and emotions, for example whether they are sad or angry. I also have many beliefs about their thoughts and desires, for example that they believe it is raining or fancy a beer. More fundamentally, and underlying this, I believe that each person has their own mind with their own experiences, and that much of what they do is because of what they believe and desire. In other words, I believe that people have minds.

Now consider what evidence I have for these beliefs. In all my dealings with other people, all I ever observe are the movements of their bodies, the expressions on their faces and the words that they utter. What I cannot observe, however, are the feelings they experience nor the thoughts they are thinking. All I have to go on in supposing them to be in pain or entertaining a certain thought is their behaviour. So when I see someone stand on a nail, scream out loud and hop around holding their foot, I infer that they are experiencing pain. But we can question whether this inference is sound. I have no way of checking that other people have experiences that are anything like what I experience when I step on a nail. Their 'pain' might be very different from mine. Moreover, not only is it conceivable that other people don't really experience my kind of pain, but, worse, it may be that they don't experience anything at all! All that I can be sure of is that when they stand on nails this causes them to hop around and produce a horrible noise. All that I can be sure of is what they do, not what they think or feel. So, for all I know, I am the only person with a mind. Everyone else could be zombies.

Do you agree with the conclusion that you cannot know that anyone else has a mind? If so, will this change the way you deal with them? How?

If not, why not? What could justify the inference from their behaviour to the existence of their minds?

According to dualism, my own mind is perceived *directly* by introspection, while the external world is perceived only *indirectly* via the senses. It follows from this picture, one inherited from Descartes, that we can only know about the minds of *other* people indirectly. This inevitably raises the question of precisely *how* I can judge what state of mind some other person is in. An initial answer would have to be that I must come to such knowledge on the basis of their behaviour. As we saw in our discussion of the problem when looking at epiphenomenalism, if, for example, someone is writhing on the floor screaming, the obvious inference would seem to be that they are in pain. But this just leads us to the more fundamental question, namely how this inference is made and whether or not it is justified. All the evidence about other people consists of what they do or is done to them, yet we think we know things about what they think and feel. If, for the dualist, pain is a sensation felt in my own mind, how can I infer the existence of a pain that is not mine and not felt by me? The evidence would seem only to be sufficient for us to make the generalisation that when people sit on drawing pins they jump up sharply and emit strange noises from their mouths, not that they are in pain, for their pain is not perceived. More radically, the dualist picture raises the possibility that we lack any firm basis for positing the very existence of other minds.

> *Suppose everyone had a box with something in it: we call it a 'beetle'. No one can look in anyone else's box, and everyone says he knows what a beetle is only by looking at his beetle. – Here it would be quite possible for everyone to have something different in his box. One might even imagine such a thing constantly changing. – But suppose the word 'beetle' had a use in these people's language? – If so, it would not be used as the name of a thing. The thing in the box has no place in the language-game at all; not even as a something: for the box might even be empty.*[54]
>
> **Wittgenstein**

Wittgenstein likens the dualist picture to a situation in which each of us has his or her own box into which only he or she can look. I can see directly what I have, but no one else can; they have to rely on my report about what I have. Wittgenstein asks us to imagine that each of us calls what we have in our box a 'beetle'; and while we may suppose that everyone's beetle is the same, it is possible that we all have something different in our boxes. Because we can never compare what is in our boxes, we can never be sure. It is even possible that some people have nothing in their box at all! What this picture suggests is that when I talk about my beetle, no one else can truly understand what I mean by the term, since it refers to a wholly private object. It could be that we are all talking at cross-purposes, and using words to refer to private sensations which are very different from each others.

Wittgenstein thinks this consequence is enough to raise serious doubts about the way dualism sets up the situation in the first place, as we will see below (see pages 283–87). And Gilbert Ryle is another philosopher who agrees that the problem arises because of a mistaken view of how we acquire knowledge of other minds in the first place. According to Ryle, dualism would entail that 'each of us lives the life of a ghostly Robinson Crusoe'.[55] If, as dualists suppose, our language of mental states refers only to private mental states, we could never be sure that they are being correctly applied to others; a situation which suggests that 'absolute solitude is ... the ineluctable destiny of the soul'.[56] For Ryle, this consequence of dualism was one reason (of many reasons) to reject it.

However, dualists have tried various strategies to try to avoid this sceptical conclusion. To do this, they need to argue that the inference to the conclusion that others have minds is justified, and two major defences of its legitimacy are traditionally offered: namely the *argument from analogy*, and the *argument from the best explanation*. (Ryle's own solution, rather than answer the problem directly, tries to defuse it and we'll be looking at that below when discussing analytical behaviourism.)

The argument from analogy with my own case

The argument from analogy contends that we learn the connection between behaviour and mental states by observing it in our own case. Subsequently we suppose that there is an analogous connection between the behaviour of other people and internal states. John Stuart Mill, who appears to be the first philosopher to articulate the argument, wrote:

> *I conclude that other human beings have feelings like me, because, first, they have bodies like me, which I know, in my own case, to be the antecedent conditions of feelings; and because, secondly, they exhibit the acts, and other outward signs, which in my own case, I know by experience to be caused by feelings.*[57]
>
> Mill

Here Mill is arguing that I learn there are law-like connections between occurrences in my body and in my mind. My foot steps on a nail and I feel a pain in my mind. The pain in my mind is typically followed by shouts and screams, efforts to remove the source of the pain and so on. So when I observe someone else behaving in similar ways in response to similar occurrences in their bodies, I infer that they have similar conscious experiences. This inference is based on an analogy. That is, it begins by drawing a parallel between observable similarities between my case and others (similar bodies, similar behaviours), and it then infers that others are also similar to me in certain unobserved (and unobservable) ways (other minds).

Figure 2.12 The argument by analogy with my own case
When I step on a nail it causes a pain. The pain in turn causes pain behaviour. When others step on nails they also exhibit pain behaviour. So, by using my own case as an analogy, I am able to infer that they, like me, experience pain.

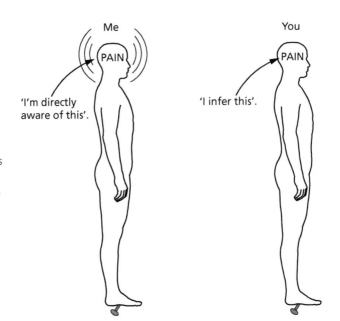

Problems with the argument by analogy

Criticism 1

What is the justification for the assumption that other people are analogous to my own case? Is the evidence of my own case sufficient to generalise to all other people? In general, to argue by analogy with a single case is not a very strong procedure. For example, if I came across one black bird with a red beak, I would surely not be justified in inferring that all black birds have red beaks. Inductive generalisations surely require rather greater evidence than that.

The argument by analogy may be defended against this objection by pointing out that the idea that others are similar to me has rather more going for it than a simple inductive generalisation based on one observation. There is a great range of ways in which my body and behaviours are similar to others' bodies and behaviours. Other people are very like me not just in the way they react to standing on nails. Their bodies are composed of the same kind of stuff, they have the same limbs, and sense organs. And their behaviour is like mine in a whole range of complex ways. Language use is just one striking example of complex behaviour which is causally connected in my own case in a systematic way to thought processes. This complexity and the regularity of the connections between the inside of my mind and the outside of my behaviour, may give us greater reason to suppose that others also have similar internal processes when they exhibit similar behaviour.

Moreover, we are members of the same species. And we know that members of the same species tend to be very similar in respect of a whole range of characteristics, including things we tend not directly to observe, such as the structure of their internal organs. It would be rather odd, we might think, if others were different from me when it comes to having a mind. After all, my mind is a very important part of what I am.

So important that it is reasonable to suppose that it is an essential component of what it is to be a typical human. Surely, then, we have very strong reasons for supposing that all humans have a mind, not just me.

Criticism 2

However, the inference from my own case may still appear problematic. For what makes an analogical inference reasonably secure is that there is some possibility of making independent checks. Thus, if I reason from the similarities between the external appearance of two human bodies that they both have similar internal organs it is possible for me directly to check whether the analogy holds. So suppose I listen to someone's chest and hear beating and infer on the basis of other similar beatings that they have a heart. In this case, it is always possible, at least in principle, to cut them open to check. But in the case of other minds there is no possible means of checking, and so no possible way of ever verifying the claim that others do indeed have minds. It's not just that we cannot check as a matter of contingent fact. It is impossible to check whether others have minds, *in principle*. 'Since ... one person cannot in principle visit another person's mind ... there could be no way of establishing the necessary correlation' between their external behaviour and internal mental states. [58] And it is this, Gilbert Ryle argued, that makes the analogical inference in this case ungrounded.

However, it is not obvious that the inability to make independent checks completely undermines the inference. If, as dualists hold, minds are by their nature private, then it is going to be impossible to check, but this doesn't mean I have no basis for making the inference. Certainly it makes it impossible to guarantee the soundness of the reasoning, but it may still have some force.

Learn More

The argument by analogy leaves the existence of other minds probable at best, and this has struck many philosophers as unsatisfactory, in part because it doesn't sit well with our everyday conviction that they do exist. Those, such as Wittgenstein, who reject this attempt to explain our belief in the reality of other minds often claim that the whole problem derives from the dualist approach which begins with the idea that knowledge of my own mind is secure, while that of others is problematic. As normally conceived, the problem is a direct consequence of Cartesian dualism – a consequence of regarding *mind* as something inner and private, which is accessible only through introspection, while other people's bodies form part of the public world, and propositions about them can be shown to be true or false in the same way as any physical object statement. A theory of mind which allows that you know that you have a mind while leaving the possibility of other minds in doubt, cannot really be a satisfactory theory of mind. And if we do not, as Descartes did, insist upon this sharp distinction between mind and body, or at least, do not make a distinction between them in quite the way that he did, we need not, it is claimed, inherit the problem in the same way at all.

Wittgenstein develops his attack on dualism and the argument from analogy by arguing that I would find it impossible even to form a coherent concept of someone else's experiences on the basis of acquaintance only with my own. If I learn the meaning of the word 'pain' from my own case, how can I make sense of the idea of someone else's pain? For if 'pain' means *pain that I feel*, then someone else's pain would be a pain that I don't feel and so wouldn't be something I could understand. A pain that is not felt by me would surely be a contradiction in terms, if the only basis for understanding the word was my own experience of it.

Further, according to Wittgenstein, in order for me to be able to judge that this particular sensation is a pain that *I'm* feeling I need first to have something to contrast it with, namely pains that *others* feel. The idea of a pain that *I* feel only makes sense in the context of pains in general which are felt by others. If this is right, then the argument by analogy with my own case can't get off the ground, since I cannot judge myself to be having particular experiences, such as pains, if I've not *already* made judgements about other minds. Knowledge of my own mind without prior knowledge of others is impossible, and so it cannot be the basis for knowledge of other minds.[59] In other words, to have a concept of myself as a **subject of experience** I must have the concept of subjects of experience other than myself.

Wittgenstein also tries to show that the idea of ascribing mental states to others by analogy with my own case is far more problematic than the dualist recognises. This is because, according to the Cartesian picture, there is no conceptually necessary connection between having a certain sort of physical form and having a mind, or between certain events occurring in your body and your mind experiencing certain sensations. That is, it is a purely contingent matter that my behaviour happens to be caused by my mental states and that sensory information conveyed to my brain happens to cause me to have certain types of sense experience. This is why, according to dualism, the ideas, of spectrum inversion and philosophical zombies are conceivable. But if there is no conceptual connection, then surely any behaviour and any physical form could be secretly attached to a mind. I would therefore have no good reason for singling out other human beings from among all the physical things around me, as those to consider minded. Why not suppose that my toaster or my teapot has a mind? If Descartes were right, this should be quite easy to do. And it should also be easy to imagine that someone writhing on the floor with a nail in their foot is not really in pain. But can you actually do this in real life? Wittgenstein asks us whether we can make proper sense of the idea of attributing thoughts to a teapot or denying pain to a person in obvious distress. The fact that both of these are impossible for us seriously to imagine, suggests a closer connection between the behaviour and physical form of human beings and the workings of their minds.

According to Wittgenstein, the connection may be understood in terms of the conditions under which we ascribe mental states to others. In other words, there are certain criteria or rules which we apply which specify when someone is in a particular mental-state. Take for example being in pain. The criteria for ascribing a toothache to someone might be that they are groaning, holding their jaw, searching for aspirin and so on. And if someone is exhibiting all these symptoms then one is justified in concluding that they have a toothache. Wittgenstein argues that there must be criteria such as these which are publicly observable since otherwise we would be unable to learn the language of mental states. If dualism were true, we would be unable to ascribe mental states to others, since we could never know whether we were correctly ascribing the terms or not. Since we do, for everyday purposes, have little trouble using mental-state terms when talking about other people ('Greta has toothache'; 'Mathilda loves chips and curry sauce'), we must have a good command of the rules for correct and incorrect ascription. And these must be conceptually connected to behaviour – behaviour which is publicly observable. How else could a child ever learn to ascribe pain to others unless they did so on the basis of what they can observe? It is for this reason that we cannot meaningfully ascribe mental states to teapots – they just lack the requisite behaviours. And it is why it is not practically possible to doubt that someone is in pain when obviously injured and screaming: these just are the kinds of behaviour which entail that they are in pain.

Wittgenstein's 'private language' argument

Wittgenstein's so-called 'private language' argument is found in his *Philosophical Investigations* (1953)[60] and represents an attempt to undermine the Cartesian approach to epistemology. Wittgenstein's arguments try to show that no coherent sense can be made of the **solipsistic** position that Descartes entertains, since it implicitly relies on what it claims to doubt. In other words, his argument questions the assumption of the primacy of knowledge of our own minds over those of others, by trying to show that the identification of private mental states is only possible if one presupposes a world of publicly observable objects, and therefore presupposes the reality of other minds.

Wittgenstein's argument begins by pointing out that the ability to identify specific elements within one's own experience, such as qualia, requires some kind of classification system, in other words, something akin to a *language*. The Cartesian approach must presuppose such a language since only by the use of one could I classify and re-identify my experiences, and on that basis hope to build up knowledge about the external world and of other minds. The sort of world Descartes inhabits in the second *Meditation* in which he can identify his own private experiences but is not certain of the existence of the external world is just the sort of world that would be inhabited by a 'private language' user.

Note that the private language I would have to use will only be comprehensible to me, since its terms refer to my own immediate and private mental states, and such mental states cannot be properly known to anyone else because such things are private. In other words, their meanings are given by *me*, and not by any public agreement.

The next step is to point out that any system of classification, including a private language, must allow for a distinction between correct and incorrect use of its terms. For if there were no distinction, then whatever is being classified could no more be said to be one thing than another. Any language must be able to distinguish between correct and incorrect usage, since otherwise we couldn't determine whether a term meant one thing rather than another.

Now, our ordinary *public* language clearly has criteria for distinguishing between the correct and incorrect use of terms. When someone misuses a word this can be pointed out to them. We have dictionaries and grammar books and so on, which tell us how to use words properly. It is the existence of such publicly available rules that allows language to operate as, among other things, a system of classification. So now the question becomes whether a *private* language could satisfy these conditions. Could the Cartesian solipsist devise a language in which to classify his or her own experiences?

Wittgenstein claims that he or she could not and does so through the following thought experiment. Suppose, in the world of Cartesian solipsism, we experience a quale and identify it with a name 'S'. Here we appear to have instituted a private name for a private sensation. But have we? A necessary condition for having successfully named something is that we could recognise a second instance of the same thing. But if we experience a second sensation, how are we to decide if it is an 'S' or not? In other words, how are we to tell whether this second sensation is similar to the original one in the relevant respect? How are we to be sure that we are not making a mistake?

The solipsist's answer is that so long as the new sensation *appears* to be 'S' then it *is* 'S'. For when it comes my own qualia, appearance and reality are one. In a private language, the rules would be just those which it seems right to apply on this or that occasion. And this is what is meant by saying that here I cannot make an error. I can be absolutely certain of the way things appear to me. But, complains Wittgenstein, if there is no chance of going wrong here, there is no legitimate sense in which we can be said to go right either. If the 'private language' user does not risk the possibility of going wrong in his or her re-identification of a sensation then he or she is not actually re-identifying the sensation at all. For if there are no objective criteria for determining correct identification, then we haven't succeeded in instituting a legitimate rule for classification.

Considerations such as these led Wittgenstein to suppose that the public world is primary, and is a necessary condition for the possibility of talking about our mental life. He suggests that the terms that describe our minds, emotions, sensations, etc., are acquired in the same way as any other term in our language, by our being shown how such terms are used. It follows that the attempt of traditional dualism to begin with the immediate data of consciousness is misguided because it cannot make the first move. That is, I cannot even identify those immediate data. The mistake is to think that I can know what terms such as 'red' or 'pain' mean by direct acquaintance with the private objects they supposedly stand for. Whereas the only reason we are able to use such terms properly is because there is a public world in which correct and incorrect usage is determined.

The argument to the best explanation

The argument to the best explanation accepts the dualist picture according to which it is at least conceivable that the objects I call persons are zombies, but insists that I have sufficient reasons for thinking that they are not. These reasons are similar to those that lead scientists to believe in the existence of unobservable entities such as atoms. No one has directly seen such entities and yet atomic theory is the best explanation of the phenomena we can and do observe. For example, it predicts that heated copper will gain weight because oxygen atoms from the atmosphere will combine with copper atoms to create a film of copper oxide. Similarly the supposition of the existence of other minds with their own thoughts and feelings, that is to say, the hypothesis of our everyday folk psychology, is the best explanation of the elaborate behaviour we observe in other human beings. The supposition that someone is in *pain* when they are writhing on the floor and screaming with a nail in their foot, or that they are having thoughts about philosophy when discussing the problem of other minds with you, is the best 'theory' available to account for their behaviour. And it is not just that folk psychology *explains* human behaviour. It is because I suppose others have beliefs, desires and sensations of different kinds that I can also *predict* their behaviour in a range of circumstances. Standing on a nail causes pain. Pain is undesirable. If it is extreme enough it causes people to scream. So folk psychology predicts that someone who stands on a nail is likely to scream and remove the nail from their foot.

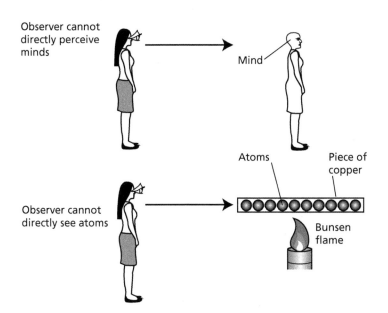

Observer cannot directly perceive minds

Mind

Observer cannot directly see atoms

Atoms

Piece of copper

Bunsen flame

Figure 2.13 Atoms beneath a piece of metal being heated
Atomic theory explains and predicts the behaviour of matter in a range of circumstances. So it is reasonable to believe in atoms, even though we cannot directly observe them. In the same way, it is reasonable to believe in beliefs and desires even though we can't observe them directly, since they successfully explain and predict human behaviour.

Note that those persuaded by the best-explanation argument may also appeal to the inconceivability of the idea that other human beings could act in the complex ways that they do if they did not have minds. Why would they talk if they did not have thoughts? What possible explanation for this complex behaviour could there be, other than that they are trying to communicate their inner ideas? Also, if others don't have minds, why do they act as if they do? Why do they *say* that they do when asked? And why are they able to describe an inner life so similar to mine, if they possess no such thing? No other answer to these questions comes near to being as plausible as the hypothesis that they do indeed have minds.

No matter how plausible a hypothesis folk psychology might be, it may well turn out to be false. That is, the unobserved entities that it posits may not actually exist. Just as concepts used in the past to explain behaviour such as possession by demons, fate or curses are not now thought to correspond to anything in reality, so our concepts of beliefs, desires, intentions, etc. may turn out to be inadequate in a more complete explanation of human behaviour. Compare this possibility with advances in science where theories are superseded by new theories which explain the phenomena more adequately. As we have seen, eliminativists argue that the neuroscience of the future will supersede it. But supporters of the argument to the best explanation emphasise that folk psychology is by far the best theory available and that we are, therefore, justified in accepting it.

In his *Discourse on Method* (1637) Descartes offers a version of this argument to show that others must have immaterial minds. He argues that there are two ways to test whether 'machines bearing the image of our bodies, and capable of imitating our actions' were genuinely minded, namely their use of language and of reason. For language and reason cannot be explained mechanically. What he has in mind here is that competent language use involves the ability to construct completely novel sentences that no one has ever uttered before. It also allows us to understand such sentences. But, thinks Descartes, something purely physical could never create or comprehend novelty since it would be bound to behave and respond in a preprogrammed or reflex manner. Understanding is also required for genuinely intelligent behaviour which can respond appropriately to new situations. Any purely physical device, no matter how complex, would, therefore, not be able to cope with unexpected situations or solve the most basic of practical problems since they would be bound to repeat reflex behaviours. Read the quotation below for Descartes' own account of this argument.

> for we may easily conceive a machine to be so constructed that
> it emits vocables, and even that it emits some correspondent to
> the action upon it of external objects which cause a change in
> its organs; for example, if touched in a particular place it may
> demand what we wish to say to it; if in another it may cry out that it
> is hurt, and such like; but not that it should arrange them variously
> so as appositely to reply to what is said in its presence, as men of the
> lowest grade of intellect can do. The second test is, that although such
> machines might execute many things with equal or perhaps greater
> perfection than any of us, they would, without doubt, fail in certain
> others from which it could be discovered that they did not act from
> knowledge, but solely from the disposition of their organs: for while
> reason is an universal instrument that is alike available on every
> occasion, these organs, on the contrary, need a particular arrangement
> for each particular action; whence it must be morally impossible that
> there should exist in any machine a diversity of organs sufficient to
> enable it to act in all the occurrences of life, in the way in which our
> reason enables us to act.[61]

Descartes

Heidegger and 'being with others'

Martin Heidegger (1889–1976) argues that the appeal of the problem of other minds lies in a mistaken picture of how we acquire knowledge in the first place. Like Wittgenstein, he sees it as a mistake to suppose that we must infer the existence of other minds from others' behaviour. But, he argues, I don't need to discover the other's mind by inference from my experience because I have an a priori recognition of their consciousness *within* the structure of my own experience. Heidegger argues that human experience from the outset involves the recognition of other consciousnesses. We inhabit a world which is always intersubjective and we cannot uncover any solipsistic starting point from which intersubjectivity would be derived. In other words, for Heidegger it is a mistake to suppose that we ever were conscious only of the self as isolated from others, subsequently to have to discover them. Rather, our primary mode of experience is already what he calls 'being with others'. So the problem is not how to reach out to others, but how to separate ourselves off from them in order to come to see oneself as a distinct individual.

If we do have an innate sense of 'being with others', a primordial sense of their consciousness, then this may well be something which is hard wired into our biology (although such empirical evidence is not something Heidegger explores). A social animal such as ourselves is arguably one which has an innate capacity for its sense of 'being with' members of its own species. Babies will imitate facial expressions, showing that there exist hard-wired mechanisms whereby they can recognise the same action or expression performed by another. Such hard wiring allows for the development of our consciousness and our sense of self within a social context. Contemporary attachment theory in psychology also supports the idea that our sense of self and our ability to read and interact successfully with other minds is based on the nature of our relationships with our caregivers in our earliest years. Such empirical evidence also suggests that by the time we develop self-consciousness we are already enmeshed within an intersubjective world.

Sartre on other minds and self-consciousness

Similar conclusions have been reached by Jean-Paul Sartre (1905–80) in his analysis of self-consciousness. For Sartre, I am *directly* aware of the existence of other minds when I encounter other people. This immediate awareness is not something inferred, but an integral part of my experience of being in the world. Consequently, the issue of whether I am justified in believing in other minds doesn't arise. I can be as sure of the existence of other minds as I am of the existence of any object of my awareness.

He argues that to be aware of one's self takes more than some isolated act of Cartesian introspection. We must encounter other consciousnesses before we become self-aware. Sartre draws our attention to the *phenomenology* of the experience of 'the other', the way it feels to me, to encourage us to recognise this primordial truth about ourselves. Without others I can go about my business with no sense of self at all. My conscious life is completely absorbed by what I am doing. It is directed away from myself into the world. We might imagine a Robinson Crusoe who never met another soul from birth, never focusing attention inwards on himself. No conscious distinction would be drawn by such an individual between self and world. But as soon as I encounter someone else who is looking at me, for example, I become aware of myself as an object of their consciousness. And with this experience I become for the first time self-conscious. So self-consciousness actually presupposes awareness of other minds, rather than the other way round.

2.2 Materialism: The mind is not ontologically distinct from the physical

2.2.1 Analytical behaviourism[1]

> *The distinction between a conscious man and an unconscious machine resolves itself into a distinction between different types of perceptible behaviour ... When I assert that an object is conscious, I am asserting no more than that it would, in response to any conceivable test, exhibit the empirical manifestations of consciousness. I am not making a metaphysical postulate concerning the occurrence of events which I could not, even in principle, observe.*[2]
>
> Ayer

An alternative solution to the problem of other minds, which has affinities with Wittgenstein's line of thought explored in the last section (see pages 283–87), consists in the denial that there is anything beyond the behaviour of others the existence of which needs to be inferred. Since dualists are saying that other people's minds cannot even in principle be detected, it may be argued that the notion that they are real entities is idle and meaningless. For something which cannot be detected, on such a view, is not something we can meaningfully regard as real. In other words, the solution is that what you directly observe is all there is.

Analytical behaviourism claims that minds are just what people say and do. Thus all statements concerning mental states or processes are not really, as dualists claim, concerned with a private world which each of us is directly aware of through introspection. Rather, talk about minds is completely *reducible* without remainder to talk about people's *behaviour*. It is termed 'analytical' behaviourism, because *analysis* of the meanings of the language of mind will reveal that it all boils down in the end to statements about behaviour. This is termed an '**analytic reduction**', meaning that statements about minds mean the same as statements about behaviour in the same way that 'mother' means the same as 'female parent'. What this means is that statements about emotions, sensations, beliefs and desires are not about hidden processes going on 'inside' people, but are rather a shorthand way of talking about publicaly observable actual and potential patterns of behaviour; so, they are concerned with what we can all directly see. If this is right, then there is no longer a problem of whether belief in the existence of other minds is justified. If you can observe what another person says and does, since saying and doing *is* mind, you are amply warranted in believing that the person is minded.

Arguments for analytical behaviourism

The motivation for such a view is firstly that, as a matter of fact, we do only have access to the behaviour of others, and consequently that that behaviour must be the basis for all our language about other people. Those, like Ayer, who consider that meaningful propositions must be to do with what can enter into our experience, reject as confused the idea that other minds could be isolated from any possibility of detection. Talk of things the existence of which cannot be verified is meaningless. It is the failure to recognise this that allows dualists to become embroiled in the pseudo-problem of other minds. Behaviourism, by equating mind with what is observable, eliminates the problem.

Secondly, the behaviourist position overcomes the problem of interaction that, as we have seen, plagues all forms of dualism. For if the mind is not a distinct **substance** mysteriously linked to the body, then there is no causal interaction to account for.

Thirdly, if words acquire their meaning from the public context in which they are used, then there must be rules governing their use. This means it must be possible to determine whether they are being used correctly by reference to what is publicly observable. But if mental-state terms got their meaning by reference to private experiences within each of our minds, it would be impossible to tell whether the words were being used correctly or not. Communication with others about our minds would not just be subject to occasional misunderstanding, it would be literally impossible to talk about our own or others' mental states (see Wittgenstein on the argument from analogy, page 284). So, given that we can talk about minds, and generally have little difficulty ascribing mental states to people, we must be talking about what is publicly observable, namely behaviour.

Hard behaviourism

> *The proposition ... about someone's 'pain', is ... simply an abbreviated expression of the fact that all its test sentences are verified. ... It can be re-translated without loss of content into a proposition which no longer involves the term 'pain', but only physical concepts. Our analysis has consequently established that a certain proposition belonging to psychology has the same content as a proposition belonging to physics.*[3]
>
> Hempel

There are different versions of behaviourism, and we will be focusing on the so-called 'soft' behaviourism of Gilbert Ryle in this section. However, it is worth briefly looking at the 'hard' behaviourism of Carl Hempel (1905–97) as this will provide us with a useful introduction to the issues.

Hempel was a member of the Vienna Circle, a group of philosophers active in the 1920s and 1930s in the promotion of **logical positivism**. Logical positivism is a form of empiricism which insists that meaningful propositions must have empirical content and so make positive claims about our experience. So Hempel adhered to the verificationist account of meaning, according to which all meaningful propositions are either **analytic** and so trivial or they must be provable by reference to observation statements. Since other minds cannot be observed, talk about them is either meaningless or reducible to what can be observed. Ultimately, for Hempel, this means that if we are to talk meaningfully about human beings' minds, we have to be able to show just how our claims about them can be reduced to behavioural descriptions. So his project was to replace the language of mental states with descriptions in terms of physical movements which could ultimately be rendered in the language of physics.

So how exactly would such a translation from the language of mind to that of behaviour work? An initial example may be useful here so that we can get the idea. Suppose your friend Dolores has trodden on a nail. She is swearing at the top of her lungs and jumping around on one leg, making efforts to remove the nail from the sole of her foot. According to Hempel, such behaviour must constitute what it means to say that she is in pain. The pain is not a private experience causing Dolores' behaviour, it just is the behaviour.

Experimenting with ideas

We've given a rather crude characterisation of behaviourism up to this point, but this is still a good moment to begin to reflect on the difficulties it faces.

1   Using the example of Dolores above, can you think of any problems with reducing talk of her pain to purely physical descriptions of her behaviour?
2   Try translating these statements about other minds into behavioural language.
    a) Beatrice is elated.
    b) Eli has an itch on his knee.
    c) Solomon likes football.
    d) Rowena is hungry.
    e) Konstantin wants to be rich.
    If you are in a class, work with a partner to see whether you can straightforwardly read off their mental states from what you can observe of their behaviour.
How did you do, making your behavioural translations? One test of their success is whether you were able completely to eliminate all reference to mental states. For if the reduction is going to work, we must translate into the language of what is observable without making any reference, implicit or otherwise, to minds. Mental states need to be completely analysed away since otherwise the analysis would be circular – it would be reintroducing the mind instead of making reference exclusively to behaviour. So have another look at your translations. Do they refer only to bodily movements?

Criticism
Issue with defining mental states adequately: circularity and multiple realisability

One important issue with Hempel's version of behaviourism is that in order to complete his reduction to the language of behaviour, he cannot be satisfied with expressions like 'Beatrice punches the air', 'Eli scratches his knee', or 'Candice kicks the ball'. This is because such expressions make implicit reference to human agency, that is, to the notion that the person acted intentionally, that he or she willed this action. And to say that someone acted intentionally is to make implicit reference to a mental state. So in order to completely replace the language of mind we need to translate such expressions into those of pure bodily movements. Thus, 'Candice kicked the ball' would need to be rendered as something like 'Candice's foot lifted from the ground, the knee flexed and her leg swung forward causing the foot to impact with the ball.' In this way, all reference to supposedly hidden mental-state terms can be eliminated and we have a scientifically respectable and verifiable description of what's happened.

However, a problem is that there doesn't appear to be a way of translating particular types of action defined partly in terms of mental states, into particular types of bodily movement. This is because the same bodily movement may, on different occasions, manifest itself in any number of different actions. For example, impacting your foot on a ball may be an attempt to score a goal, returning the ball to its owner, a gesture of contempt for a refereeing decision, a demonstration of how to kick a ball, testing to see if the ball is pumped up, tripping over a ball, squashing a mosquito that's alighted on the ball, trying to relieve an itch on your toe, and so on.

▶ ACTIVITY

Below are five bodily movements. (Note that arguably some still make some implicit reference to human agency, but they will do as shorthand versions of pure bodily movements.) Examine them and list how many different actions each could be.

1 Your knees bend and your bottom rests on a rock.
2 You raise a finger in the air.
3 Your hand grips a glass and lifts it from a table.
4 Your grip loosens on a pen so that it falls to the floor.
5 Air blows out of your mouth.

Hopefully you have seen from the activity that a given bodily movement can represent different actions. But this presents a problem for analytical behaviourism since in order to reduce actions to bodily movements, it would need to be able to show some differences in the bodily movements that would account for them being different actions. Otherwise the reduction cannot adequately account for the range of mental states we attribute to people. At the same time, the same action may be manifested by very different bodily movements. The action of greeting someone may be achieved by raising a hand, uttering certain words, punching the air, kicking a ball to them, raising your eyebrows and so on, so that, again, no one-to-one correspondence seems to obtain between actions and bodily movements. The fact that the same action may be manifested in a great variety of bodily movements may be expressed by saying the action is **'multiply realisable'** in behaviour.

Experimenting with ideas

Imagine watching a game of football with a Martian. The Martian is interested to know what is going on, but, because Martians know nothing of minds, doesn't understand mental-state terms or references to the intentions of human agents. Can the game be reduced to a purely physical explanation, one that refers only to the laws of motion and attraction of physical objects such as balls, and human bodies? Even if a complete description of the game could be given, would the Martian now understand what was going on?

It also seems clear that being in a particular mental state need not always lead to a specific type of action. Suppose I am feeling thirsty. This might lead me to exclaim 'I'm thirsty!', or (if I am in a library for example), I might keep quiet. I might go to a cafe for a cup of tea, a pub for a beer, or home for a glass of water. Or I might do none of these and wait for the feeling to go away on its own. All of these and an infinite number of others are possible behaviours that the mental state could be associated with so that a full analysis of it couldn't be completed. When it comes to my holding certain abstract beliefs, such as that philosophy is hard or that Britain should leave the European Union, the range of ways such mental states might manifest themselves is bewildering. But if the analysis cannot be completed, not even in principle, then the project of reducing mental states to pure behaviour must fail.

The failure to complete the reduction occurs not just because it would be infinitely long, but also because it necessarily would reintroduce agency and mental-state terminology into it. Consider that a mental state, such as a desire to drink beer, would only lead one to drink a beer, if you didn't also have the belief that you had to drive later or that the beer was poisoned or that this pub doesn't keep its beer properly, and so forth. But if our analysis of 'desires a beer' needs to take account of this, then it needs to translate these mental states into behavioural language as well. But the attempt to analyse 'believes she must drive later', 'believes the beer is poisoned' in terms of its behavioural manifestations will also have to reintroduce mental-state terminology. This means that the reduction cannot be completed without circularity; that is, without reintroducing at each level of the analysis, precisely what the analysis is supposed to be eliminating: the mind.

This suggests that the reduction to purely physical descriptions which make no mention of human agency is not going to work and that the language by which we describe human behaviour necessarily involves reference to actions.

Ryle's project

Ryle's version of behaviourism is less ambitious in the sense that he doesn't think a reduction of the language of the mind to pure bodily movements is possible, and for this reason it is often called 'soft' behaviourism. Before examining his positive account of the mind, it is worth examining the extended critique of substance dualism that he offers in the first chapter of *The Concept of Mind* (1949).[4] His intention in the book is, Ryle explains, to 'explode the myth' of Cartesian dualism, a picture of mind and body which he thinks fuddles our thinking and which generates the various problems we've been grappling with – including the problem of other minds and the problem of interaction. Once we have clarified the proper ways in which the language of the mind is used in everyday discourse, these problems should dissolve.

Ryle likens the Cartesian philosopher who wonders what kind of thing the mind could be and how it might interact with the body, to a foreigner in England who watches a cricket match for the first time and who is taught to recognise who is responsible for the batting, the bowling, the wicket-keeping and so on, but then asks who is responsible for the team spirit. The point is that the team spirit is not another cricketing task but rather a way of talking about the way the team performs, that is to say, a manner of talking about the players' tendency to play well together.[5] In this story, the foreigner misunderstands how the term 'team spirit' functions. Its function is not to refer to a specific operation performed in the game, but to how well all of them are performed. Ryle calls a misunderstanding of this kind a 'category mistake'.

anthology 2.11

Now, according to Ryle, Descartes was led astray in a similar way to the foreigner at the cricket match. He noted that people eat, walk, talk and sleep and all these actions are performed physically, so they are easy for us to see. But we also talk a great deal about people thinking, imagining, sensing and so on. But when we say they are doing these sorts of things, Descartes couldn't find any obvious behaviours that our talk referred to. And when we talk about the mind, we are not able to point to any physical object corresponding to the word. This led him to wonder what kind of a thing the mind could be if it cannot be seen or touched and doesn't exist in space. His answer was that it must be a *very special kind of thing*: one that has none of the characteristics of normal (i.e. physical) things – it has no spatial dimensions, no capacity for being divided, is not subject to physical laws, and so on. The mistake here is that Descartes held on to the idea that the mind is a kind of *thing*. For the mind is not a weird type of substance; it is not a substance at all. Rather it is a way of talking about the capacities, of human beings to perform a whole range of actions. By understanding just how our talk about the mind can be made sense of in terms of human behaviour we will be freed from the spell cast on our thinking by 'Descartes' Myth'.[6]

The distinction between our talk about minds and our talk about bodies is then not talk about two different sorts of substance. For, according to Ryle, mental concepts are not of the same *category* as those of material bodies. So the difference between deliberate and non-deliberate behaviour is not to be explained in terms of the one being caused by the mind and the latter by bodies, but rather in terms of publicly observable behavioural differences. When we talk of other minds 'we are not referring to occult episodes of which their overt acts and utterances are effects; we are referring to those overt acts and utterances themselves'.[7] Ryle's task therefore is to analyse our ordinary talk about the mental and the physical and show that while it may invite the idea that there is substantial distinction between an observable body and an unobservable mind, a proper understanding of its logic shows the distinction to be explicable in terms of differences in observable *behaviour*.

We have already seen that a crude reduction of mind to behaviour would claim, for example, that to say that someone has a toothache *really* means that they are moaning, rubbing their jaw, looking for pain killers, asking for the dentist and so on. But one obvious difficulty, which you may well have already considered when doing the activity on hard behaviourism on page 293, is that these observable pieces of behaviour are not sufficient to determine that the person really *is* in pain. They could be pretending, for example. In such a case it seems the person exhibits pain behaviour without being in pain. This suggests that actual behaviour cannot be sufficient for the ascription of pain to people and the analysis will need to be a little more sophisticated.

Another example might be the analysis of a desire. To say that Myrtle wants a beer need not be reducible to any actual piece of behaviour. For it may be the case that Myrtle has a strong desire to drink a warming pint of her favourite stout, but that she does nothing to satisfy her desire. We can imagine her spending a few hours in the pub with friends, harbouring this desire, but that she repeatedly turns down each offer of a drink. Because she shows no signs of wanting a drink, can we safely conclude that she has no such desire? The answer is surely not – she may be turning down the drinks because she has to drive. So the fact that her behaviour gives no immediate indication of a desire doesn't warrant us in concluding that she doesn't have it. And this shows that any simplistic reduction of mental states to behaviour is not going to work.

Figure 2.14 Myrtle sits in the pub for hours, nursing one glass of orange juice. She turns down several offers of a pint. So her behaviour gives no indication of any desire for a stout. Despite this, there is nothing she would enjoy more than a pint of Winter Wobbler, and it is only because she knows she must drive that she chooses not to satisfy her desire. So how can her mental states be reduced to her behaviour?

Ryle's dispositional analysis

How then is the behaviourist going to make the reduction more plausible? The answer is that the analysis of mental terms is not conducted in terms of *current* behaviour but in terms of *dispositions* to behave. It is in Chapter 5 of *The Concept of Mind* (1949) that Gilbert Ryle gives his analysis of dispositional properties. A dispositional property of something is its liability, or proneness to act or react in a certain way. For example, the property of being soluble is a liability or proneness to dissolve if placed in water. To say of sugar that it is soluble is not to say that it is *currently* being dissolved, or indeed that it is *doing* anything, but only that it is *disposed* to dissolve under certain conditions. And this in turn is equivalent to saying that *if* the sugar were put in water *then* it would dissolve. Thus the sentence 'sugar is water soluble' is logically equivalent (or translatable into) 'if sugar were put in water then it would dissolve'. Dispositions are to be contrasted with occurrences, that is processes and events which are identified as actually happening. So to say that a sugar cube is soluble is not to say that the sugar cube enjoys some *current* but ghostly inner state of solubility, but that certain **hypothetical propositions** (i.e. *if ... then ...* propositions) about its non-actual behaviour are true of it.

According to Ryle, a similar analysis holds for mental states. Thus, to say that someone wants a pint of stout is simply to say things like, (1) 'If asked whether stout is what she wants, she would answer yes'; (2) 'If given a choice of stout or lager, she would choose the stout'; (3) 'If she is in the pub and she isn't driving, she will drink stout', and so forth. A similar analysis holds for beliefs. A belief is not a state of mind hidden from view, causing various behaviours, but signifies someone's tendency to do certain things. Mental states, in other words, are ultimately *dispositions* to behave in certain ways and sentences expressing dispositional properties are always, in the final analysis, hypothetical in form. They sum up past behaviour in a law-like way and are used to make predictions about future behaviour. Because dispositions are behaviour patterns, people do not possess them as a state of themselves but rather display them through what they do in various situations and so we need not think of mental terms as signifying 'ghostly processes',[8] as Ryle disparagingly refers to the dualist conception of mental states, but simply dispositions. So 'to explain an action as done from a certain motive is not to correlate it with an occult cause, but to subsume it under a propensity or behaviour-trend'.[9] And so, 'to explain an act as done from a certain motive is not analogous to saying that the glass broke, because a stone hit it, but to the quite different type of statement that the glass broke, when the stone hit it, because the glass was brittle'.[10] This being the case, mental concepts behave differently from the way the dualist model supposes, i.e. they are not 'occult causes and effects'[11] but what Ryle calls 'inference tickets',[12] ways of inferring future behaviour or of forming hypotheses about persons' likely behaviour based on their past behaviour.

Figure 2.15 To say that a sugar cube is soluble is not to say that anything is currently happening hidden within the cube. Rather it is to say that *if* it were placed in liquid, *then* it would dissolve. It means, in other words, that the sugar is *disposed* to dissolve. In the same way, to say that someone is thirsty is not to say that they have a ghostly invisible thing within them which causes them to drink. Rather it is to say that *if* the circumstances were right, *then* they would drink. In other words, to be thirsty is to be disposed to drink.

▶ ACTIVITY

Now that you have an idea of how Ryle's dispositional analysis of beliefs and desires is supposed to work, try to translate the following propositions about people's mental states into behavioural language.

1   Kev loves to discuss philosophy with his friends.
2   Angela is afraid of spiders.
3   Olly is in pain because of an infected appendix.
4   Liz believes that giraffes don't wear ties.
5   Craig hopes one day to become a long-distance runner, but is embarrassed to admit this to anyone.
6   Emma has secret doubts about whether God exists.
7   Steph is pretending to understand philosophical behaviourism.
8   Giles is day-dreaming about his childhood in Zanzibar.
9   Lucy hates her mother's Brussel sprouts, but will never let on.
10   John has an odd twinge in his earlobe which he immediately forgets about.

What difficulties did you encounter? See if you can use any difficulties as the basis for an objection to analytical behaviourism. Is there any reason to think it may be impossible to translate any and all claims about our minds into behavioural terms?

Further issues with analytical behaviourism

Criticism 1
The evidence of introspection

Perhaps the most intuitively obvious objection to behaviourism is that it involves denying what appears evident in my own case, namely the reality of any 'inner' aspect of my mental states, that is, the reality of qualia. To have a pain, for example, seems not to be (or at least not to be merely to be) a matter of being inclined to moan, to wince, to take an aspirin, and so on. Pains also have an intrinsic qualitative nature (a horrible one) that is revealed in introspection, and any theory of mind that ignores or denies qualia fails to do justice to our knowledge of our own mental life. So while behaviourism might make sense of how we learn to ascribe mental states to others, it doesn't appear to do justice to the subjective point of view and the direct awareness I enjoy of my own mental states. We might say that the behaviourist is effectively claiming not simply that everyone else is a zombie, but that *I* am too. And yet all I have to do is look inwards to plainly see that there is more to my mind than outward behaviour.

Criticism 2
The asymmetry between self knowledge and knowledge of others
In defence of the view that we are directly aware of our mental states via introspection, we may also point out that the subject of experience has no need of behavioural evidence in their own case in order to discover the contents of their mind. I can know I'm in pain without having to check by examining my behaviour. So while I may observe you groaning, holding your jaw and searching in the medicine cabinet and then infer that you have a toothache, it would be absurd to suppose that I learn that I have a toothache by observation of similar behaviour in myself. So while it is doubtless true that I have to observe the behaviour of others in order to know what they are thinking or feeling, I can know similar things about myself without taking any notice of my behaviour. Indeed, one absurd consequence of behaviourism would seem to be that others would have a better idea than I do of what I am thinking and feeling, because they have a better view of my behaviour. What this shows is that there is an 'asymmetry' between my knowledge of my own mind and my knowledge of other people's minds. We do not gain such knowledge in the same way and Ryle's account glosses over this crucial difference.

Criticism 3
In defence of interaction
We have seen during our discussion of epiphenomenalism that the interactionist thesis appears to have powerful support from common experience and the evidence of introspection. By denying that beliefs, desires and sensations causally interact with our behaviour, Ryle seems to fly in the face of common sense. Surely it is because I want a cup of tea that I make one. And it is because of the pain in my foot, that I jump about screaming. And I don't remove the nail from my foot simply to change my behaviour, but because it hurts!

Criticism 4
Circularity
But it is not just that interactionism sits well with our common sense understanding. It also gives us an effective *explanation* for people's behaviour. If we suppose pains cause pain behaviour, and desires cause people to seek out the objects of their desires and so on, then we have a causal explanation for their actions. But if these mental states just are these actions, then there is nothing to explain them. If the desire and the sensation are translated into behaviour, then they cannot explain behaviour without circularity. We would be trying to explain behaviour in terms of behaviour.

The conceivability of mental states without the associated behaviour

> *Imagine a community of '**super-spartans**' or 'super-stoics' – a community in which the adults have the ability to successfully suppress all involuntary pain behavior. They may, on occasion, admit that they feel pain, but always in pleasant, well-modulated voices – even if they are undergoing the agonies of the damned. They do not wince, scream, flinch, sob, grit their teeth, clench their fists, exhibit beads of sweat, or otherwise act like people in pain or people suppressing the unconditioned responses associated with pain. However, they do feel pain, and they dislike it (just as we do). They even admit that it takes a great effort of will to behave as they do. It is only that they have what they regard as important ideological reasons for behaving as they do, and they have, through years of training, learned to live up to their own exacting standards.[13]*
>
> Putnam

The contemporary philosopher Hilary Putnam (1926–) defends a functionalist account of mental states in 'Psychological predicates', one of the Anthology extracts which we will be examining later. Putnam is also a critic of analytical behaviourism and argues that we can conceive of cases where someone may be in a particular mental state but without there being any behavioural manifestation. He asks us to imagine a community of 'super-spartans', who have trained themselves to suppress any outward signs of the pains they endure (see Anthology extract 2.13). If analytical behaviourism were correct, then it would seem to follow that super-spartans don't experience pain.

Now, as we have already seen, Ryle has a response to this sort of objection. The super-spartans may not display any actual pain behaviour, but they remain *disposed* to display the behaviour were it not for the fact that they have Putnam's 'important ideological reasons' for not doing so. So, *if* the super-spartan were placed in a situation where these reasons didn't apply – perhaps she stands on a nail while perfectly alone, secure in the knowledge that no one will observe her – *then* she would wince, scream and so on.

To deal with this response, Putnam introduces the idea of *super-super-spartans*:

> *These have been super-spartans for so long, that they have even begun to suppress talk of pain … [they] do not even admit to having pains. They pretend not to know either the word or the phenomenon to which it refers …[14]*
>
> Putnam

If such a fantasy is not self-contradictory in some way, then it shows, says Putnam, that a reduction of pain to behaviour cannot work. For here we have a race who, according to the scenario we are imagining, are not even disposed to pain behaviour.

Putnam concludes that behaviourism confuses the evidence we use to ascribe mental states with the mental states themselves. He uses the analogy of a disease, such as polio. Before people knew what caused polio they would identify the disease by its symptoms. But later when they discovered the virus that causes it, they came to see that having the virus is necessary and sufficient for having the disease, irrespective of whether the patient exhibits the symptoms. Someone may have the virus without displaying any symptoms; or, they may display the symptoms without having the virus. So while the symptoms are evidence of having the disease, they do not constitute having it.

In the same way, we may identify people's pains by the symptoms – the pain behaviour. But this doesn't mean that the symptoms exhaust the meaning of the word 'pain'; or that pain just is the behaviour. Pains are not equivalent in meaning to pain behaviour, but are the cause of pain behaviour, and this is why it is possible to be in pain without exhibiting the behaviour, and possible to exhibit the behaviour without being in pain.

Putnam's super-super-spartans also represent a problem for dualism, however. For if they show no symptoms, then there would be no way of ever telling that they are in pain. Putnam, though, is a physicalist and so thinks there must be some physical basis for telling that someone is in pain even if they exhibit no behavioural manifestations. The physical basis, according to Putnam, is the state of their brains. For if the super-super-spartans are like normal human beings and we can correlate pain with certain spikes in the activity of specific regions of our brains, then if the super-super-spartans also exhibit those same brain activities, then we can infer that they experience pain. The idea that it is to the brain that we need to look to understand mentality is one we can now turn to.

2.2.2 The mind–brain identity theory

The central claim of the identity theory is that the mind is the brain, and so each mental state or process is literally one and the same thing as a state or process within the brain. What this means is that facts about the mind are *reducible* to physical facts about the brain, so that pains, beliefs, desires and so forth, are nothing more and nothing less than neurological (i.e. brain) states. Now, clearly, at present we do not know enough about the intricate workings of the brain to be able to say exactly what all mental states are in neurological terms, but the identity theory is committed to the idea that research can (and hopefully will) eventually identify what each thought, feeling or desire is in the brain.

Numerical and qualitative identity

In order to be clear about what the identity theory is saying, we need to be clear about what is meant by 'identity' in this context. Philosophers traditionally oppose **numerical identity** and **qualitative identity**. Identical twins, for example, may have identical *qualities*, they look the same, talk the same, dress the same, etc., while they nonetheless count as two people. So they may be said to be qualitatively identical but not numerically identical. Note that according to Leibniz's Law, which we encountered in our discussion of Descartes' arguments for dualism (see page 221ff.), if we come across what appear to be two things, but discover that they literally share *all* their qualities, then they must in fact be *one* thing.

So if you meet someone on the bus who looks just like your dentist, to determine whether it is indeed your dentist rather than her twin sister, you would need to determine whether what it is true of your dentist is also true of the person on the bus. And if the person on the bus is not your dentist, then there must be at least one thing by which they might be distinguished. For example, the person on the bus might have a different first name from your dentist. Identical twins, after all, do not share *all* their qualities, if only because they do not occupy the same portion of space. On the other hand, if it turns out that everything that's true of the person on the bus is also true of your dentist (including where she is at any given moment), then the person on the bus must *be* your dentist rather than her twin. Now, what the identity theory claims is that everything that is true of the brain, all of its qualities, are identical with the qualities of the mind and therefore that the terms 'brain' and 'mind' – like 'your dentist' and 'person on the bus' – refer to the same thing.

Note that the type of reduction involved here is importantly different from the one the reduction analytical behaviourists try to perform. The identity theorist is not saying that our talk of the mind *means* the same as our talk about the brain. It clearly does not. For when I say I am experiencing a certain sensation or that I hold a specific belief, I do not mean the same as when I say that certain neurons are firing in my brain. So to say 'the mind is the brain' is not to claim that the terms 'mind' and 'brain' are synonymous and so it is not something

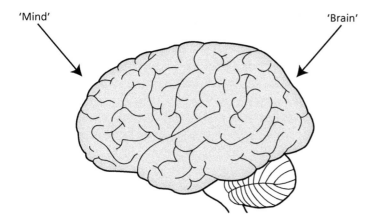

'Mind' 'Brain'

Figure 2.16 The terms 'mind' and 'brain' do not have the same meaning so analysis of our talk about the mind will not demonstrate that it is really talk about the brain. Rather, the identity theorist is saying that the two terms refer to the same object. This claim is a hypothesis to be proved by scientific investigation into the brain and its operations.

that can be demonstrated a priori by the analysis of our talk about minds. Rather, what is being claimed is that the mind and the brain happen, as a matter of empirical fact, to be the same. It is, in other words, a scientific hypothesis that these terms refer to the same object and so the truth of the identity theory is to be established by empirical investigation, not by philosophical analysis.

Other ontological reductions in science

This kind of reduction proposed by the identity theory is termed an **'ontological reduction'**. **Ontology** concerns the nature of being or existence, and ontological reductions involve showing that beings or entities of one kind are in reality the same as entities of another kind. The successful reduction of the mental to the neural predicted by identity theorists has parallels in the history of science. For example, it has been shown that sound is identical with a train of compression waves travelling through the air; that water is identical with H_2O; and that lightning is identical with an electrical discharge. In the same way, the identity theorist claims that what we call 'mental states' will turn out to be identical with brain states, and that neuroscience will eventually be able to reduce our folk-psychological concepts to neurological phenomena.

 Experimenting with ideas

Think back to the arguments for dualism that we explored above Section 2.1

Which could be used to criticise the identity theory?

Try to turn one argument for dualism into an attack on the identity theory.

Arguments for the identity theory

> [S]cience is increasingly giving us a viewpoint whereby
> organisms are able to be seen as physiochemical mechanisms:
> it seems that even the behaviour of man himself will one day
> be explicable in mechanistic terms. There does seem to be,
> so far as science is concerned, nothing in the world but increasingly
> complex arrangements of physical constituents .... That everything
> should be explicable in terms of physics ... except the occurrence of
> sensations seems to me to be frankly unbelievable. Such sensations
> would be 'nomological danglers'.[15]
>
> J.J.C. Smart (1920–2012)

Identity theorists defend their position by pointing to the physical processes which we know have been responsible for the development of human beings, both as individuals and as a species. As we have seen in the discussion of Descartes' conceivability argument (see pages 238–9), it is hard make sense of the idea that an immaterial substance should become attached to our brains at some point in our evolutionary history or in our development from conception. A physicalist account of our origins, therefore, fits far better with our current scientific understanding.

What is more, modern neuroscientific exploration into the structure and workings of the brain and nervous system is making great advances in its understanding of the mechanisms underlying human behaviour and our various mental capacities. The physicalist argues that we know the brain exists; what it is made of; something about its internal structure; how it is connected to the muscles and sense organs and so forth. The neuroscientist can tell us a great deal about the brain, about its constitution and the processes that occur within it; and can explain much of our behaviour in terms of its physical, chemical and electrical properties. This knowledge is unfavourably compared with the lack of detailed or precise information the dualist can provide about the nature and workings of spiritual substance.

Not only does the idea that the mind is the brain hold out the promise that we should be able to understand our minds better by investigation of the brain, but it is increasingly evident that there is a precise and systematic correspondence between different types of mental process and processes in the brain. The evidence of real-time imaging techniques shows that subjects engaged in specific mental activities, such as mental arithmetic, imagining performing some activity, recalling events in the past, and so on, are correlated with specific areas of the brain becoming active. If the identity theory is correct, this is exactly what we would expect to see.

Now, as we have seen, property dualism also recognises the dependence of the mind on the brain, and so is also consistent with this evidence. But the identity theorist argues that a thoroughgoing **physicalism** is to be preferred on the grounds of simplicity. To allow immaterial properties just looks untidy, given that everything else appears to be explicable in terms of physics. Smart says that if states of consciousness cannot be accommodated within the physicalist picture, they would be '**nomological danglers**', meaning they would not fit into the system of laws which govern everything else in the universe[16] and this offends against **Ockham's razor** – the methodological principle that, given two competing hypotheses, if their explanatory power is equal, then the simpler should be preferred. (The principle is named after the medieval philosopher William of Ockham (c.1287–1347).) So if we can explain mental phenomena in terms of the physical brain, and dualism has no explanatory advantage, then a physicalist account should be preferred.

Another important consideration concerns the problem of interaction, that is the difficulty dualist theories have explaining our common sense conviction that my decisions or volitions can cause my actions and, conversely, that events in my body can cause sensations in my mind. The difficulty for a substance dualist like Descartes is that if mind and body are distinct substances with no properties in common, it's hard to see how they can come into contact with each other. Moreover, as we have seen, the idea that mind can influence body appears to contradict the principle of the conservation of energy. Property dualism may also appear less than satisfactory as an account of the relationship, since it too has difficulty explaining how mind can influence behaviour. However, if the identity theory is correct and the mental *is* the physical then clearly the difficulty disappears.

The identity theory may also be regarded as preferable to analytical behaviourism because it can allow a causal role for our mental states. As we saw above, one of the main problems for behaviourism is the fact that it cannot explain behaviour; if mental states are nothing more than behaviour, then there is nothing to account for why we act as we do. But if the identity theory is right, then behaviour is caused and so can be explained by mental states and processes – just as our common sense suggests they are.

These considerations support some form of physicalism, but not the precise claim that there is a one-to-one correspondence between types of mental state and types of brain state. However, the identity theorist argues that no conclusive *philosophical* arguments are to be expected. As far as philosophy is concerned, the mind could be any bodily organ, the liver, the heart or whatever. But there are good scientific reasons for thinking the brain is responsible for consciousness. And if scientists eventually discover that there is indeed a one-to-one correspondence between all mental phenomena and structures and events in the brain, then the identity theory will be well established. Ultimately we need to wait to find out whether this will turn out to be the case.

Issues with the identity theory

Criticism 1

Talk about the brain doesn't mean the same as talk about the mind

Many philosophers believe that the statement 'pain is a brain state' violates some rules or norms of English.[17]

Putnam

In the Anthology extract 2.13, Putnam considers a common objection to the identity theory, namely that it is initially implausible since the words we use to talk about our mental states and processes do not *mean* the same as our vocabulary of physical states and processes occurring in the brain. When I say that I fancy a drink I do not *mean* that my brain is in a certain state. Similarly, if instead of saying that I have a headache I say that a certain neural pathway is being activated, don't I lose something in the translation? If I complain that my C-fibres[18] are firing, even if we know that this always happens when someone has a headache, surely this is not to say the same thing as when I complain of a headache.

Smart also considers this objection and observes that someone who has no knowledge of the brain can still speak meaningfully about his or her mental states. The 'illiterate peasant' in the quotation in Anthology extract 2.14, is fully conversant with the vocabulary of folk psychology; he knows what he means by 'after image', 'ache' and 'pain', and so knowing the meanings of mental vocabulary doesn't involve knowing anything about the brain. It follows, according to this objection, that we are talking about different things when we talk about our mental states from what we are talking about when talking about our brains. So any reduction of folk-psychological talk to talk about brain states will change the meaning of the terms.

Meaning and reference

To deal with this difficulty, the identity theorist can draw on a philosophical distinction between '**meaning**' and '**reference**'.[19] The *meaning* of a term or phrase is the way the thing it identifies is presented to the mind; it is the way an object is conceived. On the other hand, the *reference* is the actual thing in the world to which the term refers. If we draw this distinction, what is clear is that it is quite possible for two terms which have different meanings to have the same reference.

This distinction will be clearer if we illustrate it through an example (see the discussion of Anthology extract 2.14 above). The terms 'Morning Star' and 'Evening Star' clearly have different meanings. The idea of a star which appears in the morning is different from that of a star appearing in the evening. However, as it happens, they both refer to the same object, namely the planet Venus. So the two terms have the same reference.

Now, according to identity theorists, the same thing is going on with our talk of minds and of brains. They accept that our vocabularies of mental and physical states have different *meanings*. However, their claim is that they nonetheless *refer* to the same things.

This means that when we say 'Pain is a C-fibre firing in the brain' the identity in question is not an identity of meanings. To say that C-fibres are firing does not *mean* the same as to say that pain is occurring. If the two meant the same then this proposition would be *analytic* (i.e. true by definition). But, says the identity theorist, it is not an analytical or necessary identity of *meanings* which is being claimed, but rather, an empirical identity of *things*. In other words, it is an ontological reduction rather than an analytical reduction. The point is not that the words we use to describe our minds *mean* the same as those we use to describe our brains, but rather that both vocabularies *refer* to the same things.

It is important to realise that this means that the identity theorist wants to claim that there is a **contingent identity** (not a necessary one) between mental states and brain states. As Smart puts it, the claim is that to report that you have a mental state such as a pain is to report a process that *happens* to be a brain process, as a matter of empirical fact, and so it is not a claim about the meanings of our mental-state terminology. Sensation statements don't *mean* the same as statements about brain states and the one cannot be translated into the other. It is for this reason that the identity theory can only be established empirically, by advances in our understanding of neurophysiology. As has already been pointed out, science in many other fields has been successful in achieving a reduction of complex phenomena to a material basis, such as lightning to an electrical discharge, or clouds to droplets of water.

anthology
2.15

Criticism 2
The spatial location problem
Leibniz's Law states that if one thing is identical with another then everything that is true of one must be true of the other. Thus if we can identify a property of mental states that brain states don't have, the identity theory would be refuted.

Now, spatial properties have often been cited to this end. The argument runs that since brain states must have some spatial location, a specific size and shape, the identity theorist is committed to saying that mental states have the very same location, size and shape. But, it is nonsensical to say that my belief that rabbits have long ears is two centimetres to the right of my desire for spaghetti bolognese; that it is pear-shaped or four nanometres wide. Mental states are just not the sorts of things that have spatial location, size or shape.

Dealing with this objection

The identity theorists can defend themselves against this objection by saying that the fact that it sounds strange to ascribe spatial properties to mental states is just because ordinary language lags behind the neuroscientific advances we are now making. Once our understanding of the brain has developed sufficiently, and once we become well versed in its terminology, we may all find ourselves complaining that our C-fibres are firing, rather than talk about pains, and will no longer find it odd to talk about a belief being two nanometres long, and located in the cerebellum.

Moreover, it can be pointed out that just because it makes no sense to ascribe certain spatial properties to states of mind, doesn't establish that they are not physical states. Take examples of obviously physical states, such as being wet, or running. It makes no sense to say that being wet is square, or running is three metres long, but this doesn't mean that they are not physical states. Such states are conditions of physical beings, not physical objects in their own right, which explains why we cannot ascribe shapes and sizes to them. In the same way, a belief or a desire may be a condition realised in someone's brain. And just as we can say meaningfully that Rodney is running in the park and that Winny is wet in the bathroom, surely we can also say that Anna's musing that her cat is very wise is also taking place in the park where she is taking her stroll, and that Gemma's desire for hot chocolate is also happening in the bath where she is daydreaming. These mental states cannot be given precise shapes and sizes, but they do take place where the person having them is, and so do have spatial characteristics on a par with other types of physical state.

Putnam considers a slightly different version of this objection in 'Psychological predicates'.[20] It seems reasonable to suppose that for one phenomenon to be reduced to another, they have to occupy the same spatial location. If lightning is an electrical discharge, then the lightning flash and the electrical discharge occur in the same physical location. And, if temperature is reducible to the mean kinetic energy of molecules in an object, then the temperature and the vibrating molecules must be in the same physical place. But, a pain in the arm and a brain state are in different spatial locations – one is in the arm the other in the brain. And so the one cannot be reduced to the other.

Putnam himself dismisses this objection on the grounds that the principle that a reduction requires that the two phenomena occupy the same space is not sound. To show this he uses the example of a mirror image which is located behind the surface of the mirror but which can be explained in terms of the way light reflects from an object and then from the surface of the mirror before entering the eye. The reduction and the phenomenon being reduced are in different spatial locations, but this doesn't mean the reduction fails. In the same way, the apparent location of pains in parts of the body doesn't mean that they are not in fact brain states.

Criticism 3
Dualist arguments: appeal to the evidence of introspection

Introspection reveals to me a world of thoughts, sensations, emotions, etc., not a domain of electrochemical impulses in an organ in my head. Mental states and properties are radically unlike neurophysiological states and properties, and therefore they cannot be the very same things. Another way of making the point is by reference to the supposed irreducibility of subjectivity. In other words, the claim is that the subjective experience of pain, i.e. what it feels like, is an essential part of our concept of pain. Any attempt to reduce this experience to purely objectively observable neurological processes inevitably leaves something out. For while brain processes are (in principle at least) publicly observable, my pain is a private event. No matter how much we may know about the neurological basis of pain, there remains some aspect of the conscious experience of suffering pain which must escape scientific explanation. And if this is so, by Leibniz's Law, brains and minds cannot be identical.

We have encountered considerations of this kind when exploring dualism above. Descartes' conceivability argument Section 2.1.2 and Chalmers' philosophical zombies argument Section 2.1.3 both appeal to the apparent irreducibility of the way consciousness appears to the subject of experience and to qualia.

One way the identity theorist can respond to these sorts of complaint is to point out that it is quite possible for the same thing to appear in different ways. So the way my brain appears to itself via introspection may be as a realm of conscious experiences. But when we examine the brain via our outer senses, it appears as a physical organ pulsating with impossibly complex electrochemical activity. Just as we saw when discussing the masked man fallacy as a response to Descartes (page 231), the fact that the mind appears radically unlike the brain doesn't show that it isn't in fact the brain. It may simply be that the nature of the access that introspection provides to the goings on of our brains is very different to the access provided by our eyes.

Consider the fact that when our external senses discriminate between colours or sounds, they are actually making distinctions between subtle physical differences in objects which we are not directly aware of. Colour differences are produced by differences in the ways the surfaces of objects absorb and emit different wavelengths of electromagnetic radiation. But when I see red, I am not aware of the wavelength of the light which produces this sensation in me. In the same way, it shouldn't be any real surprise that our introspective sense should not be particularly penetrating in the way it discriminates the physical states and properties of the brain. Introspection may reveal to us the goings on in our brains, but only in a rather confused way. And we may well be able to discriminate between a great variety of neural states by introspection, without being aware of the detailed nature of those states.

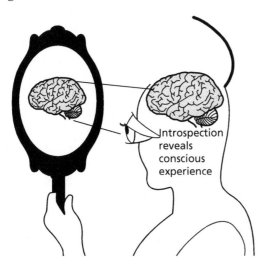

Introspection reveals conscious experience

Figure 2.17
The brain may appear in two different ways
By introspection my brain and its processes appear as a realm of conscious experiences. But when I examine my brain using my eyes, it appears to be a physical organ. These radically different appearances, though, need not indicate that I am dealing with two actually distinct things.

Criticism 4
The irreducibility of intentionality

Sceptics about the possibility of reducing consciousness to the brain may appeal to another feature of mental states that we haven't considered yet, namely **intentionality**. Intentionality is the property of certain conscious states, such as beliefs, desires, hopes and fears, that makes them represent or point to states of affairs which lie beyond them. So, I cannot simply believe, or desire, or hope; I must believe *something*, desire *something* or hope for *something*. So these states of mind are necessarily *about* something, and 'intentionality' denotes the quality these mental states have that enables them to be *about*. Now, it is often claimed that no purely physical system can represent, or be *about* something in this sense. For it is hard to see how an arrangement of material particles could come to represent anything. Surely physical material can only ever be what it is and cannot point beyond itself to something else. If this is right, then brain states cannot be intentional, and so mental states cannot be reduced to the brain.

To see why it may be thought impossible for intentionality to be explained physically consider just how remarkable this feature of our mentality is. My mind is able to wander freely around the universe. I can wonder where I put my keys, think about the weather in Moscow and the next moment speculate about objects on the far side of the solar system, and beyond. One reason the mind's capacity to do these things seems difficult to explain physically is that there would appear to be no physical connection between me and what I'm thinking about. If there were a physical connection, then surely it would take longer to think about things the further away they are, and yet I can think about the Moon or the Crab Nebula as quickly as I can think about the objects close to hand on my desk. My mind can also go back into the distant past and latch onto long-dead figures such as Cleopatra, or even extinct species from millions of years ago. Again, this cannot be a physical process since no physical thing can go back in time. I am also able to think about the future, as when I plan a holiday in Broadstairs, in which case I'm thinking about something that hasn't even happened and may never happen. A future event surely cannot be physically connected to a current one precisely because the future is not physically with us. Even more extraordinary, I can think about things that never have and never will exist. I can be afraid of monsters under the bed or wish I had my own unicorn. Such mental states have intentionality; they are directed beyond themselves and represent something, even though there is no actual thing out in the world that they are directed at. Again, we can wonder how it could be possible for such mental states to be physical since I cannot be physically influenced by the things they are about.

One way of explaining how intentionality might be a feature of physical states is to explain it in terms of resemblance. Perhaps my brain is able to represent the Moon because its inner workings are able to picture the Moon in some way. The difficulty here is that even if we can make sense of the idea that a brain state could resemble something, it still doesn't seem enough to explain intentionality. We might imagine that something within the microstructure of our brains is systematically arranged in a way as to resemble an object in the world, but we still wouldn't seem to have explained why this resemblance should make the brain state *about* the world. After all, my brain resembles a walnut, but this doesn't mean it is *about* a walnut.

Another account suggests that brain states can be about a feature of the world if they are caused in the right way by that feature. If my brain is in a particular state because of the Moon – perhaps the Moon has impacted on my sense organs and so been causally involved in producing it – then that brain state might be about the Moon. We might think here of animal tracks indicating that an animal has passed that way. Aren't the tracks, in a sense, about the animal? Those who oppose such efforts to give a physical explanation of intentionality will insist that they are not. There is a causal connection, but the ability to see the tracks as an indication that an animal has passed requires a mind. If there were no one to interpret them, they would represent nothing.

Criticism 5
The chauvinism of the type–type identity theory

*[P]hysicalism is a **chauvinist** theory: it withholds mental properties from systems that in fact have them. In saying mental states are brain states, for example, physicalists unfairly exclude those poor brainless creatures who nonetheless have minds.*[21]

Ned Block (1942–)

The version of the identity theory we have so far been considering is known as the type–type theory. To understand why it is called this we need to draw a technical distinction between '**types**' and '**tokens**'.

A type is a general class and a token is a particular instance of that class. For example, the word 'oak', as it is printed here, is a particular instance or 'token' of the word and instances like this can be repeated. But these instances are all members of a general class or 'type'. In the same way, a specific oak tree is a token of the type or species of tree that it is a member of. Turning to the mind, if I wish it were Friday on Thursday this week and wish it were Friday on Thursday last week, then these mental states would be different tokens of the same type of mental state. The type of mental state called 'wishing it were Friday' can be instantiated in the same person at different times and each occasion would represent a different token of that same type. At the same time, tokens of this type can (and do) occur in different people. So both you and I might now wish it were Friday, in which case we'd both be enjoying a different token of the same type of mental state.

Now, what the type–type theory says is that every type of mental state, e.g. seeing red, or wishing it were Friday, is identical with a particular type of brain state; let's call these brain states 'R-fibre firing' and an 'F-fibre firing' respectively. This means that seeing red occurs if and only if the R-fibre fires in the visual cortex; and wishing it were Friday occurs if and only if the F-fibre is firing (presumably in some other part of the brain).

This version can seem plausible for mental events like seeing colours and experiencing pains which might be expected to have a relatively straightforward neurophysiological basis. After all, it seems likely that similar things go on in all human brains when our nervous systems are similarly stimulated. The type–type theory implies that if my brain were damaged and the R-fibres in my visual cortex were destroyed, then I would cease to be able to see red. Or if the part of the brain responsible for receiving sensory information from my arm were damaged, I might cease to be able to feel pain there. However, it is less plausible for other states of mind, such as beliefs or desires.

Consider someone driving home wishing it were Friday, who meets with a terrible accident and damages the F-fibres in their brain. In the process we can suppose that the wish that it were Friday is destroyed. If the person then recovers to live a normal life, are we going to want to say that this person could never have this wish again? Surely not. And yet this is what is implied by the type–type theory. The recovery of stroke victims also suggests that the brain can regain all kinds of functions by using different parts of itself to do the work, so it seems unlikely that a particular type of wish or belief could be numerically identical with a particular type of brain state. In other words, the evidence suggests that, at least for certain mental states, we cannot expect precisely the same type of brain state to be responsible, either between different individuals or even in the same individual at different times.

Another unhappy consequence of the type–type theory concerns the status of the mental life of other species. For consider that other animals have different types of brain from human beings. So when an animal exhibits pain behaviour, the brain events causing this will be different from the brain events that go on in humans when we judge them to be in pain. But if pain *is* a human brain process, then it seems to follow that animals without human brains cannot be in pain. A further consequence is that any aliens we might one day encounter with very different types of brain from us would also be incapable of experiencing mental life. A Martian with spaghetti in its head rather than human grey matter could never be in pain, even though it might act very much as though it were in response to damage to its body. What these considerations are taken to suggest is that the type–type theory is overly *chauvinistic*, meaning it singles out human beings as the only proper possessors of mental states, and unfairly denies them to all other species. This not only goes against our intuition about animal mentality, but also against our sense that a creature that behaves as though it is in pain should be judged to be in pain regardless of what kind of a brain it has (or perhaps even if it has no brain at all).

To deal with this objection the identity theorist may adopt the token–token approach. This amounts to saying that different types of brain state can be the same type of mental state at different times in one brain or in different individual brains. So while each token mental state is identical with a particular token brain event, there is no type–type identity. What this would mean is that mental states are multiply realisable. Each type of mental state, such as the belief that it is Friday, can be identical with a different type of brain state. Moreover, different creatures can have different types of brain and brain states, which nonetheless are identical with the same mental states that we enjoy, such as pain. So we no longer need to deny that dogs and Martians can suffer.

The idea that the mind is multiply realisable is closely linked to the concept of **supervenience.** Mental states are said to 'supervene' on brain states if they depend on brain states for their existence and if there can be no changes in mental states without corresponding changes in brain states. At the same time, though, there can be changes in brain states without changes in mental state. The relationship of supervenience holds, for example, between an object and its shadow. The shadow depends for its existence on the object and no changes can occur in a shadow without changes occurring in the object. However, it is possible for changes to occur in the object without there being any change in the shadow. Those who believe that the mental is supervenient on the brain reckon that different things can be going on in the brain to produce the same mental event – in other words, mental states are multiply realisable – but that something must go on in the brain for there to be mental states.

There is a difficulty for this move, however. For although it seems to allow for different species to experience pain despite their possession of different types of brain, we now have as many different types of pain as there are creatures with brains. There is dog pain, hedgehog pain, Martian pain and so on. But if each type of brain has its own type of pain, we have no way of specifying what it is about these different brain states that makes them all pains. What is it that these various pain-states have in common in virtue of which they are painful? If the only answer is that creatures in these states act as though they are in pain we seem to have retreated to a behaviourist definition of pain and abandoned the effort to identify it neuro-physiologically.

In the previous section we entertained the possibility of a Martian with a very different type of brain from humans experiencing the same type of mental states as us. If this possibility is conceivable, then it seems we are committed to saying that it is metaphysically possible for brain states not to be identical with mental states and therefore for someone to be in pain without having the appropriate brain activity. But, in this case, we might wonder, how can there be said to be a numerical identity between brain and mind? For if the mind is the brain, and pain is C-fibres firing, it must be impossible to be in pain without one's C-fibres firing.

Learn More

The response to this is to remind us that the identity theorist accepts the metaphysical possibility that someone could be in pain without their C-fibres firing, but insists that, *as a matter of empirical fact*, it never happens. If it did, of course, this would disprove the theory. So if we had good reasons to believe that an alien were in pain, even though its brain were made of spaghetti, this would disprove the numerical identity of pain with certain brain states. In other words, the identity being argued for, as we have seen, is said to be a *contingent* one.

However, we may counter by asking whether it makes sense to speak of a 'contingent' identity, that is, of two apparently distinct entities just happening to turn out to be the same thing. If we look at the example of the 'Morning Star' and the 'Evening Star' once again, it is clear that since, as has been established, both terms refer to the same object, then there plainly is only one object out there to which they refer. Given this, it is impossible for the terms to refer to different things. To take a different example, if it is the case that water is H_2O, then it is not possible, and never was possible, for water not be H_2O. In other words, there is no possible world in which water turns out to have a different molecular structure, for if what the people there call 'water' did have a different composition, then it wouldn't really be water. So if two apparently distinct things turn out to be numerically identical there is no sense in which they *could* be distinct and this means that the very idea of a contingent identity is incoherent. We may have been unsure of whether the Morning Star really was the Evening Star, but this is not to say that the Morning Star might not have been the Evening Star. It follows, the argument runs, that the identity between mind and brain which the identity theory claims holds can only be a *necessary* identity even though it is only discoverable through empirical means. But if this is right then it would be logically impossible for the mind not to be the brain, and so impossible to conceive of brainless aliens, which, it is argued, is plainly absurd.[22]

2.2.3 Functionalism

> *I shall, in short, argue that pain is not a brain state, in the sense of a physical-chemical state of the brain ... but another kind of state entirely. I propose the hypothesis that pain, or the state of being in pain, is a functional state of a whole organism.*[23]
>
> Putnam

We have seen that common sense is on the side of the interactionist thesis that our mental states cause some of our actions. The epiphenomenalist's denial of this apparent aspect of our everyday experience strikes many as reason enough for us to reject it. Similarly, analytical behaviourism seems to get things the wrong way around when it claims that having a pain is simply to be disposed to behave in certain ways, such as to pronounce the words 'I am in pain'. Surely, we might think, it is the pain which disposes us to pronounce these words, rather than the pain simply *being* our disposition to pronounce them. The problem with behaviourism is the strangeness of its insistence that my desire for a drink, for example – an apparently private state – is no more than a disposition to drink under certain circumstances, while normally we are inclined to assume that it is the *cause* of my drinking. If we are dissatisfied with epiphenomenalism and behaviourism, we may be inclined to look for a theory which allows mental states to play some causal role in human behaviour, and if dualism and the identity theory are considered unsatisfactory, we may turn to *functionalism*. The American philosopher Hilary Putnam (1926–) urges us to do just this in his 1967 paper 'Psychological predicates' which is part of the Anthology (see extract 2.13).

Reducing mental states to functional roles

The functionalist identifies mental states with **functional states**. To understand what is meant by a functional state, consider first that many everyday objects are defined less by what they are made of, or how they are designed, than by what task they are intended to perform. If you open the kitchen drawer you will find an array of devices created for specific functions. The can-opener, corkscrew, knife sharpener, garlic crusher and so on. Each of these comes in a range of different designs and is made from different sorts of material. Your can-opener could be the sort you get on pen knives which you have to lever into the can lid and use to make a series of incisions; or it may be the kind which pierces and clips onto the lid and you then turn the handle; or perhaps you have a modern battery-operated contraption that latches onto the lid with magnets and automatically rotates, cutting into the side as you look on in wonder. These different types of can-opener look very different, they are made out of different materials, but this doesn't prevent them from all being tin openers. This is because what makes something a can-opener is the fact that it opens cans. It is defined by its *function*, that is, by what it does or is used for, rather than in terms of the stuff of which it is made or the details of its design.

Think also of a bodily organ such as the heart. What makes something a heart is not what it is composed of or precisely how it is put together, but what it does. Anything that pumps blood around the body counts as a heart and different animals have hearts of different designs and materials. We now have artificial hearts composed of metal and plastic, but for all that, they are still hearts. What makes them hearts is the task they perform.

▶ **ACTIVITY**

Which of the following is best defined functionally? Which is best defined in some other way, such as in terms of what it is composed of, or the processes that brought it into being?

  1 A wheel
  2 The Moon
  3 A screwdriver
  4 A mobile phone
  5 A rabbit
  6 A pound coin
  7 An ear
  8 Salt
  9 The prime minister
10 A carburettor

Come up with your own example of something that is best defined functionally.

Now, functionalists believe that mental states are best understood as being functional entities like hearts, or can-openers. On this view, the essential or defining feature of any type of mental state is the set of causal relations it bears to (1) environmental effects on the body, (2) other types of mental states, and (3) bodily behaviour. Put another way, functionalism explains mental phenomena in terms of the *causal* (or *functional*) role it plays within a sequence of events. To be a particular sort of mental state is to have a particular sort of functional role. A pain in the foot or the belief that it is raining should be defined in terms of the role that they play in mediating between sensory inputs, other mental states and behavioural outputs. So a functional definition of pain would treat it as that mental state which is produced by damage to the body and whose role is to trigger other mental states such as wanting to avoid the source of the pain as well as pain behaviour such as inspecting the damage, wincing or hopping on one leg. And *any* state that plays exactly that functional role *is* a pain. Similarly, my belief that it is going to rain is the mental state caused by the perception of an overcast sky which when coupled with my desire to keep dry, causes me to wear a raincoat and take an umbrella when I go out.

Now, just as can-openers and corkscrews can be made of very different substances, so the belief that it is raining need not be instantiated by any particular type of stuff. For if being minded is a matter of being organised in the right way, a great range of substances could realise minds. Indeed, it is possible for a functionalist to be a dualist and claim that it is mind-stuff or spirit, arranged in a particular way, that happens to instantiate human minds.[24] In practice, functionalists are generally physicalists and view the brain as the material basis for consciousness. This means that functionalism holds that mental states depend upon physical states and their causal powers, and so mental properties *supervene* on states of the brain. Thus there can be no change in mental states without some change in the physical organisation of the brain. But because the precise material is not what defines a mental state, I can hold the same type of belief as you without precisely the same type of brain process taking place. So functionalism allows for the multiple realisability of mental states which we saw in our discussion of the identity theory is preferable to a type–type reduction of mental to neural. For this reason, functionalism is fairly liberal about what kinds of entity might be minded. Aliens might have very different types of stuff in their skulls, but so long as it was organised in the right way, then aliens can be minded.

Functionalists were originally inspired by the analogy between computational systems and the operations of the mind. Computers receive inputs, react by following a series of rules, and produce an output, and living organisms similarly process sensory inputs and convert them into behavioural outputs. These parallels suggest that a further analogy can be drawn between, on the one hand, the computer *hardware* and our physiological make-up (the brain), and between, on the other, the *software* and the mental functioning or thinking of the mind. This analogy provides an unmysterious account of the relation of mind to body. For hardware and software are not different entities, still less different substances, but nor are they identical with one another. Rather, it is the way the brain is organised and the manner of its operations that enables it to be minded. Even if computers are not yet sufficiently complex to count as minded, the claim is that for them to be so all that is necessary is to run a sophisticated enough software program on a sufficiently powerful hardware platform for it to instantiate the relevant functional economy. Organic brains, in other words, are not necessary.

'**Machine state functionalism**' is the term given to the view that minded human beings are to be understood as a complex system of inputs and outputs, the inputs being sensory and the outputs behavioural. A very simple input/output device is a vending machine – it receives coins as inputs and follows a set of instructions in its program to deliver various products as the outputs. Now, we can capture the operations of such a machine in a diagram termed a **machine table**. A machine table specifies which inputs will produce which outputs and the changes in internal states that mediate between them.

	S_1	S_2
50p input	Emit no output Go to S_2	Emit a coke Go to S_1
£1 input	Emit a coke Stay in S_1	Emit a coke & 50p Go to S_1

Figure 2.18 The machine table for a simple drinks vending machine. Adapted from Ned Block's example given in 'Troubles with functionalism' (page 267).

Ned Block gives an example of a simple machine table which captures the functioning of a drinks dispensing machine (see Figure 2.18). What the table shows is how the machine reacts to two different inputs: pound coins and 50p pieces. The machine has two internal states, S_1 and S_2. S_1 is its original state as it waits for a customer. If you enter £1, the machine will deliver a coke and stay in S_1. However, if you input 50p the machine will not deliver a drink, but will move from S_1 to S_2. If you now insert another 50p it will emit a drink and return to S_1. And if you input a £1 while it is in S_2 it will have too much money and so will emit a drink and 50p.

One point to note is that the internal states of the machine could be realised by a range of different hardwares. The internal mechanism could be one of weights, springs and pullies; it could be electronic; or there could even be a trained monkey inside following the rules specified in the machine table. In other words, the machine table is multiply realisable, and in the same way, it is held, mental states may be realised in a variety of different ways.

Now, functionalists do not generally claim that simple machines of this sort have mental states, but the internal states specified by the machine table are regarded as analogous to mental states in human beings so that, in principle at least, a machine table could be written specifying the functional economy of a human being in response to the great range of possible inputs it might encounter. The machine table for a human being would bewilderingly complex with countless serially nested subsystems. And Putnam and others don't consider humans to be deterministic automatons like the vending machine, but *probabilistic*. That is, our programming doesn't specify a determined reaction to a specific input, but instead the probability that we will change into certain states or produce certain outputs. Still, the basic idea is that the difference between the vending machine and a human being is one of degree rather than of kind.

Advantages over behaviourism

There are some obvious similarities with behaviourism, but also one fundamental difference. Where the behaviourist hoped to define each type of mental state solely in terms of environmental input and behavioural output, the functionalist denies that this is possible. An adequate characterisation of a mental state cannot be confined to what is observable on the outside, but must involve reference to a variety of other mental states with which it is causally connected. Thus, there is a cluster of events that form around the state of any person and it is how they combine that determines his or her mental state. In sum, functionalists recognise the role mental states have in causing behaviour and other mental states and this accords far better with our common understanding of the nature of the mind. [25]

Advantages over the identity theory

We have seen that the functionalist agrees with the identity theorist in regarding a mental state such as a pain as the cause of pain behaviour. The important difference in their positions, however, emerges out of a consequence of the type–type identity theory, namely that no being whose brain is not made out of the same basic stuff as ours has a mind. And yet to claim that a Martian displaying characteristic pain behaviour when its body is injured would not be in pain simply because its brain were made of spaghetti seem implausible. In response, the identity theorist claims that we can conceive a spaghetti-brained Martian with a mind because the identity between mind and brain is not a conceptual one. It is a contingent identity of things rather than an identity of meanings. So, on this view, evidence of a Martian in pain would count against the identity theory, were it ever to be an empirical reality. But, their bet is that we never will encounter such creatures. However, as we have seen, the coherence of the idea of a contingent identity can be questioned. For the claim that there is a contingent identity can only mean that there *might have been* two distinct things – to which the words 'mind' and 'brain' refer, but that, as a matter of (contingent) fact, they refer to one and the same thing. So it would mean that there are possible worlds in which Martians have minds. But if they are simply two terms for the same thing, then there is (necessarily) only one thing, and things could not have been otherwise. If 'mind' and 'brain' refer to the same thing then there could not possibly be any other thing for the terms to refer to and so there can be no possible world in which a creature with spaghetti rather than brains can be minded, just as there is no possible world in which water is something other than H_2O. What this suggests is that if the identity theory is right then it is empirically necessary, and so logically speaking our Martian could not have a mind. And since it would seem logically possible for such a being to have a mind, the identity theory must be false.

Now functionalists are able to deal with this problem by allowing that an alien with a physiology very different from ours might nonetheless be functionally equivalent to the extent that they instantiate a similar set of internal states. In other words, the machine table which describes the functionings of the Martian is the same as that which describes us, even though it has spaghetti for brains. So if when the Martian damages its body it attends to the affected area, avoids the source of the pain and so on, then it would appear that from a functional point of view its internal state is a functional parallel of a human pain state and since mental states *are* functional states we can confidently assert that the alien feels pain.

 Experimenting with ideas

Suppose for some reason you need to go to hospital for a brain scan. After a while, you notice a group of hospital staff have gathered around the monitor scratching their heads in disbelief. When you make inquiries, it turns out that you don't have a brain! Instead, inside your head is a swarm of flea-like creatures, apparently organised into a bafflingly complex arrangement and functioning to control your behaviour in response to sensory stimuli entering your skull via your sense organs and spinal column.

Is this conceivable? If it is, does it show that brains are not necessary for consciousness?

If it is not conceivable, does this mean functionalism must be false? [26]

Arguments against functionalism

Criticism 1
Inverted qualia
A standard objection to physicalist theories is also one levelled at functionalism, namely that it fails to account for the intrinsic qualitative nature of our mental states. Dualists will claim that any theory of mind must explain qualia and that reductive approaches such as functionalism necessarily leave the first person perspective out of the picture. The first argument we will examine that tries to expose this difficulty employs the inverted spectrum thought experiment, which we considered earlier (see 'Qualia do not exist and so Mary gains no new propositional knowledge', page 253). The basic idea is that the spectrum of private colour qualia that I experience might be systematically inverted by comparison to yours. So the quale I experience when looking at a banana is like the quale you experience when you look at the sky and vice versa. Because this has been our situation since birth, we use the vocabulary of colour terms in the same way and so never notice the difference.

Now, if this were the case, from a functional point of view we would be identical to each other. I react in the same way as you to the same sensory stimulations. We both call bananas 'yellow' and describe the sky as a beautiful, unfathomable blue. And internally, the mental states caused by bananas and the sky play the same role in relation to other mental states. Bananas remind us both of cornfields and the sun. The sky makes us both feel calm and wistful. So a machine table describing our internal states would be identical. But if we are functionally equivalent, then, according to the functionalist definition of mental states, we must be experiencing the same visual sensations. Thus the possibility of spectrum inversion is ruled out by definition. And yet, the objection runs, it remains quite conceivable, and so functionalism must be false. It is conceivable because qualia appear to have intrinsic qualities which are what they are regardless of how they relate to other mental states or to sensory inputs and behavioural outputs.

But is it really conceivable? If the hypothesis is both irrefutable and unconfirmable we may be inclined to conclude that the idea of inverted qualia is nonsensical. We cannot make coherent sense of the supposed difference between you and me if we cannot point to anything in the world that would establish the difference. And, as we have seen, physicalists in general may reject the objection on these grounds (see the discussion of Dennett, pages 253–59). Yet, if we modify the thought experiment slightly we can generate a problem which is specific to functionalism rather than materialism generally. Suppose I was born with normal vision, but that an operation was performed on me at birth to switch the neural pathways travelling from the optic nerve to the visual cortex. If this were to happen, it seems we would have good empirical reasons to suppose that my qualia were now inverted relative to yours. And yet, although my visual system is no longer physically identical with yours, we could imagine me learning the vocabulary of colour words to become fully functionally equivalent to you and everyone else. Surely, this shows that there is more to qualia than what can be captured by a functionalist account.

In response to this, functionalists can still deny that I have different qualitative experiences from you. If we react in similar and complex ways to the same stimuli in a great variety of situations, then this is all we need to be sure that we are in the same mental state. And if the range of qualia really were to play the same complex role in relation to other mental states and behaviour right down to our tendency to find blue calming, red exciting, green peaceful and so on, it certainly becomes harder to hold on to the intuition that they could nonetheless have distinct intrinsic natures. Nonetheless, some functionalists concede that in the version of the thought experiment just considered, the intrinsic physical differences would produce a different qualitative feel, and so concede that qualia cannot be given a complete functional definition. In conceding this, however, functionalists need not give up on the theory as an account of most of our mental states such as beliefs and desires.

Criticism 2
The knowledge argument revisited

We have discussed Jackson's knowledge argument and the attempt to show that no reduction of mentality to the physical is possible. The same argument can be employed against functionalism. For if Mary were to know all the physical facts, including all the functional facts, about what happens when humans experience colours, and yet learn something new when she herself sees colour for the first time, then there is more to experiencing qualia than is captured in a complete functionalist story (for a fuller discussion of this objection, see Section 2.1.4).

Functionalism can be defended, however, and Jackson himself came to reject his own anti-reductivist argument and accept that a functionalist account of qualia could be correct. On this view, qualia provide us with a short-cut by which we represent complex functional and relational information. It is clearly going to be useful to an organism that needs to survive in a hostile environment to recognise when its body is damaged, but having an explicit and detailed grasp of the nature of the damage and of one's physiological reactions to it is not needed or practically possible to attain. A complete functional analysis of pain would involve bringing together a great range of information about the physiological reactions undergone in the nervous system and the brain. And similarly with colour experiences. A complete functionalist account would be fiendishly complex. When we experience colour we get access to this information more quickly than would be possible if we came to an explicit understanding of all that is really going on. Because we acquire it in this way, it appears as though we are aware of something different from a set of functional and relational properties – but this is, nonetheless, what they are. So if qualia are really confused representations of functional states, then there is no reason why Mary wouldn't be able to deduce their nature from her complete knowledge of the physical facts.

Criticism 3
Absent qualia

In 'Troubles with functionalism' Block accuses functionalism of **'liberalism'**, that is, the tendency to ascribe minds to things that do not have them. He outlines two systems which could be functionally equivalent to a human being but which we would be reluctant to ascribe mentality to. Imagine a body like yours on the outside but with the head hollowed out and replaced with a set of tiny people whose job is to realise the same machine table as you. Clearly, the overall task would be immensely complex but we can suppose that each individual's job would be fairly simple. Now, according to the functionalist account of mentality, this 'homunculi-head' (i.e. head full of people, *homunculus* being Latin for 'little man') would have a mind just like you do, including experiences of pain, colours and also intentional states such as beliefs and desires. However, Block argues, we have a strong intuition that such a system would not be minded – there is nothing it is like to be the homunculi-head.

Block then modifies the thought experiment so that the billion or so citizens of China are engaged in realising the same machine table, this time with radios connecting them with each other and the body. Suppose that the body now stands on a nail. The people of China would have a busy time of it reacting to the input signals and would – we must imagine – successfully cause the body to hop on one leg, yelp and make efforts to remove the nail. But would anyone feel any pain? If we think not, the system can be in a state which is functionally equivalent to feeling pain in you, but not actually be in pain. So once again we are saying that functionalism is too liberal and so not an adequate account of mentality.

In response, functionalists may question the intuition that such systems would not be minded. After all, it may be mere prejudice that makes us suspicious of genuine mentality being found in things so very different from the kinds of bearers of minds our experience typically encounters. And if the system really were complex enough to succeed in realising an equivalent machine table to a human being, then perhaps conscious states would indeed emerge. We may note also that it remains mysterious just how qualia emerge from the complex arrangement and actions of neurons in the brain, but, unless we are substance dualists, we must suppose that somehow they do it. As Block himself admits:

> *No physical mechanism seems very intuitively plausible as a seat of qualia, least of all a brain. Is a hunk of quivering gray stuff more intuitively appropriate as a seat of qualia than a covey of little men? If so, perhaps there is a prima facie doubt about the qualia of brain-headed systems too.*[27]

(Block, though, goes on to give arguments for supposing that the doubt about homunculi-heads is reasonable after all. See 'Troubles with functionalism'.)

Could computers have minds?

If, as functionalist accounts of the nature of mind claim, there is nothing mysterious to being conscious over and above the functional arrangement of particular organisms, the way would seem to be left open to the possibility of our constructing a conscious machine. For, as we have seen, a purely functional description of the operations of a given 'system', such as a human being, Martian or robot, makes no *ontological* commitment to the kind of stuff of which it is made, and so if functionalism is the correct account of the nature of mentality, then a sufficiently powerful computer could one day be minded.

Experimenting with ideas

Consider whether you think it is conceivable that a mechanical device could have a mind. For example, do you believe a vending machine has desires and beliefs? Can it want more money, or believe it must deliver change? What about the various computer programs you can access via the internet for information, such as to plan a train journey. Does it understand that you will be travelling during the busy period when it apologises that it can't make a seat reservation? Is it genuinely sorry? Think of why you answer these questions as you do.

Next think of some of the artificial minds appearing in science fiction films, such as HAL from *2001: A Space Odyssey*, or the robots in *I, Robot* or C3PO or R2D2 from *Star Wars*. Do you think it is possible that we could build such machines? If you encountered a machine that behaved in this way, would you be persuaded it had a mind, or would you think it was just an unconscious machine?

The Turing test

The mathematician and cryptanalyst Alan Turing (1912–54) was instrumental in the early development of computers and played a key role in helping to break the German 'enigma' code during the Second World War.[28] In philosophical circles he tends to be better known for his proposal for a test of whether a computer could be said to have a mind. If a computer could communicate with a human being via a keyboard in such a way that the human being could not tell the difference between conversing with the computer and conversing with another human being, then to all intents and purposes, Turing suggested, the computer should be considered minded. According to the **Turing test**, then, competence in linguistic conversation is the criterion for the possession of beliefs and other intentional states by an artificial intelligence.

In support of the view that computers *already* have minds (as proponents of Artificial Intelligence – AI – sometimes do) we may point to our ordinary understanding of their basic operations. We say that a computer has so much 'memory', that it processes information, uses language, calculates, obeys commands, follows rules and so forth. On the face of it, it may seem as though computers carry out the same functions carried out by human beings with minds. And if we think back to the vending machine from earlier (pages 318–19), perhaps it is not too much of a stretch to characterise S_1 as a simplified version of what goes on in us when we want £1.

The American philosopher John Searle (1932–) is well known for his opposition to the machine functionalist's claim that organic brains are not required for consciousness. Searle insists that mental states are essentially natural phenomena. They are the product of human evolution and in this respect no different to all other biological functions such as digestion and respiration. This means that it is essential to being minded that one have a certain neurophysiology, i.e. a living brain, and so Searle insists that no artificial intelligence could be conscious. His attack on functionalism tries to show that a computer which was functionally equivalent to a human being with respect to linguistic behaviour, and so could pass the Turing test, still wouldn't be conscious. To show this he constructs his well-known thought experiment, the Chinese room.

The Chinese room argument

Searle's focus in this argument is on intentionality, the feature of our mental states which enables them to be *about* things. He distinguishes different sorts of intentionality. There is what he calls *as-if* intentionality, which is possessed by things like rivers as they flow towards the sea, or plants as they grow towards the light. Here there is the appearance that the water 'wants' to flow downhill, or that it is 'trying' to reach the sea, but in such cases most people would not say that the river truly has desires and intentions and it is not able to think about the sea. Rather we should say that this is a short-hand manner of speaking, or that it is merely a way we might choose to represent the river, but not something really possessed by the river itself. Similarly, we might, in certain moods, speak of the beliefs or desires of flowers to attract insects, or of a swarm of bees to protect the queen, while strictly we would be disinclined to ascribe intentional states to them. *Intrinsic* intentionality, by contrast, is the real thing: the sort that is supposedly only possessed by *minds*.

Searle's thought experiment goes roughly as follows:

Suppose a man who speaks only English is locked inside a room with only a slot through which to communicate with people in the outside world. Outside is a Chinese speaker who is eager to discover whether the person inside speaks Chinese and who passes messages into the room written in Chinese. The English speaker has several baskets containing Chinese symbols and a rule book written in English which he consults to determine how to respond to the messages. The Chinese characters are completely meaningless to the English speaker, but nonetheless, because of the sophistication of the rule book, he is able to respond in ways which are meaningful to the Chinese speaker outside the room. In other words, we must imagine that the person in the room passes the Turing test and fools the Chinese person into thinking he is a fluent speaker of Chinese.

Searle contends that the Chinese room undermines the notion that computers have intrinsic intentionality. For the set-up contains everything relevant to a computer. The person in the room functions like the central processor of a computer. He manipulates physical symbols and uses an instruction book which can represent the computer program. The baskets full of symbols would be the database; the messages that are handed in are the input and the replies handed out are the output.

While it is unapparent to outside observers, it is clear to us that the person in the room does not understand Chinese. Also clear, contends Searle, is that the entire system of the room plus the person and its contents is ignorant of Chinese as well. None of the responses made has any intrinsic *intentionality* or *means* anything, except as it is viewed by outside observers. And it follows, according to Searle, that computers also cannot have intrinsic intentionality. For if the person in the room does not possess intrinsic intentionality (does not understand Chinese) solely on the basis of following a set of instructions or program, then neither could any computer. Like the man in the room, or an ants' nest, a computer only has as-if intentionality.

Searle's thought experiment tries to undermine the functionalist thesis that the mind is in the same relation to the brain as computer software is to computer hardware. For what a functionalist in essence claims is that it is not the physical instantiation which is of importance to having a thinking thing, so long as it is compatible, as it were, with the *software*. Searle, along with linguists, calls rule following or grammar in language, '**syntax**', and the meaning we construct from those rules, '**semantics**'. The idea, in other words, is that a computer does not deal with *meanings* (semantics) but simply follows *rules* of syntax. It cannot understand what the Chinese figures mean, since it merely follows rules for manipulating symbols. Thus, Searle concludes, a computer can only ever simulate consciousness, but never duplicate it.[29]

Counter arguments

Criticism 1

One response that Searle considers is what he calls the systems reply. This basically says that while the person in the room may not understand Chinese, the entire system – baskets of symbols, rule book, and so on – does. The English speaker is just one part of a complex system responding in Chinese, including a huge database and complex set of rules. As a whole, if such a system could genuinely pass the Turing test then it would demonstrate genuine understanding.

Searle's response to this is that we can imagine the person in the room internalising the database and the rule book. He could then leave the room and even convince Chinese speakers that he can speak Chinese. However, he would still only have learnt a set of instructions and memorised a huge number of meaningless squiggles and so still wouldn't possess intrinsic intentionality.

Criticism 2

Another response is to accept that neither the person in the room, nor the system as a whole would be able to understand Chinese, but insist that this does not show that more sophisticated kinds of machines could not. Searle's thought experiment evokes an overly simplistic mechanism which, while it could not understand Chinese, surely would not fool anyone in a conversation either. In fact, it may not be as obvious as Searle supposes that we would be reluctant to grant intrinsic intentionality to a system that actually *can* hold its own in a complex conversation. In the end, Searle's argument rests on our intuition that machines could not be conscious and yet intuitions are not necessarily reliable. In the future, when we are used to talking machines, we may find our intuitions change. In making this point, Stephen Pinker (1954–) asks us to imagine a race of intelligent aliens with very different physiology from ours, who cannot believe that we humans are conscious because our brains are made of meat. If their experience to date is exclusively of minds in silicon-brains, then they might well find it inconceivable that our sort of brain could produce consciousness. [30]

Criticism 3

Critics of Searle may point out that we are in the same position with respect to others as we are to the Chinese room in deciding whether to ascribe genuine understanding. The only basis we have for ascribing minds to others is that they behave appropriately, for example, in conversation; so if we are happy to ascribe mentality to other humans we should be happy to do so to a machine capable of behaving in the same way. Any other attitude would be chauvinistic – denying mentality to the machine, simply because it is a machine. We would be behaving like Pinker's aliens. Moreover, aren't we in search of some wholly mysterious property if we insist the machine must possess supposedly *intrinsic* intentionality? After all, it's not obvious that any theory of mind is able to explain this feature of consciousness. If the dualist insists that a purely material mechanism could not be intentional, her or she still needs to account for how an *immaterial* mind-substance *is* able to be intentional. Simply to assert that it is essential to thinking substance that it be capable of intrinsic intentionality, is to present a non-solution to the general problem of how things represent, much as to explain why it is that opium puts people to sleep by saying it possesses 'dormitive power'.

Criticism 4

This may lead us to consider whether we can deny that *anything* – computer, Chinese room or human being – possesses *intrinsic* intentionality. After all, as we have seen in our discussion of the identity theory, it is not easy to see how intentionality is to be incorporated into a physicalist picture of mind. Since the very notion of intrinsic intentionality is highly elusive, perhaps the only kind of intentionality is of the as-if kind. On this way of viewing the situation, we are subject to a kind of illusion in supposing that we have beliefs and desires that genuinely point to the world. In reality, this is just a way of interpreting and predicting human behaviour that is ultimately reducible to a set of causal relations. Complex mechanisms like us can be usefully understood as having internal states which are directed outwards to their environments, and any system the behaviour of which be reliably predicted in this way can be considered to have intentionality. In reality, though, the only difference between our desires and the internal states of a vending machine concerns the level of organisational complexity. [31]

Criticism 5

A final response we will consider is called the robot reply. What Searle's scenario seems to show is that a computer might well be able to manipulate symbols and respond appropriately to verbal stimuli, but for it to understand what is being spoken *about* it would need to be able to recognise what things in the world the words refer to. Otherwise, as Searle rightly says, it will be manipulating symbols but with no understanding of what they mean. But if it were to be given access to its environment and so to the world that gives the Chinese symbols their meaning, couldn't it then develop genuine understanding? Suppose we equip the Chinese room with sensors of various sorts and provide it with a robotic body that can move around and interact with the environment. In this scenario, the robot would be more in the position of an organic being, in that it would be able to learn about the objects around it and so attach meanings to the symbols it manipulates. Since this is how we learn the meanings of words, surely such a robot might be able to do the same.

Searle's response is that even in this scenario, it is still only data inputs that the person in the room would receive via the sensors and so he would still be in the same position as before. For if the room were now mounted on a robot, the information about the robot's movements and what its sensors detect would have to be fed into the room as syntactical information, and so the person in the room would simply have more meaningless squiggles to deal with and still no way of making the leap to genuine understanding.

2.2.4 Eliminative materialism

> Eliminative materialism is the thesis that our common sense conception of psychological phenomena constitutes a radically false theory, a theory so fundamentally defective that both the principles and the ontology of that theory will eventually be displaced, rather than smoothly reduced, by completed neuroscience.[32]
>
> Paul Churchland

Reduction or elimination?

In the past, people were well acquainted with water, but they didn't know what it was made of. The ancient Greeks supposed it was a basic element, that is, something that couldn't be broken down into anything simpler. Indeed, the thinker credited with being the first philosopher, Thales (c.624– c.546BC), believed that it was *the* basic element out of which everything else was made. With the development of modern chemistry, however, it has been shown that water is composed of molecules of hydrogen and oxygen. In other words, water has been *reduced* to more basic elements. This reduction, however, leaves the existence of water intact. We wouldn't want to say that water doesn't exist because it is *really* just hydrogen and oxygen. Water is still a real thing, it's just that we now have a fuller grasp of what it is. In the same way, as we have seen above, the identity theory claims that mental states will be reduced to brain states, and that when we have discovered the various identities, our vocabulary of mental states will remain intact and we will still be able truthfully to talk about our possession of beliefs, desires and sensations.

Eliminative materialism (or simply eliminativism), however, is sceptical about the chances of the neuroscience of the future being able to account for our folk-psychological concepts in terms of the brain. There will, in other words, be no 'smooth reduction' of mental states to the physical. The reason for their scepticism, however, is not that eliminativists believe the mind is ultimately non-physical. Rather they consider that mental states as they are currently understood *do not exist*.

To understand what this claim amounts to, consider a parallel story to the one about water. When a plague ravaged Europe between 1346 and 1353, people became all too familiar with the disease. They called it the Black Death and they could accurately identify victims by their symptoms, which many believed were brought on by exposure to 'bad air'. With the advance of germ theory, we are now pretty confident the disease was caused by a pathogen, most probably a bacterium called *Yersinia pestis*, and was spread by fleas carried by rats.[33] Germ theory has shown that 'bad air' has nothing to do with the spread of disease, indeed, we would probably want to say that 'bad air' doesn't really exist. The concept of 'bad air' is part of a way of seeing the world which misrepresents the phenomena of disease so seriously that we have decided it can have no place in a proper account of the Black Death. By explaining the disease in terms of a bacterium we have been able to *eliminate* bad air from our vocabulary and from our picture of what exists (i.e. from our *ontology*). In the same way, the eliminativist argues that our vocabulary of mental states will be eliminated once we have a more advanced understanding of what makes us tick. Like 'bad air' our folk-psychological concepts present an inaccurate conception of what there is and need to be eliminated.

What the parallel with the Black Death brings out is the idea that our common sense talk about the mind makes use of a *theory*. We've come across this idea before when discussing the problem of other minds where we saw that folk psychology may be considered a theoretical framework by which we interpret and predict human behaviour (see page 255). Now, what eliminativism is claiming is that this theory – folk psychology – is literally *false*. In other words, our talk about beliefs, sensations, memories, etc. is fundamentally flawed and misleading as an account of the causes of human beings' behaviour and cognition and the nature of their internal states. What is needed therefore is a neuroscience which can explain what is really going on with human beings, and which makes no reference to the terminology we currently use to talk about the mind.

anthology
2.17

Paul Churchland begins his defence of eliminativism in the Anthology paper, 'Eliminative materialism and the propositional attitudes'[34] by defending the claim just outlined that folk psychology is indeed a theory. To this end he draws attention to many common sense or 'folk' ways of viewing different phenomena, which we now recognise to be theories which turned out to be false. For example, it used to be thought that the sky was a great sphere that turns daily, allowing the sun and other heavenly bodies to rise and set.[35] We now know that it is the rotation of the Earth that produces the appearance of a sun which 'rises' at dawn and 'sets' at dusk, and so this 'folk' understanding has had to be abandoned. In the same way, we should be prepared to allow our folk psychology to be superseded by a fuller scientific account.

The eliminativist can look to the history of science for further parallels in which the development of a new theory leads to the junking of an old ontology. To return to the example we used earlier (page 255), it was once thought that heat was a very subtle fluid called caloric which was suffused through material bodies. With the development of modern atomic theory it was established that heat is in fact the mean kinetic energy of the molecules making up physical bodies and caloric was dispensed with. Note that this process is different from a *reduction* of talk of a caloric fluid to talk mean kinetic energy. Rather, talk of caloric has been *eliminated* because it posits the existence of an entity which does not in fact exist. Another example of entities that have been eliminated from our current ontology are sound particles. It was once thought that sound particles of different sorts occupied different substances and were dispersed into the air when these substances were hit. So, for example, a table might contain woody sound particles and so when struck with a hammer it emits these particles into the air which we detect with our ears. Nowadays it is thought that sound is actually produced by compression waves in the air. And, according to eliminativism, once neuroscience has advanced sufficiently all our folk-psychological concepts can be dispensed with, just as caloric and sound particles have been. Hopes, fears, sensations, etc. will be shown not really to exist; all there are are different states and processes of the brain.

In defence of what is, at first glance, a somewhat implausible thesis, the eliminativist points to the failure of folk psychology accurately to explain much of how we function. We don't understand, for example, how we learn things, nor how memory works, why we sleep, or what happiness is. The concepts used even in modern psychiatry, grounded as they are in our ordinary folk-psychological concepts, are deeply inadequate as an account of what goes on in mental illness. So just as we no longer explain people's behaviour by reference to their being possessed by devils, so too we will someday dispense with talk of paranoid delusions and stress.

Figure 2.19 For most of their time on the planet, human beings have explained a range of natural phenomena in intentional terms. 'The wind could know anger, the Moon jealousy, the river generosity, the sea fury, and so forth.'[36] With the advance of naturalistic explanations, we have come to recognise this way of thinking as mere superstition. So too, the eliminative argues, we will come to see human behaviour as better understood without reference to intentional terms.

Moreover, folk psychology is a theory which hasn't developed for thousands of years. Its basic elements and the theoretical rules governing how they operate which are current today haven't changed much since the time of the ancient Greeks (at least). This, says Churchland, 'is a very long period of stagnation and infertility for any theory to display'.[37] His point here is that successful scientific theories are able to develop and expand, and so provide us with a deeper and richer understanding of some phenomenon. Those that fail to do so should be regarded with suspicion and as in need of overhaul. Moreover, folk psychology harmonises poorly with the rest of our scientific understanding of human beings, for example, in the areas of biology, evolutionary theory and neuroscience. We seem to be as far as we have ever been from being able to explain intentionality in physicalist terms. And if intentional states cannot be accommodated within the rest of science then this gives us good reason to jettison them. Churchland likens the current position of folk psychology to that of alchemy when modern chemistry was developing as we begin to see that its categories are fundamentally muddled.

Another advantage of eliminativism is that its approach provides a solution to the problem of other minds. For, if folk psychology is indeed a theory, then we are justified in supposing others have minds on the basis that it is the best theory we have for explaining and predicting others' behaviour. To the extent that it is successful, it is a reasonable hypothesis that others have minds (see page 287 above on the argument to the best explanation). But, of course, the eliminativist is also saying that once we have a *better* theory we will be able to give up on the claim that others have minds, and within the new theoretical framework of a future neuroscience the problem will not arise.

▶ ACTIVITY: Elimination or reduction?

Which of the following terms do you think pick out real features of the world?

Which exist but can be *reduced* to some more basic entities?

Which should be eliminated from a complete scientific picture of what exists?

1	Hydrogen	11	Gravity
2	Masculinity	12	Medicine
3	Chairs	13	Grandmothers
4	Monsters	14	Great Britain
5	Dyslexia	15	Music
6	Metal	16	Evil
7	Time	17	Love
8	Average income	18	Life
9	Hurricanes	19	Green
10	Mondays	20	Austerity

Arguments against eliminativism

Criticism
The intuitive certainty of the reality of mental states
Perhaps the most obvious objection is to appeal to the deliverances of introspection, that is to my own experience of my interior mental life. Surely, you might say, I am directly aware of the existence of desires, thoughts and pains, and therefore any theory that denies their existence has to be false. My conviction that I experience such mental states trumps any other consideration. It is something I am more sure of than I could be of any philosophical argument to show the contrary. We may recall Descartes' sceptical arguments from *Meditations 1* and *2*, which lead him to conclude that I cannot reasonably doubt that I am aware of the contents of my own mind, such as that I am doubting that I am awake or that I am experiencing a headache.

This objection, however, need not be fatal. Consider an analogous argument that might have been made by a believer in caloric against modern theories of heat. How, they might ask, can you doubt the existence of caloric when I can feel it with my own hands as I place them by the fire? Similarly, a believer in bad air might insist that it is real on the grounds that they can directly see people dying of its effects! Those who doubted Galileo's claim that the Earth spun on its axis and orbited the sun pointed out that they could directly feel that the Earth wasn't moving. And how can anyone deny that the sun rises when we can see it doing so daily with our own eyes!

Clearly we would not today be particularly impressed by such arguments. The problem with them is that they assume that observation of a phenomenon can occur independently of a conceptual framework; that experience delivers to us the nature of what we observe with no mediation from our theoretical expectations. But what these observations actually do is interpret the experience in terms of the conceptual framework the people making them already possess. What this shows is that we cannot assume that entities are identifiable in isolation from the concepts we use when identifying them. So in the same way, we may be in thrall to our folk-psychological concepts when we think we are directly aware of our states of mind. We are allowing our concepts of belief and pain to determine how we interpret the phenomena. What the eliminativist is saying is that we need to rethink the background assumptions within which we identify beliefs, pains and so forth. Once we have a more sophisticated way of theorising our selves, our internal states and behaviour, the phenomena will be conceived in different ways and we will no longer feel the force of the intuition that we are directly aware of the existence of entities corresponding to our folk-psychological concepts.

Churchland makes the point by saying that judgements about your own mind don't have any privileged status, rather it is an acquired habit which depends upon the conceptual framework with which one is operating: 'Accordingly, one's *introspective* certainty that one's mind is the seat of beliefs and desires may be as badly misplaced as was the classical man's *visual* certainty that the star-flecked sphere of the heavens turns daily.'[38]

Criticism

Folk psychology has good predictive and explanatory power

Churchland admits that folk psychology 'does enjoy a substantial amount of explanatory and predictive success'[39] while nonetheless arguing that its shortcomings are so serious that we need to reject it. However, are these failings really as terrible as he suggests? Churchland complains that it fails to explain mental illness, the mechanisms underlying memory, how we learn, or why we sleep. To say we need sleep because we need to rest is not satisfactory since no matter how much rest we get, we still need to sleep. And to say that we need sleep because we become tired explains nothing, since tiredness is simply a desire for sleep. Still, to focus on areas where folk psychology has little useful to say, may be unfair. If we consider it to be first and foremost a theory of human behaviour used to predict our actions, it performs quite well. Armed with this theory we can predict and explain a good deal of what we observe in our own and others' behaviour in a range of circumstances, from why you are sitting staring at this book (e.g. you are reading it, to try to understand about philosophy of mind), to what happens when someone shouts 'Fire!' in a crowded theatre (we can predict everyone will suddenly stand and make for the exits). We can also use the concept of tiredness and the fact that it tends to increase in intensity the longer you're awake, to predict that someone will go to bed by a certain hour. Does any neuroscience come anywhere near giving us an alternative? Certainly it hasn't yet, and so at the very least we may defend folk psychology as the only game in town, putting the onus on the eliminativist to show us a better one. Until that happens, we have a right to be sceptical that elimination is a genuine possibility.

Defenders of folk psychology may also ask just how and why folk psychology has managed to endure so well if its failings are really as significant as Churchland suggests. Moreover, folk psychology is a human universal; every culture employs the same basic concepts. Again, what explains this if it provides so misleading an account of our inner life and actions? Certainly it would appear that the adoption of this theory has had a good deal to do with our success as a species. Can we imagine the great civilisations being built if the people involved did not employ folk-psychological concepts to communicate and predict each other's behaviour? Surely a theory of such remarkable antiquity and ubiquity must have something going for it.

Even supposing, for the sake of argument, that we do develop an alternative, neuroscientifically respectable theory of human behaviour and mentality. Would we ever actually give up talking with each other about our thoughts, feelings and desires? If we take examples from the history of science, examples which Churchland himself uses of successful elimination, we note that it is quite common for the 'folk' ways of talking to persist. We still talk about the sun rising and setting even though we know that in reality the Earth is turning. In the same way, we may continue to use folk psychology for everyday human social exchange no matter what the neuroscience of the future teaches.

In support of this response to eliminativism, we may also argue that the examples where theoretical entities have been eliminated, don't actually suggest that we are likely to give up on folk psychology. The Black Death may have turned out to be caused by a bacterium rather than bad air, and yet we still talk about the disease. Heat may be the mean kinetic energy of molecules instead of caloric; sound may be compression waves of air, not sound particles, but heat and sound are as real as ever. Surely, the argument here is over how to reduce these phenomena and what is being rejected is the ontology of a failed theory, not the ontology of the original phenomena requiring explanation. So just as we still talk about the Black Death, sound and heat, so too we will surely still talk about beliefs and desires, whatever it is that these turn out to be.

We can also question Churchland's claim that it represents a 'degenerating research programme',[40] that is, a stagnating theory which is not keeping pace with developments elsewhere in our understanding of the world and human nature. We may, for example, point to contemporary theoretical work in the area of clinical psychology directed at helping people with mental ill-health which employs the basic framework of folk psychology. Cognitive Behavioural Therapy, for example, is one of the most successful treatments for conditions such as anxiety and depression; far more successful than drug treatments which concern themselves directly with neurological mechanisms. And yet it is grounded in folk-psychological notions such as that thoughts, feelings and sensations are causally interconnected. It encourages patients to *reflect* on their *inner mental life* in order to *learn* new *patterns of thought*. It tells us *we can change our emotional landscape* by *consciously changing our behaviour*. All this buys into the folk-psychological picture of a conscious realm of desires, emotions and so on, all causally interrelated and linked to behaviour, and the prospects for us improving our understanding of ourselves by developing rather than junking this basic framework currently look pretty good.

We may also argue that folk psychology may not be like scientific theories that can be learnt and replaced. It may be that our folk-psychological concepts are part of our evolutionary heritage such that we would be incapable of social intercourse without them. Experiments on young children suggest that we gradually develop proficiency in employing folk-psychological concepts, but that this process is a consequence of our hard wiring rather than like learning an artificial skill such as swimming or riding a bike. People on the autistic spectrum find it hard to become proficient in utilising folk psychology and as a consequence find it hard to make sense of other people's behaviour and may have difficulty forming relationships. This syndrome appears to have a neurological basis, suggesting that interpreting others as possessors of minds with a subjective point of view and a private world of desires, beliefs, emotions and sensations is an integral part of the normal social development of individuals of our species.

Eliminative materialism as a theory is self-refuting

> [T]he statement of eliminative materialism is just a meaningless string of marks or noises, unless that string is the expression of a certain belief, and a certain intention to communicate, and a knowledge of the grammar of the language, and so forth. But if the statement of eliminative materialism is true, then there are no such states to express. The statement at issue would then be a meaningless string of marks or noises. It would therefore not be true.[41]
>
> Paul Churchland

A final objection to eliminative materialism that Churchland considers in the quotation above is that it is self-refuting. For if it is true, then there are no such things as beliefs. But if there are no beliefs, then the proponent of eliminativism cannot believe the theory to be true, but in this case why should we take seriously what they are saying? In other words, the belief expressed by the eliminativist can have no sense if it is true. On the other hand, if it is meaningful it must express a genuine belief. But, in this case, since it denies there are such things as beliefs, it must be false. So, either way, we don't need to take it seriously.

Churchland responds by pointing out that this objection presupposes the truth of folk psychology in order to claim that the proponent of eliminativism cannot be making sense. And he gives an analogous argument to show the circularity in the reasoning. In the eighteenth century people believed in a substance called 'vital spirit' which was supposed to animate living things and so distinguish them from inanimate objects like stones or clocks. Suppose someone who denied the existence of vital spirit were challenged by the following argument:

> The antivitalist says that there is no such thing as vital spirit. But this claim is self-refuting. ... For if the claim is true, then the speaker does not have vital spirit and must be dead. But if he is dead, then his statement is a meaningless string of noises, devoid of meaning and truth.[42]
>
> Paul Churchland

This defence of vitalism presupposes the existence of vital spirit in order to say that someone who denies its existence must be dead. But those who reject vital spirit are giving an alternative account of what it is to be alive. In the same way, the denial that beliefs are real would involve an alternative account of humans' internal life and behaviour.

However, we may not be impressed by this analogy since what eliminativism denies is the very idea of meaning and of the notion that a belief could be true or false, well or poorly supported by reasoning. So the status of the eliminativist's claims looks precarious – it seems we can make no sense of supposing them to be true or well evidenced. What would be needed for the analogy with vitalism to work would be some account of an alternative to intentional states in which to frame the theory, but without this we can't even make sense of the claim that folk psychology is false since making sense of the claim involves presupposing that it is true.

Section 3: Anthology extracts

Taken from the AQA online Anthology

In the AS-level textbook we outlined five lenses that would help you to read the original (or at least translated) philosophical texts given in the AQA Anthology. You should apply these lenses to each of the extracts below, building towards the final task of putting the extract into your own words and really highlighting the structure of the extract.

 When was the extract written? Who wrote it? Why did they write it?

 What words are being used in a technical way? What is their meaning?

 What are the recurring ideas in the extract? How would you summarise these?

 Is there an argument being put forward? What are its key elements?

 Write out the extract in your own words, using separate, numbered 'chunks'.

AQA have recommended the Early Modern Texts website www.earlymoderntexts.com as a free online source for some of the texts in this Anthology section. Academics on this website have 'translated' older philosophy texts into modern language so that they are more easily understood. One of the extracts below is taken from Early Modern Texts, and so will differ from the original text of the philosopher, and we have marked this extract: EMT.

Section 1: Ethics

Bentham's principle of utility

anthology 1.1

I Nature has placed mankind under the governance of two sovereign masters, pain and pleasure. It is for them alone to point out what we ought to do, as well as to determine what we shall do. On the one hand the standard of right and wrong, on the other the chain of causes and effects, are fastened to their throne. They govern us in all we do, in all we say, in all we think: every effort we can make to throw off our subjection, will serve but to demonstrate and confirm it. In words a man may pretend to abjure their empire: but in reality he will remain subject to it all the while. The principle of utility recognises this subjection, and assumes it for the foundation of that system, the object of which is to rear the fabric of felicity by the hands of reason and of law. Systems which attempt to question it, deal in sounds instead of sense, in caprice instead of reason, in darkness instead of light.

But enough of metaphor and declamation: it is not by such means that moral science is to be improved.

II The principle of utility is the foundation of the present work: it will be proper therefore at the outset to give an explicit and determinate account of what is meant by it. By the principle of utility is meant that principle which approves or disapproves of every action whatsoever, according to the tendency it appears to have to augment or diminish the happiness of the party whose interest is in question: or, what is the same thing in other words, to promote or to oppose that happiness. I say of every action whatsoever, and therefore not only of every action of a private individual, but of every measure of government.

III By utility is meant that property in any object, whereby it tends to produce benefit, advantage, pleasure, good, or happiness, (all this in the present case comes to the same thing) or (what comes again to the same thing) to prevent the happening of mischief, pain, evil, or unhappiness to the party whose interest is considered: if that party be the community in general, then the happiness of the community: if a particular individual, then the happiness of that individual.

Jeremy Bentham, *Introduction to the Principles of Morals and Legislation*

Mill – Is it better to be a fool satisfied?

Now, it is an unquestionable fact that the way of life that employs the higher faculties is strongly preferred to the way of life that caters only to the lower ones by people who are equally acquainted with both and equally capable of appreciating and enjoying both. Few human creatures would agree to be changed into any of the lower animals in return for a promise of the fullest allowance of animal pleasures:

- no intelligent human being would consent to be a fool,
- no educated person would prefer to be an ignoramus,
- no person of feeling and conscience would rather be selfish and base,

even if they were convinced that the fool, the dunce or the rascal is better satisfied with his life than they are with theirs. ... If they ever think they would, it is only in cases of unhappiness so extreme that to escape from it they would exchange their situation for almost any other, however undesirable they may think the other to be. Someone with higher faculties requires more to make him happy, is probably capable of more acute suffering, and is certainly vulnerable to suffering at more points, than someone of an inferior type.

John Stuart Mill, *Utilitarianism* (EMT)

Peter Singer on vegetarianism

anthology 1.3

Given that an animal belongs to a species incapable of self consciousness, it follows that it is not wrong to rear and kill it for food, provided that it leads a pleasant life and, after being killed, will be replaced by another animal that will lead a similarly pleasant life and would not have existed if the first animal had not been killed. This means that vegetarianism is not obligatory for those who can obtain meat from animals that they know have been reared in this manner. In practice, I think this exemption will only apply to those who are able to rear their own animals, or have personal knowledge of the conditions under which the animals they eat were raised and killed. ...I am sure that some will claim that in taking this view of the killing of some non human animals I am myself guilty of 'speciesism' – that is, discrimination against beings because they are not members of our own species. My position is not speciesist, because it does not permit the killing of non human beings on the ground that they are not members of our species, but on the ground that they lack the capacity to desire to go on living. The position applies equally to members of our own species who lack the relevant capacity. This last consequence strikes many as shocking.

Peter Singer, 'Killing Humans and Killing Animals'

Kant on good will

anthology 1.4

Nothing can possibly be conceived in the world, or even out of it, which can be called good, without qualification, except a good will. Intelligence, wit, judgement, and the other talents of the mind, however they may be named, or courage, resolution, perseverance, as qualities of temperament, are undoubtedly good and desirable in many respects; but these gifts of nature may also become extremely bad and mischievous if the will which is to make use of them, and which, therefore, constitutes what is called character, is not good. It is the same with the gifts of fortune. Power, riches, honour, even health, and the general well-being and contentment with one's condition which is called happiness, inspire pride, and often presumption, if there is not a good will to correct the influence of these on the mind, and with this also to rectify the whole principle of acting and adapt it to its end. The sight of a being who is not adorned with a single feature of a pure and good will, enjoying unbroken prosperity, can never give pleasure to an impartial rational spectator. Thus a good will appears to constitute the indispensable condition even of being worthy of happiness.

Immanuel Kant, *Groundwork of the Metaphysics of Morals*

Kant on duty and prudence

anthology 1.5

For example, it is always a matter of duty that a dealer should not over charge an inexperienced purchaser; and wherever there is much commerce the prudent tradesman does not overcharge, but keeps a fixed price for everyone, so that a child buys of him as well as any other. Men are thus honestly served; but this is not enough to make us believe that the tradesman has so acted from duty and from principles of honesty: his own advantage required it; it is out of the question in this case to suppose that he might besides have a direct inclination in favour of the buyers, so that, as it were, from love he should give no advantage to one over another. Accordingly the action was done neither from duty nor from direct inclination, but merely with a selfish view.

Immanuel Kant, *Groundwork of the Metaphysics of Morals*

Kant's universal law

anthology 1.6

When we decide what we do, we in effect proclaim our wish that our conduct be made in to a 'universal law'. Therefore when a rational being decides to treat people in a certain way, he decrees that in his judgment *this is the way people ought to be treated.* Thus if we treat him the same way in return, we are doing nothing more that treating him as *he has decided* people are to be treated. If he treats others badly, and we treat him badly, we are complying with his own decision. ... We are allowing *him* to decide how he is to be treated – and so we are, in a perfectly clear sense, respecting his judgment, by allowing it to control our treatment of him. Thus Kant says of the criminal 'His own evil deed draws the punishment upon himself.'

James Rachels, *The Elements of Moral Philosophy*

Aristotle's function argument

anthology 1.7

Presumably, however, to say that happiness is the chief good seems a platitude, and a clearer account of what it is still desired. This might perhaps be given, if we could first ascertain the function of man. For just as for a flute-player, a sculptor, or an artist, and, in general, for all things that have a function or activity, the good and the 'well' is thought to reside in the function, so would it seem to be for man, if he has a function. Have the carpenter, then, and the tanner certain functions or activities, and has man none? Is he born without a function? Or as eye, hand, foot, and in general each of the parts evidently has a function, may one lay it down that man similarly has a function apart from all these? What then can this be? Life seems to be common even to plants, but we are seeking what is peculiar to man. Let us exclude, therefore, the life of nutrition and growth. Next there would be a life of perception, but it also seems to be common even to the horse, the ox, and every animal. There remains, then, an active life of the element that has a rational principle; of this, one part has such a principle in the sense of being obedient to one, the other in the sense of possessing one and exercising thought. And, as 'life of the rational element' also has two meanings, we must state that life in the sense of activity is what we mean; for this seems to be the more proper sense of the term.

Aristotle, *Nicomachean Ethics*

Function, soul and *eudaimonia*

Now if the function of man is an activity of soul which follows or implies a rational principle, and if we say 'so-and-so' and 'a good so-and-so' have a function which is the same in kind, e.g. a lyre, and a good lyre-player, and so without qualification in all cases, eminence in respect of goodness being added to the name of the function (for the function of a lyre-player is to play the lyre, and that of a good lyre-player is to do so well): if this is the case, and we state the function of man to be a certain kind of life, and this to be an activity or actions of the soul implying a rational principle, and the function of a good man to be the good and noble performance of these, and if any action is well performed when it is performed in accordance with the appropriate excellence: if this is the case, human good turns out to be activity of soul in accordance with virtue, and if there are more than one virtue, in accordance with the best and most complete.

Aristotle, *Nicomachean Ethics*

The doctrine of the mean

anthology 1.8

In everything that is continuous and divisible it is possible to take more, less, or an equal amount, and that either in terms of the thing itself or relatively to us; and the equal is an intermediate between excess and defect. By the intermediate in the object I mean that which is equidistant from each of the extremes, which is one and the same for all men; by the intermediate relatively to us that which is neither too much nor too little – and this is not one, nor the same for all. For instance, if ten is many and two is few, six is the intermediate, taken in terms of the object; for it exceeds and is exceeded by an equal amount; this is intermediate according to arithmetical proportion. But the intermediate relatively to us is not to be taken so; if ten pounds are too much for a particular person to eat and two too little, it does not follow that the trainer will order six pounds; for this also is perhaps too much for the person who is to take it, or too little – too little for Milo, too much for the beginner in athletic exercises. The same is true of running and wrestling. Thus a master of any art avoids excess and defect, but seeks the intermediate and chooses this – the intermediate not in the object but relatively to us.

Aristotle, *Nicomachean Ethics*

Practical wisdom and *ethica arete*

anthology
1.9

It is clear, then, from what has been said, that it is not possible to be good in the strict sense without practical wisdom, nor practically wise without moral virtue. But in this way we may also refute the dialectical argument whereby it might be contended that the virtues exist in separation from each other; the same man, it might be said, is not best equipped by nature for all the virtues, so that he will have already acquired one when he has not yet acquired another. This is possible in respect of the natural virtues, but not in respect of those in respect of which a man is called without qualification good; for with the presence of the one quality, practical wisdom, will be given all the virtues. And it is plain that, even if it were of no practical value, we should have needed it because it is the virtue of the part of us in question; plain too that the choice will not be right without practical wisdom any more than without virtue; for the one determines the end and the other makes us do the things that lead to the end.

Aristotle, *Nicomachean Ethics*

Involuntary acts and the virtue of justice

anthology
1.10

A man acts unjustly or justly whenever he does such acts voluntarily; when involuntarily, he acts neither unjustly nor justly except in an incidental way; for he does things which happen to be just or unjust. Whether an act is or is not one of injustice (or of justice) is determined by its voluntariness or involuntariness; for when it is voluntary it is blamed, and at the same time is then an act of injustice; so that there will be things that are unjust but not yet acts of injustice, if voluntariness be not present as well. By the voluntary I mean, as has been said before, any of the things in a man's own power which he does with knowledge, i.e. not in ignorance either of the person acted on or of the instrument used or of the end that will be attained (e.g. whom he is striking, with what, and to what end), each such act being done not incidentally nor under compulsion (e.g. if A takes B's hand and therewith strikes C, B does not act voluntarily; for the act was not in his own power) … Therefore that which is done in ignorance, or though not done in ignorance is not in the agent's power, or is done under compulsion, is involuntary.

Aristotle, *Nicomachean Ethics*

Actions caused by desire are not involuntary actions

anthology
1.11

Since that which is done under compulsion or by reason of ignorance is involuntary, the voluntary would seem to be that of which the moving principle is in the agent himself, he being aware of the particular circumstances of the action. Presumably acts done by reason of anger or appetite are not rightly called involuntary. For in the first place, on that showing none of the other animals will act voluntarily, nor will children; and secondly, is it meant that we do not do voluntarily any of the acts that are due to appetite or anger, or that we do the noble acts voluntarily and the base acts involuntarily? Is not this absurd, when one and the same thing is the cause? But it would surely be odd to describe as involuntary the things one ought to desire; and we ought both to be angry at certain things and to have an appetite for certain things, e.g. for health and for learning.

Aristotle, *Nicomachean Ethics*

Mill's naturalistic foundations for utilitarianism

anthology 1.12

The only proof capable of being given that an object is visible, is that people actually see it. The only proof that a sound is audible, is that people hear it. ... The sole evidence that it is possible to produce that anything is desirable, is that people do actually desire it. No reason can be given why the general happiness is desirable, except that each person, so far as he believes it to be attainable, desires his own happiness. This, however, being a fact, we have not only all the proof which the case admits of, but all which it is possible to require, that happiness is a good: that each person's happiness is a good to that person, and the general happiness, therefore, a good to the aggregate of all persons.

John Stuart Mill, *Utilitarianism*

Moore – Some concepts are incapable of definition

anthology 1.13

Consider yellow, for example. We may try to define it, by describing its physical equivalent; we may state what kind of light-vibrations must stimulate the normal eye, in order that we may perceive it. But a moment's reflection is sufficient to show that those light-vibrations are not themselves what we mean by yellow. *They* are not what we perceive. Indeed, we should never have been able to discover their existence, unless we had first been struck by the patent difference of quality between the different colours. The most we can be entitled to say of those vibrations is that they are what corresponds in space to the yellow which we actually perceive.

Yet a mistake of this simple kind has commonly been made about good. It may be true that all things which are good are *also* something else, just as it is true that all things which are yellow produce a certain kind of vibration in the light. And it is a fact, that Ethics aims at discovering what are those other properties belonging to all things which are good. But far too many philosophers have thought that when they named those other properties they were actually defining good; that these properties, in fact, were simply not other, but absolutely and entirely the same with goodness. This view I propose to call the naturalistic fallacy.

G.E. Moore *Principia Ethica*

Warnock's criticism of Intuitionism

anthology
1.14

Intuitionism seems, in retrospect, so strange a phenomenon – a body of writing so acute and at the same time so totally unilluminating – that one may wonder how to explain it, what its genesis was. The idea that there is a vast corpus of moral facts about the world – known, but we cannot say how: related to other features of the world, but we cannot explain in what way: overwhelmingly important for our conduct, but we cannot say why – what does this really astonishing idea reflect? One may be tempted to say: the absence of curiosity. And what the absence of curiosity reflects may be the absence of doubt … Certainly the intuitionist philosophers of the early part of this century do not strike one as men much beset by moral uncertainty …. What they called 'the facts' of morality were for them simply there, simply given, in the nature of things, standing in need from the theorist of nothing but clear recognition.

G.J. Warnock, *Contemporary Moral Philosophy*

Mackie's justification of Error Theory

anthology
1.15

Moral scepticism must, therefore, take the form of an error theory, admitting that a belief in objective values is built into ordinary moral thought and language, but holding that this ingrained belief is false … The considerations that favour moral scepticism are: first the relativity or variability of some important starting points of moral thinking …; secondly, the metaphysical peculiarity of the supposed objective values, in that they would have to be intrinsically action guiding and motivating; thirdly, the problem of how such values could be consequential or supervenient on natural features; fourthly the corresponding epistemological difficulty of accounting for our knowledge of value entities or features …; fifthly the possibility of explaining … how, even if there were no such objective values people might have to come to suppose that there are but also might persist firmly in that belief. These five points sum up the case for moral scepticism.

J.L. Mackie, *Ethics: Inventing Right and Wrong*

Hume – Morality is based on emotion, not reason

anthology
1.16

Can there really be any difficulty in proving that vice and virtue are not matters of fact whose existence we can infer by reason? Take any action that is agreed to be vicious – willful murder, for instance. Examine it in all lights, and see if you can find the matter of fact or real existence that you call 'vice'. However you look at it, all you'll find are certain passions, motives, volitions, and thoughts; those are the only matters of fact in the case. The vice entirely escapes you as long as you focus on the object, i.e. the individual action, the murder. You can never find it until you turn your reflection into your own breast and find a sentiment of disapproval that arises in you towards this action. Here is a matter of fact, but it is the object of feeling, not of reason. It lies in yourself, not in the object. So when you say of some action or character that it is vicious, all you mean is that you have a feeling or sentiment of blame from contemplating it. So vice and virtue may be compared to sounds, colours, heat, and cold, which modern philosophy says are not qualities in objects but perceptions in the mind.

David Hume, *A Treatise on Human Nature*

Ayer's principle of verification

My own version of [the verifiability principle] … was that 'a sentence is factually significant to any given person, if, and only if, he knows how to verify the proposition which it purports to express – that is, if he knows what observations would lead him, under certain conditions, to accept the proposition as being true, or reject it as being false'. Meaning was also accorded to sentences expressing propositions like those of logic or pure mathematics, which were true or false only in virtue of their form, but with this exception, everything of a would be indicative character which failed to satisfy the verification principle was dismissed as literally nonsensical.

anthology 1.17

A.J. Ayer, *The Central Questions of Philosophy*

Ayer on the meaning of ethical statements

We begin by admitting that the fundamental ethical concepts are unanalysable, inasmuch as there is no criterion by which one can test the validity of the judgements in which they occur. So far we are in agreement with the absolutists. But, unlike the absolutists, we are able to give an explanation of this fact about ethical concepts. We say that the reason why they are unanalysable is that they are mere pseudo-concepts. The presence of an ethical symbol in a proposition adds nothing to its factual content. Thus if I say to someone, 'You acted wrongly in stealing that money,' I am not stating anything more than if I had simply said, 'You stole that money.' In adding that this action is wrong I am not making any further statement about it. I am simply evincing my moral disapproval of it. It is as if I had said, 'You stole that money,' in a peculiar tone of horror, or written it with the addition of some special exclamation marks. The tone, or the exclamation marks, adds nothing to the literal meaning of the sentence. It merely serves to show that the expression of it is attended by certain feelings in the speaker.

anthology 1.18

A.J. Ayer, *Language, Truth and Logic*

Hare – Moral judgements entail imperatives

anthology
1.19

But to guide choices or actions, a moral judgement has to be such that if a person assents to it, he must assent to some imperative sentence derivable from it; in other words, if a person does not assent to some such imperative sentence, that is knock-down evidence that he does not assent to the moral judgement in an evaluative sense – though of course he may assent to it in some other sense (e.g. one of those I have mentioned). This is true by my definition of the word evaluative. But to say this is to say that if he professes to assent to the moral judgement, but does not assent to the imperative, he must have misunderstood the moral judgement (by taking it to be non-evaluative, though the speaker intended it to be evaluative). We are therefore clearly entitled to say that the moral judgement entails the imperative; for to say that one judgement entails another is simply to say that you cannot assent to the first and dissent from the second unless you have misunderstood one or the other; and this 'cannot' is a logical 'cannot' – if someone assents to the first and not to the second, this is in itself a sufficient criterion for saying that he has misunderstood the meaning of one or the other. Thus to say that moral judgements guide actions, and to say that they entail imperatives, comes to much the same thing.

R.M. Hare, *The Language of Morals*

Section 2: Philosophy of Mind

Chalmers – The hard problem of consciousness

anthology
2.1

'The hard problem of consciousness is the problem of experience. Human beings have subjective experience: there is something it is like to be them. We can say that a being is conscious in this sense – or is phenomenally conscious, as it is sometimes put – when there is something it is like to be that being. A mental state is conscious when there is something it is like to be in that state. Conscious states include states of perceptual experience, bodily sensation, mental imagery, emotional experience, occurrent thought, and more. There is something it is like to see a vivid green, to feel a sharp pain, to visualize the Eiffel tower, to feel a deep regret, and to think that one is late. Each of these states has a phenomenal character, with phenomenal properties (or qualia) characterizing what it is like to be in the state'.

Chalmers defines 'qualia' in a footnote as 'simply those properties that characterize conscious states according to what it is like to have them'.

David Chalmers, 'Consciousness and its place in nature'

Ryle outlines what he calls the 'official doctrine', i.e. the main tenets of substance dualism

anthology
2.2

[E]very human being is both a body and a mind. His body and his mind are ordinarily harnessed together, but after the death of the body his mind may continue to exist and function. Human bodies are in space and are subject to the mechanical laws which govern all other bodies in space. Bodily processes and states can be inspected by external observers. So a man's bodily life is as much a public affair as are the lives of animals and reptiles and even as the careers of trees, crystals and planets. But minds are not in space, nor are their operations subject to mechanical laws. The workings of one mind are not witnessable by other observers; its career is private. Only I can take direct cognisance of the states and processes of my own mind. A person therefore lives through two collateral histories, one consisting of what happens in and to his body, the other consisting of what happens in and to his mind. The first is public, the second private. The events in the first history are events in the physical world, those in the second are events in the mental world.

Gilbert Ryle, *The Concept of Mind*

The indivisibility argument for substance dualism

anthology
2.3

[T]here is a great difference between mind and body, inasmuch as body is by nature always divisible, and the mind is entirely indivisible. For, as a matter of fact, when I consider the mind, that is to say, myself inasmuch as I am only a thinking thing, I cannot distinguish in myself any parts, but apprehend myself to be clearly one and entire; and although the whole mind seems to be united to the whole body, yet if a foot, or an arm, or some other part, is separated from my body, I am aware that nothing has been taken away from my mind. And the faculties of willing, feeling, conceiving, etc. cannot be properly speaking said to be its parts, for it is one and the same mind which employs itself in willing and in feeling and understanding. But it is quite otherwise with corporeal or extended objects, for there is not one of these imaginable by me which my mind cannot easily divide into parts, and which consequently I do not recognise as being divisible; this would be sufficient to teach me that the mind or soul of man is entirely different from the body, if I had not already learned it from other sources.

Descartes, *Meditation 6*

The conceivability argument for substance dualism

anthology 2.4

And first of all, because I know that all things which I apprehend clearly and distinctly can be created by God as I apprehend them, it suffices that I am able to apprehend one thing apart from another clearly and distinctly in order to be certain that the one is different from the other, since they may be made to exist in separation at least by the omnipotence of God; and it does not signify by what power this separation is made in order to compel me to judge them to be different: and, therefore, just because I know certainly that I exist, and that meanwhile I do not remark that any other thing necessarily pertains to my nature or essence, excepting that I am a thinking thing, I rightly conclude that my essence consists solely in the fact that I am a thinking thing [or a substance whose whole essence or nature is to think]. And although possibly (or rather certainly, as I shall say in a moment) I possess a body with which I am very intimately conjoined, yet because, on the one side, I have a clear and distinct idea of myself inasmuch as I am only a thinking and unextended thing, and as, on the other, I possess a distinct idea of body, inasmuch as it is only an extended and unthinking thing, it is certain that this I [that is to say, my soul by which I am what I am], is entirely and absolutely distinct from my body, and can exist without it.

Descartes, *Meditation 6*

Chalmers' zombie world argument

anthology 2.5

According to this argument, it is conceivable that there be a system that is physically identical to a conscious being, but that lacks at least some of that being's conscious states. Such a system might be a zombie: a system that is physically identical to a conscious being but that lacks consciousness entirely. ... These systems will look identical to a normal conscious being from the third-person perspective: in particular, their brain processes will be molecule-for-molecule identical with the original, and their behavior will be indistinguishable. But things will be different from the first-person point of view. ... there is nothing it is like to be a zombie. There is little reason to believe that zombies exist in the actual world. But many hold that they are at least conceivable: we can coherently imagine zombies, and there is no contradiction in the idea that reveals itself even on reflection. As an extension of the idea, many hold that the same goes for a zombie world: a universe physically identical to ours, but in which there is no consciousness. ... From the conceivability of zombies, proponents of the argument infer their metaphysical possibility. Zombies are probably not naturally possible: they probably cannot exist in our world, with its laws of nature. But the argument holds that zombies could have existed, perhaps in a very different sort of universe. For example, it is sometimes suggested that God could have created a zombie world, if he had so chosen. From here, it is inferred that consciousness must be nonphysical. If there is a metaphysically possible universe that is physically identical to ours but that lacks consciousness, then consciousness must be a further, nonphysical component of our universe. If God could have created a zombie world, then (as Kripke puts it) after creating the physical processes in our world, he had to do more work to ensure that it contained consciousness.

David Chalmers, 'Consciousness and its place in nature'

Jackson's knowledge argument. What Mary didn't know

📖 anthology 2.6

Mary is a brilliant scientist who is, for whatever reason, forced to investigate the world from a black and white room via a black and white television monitor. She specialises in the neurophysiology of vision and acquires, let us suppose, all the physical information there is to obtain about what goes on when we see ripe tomatoes, or the sky, and use terms like 'red', 'blue', and so on. She discovers, for example, just which wave-length combinations from the sky stimulate the retina, and exactly how this produces via the central nervous system the contraction of the vocal chords and expulsion of air from the lungs that results in the uttering of the sentence 'The sky is blue'. (It can hardly be denied that it is in principle possible to obtain all this physical information from black and white television, otherwise the Open University would of necessity need to use colour television.) What will happen when Mary is released from her black and white room or is given a colour television monitor? Will she learn anything or not? It seems just obvious that she will learn something about the world and our visual experience of it. But then it is inescapable that her previous knowledge was incomplete. But she had all the physical information. Ergo there is more to have than that, and Physicalism is false.

Frank Jackson, 'Epiphenomenal Qualia'

Princess Elisabeth of Bohemia outlines the problem of interaction

📖 anthology 2.7

The question arises because it seems that how a thing moves depends solely on (i) how much it is pushed, (ii) the manner in which it is pushed, or (iii) the surface-texture and shape of the thing that pushes it. The first two of those require contact between the two things, and the third requires that the causally active thing be extended. Your notion of the soul entirely excludes extension, and it appears to me that an immaterial thing can't possibly touch anything else.

Letter from Princess Elisabeth of Bohemia to Descartes

Jackson on why pain does not cause behaviour

📖 anthology 2.8

It is supposed to be just obvious that the hurtfulness of pain is partly responsible for the subject seeking to avoid pain, saying 'It hurts' and so on. But, to reverse Hume, anything can fail to cause anything. No matter how often B follows A, and no matter how initially obvious the causality of the connection seems, the hypothesis that A causes B can be overturned by an over-arching theory which shows the two as distinct effects of a common underlying causal process. To the untutored the image on the screen of Lee Marvin's fist moving from left to right immediately followed by the image of John Wayne's head moving in the same general direction looks as causal as anything. And of course throughout countless Westerns images similar to the first are followed by images similar to the second. All this counts for precisely nothing when we know the over-arching theory concerning how the relevant images are both effects of an underlying causal process involving the projector and the film. The epiphenomenalist can say exactly the same about the connection between, for example, hurtfulness and behaviour. It is simply a consequence of the fact that certain happenings in the brain cause both.

Frank Jackson, 'Epiphenomenal Qualia'

Jackson rejects the evolution objection to epiphenomenalism

anthology
2.9

[An objection to epiphenomenalism] relates to Darwin's Theory of Evolution. According to natural selection the traits that evolve over time are those conducive to physical survival. We may assume that qualia evolved over time – we have them, the earliest forms of life do not – and so we should expect qualia to be conducive to survival. The objection is that they could hardly help us to survive if they do nothing to the physical world. The appeal of this argument is undeniable, but there is a good reply to it. Polar bears have particularly thick, warm coats. The Theory of Evolution explains this (we suppose) by pointing out that having a thick, warm coat is conducive to survival in the Arctic. But having a thick coat goes along with having a heavy coat, and having a heavy coat is *not* conducive to survival. It slows the animal down. Does this mean that we have refuted Darwin because we have found an evolved trait – having a heavy coat – which is not conducive to survival?

Clearly not. Having a heavy coat is an unavoidable concomitant of having a warm coat (in the context, modern insulation was not available), and the advantages for survival of having a warm coat outweighed the disadvantages of having a heavy one. The point is that all we can extract from Darwin's theory is that we should expect any evolved characteristic to be *either* conducive to survival *or* a by-product of one that is so conducive. The epiphenomenalist holds that qualia fall into the latter category. They are a by-product of certain brain processes that are highly conducive to survival.

Frank Jackson, 'Epiphenomenal Qualia'

Ryle outlines how dualism may lead to the problem of other minds

anthology
2.10

There is thus a polar opposition between mind and matter, an opposition which is often brought out as follows. Material objects are situated in a common field, known as 'space', and what happens to one body in one part of space is mechanically connected with what happens to other bodies in other parts of space. But mental happenings occur in insulated fields, known as 'minds', and there is, apart maybe from telepathy, no direct causal connection between what happens in one mind and what happens in another. Only through the medium of the public physical world can the mind of one person make a difference to the mind of another. The mind is its own place and in his inner life each of us lives the life of a ghostly Robinson Crusoe. People can see, hear and jolt one another's bodies, but they are irremediably blind and deaf to the workings of one another's minds and inoperative upon them.

Gilbert Ryle, *The Concept of Mind*

Ryle on category mistakes – The cricket example

anthology 2.11

A foreigner watching his first game of cricket learns what are the functions of the bowlers, the batsmen, the fielders, the umpires and the scorers. He then says 'But there is no one left on the field to contribute the famous element of team-spirit. I see who does the bowling, the batting and the wicket-keeping; but I do not see whose role it is to exercise esprit de corps.' Once more, it would have to be explained that he was looking for the wrong type of thing. Team-spirit is not another cricketing-operation supplementary to all of the other special tasks. It is, roughly, the keenness with which each of the special tasks is performed, and performing a task keenly is not performing two tasks. Certainly exhibiting team-spirit is not the same thing as bowling or catching, but nor is it a third thing such that we can say that the bowler first bowls and then exhibits team-spirit or that a fielder is at a given moment either catching or displaying esprit de corps.

Gilbert Ryle, *The Concept of Mind*

Ryle on dispositions

anthology 2.12

When we describe glass as brittle, or sugar as soluble, we are using dispositional concepts, the logical force of which is this. The brittleness of glass does not consist in the fact that it is at a given moment actually being shivered. It may be brittle without ever being shivered. To say that it is brittle is to say that if it ever is, or ever had been, struck or strained, it would fly, or have flown, into fragments. To say that sugar is soluble is to say that it would dissolve, or would have dissolved, if immersed in water. A statement ascribing a dispositional property to a thing has much, though not everything, in common with a statement subsuming the thing under a law. To possess a dispositional property is not to be in a particular state, or to undergo a particular change; it is to be bound or liable to be in a particular state, or to undergo a particular change, when a particular condition is realised. The same is true about specifically human dispositions such as qualities of character. My being an habitual smoker does not entail that I am at this or that moment smoking; it is my permanent proneness to smoke when I am not eating, sleeping, lecturing or attending funerals, and have not quite recently been smoking.

Gilbert Ryle, *The Concept of Mind*

Putnam on mind–brain identity

anthology
2.13

For example, if the fact that I can know that I am in pain without knowing that I am in brain state S shows that pain cannot be brain state S, then, by exactly the same argument, the fact that I can know that the stove is hot without knowing that the mean molecular kinetic energy is high (or even that molecules exist) shows that it is false that temperature is mean molecular kinetic energy, physics to the contrary. In fact, all that immediately follows from the fact that I can know that I am in pain without knowing that I am in brain state S is that the concept of pain is not the same concept as the concept of being in brain state S. But either pain, or the state of being in pain, or some pain, or some pain state, might still be brain state S. After all, the concept of temperature is not the same concept as the concept of mean molecular kinetic energy. But temperature is mean molecular kinetic energy.

Hilary Putnam, 'Psychological predicates'

Smart defends the identity theory against a common objection

anthology
2.14

Objection 1. Any illiterate peasant can talk perfectly well about his after-images, or how things look or feel to him, or about his aches and pains, and yet he may know nothing whatever about neurophysiology. A man may, like Aristotle, believe that the brain is an organ for cooling the body without any impairment of his ability to make true statements about his sensations. Hence the things we are talking about when we describe our sensations cannot be processes in the brain.

Reply. You might as well say that a nation of slug-abeds, who never saw the morning star or knew of its existence, or who had never thought of the expression 'the Morning Star', but who used the expression 'the Evening Star' perfectly well, could not use this expression to refer to the same entity as we refer to (and describe as) 'the Morning Star'. You may object that the Morning Star is in a sense not the very same thing as the Evening Star, but only something spatiotemporally continuous with it. That is, you may say that the Morning Star is not the Evening Star in the strict sense of 'identity' that I distinguished earlier. I can perhaps forestall this objection by considering the slug-abeds to be New Zealanders and the early risers to be Englishmen. Then the thing the New Zealanders describe as 'the Morning Star' could be the very same thing (in the strict sense) as the Englishmen describe as 'the Evening Star'. And yet they could be ignorant of this fact.

There is, however, a more plausible example. Consider lightning. Modern physical science tells us that lightning is a certain kind of electrical discharge due to ionization of clouds of water-vapor in the atmosphere. This, it is now believed, is what the true nature of lightning is. Note that there are not two things: a flash of lightning and an electrical discharge. There is one thing, a flash of lightning, which is described scientifically as an electrical discharge to the earth from a cloud of ionized water-molecules. The case is not at all like that of explaining a footprint by reference to a burglar. We say that what lightning really is, what its true nature as revealed by science is, is an electric discharge. (It is not the true nature of a footprint to be a burglar.)

J.J.C. Smart, 'Sensations and brain processes'

Smart on contingent identity

anthology 2.15

Let me first try to state more accurately the thesis that sensations are brain processes. It is not the thesis that, for example; 'after-image' or 'ache' means the same as 'brain process of sort X' (where 'X' is replaced by a description of a certain sort of brain process). It is that, in so far as 'after-image' or 'ache' is a report of a process, it is a report of a process that *happens to be* a brain process. It follows that the thesis does not claim that sensation statements can be *translated* into statements about brain processes. Nor does it claim that the logic of a sensation statement is the same as that of a brain-process statement. All it claims is that in so far as a sensation statement is a report of something, that something is in fact a brain process. Sensations are nothing over and above brain processes. Nations are nothing 'over and above' citizens, but this does not prevent the logic of nation statements being very different from the logic of citizen statements, nor does it insure the translatability of nation statements into citizen statements. (I do not, however, wish to assert that the relation of sensation statements to brain-process statements is very like that of nation statements to citizen statements. Nations do not just *happen to be* nothing over and above citizens, for example. I bring in the 'nations' example merely to make a negative point: that the fact that the logic of A-statements is different from that of B-statements does not insure that A's are anything over and above B's.)

J.J.C. Smart, 'Sensations and brain processes'

Ned Block's Chinese mind

anthology 2.16

I shall describe a class of devices that are *prima facie* embarrassments for all versions of functionalism in that they indicate functionalism is guilty of liberalism – classifying systems that lack mentality as having mentality.
Consider the simple version of machine functionalism already described. It says that each system having mental states is described by at least one Turing-machine table of a certain kind, and each mental state of the system is identical to one of the machine-table states specified by the machine table. I shall consider inputs and outputs to be specified by descriptions of neural impulses in sense organs and motor-output neurons. ...
Imagine a body externally like a human body, say yours, but internally quite different. The neurons from sensory organs are connected to a bank of lights in a hollow cavity in the head. A set of buttons connects to the motor-output neurons. Inside the cavity resides a group of little men. Each has a very simple task: to implement a 'square' of an adequate machine table that describes you. On one wall is a bulletin board on which is posted a state card, i.e., a card that bears a symbol designating one of the states specified in the machine table. Here is what the little men do: Suppose the posted card has a 'G' on it. This alerts the little men who implement G squares – 'G-men' they call themselves. Suppose the light representing input 'I' goes on. One of the G-men has the following as his sole task: when the card reads 'G' and the 'I' light goes on, he presses output button 'O', and changes the state card to 'M'. This G-man

is called upon to exercise his task only rarely. In spite of the low level of intelligence required of each little man, the system as a whole manages to simulate you because the functional organization they have been trained to realize is yours. .... Through the efforts of the little men, the system realizes the same (reasonably adequate) machine table as you do and is thus functionally equivalent to you.

I shall describe a version of the homunculi-headed simulation, which has more chance of being nomologically possible. How many homunculi are required? Perhaps a billion are enough.

Suppose we convert the government of China to functionalism, and we convince its officials to realize a human mind for an hour. We provide each of the billion people in China (I chose China because it has a billion inhabitants) with a specially designed two-way radio that connects them in the appropriate way to other persons and to the artificial body mentioned in the previous example. We replace each of the little men with a citizen of China plus his radio. Instead of a bulletin board we arrange to have letters displayed on a series of satellites placed so that they can be seen from anywhere in China.

The system of a billion people communicating with one another plus satellites plays the role of an external 'brain' connected to the artificial body by radio. ...

It is not at all obvious that the China-body system is physically impossible. It could be functionally equivalent to you for a short time, say an hour.

Ned Block, 'Troubles with functionalism'

Churchland on why folk psychology (FP) might be false

anthology 2.17

When one centers one's attention not on what FP can explain, but on what it cannot explain or fails even to address, one discovers that there is a very great deal. As examples of central and important mental phenomena that remain largely or wholly mysterious within the framework of FP, consider the nature and dynamics of mental illness, the faculty of creative imagination, or the ground of intelligence differences between individuals. Consider our utter ignorance of the nature and psychological functions of sleep, that curious state in which a third of one's life is spent. Reflect on the common ability to catch an outfield fly ball on the run, or hit a moving car with a snowball. Consider the internal construction of a 3-D visual image from subtle differences in the 2-D array of stimulations in our respective retinas. Consider the rich variety of perceptual illusions, visual and otherwise. Or consider the miracle of memory, with its lightning capacity for relevant retrieval. On these and many other mental phenomena, FP sheds negligible light. ...

Failures on such a large scale do not (yet) show that FP is a false theory, but they do move that prospect well into the range of real possibility, and they do show decisively that FP is at best a highly superficial theory, a partial and unpenetrating gloss on a deeper and more complex reality. Having reached this opinion, we may be forgiven for exploring the possibility that FP provides a positively misleading sketch of our internal kinematics and dynamics, one whose success is owed more to selective application and forced interpretation on our part than to genuine theoretical insight on FP's part.

Paul Churchland, 'Eliminative materialism and the propositional attitudes'

Glossary

Section 1: Ethics

Agency   The capacity of an **agent** to act in any given environment.

Agent   A being who is capable of action. **Agency** and action are typically restricted to human beings, because human beings have the capacity to reason, make a choice between two courses of action, then do what they've chosen.

Anti-realism   See **realism and anti-realism**.

Applied ethics   See **practical ethics**.

A priori   A Latin term that usually describes a belief (or knowledge) that is known prior to or independently from experience. A priori beliefs are contrasted with a posteriori beliefs, which are ones derived from experience.

Argument   An argument is a series of propositions intended to support a conclusion. The propositions offered in support of the conclusion are termed **premises**.

Autonomy   (from the Greek *auto* – self, and *nomos* – law) An **agent** has autonomy insofar as it is rational and free. For Kant, moral autonomy was only achieved through following the categorical **imperative**.

Autonomy of ethics   See **is/ought gap**.

Categorical imperative   See **imperative**.

Cognitivism and non-cognitivism   Cognitivism in ethics is the view that moral **judgements** are **propositions** which can be known – they refer to the world and they have a **truth-value** (they are capable of being true or false). Non-cognitivism is the view that moral judgements cannot

be known, because they do not say anything true or false about the world (they do not have a truth-value). There are many different forms of non-cognitivism such as **emotivism**, **prescriptivism** and nihilism. See also **realism and anti-realism**.

Conclusion   A belief or statement that an **argument** tries to prove. If an argument is valid and all of the premises are true, then the conclusion will also be true.

Consequentialist ethics   A type of normative moral theory which views the moral value of an action as lying in its consequences. So an action is judged to be good if it brings about beneficial consequences, and bad if it brings about harmful ones. This is in contrast to **deontology.** Egoism and **utilitarianism** are two examples of consequentialism.

Deontological ethics   A type of normative moral theory which views the moral value of an action as lying in the action itself. So an action is right or wrong in itself, whatever the consequences. Generally, deontologists (such as Kant) propose certain rules or principles that guide us as to which actions are right and which are wrong. This is in contrast to **consequentialism. Divine command ethics** and **Kantian ethics** are two examples of deontological theories.

Descriptive   See **prescriptive and descriptive**.

Dilemma   See **moral dilemma**.

Disposition   Our tendency to behave in certain ways, our character traits. This term is used by **virtue ethicists**, who believe we ought to develop virtuous dispositions.

Divine command ethics   A type of deontological ethical theory, which claims that the moral value of an action is determined by the commands of God. So an action is right if it follows one of God's commands.

Duty   An action which we are required or impelled to carry out. Kant's deontological theory places duty at its centre. For Kant, duties are experienced as **imperatives**. See also **prima facie duties**.

Emotivism/emotivist   A **non-cognitivist** theory of the meaning of moral terms and judgements. In its basic form, emotivism claims that moral judgements do not refer to anything in the world, but are expressions of feelings of approval or disapproval.

Empirical fact   A fact established by observation.

Empiricism/empiricist   The claim that our beliefs and knowledge must be based on experience.

Eudaimonia   According to many ancient Greek philosophers *eudaimonia* is the goal or 'good' we are all striving for. Sometimes translated as 'happiness', it is probably closer in meaning to 'flourishing'. Aristotle's virtue ethics is centred around *eudaimonia*.

Fallacy   This refers to an **argument** which has gone wrong, either because a mistake has been made, rendering the argument invalid; or because the argument has a form, or structure, which is always invalid (see also the **naturalistic fallacy**).

Golden rule   Versions of this rule have been proposed at various points within religion and moral philosophy (e.g. by Confucius, Jesus, Hobbes and Kant). The basic idea is that we should be impartial, and not afford ourselves special treatment: we should treat others as we should like to be treated. See also **universalisability**.

Good   Actions are good according to whether they bring about certain positive outcomes – these may be pleasure or happiness, or something more intangible (Moore believed that love of friendship and beauty were goods). **Consequentialists** believe that moral value lies in the good (or bad) consequences of an action. But 'good' also has a functional meaning, in the sense that 'good' means 'fulfilling your function well'. Aristotle believed that we had a function and hence could be good in both senses: by being good (fulfilling our function) we could reach the good (**eudaimonia**).

Hedonism/hedonistic   The claim that pleasure is the good. Many **utilitarians** are hedonists, in that they believe we ought to try to maximise pleasure (for the majority).

Hume's Law   See **is/ought gap**.

Hypothetical imperative   See **imperative**.

Imperative   In **Kantian ethics** we experience our duties as commands (imperatives) which are categorical, or absolute. These categorical imperatives are commands that we are obliged to follow no matter what, and according to Kant only these are moral imperatives. As rational **agents** we can work out the categorical imperative by asking whether the **maxim** that lies behind our action is **universalisable**. Other imperatives, things we should do in order to achieve some goal, are conditional or hypothetical imperatives, and they are not moral according to Kant.

Intuitionism/intuitionist A **realist** theory which claims that we can determine what is right or good according to our moral intuitions. For intuitionists, the terms 'right' and 'good' do refer to something objective, but they cannot be reduced to **naturalistic** terms.

Is/ought gap Hume argued that we cannot draw a conclusion which is evaluative (containing 'ought') from **premises** which are purely factual or descriptive. To some philosophers this indicated the autonomy of ethics, i.e. that the ethical realm was entirely distinct from other, factual or **naturalistic**, realms.

Judgement A moral judgement is a decision made (in advance or retrospectively) about the rightness or goodness of a course of action (our own or someone else's) or, for **virtue** theorists, of someone's character.

Kantian ethics A **deontological** ethical theory developed by Kant or influenced by Kant. At the heart of Kantian ethics is the claim that we can determine what is right, and what our duties are, through the categorical **imperative**.

Maxim A rule underlying our actions. For example, in stealing £10 from your mum's wallet, you would (perhaps unconsciously) be acting on a rule like this: 'When I need money I will take it from my parents without telling them.'

Meta-ethics Sometimes called 'second-order ethics', this is the study by moral philosophers of the meaning of moral **judgements**. This covers issues such as **realism/anti-realism, cognitivism/ non-cognitivism**, the **is/ought gap**, the **naturalistic fallacy**, and the objectivity/subjectivity of moral judgements.

Moral dilemma Any situation that an **agent** faces where there is a difficulty choosing between two or more courses of action. This difficulty arises when there are moral reasons for both choosing and not choosing a course of action. It also arises when there are moral reasons against all courses of action, but where a choice has to be made.

Naturalism The view that we can explain moral concepts, such as good, in naturalistic terms, such as happiness or pleasure.

Naturalistic fallacy G.E. Moore attacked **naturalism** because he claimed that it committed a **fallacy**, namely of trying to define the indefinable. Moore believed that moral terms such as **good** could not be defined (he held they were non-natural), and that naturalists tried to define them in naturalistic terms. He particularly singled out the **utilitarians** in his attack.

Non-cognitivism See **cognitivism and non-cognitivism**.

Normative ethics Sometimes called 'first-order ethics', this term covers moral theories that offer action-guides. These are rules, principles or standards by which we make moral **judgements**, and according to which our conduct is directed. There are three general forms of normative theory: **deontological**, **consequentialist** and **virtue ethics**.

Ontological Ontology is the study of 'being' or 'existence'. If you have an ontological commitment to something then you believe that it exists independently of you (for example, some moral realists have an ontological commitment to moral values).

Person In ordinary language this refers to human beings, but recently some philosophers have asked what is special about persons and whether a) all human beings are persons and b) some non-human beings might count as persons. The sorts of qualities that characterise persons might include **agency**, **autonomy**, rationality, self-consciousness, etc.

Practical ethics Like **normative ethics**, this is also a type of 'first-order' theory. It looks at the application of ethical theories to concrete situations and **moral dilemmas** that people face, such as abortion, euthanasia and the treatment of animals.

Premise Any reason given (usually in the form of a statement or claim) to build or support an **argument**.

Prescriptive and descriptive A prescriptive statement is one that guides action, it tells us what to do. A descriptive statement, on the other hand, simply tells us the way things are.

Prescriptivism A **non-cognitivist** view of the meaning of moral terms and judgements. Like **emotivists**, prescriptivists believe that moral language has a special use, but they believe that the purpose of moral **judgements** is to prescribe actions, in other words to urge others to act in a certain way.

Prima facie A Latin term meaning 'at first sight' or 'as things first appear'.

Prima facie duties A term used by W.D. Ross to describe the 'rough and ready' obligations that we know that we have in advance of any particular situation (such as the obligation to be honest, keep promises, not harm others). Sometimes we face dilemmas where our prima facie duties clash, and we

have to decide what our actual duties are in these circumstances, i.e. which **duty** has the stronger claim over us.

Proposition A proposition is a sentence that makes a claim about the way the world actually is. **Non-cognitivists** such as the **emotivists** claim that moral **judgements** are not propositions, in other words they are not making claims about the world and are neither true nor false.

Rationalism/rationalist The claim that our beliefs and knowledge are properly based on reason (and not, for example, on sensory experience as the **empiricists** claim).

Realism and anti-realism Moral realists believe that in some sense moral terms refer to something real, for example pleasure, or happiness, or utility, or the moral law or God's command. So, from a realist position, morality is discovered. Moral anti-realists believe that moral terms do not refer to anything real, but are something else entirely – for example, expressions of feelings (**emotivism**), prescriptions to other people (**prescriptivism**) or they refer to nothing at all (**nihilism**). See also **cognitivism and non-cognitivism**.

Relativism Moral relativism is the view that moral **judgements** vary according to (are relative to) the social context in which they are made. So, moral values or standards of conduct are different in different societies: what is right for you may not be right for me, etc.

Right Actions are right according to whether they ought to be done, irrespective of the particular situation, or the consequences that result from a course of action. **Deontological** theorists believe that moral value lies solely in what is right (rather than in what is **good**) and that we have obligations or duties to do what is right. However, **consequentialist** theorists are quite happy to redefine 'right' to mean 'actions that bring about the good'.

Rights   A right is an entitlement that I have to the protection of certain powers, interests or privileges. It is debatable whether we can have rights only because we make a contract within society, or whether we have 'natural rights' which exist independently of any contract. Rights may be seen as the converse of duties; thus if I have a right to X then you have a duty to promote X or at least not interfere in my access to X.

Summum bonum   A Latin phrase meaning 'the highest good' or simply 'The Good'. For Aristotle, this was the goal of all human life, and he argued that this consisted in ***eudaimonia***. Other moral philosophers, such as Plato, Mill, Kant and G.E. Moore have put forward very different views on what the Good is.

Tautology   A sentence that is true by definition. For example, 'all bachelors are unmarried' or 'all squares have four sides'.

Teleological   Purpose, goal or end, deriving from the Greek word *telos*. A teleological ethical theory is one that says we should be striving to achieve certain moral goals – for Aristotelians this would be virtue, for **utilitarians** the goal would be happiness. See also **consequentialism**.

Truth-value   The truth or falsity of a **proposition**. Only propositions can have truth-value. Some philosophers (**cognitivists**) claim that moral **judgements** are propositions, but other philosophers (**non-cognitivists**) claim that moral judgements are not propositions and hence do not have a truth-value.

Universalisability   A fundamental feature of most ethical theories, and a version of the **golden rule**. A principle is universalisable if it is applied to all people equally and in the same way. Some philosophers (including **prescriptivists**) have seen this as part of the very meaning of a moral **judgement** – it applies to everyone in the same situation. **Consequentialists** (Bentham and Mill), **deontologists** (Kant) and even existentialists (Sartre) have all appealed to universalisability at some point in their theories. For Kantians, the principle of universalisability has to be a more rigorous version of the golden rule: it says that we should only act on those rules which we can will to be universal laws (i.e. without contradiction or inconsistency).

Utilitarianism   A **consequentialist** moral theory, perhaps inspired by Hume (although he is closer to **virtue ethics**) and developed first by Bentham and then by Mill and Sidgwick. In most of its forms it is a **hedonistic** theory claiming that what is **good** (i.e. what we ought to strive to bring about) is as much pleasure or happiness as possible for the majority of people. In its negative forms it says we ought to strive to reduce pain or harm to the majority of people.

Utility   Welfare or use for the majority of people. For Bentham and Mill, utility came to mean 'pleasure' or 'happiness'.

Utility principle   The principle that an act or object is good in as much as it brings about something that is desired (for most **utilitarians** this is pleasure or happiness). Similarly, for most utilitarians, an act or object is bad insofar as it brings about pain or unhappiness.

Verification principle   The rule put forward by verificationists that a proposition is only meaningful if it can be shown to be true or false by experience or by analysis of the meanings of the terms involved.

Virtue   A character trait or **disposition** which is to be valued (for the ancient Greeks, it is a disposition which is excellent). Common virtues include wisdom, courage, self-control, honesty, generosity, compassion, kindness.

Virtue ethics   A **normative** ethical theory which locates value not in an action or its consequences, but in the **agent** performing the act. Virtue ethicists stress the need to develop virtuous **dispositions**, and to judge actions within the broader context of what someone is inclined to do. So a person may be judged to be virtuous or vicious through noting how they are disposed to act. Frustratingly, for many people, virtue ethicists fail to give us a formula (unlike **consequentialists** and **deontologists**) that guides us in what we ought to do in any particular situation.

Section 2: Philosophy of Mind

Acquaintance knowledge   See **propositional knowledge and acquaintance knowledge**.

Analytic   A proposition is analytic if it is true by definition. This means you can work out that it is true just by analysing the meanings of the words involved. For example, 'All sisters are female'. Analytic propositions are contrasted with 'synthetic' ones for which understanding the meanings of the words involved is not sufficient to determine whether they are true. Knowledge of such propositions therefore requires some knowledge of the way the world is as well. For example, 'All sisters are jealous of their siblings'.

Analytic reduction   To reduce one **phenomenon** to another is to explain one in terms of the other. An analytic **reduction** is concerned with the *meaning* of the language we use to talk about phenomena and claims that all that is said about one phenomenon can be translated into talk about another without loss of meaning. **Analytical behaviourism** claims that conceptual analysis of our talk about minds reveals it to have the same meaning as talk about behaviour and behavioural dispositions. Analytic reductions are contrasted with **ontological reductions** which are a reduction of things rather than meanings.

Analytical (or logical) **behaviourism** Analytical behaviourism is a theory about the meaning of our language of the mind. It claims that our talk of mental states does not involve reference to others' internal states. Rather it is a way of talking about people's behaviour and their dispositions to behave in various ways.

A priori   A priori knowledge is knowledge which can be known without the need for sense experience. By contrast, a posteriori knowledge can only be established by reference to experience. For example, we can know that no bachelors are married without conducting a survey of bachelors' marital status and so this knowledge is a priori, but we could *not* work out what percentage of bachelors are left handed except by some sort of

empirical investigation and so this knowledge is a posteriori.

Automaton (plural **automata**) A mechanism that operates and/or moves automatically, usually resembling a human being. The term is often used to refer to the idea of a being which acts without conscious awareness and so can be used as a synonym for a **philosophical zombie**. But automata may be conscious, as in Huxley's phrase 'conscious automata', used to refer to animals and humans whose actions are not controlled by conscious volitions (see **epiphenomenalism**). The term is also used to refer to a mechanism the operations of which may be described in a **machine table**.

Behaviourism Here used as short for **analytical behaviourism**.

Cartesian dualism 'Cartesian' is the adjective deriving from Descartes' name, so it describes any doctrine expounded by Descartes. 'Cartesian dualism' refers to Descartes' version of mind–body **dualism** and to versions of **substance dualism** inspired by Descartes.

Chauvinism Chauvinism is the ungrounded belief in the superiority of one's own nationality, sex or race. In philosophy of mind it is used to refer to the implication one can draw from certain theories that members of other species (either real or imaginary) could not possess certain types of mental state. This implication is usually taken to represent a problem for such theories. The opposed tendency of allowing too wide a range of beings to count as minded is termed **liberalism**, and is also considered problematic.

Compatibilism Compatibilism is the view that free will is compatible with determinism. In other words, there is no contradiction in the idea of an action which is completely causally determined and yet still free.

Consciousness All that you are directly aware of, including thoughts, emotions and sensations. The contents of the mind.

Contingent A state of affairs is contingent if it happens to be the case, but could have been otherwise. A contingent proposition is one that could be either true or false.

Contingent identity Two things are identical if they are really just one thing. Angela Merkel and the Chancellor of Germany are the same thing in this sense. A contingent identity is one where two things *happen* to be the same, but might not have been. In other words, there is a possible world in which the two are not the same. For example, it is possible for Angela Merkel not to have become Chancellor so this identity is contingent. Mind–brain identity theorists hold that a contingent identity holds between mental states and brain states, so that while they happen to be the same, it is still conceivable that they might have been something else, meaning that there is a possible world in which the mind is some other organ, say, the heart. Such identities cannot be discovered by investigation of the meanings of the terms involved and so can only be established by **empirical** investigation.

Dualism In philosophy of mind, mind–body dualism (or more simply 'dualism') is the view that the mind and body are not identical (i.e. they are *dual*) meaning that the mental cannot be reduced to the physical. Dualism is contrasted with **monism**.

Eliminativism or **eliminative materialism**   The view that **folk-psychological** concepts, such as belief, desire and sensation, do not pick out real entities. Our language of the mind is therefore fundamentally misleading and so should be replaced by terminology forged by a mature **neuroscience**.

Empirical   From experience or observation.

Empiricism/empiricist   The philosophical tendency to regard experience as the sole or most important source of our concepts and knowledge.

Epiphenomenalism   The view that mental states such as sensations and beliefs are caused by states of the brain, but that there is no reciprocal influence of mental states on the brain and body or on other mental states. Thus mental states are by-products of the physical processes that go on in the body which govern our actions.

Experimenting with ideas   The 'thought experiment' is a philosophical technique employed to explore our intuitions about conceptual possibilities and implications. Because they are concerned with what is possible, rather than what is actually the case in the real world, they are conducted in the imagination. There is some controversy about how useful explorations of our intuitions are in establishing what is and is not genuinely possible.

Folk psychology   Folk psychology is the theory of mind (or psychology) held by ordinary people (folk). It is claimed that our everyday picture of the mind as a private world of sensations, emotions, beliefs and so on, constitutes a theoretical framework which we use to explain and predict behaviour. The idea can be used to try to solve the problem of other minds, since if the theory that others possess minds is the best explanation of human behaviour then it is rational to believe in them. But, theories can also be refuted, and **eliminativists** claim that folk psychology will be superseded by the **neuroscience** of the future.

Functional state   A state which is defined in terms of its causal role rather than in terms of what it is made of. Functionalism claims that mental states are functional states of the brain, and so that it is the causal relationship to sensory inputs, other mental states and to behaviour which determines the nature of any mental state.

Hypothetical propositions   An 'if... then...' proposition, for example 'If you were offered a cup of tea, then you would accept.' In Ryle's **analytical behaviourism**, certain mental states are regarded as dispositions to act in various ways and dispositions can be translated into hypotheticals of this kind which detail what a person would do *if* certain circumstances were realised.

Idealism   Idealism is an anti-realist theory of perception. It is the view that matter does not exist independently of the mind and that all that exists are minds and their ideas. Physical objects are no more than collections of sensations appearing in minds.

Intentionality   The quality of certain mental states which directs them beyond themselves and to things in the world. It's what makes mental states such as beliefs, desires and fears *about* something. For example, my belief that it is raining is about the rain, and my fear of heights it about heights.

Interactionism   The common sense view that mind and body are in causal interaction, so that mental events such as acts of will or decisions, can cause actions and that events in the body, such as changes brought about by the impact of the environment on our sense organs, can cause mental events such as sensations.

Intersubjective   The relationship between distinct subjects of experience. The awareness one person has of other persons and other persons' consciousnesses.

Introspection   The process of looking into your own mind. The direct awareness each of us has of his or her own mental states.

Leibniz's Law   Also known as the principle of the identity of indiscernibles, the law states that no two objects can share *all* their properties; so that if what appear to be two objects turn out to have all the same properties, then they must be one object.

Liberalism   The tendency of a theory of mind to count as minded systems we would be reluctant to think of as conscious, such as computers or even simpler mechanisms.

Logical positivism   The twentieth-century school of thought that emphasised the necessity of an **empirical** basis for knowledge and rejected as meaningless 'metaphysical' claims which have no grounding in experience. Logical positivists, such as Ayer, held that all meaningful propositions must either be statements of logic or mathematics and so purely analytic, or confirmable by empirical means (that is 'verifiable').

Machine state functionalism   Machine state functionalism is the view that minded human beings are to be understood as a complex system of inputs and outputs, the inputs being sensory and the outputs behavioural. Mental states are the internal states that can be specified by a **machine table**. The mind is the software that 'runs' on the hardware of the brain.

Machine table   A representation of the set of instructions for a machine which details how it responds to different inputs.

Materialism   A synonym for **physicalism**. The view that the mind is ultimately material in nature and so is not distinct from the physical body.

Meaning and reference   Frege (in 'Über Sinn und Bedeutung', 1892) distinguished the reference (*Bedeutung*) of a term from its meaning (*Sinn*). The reference is the thing in the world that the term refers to; the meaning is the way the term presents the reference to the mind. It is possible for a term to have the same reference but different meanings. For example, the expression 'half-blood prince' has a different meaning to 'Severus Snape' and yet they refer to the same person. It is because expressions can have different meanings but the same reference that it is possible for someone not to realise that two terms refer to the same objects. According to the identity theory, the terms we use to talk about mental states have different meanings from the terms we use to talk about brain states, but they nonetheless refer to the same things.

Monism   In philosophy of mind, the view that humans are composed of just one type of substance.

Multiply realisable   Mental states are multiply realisable if the same type of mental state may be instantiated in different types of brain state. This means that a mental state, such as pain, can occur in different creatures with very different types of brain.

Neuroscience   The science of the brain.

Nomological danglers   'Nomological' concerns the formulation of a system of laws or scientific theories used to explain natural **phenomena**. A nomological dangler is a phenomenon which cannot be explained by reference to such a theory or system of laws. Smart uses the term in the Anthology article 'Sensations and brain processes' to refer to the irreducible mental properties posited by **dualists** and argues that they should be rejected because they don't fit in with the established laws of physics.

Numerical and qualitative identity   It is possible to distinguish two senses of the 'same'. Things are qualitatively the same if they share properties. Since different copies of this book share many properties they can be termed *qualitatively identical*. But one copy is still a different thing from another. They are not literally one and the same object and so are not *numerically identical*. Numerical identity is the sameness a thing has with itself and nothing else, so the copy you are holding is qualitatively identical with other copies, but can only be numerically identical with itself.

Occasionalism   The difficulty of explaining how two distinct substances, mind and body, could causally interact has led some to suppose that they instead run in parallel. Malebranche's occasionalism claims that the only true cause is God

and that he directly causes changes in the mind and the body in such a way as to produce the appearance of a direct causal connection.

Ockham's razor   The principle that when constructing hypotheses we should avoid multiplying entities beyond necessity. So if two competing theories both explain some **phenomenon** equally well, it is reasonable to prefer the one that is simpler or makes fewer assumptions. **Physicalists** sometimes invoke this principle against **dualism**, arguing that the **ontological** commitment to two substances is unnecessary.

Ontological   To do with being or real existence. An ontological category is a type of being or thing, such as minds or physical substance. An ontological commitment is a commitment to the existence of some type of thing, that is the belief or assertion that a certain type of thing exists. **Dualists** have an ontological commitment to minds as a distinct type of being from matter.

Ontological reduction   An ontological reduction is an explanation of one kind of **phenomenon** in terms of something more fundamental, as when chemists tell us water is H_2O, or the identity theory tries to explain the mind in terms of the brain. If one phenomenon can be ontologically reduced to another this means they are ultimately the same things under different descriptions. But it doesn't mean that the terms used to refer to them have the same meanings and so doesn't mean that the one can be analytically reduced to the other (see **analytic reduction**).

Ontology   An account of what exists.

Parallelism   Theories of mind that deny a direct causal interconnection between mind and body. Instead the two are coordinated, usually by the involvement of God. See **occasionalism** and **pre-established harmony**.

Phenomenal   Concerning the way things appear. The character of what one is directly aware of in the mind.

Phenomenon (plural **phenomena**) From the Greek for 'appearance', a phenomenon is anything that appears or is shown. Here the term is mostly used to refer to what appears to the mind; or that which is revealed in conscious experience. The term may also be used more generally to refer to the aspects of things that show themselves or are apparent, but which need to be explained in terms of some theory.

Physicalism (or **materialism**)   The view that everything in the universe is physical. In the philosophy of mind this means that mental states must ultimately be reducible to the physical and so mentality doesn't constitute a distinct type of **phenomenon**.

Pre-established harmony   Leibniz's account of the relationship between mind and body which denies **interactionism**. Distinct substances cannot causally influence one another directly, despite appearances. Rather God creates all substances with a pre-programmed course to follow so that each independently develops under its own internal dynamic but is coordinated with the development of all other substances.

Property   A property is something that depends on something else for its existence (see **substance and property**).

Property dualism   Unlike **substance dualism**, property dualism claims that humans are composed of just one kind of substance: matter. However, what makes it a dualist theory is the claim that we possess both mental and physical properties. Mental states are dependent on the physical, so that the mind cannot exist without the body, but at the same time mental states cannot be reduced to physical states.

Propositional knowledge and acquaintance knowledge Propositional knowledge is knowledge of facts or knowledge *that* something is the case. Acquaintance knowledge is the knowledge you obtain by encountering or experiencing something. The distinction is employed in an objection to Jackson's knowledge argument, 'Mary gains no new propositional knowledge'.

Qualia (singular **quale**)   The subjective feel, or **phenomenal** quality of certain conscious experiences, for example what it is like to smell petrol, the way an apple tastes, or how a cat's fur feels. An important problem for **physicalism** concerns whether the subjective nature of such experiences can be accounted for in objective physical terms.

Qualitative identity   See **numerical and qualitative identity**.

Reduction   To reduce one type of thing to another is to explain the first in terms of the second. See **ontological reduction** and **analytic reduction**.

Reference   See **meaning and reference**.

Semantics/syntax   Semantics concerns the meanings of words and sentences. Syntax concerns the rules governing correct linguistic usage. Searle employs the distinction in his Chinese room argument, claiming that a computer may be programmed to follow syntactic rules, and could conceivably pass the **Turing test**, but it could not understand the semantics of natural language.

Solipsism   The view that nothing beyond my own mind, including the external world and other minds, can be known to exist.

Subject of experience   That which is conscious; the self or 'I'.

Substance and property   A substance is a basic kind of stuff or thing, something which doesn't depend on anything else to exist. A property, by contrast, cannot exist on its own, but depends on a substance. While **substance dualism** claims that there are two substances and so two fundamental types of thing in the world, **physicalists** claim there is just one – matter. **Property dualists** agree with physicalists that matter is the only substance, but argue that when it is organised properly into persons with brains it also has irreducible mental properties.

Substance dualism   The view that humans are composed of two types of substance: mind and matter.

Super-spartans   In the Anthology extract 'Psychological predicates' (1967), Putnam develops a thought experiment as a refutation of **analytical behaviourism** involving people who are able to suppress all outward signs of pain. He terms them super-spartans after the Spartans of ancient Greece, who were famed for their stoicism.

Supervenience   The nature of the dependence relationship often said to hold between mind and brain. Mental states would supervene on brain states if there can be no difference in the mental without a difference in the brain. But at the same time a difference in the brain need not produce a difference in the mind.

Syntax   See **semantics**.

Turing test   A test suggested by Alan Turing in his paper 'Computing, machinery and intelligence' (1950) for determining whether a computer could be considered able to think. If a machine's linguistic competence when engaged in conversation cannot be distinguished from that of a human being then it would pass the test.

Type and **token**   A type is a general class or kind of thing; a token is a particular instance of a type. For example, there are four tokens of the word 'a' in the previous sentence and each is a token of the same type.

Type and **token identity**   The mind–brain identity theory claims that mental states are the same things as brain states. If mental states are type-identical with brain states, then each token of a type of mental state is the same as different tokens of the same type of brain state. So pain in me and pain in you will be the same type of neurological event, say C-fibres firing. But if mental states are token identical with brain states, then each token of a given type of mental state may be identical with tokens of different types of brain state. So pain in me may be a different type of brain event than in you, or a dog or a Martian.

Verificationism   Verificationism is a claim associated with **logical positivism** that a proposition is only meaningful if it is either verifiable by experience or is analytic. The idea that meaningful utterances must tell us about the world by making some difference to our experience may be used to question whether it is meaningful to speak of other minds as necessarily private, of the possibility of spectrum inversion, or of mental states with no behavioural manifestation. For claims about mental states which cannot be identified would be empty of factual significance and so meaningless. The principle may also be used to argue that the idea of **philosophical zombies** is incoherent, since no **empirical** test could be devised to distinguish them from ordinary people. Considerations inspired by verificationism may lead to **analytical behaviourism** and the idea that to speak meaningfully about minds, we must be referring to what can be observed, namely behaviour.

Volition   An act of will which leads to a bodily movement. The mental state which initiates freely chosen actions.

Will   The mental power or faculty which enables us to perform acts of volition.

Zombie or **philosophical zombie**
A philosophical zombie is a hypothetical being which is physically indistinguishable from a regular human being, but which has no consciousness or subjective awareness. The idea is discussed by Chalmers in Anthology extract 2.5.

Notes

1.1

1   Peter Singer (1974), 'Philosophers are back on the job', in P. Singer (ed. H. Kuhse) (2002) *Unsanctifying Human Life*, Blackwell, p. 62.

2   Kohlberg, L. (1981), Essays on Moral Development, Vol 1: The Philosophy of Moral Development, San Francisco: Harper & Row.

1.1.1

1   Jeremy Bentham (1789), *Introduction to the Principles of Morals and Legislation*, Clarendon Press (2nd edn 1823, reprint 1907), p. 1.

2   R. Nozick (1974), *Anarchy, State, and Utopia*, Blackwell.

3   Bentham, *Introduction to the Principles of Morals and Legislation*, p. 3.

4   Bentham (1776), 'A Fragment on Government' in J. Burns and H. Hart (eds) (1977), *The Collected Works of Jeremy Bentham*: Clarendon, p. 393. Bentham wrote the fragment in 1776, but it was not published until the twentieth century.

5   Bentham (1830), *The Rationale of Rewar*, Robert Heward, p. 206.

6   John Stuart Mill (1863), *Utilitarianism*, J. Bennett (ed.) (2005), online edition: www.earlymoderntexts.com, p. 5.

7   Ibid., p. 24 (note that we have quoted the original version, Bennett's version changes the syntax a little).

8   Ibid., p. 6.

9   Ibid., p. 7.

10 Ibid., p. 7.

11 Ibid., pp. 7–8.

12 Mill (1859), *On Liberty*, J. Bennett (ed.) (2005), online edition: www.earlymoderntexts.com, p. 7.

13 Mill, *Utilitarianism*, p. 18.

14 Ibid., p. 18.

15 Bentham, *Introduction to the Principles of Morals and Legislation*, p. 311.

16 This example is taken from T.L.S. Sprigge (1988) 'Utilitarianism', G.H.R. Parkinson (ed.) (1988), *An Encyclopedia of Philosophy*, Routledge.

17 Bentham (1827), *Rationale of Judicial Evidence, Specially Applied to English Practice*, in *The Works of Jeremy Bentham*, ed. J. Bowring (Edinburgh, 1838–43), vii 334.

18 Mill, *Utilitarianism*, p. 12.

19 Singer (1972) 'Famine, Affluence, and Morality', in *Unsanctifying Human Life*, p. 149.

20 Singer (1972) 'William Godwin and the Defense of Impartialist Ethics' in ibid., p. 174.

21 Bentham, *Introduction to the Principles of Morals and Legislation*, p. 170.

22 Ibid.

23 *Guardian*, Friday 16 January 2004 (accessed online March 2015).

24 Bentham, 'On War', in J. Bowring (ed.) (1843), *The Works of Jeremy Bentham, Volume 2*, p. 544.

25 Mill, *On Liberty*, p. 7.

26 Singer (1975), *Animal Liberation*, New York Review Books, p. 38.

27 Singer (1974), 'All Animals are Equal', in *Unsanctifying Human Life*, p. 87.

28 Singer (2006), Press release essay on the Great Ape Project, Guardian website, 27 May (accessed March 2015).

1.1.2

1   Immanuel Kant (1788), *Critique of Practical Reason*, trans. T.K. Abbott (1873), Longman, p. 260.

2   Kant (1785), *Grounding for the Metaphysics of Morals*, 3rd edn, trans. J.W. Ellington (1993), Hackett, p. 30. This is a clearer version of the first formulation than the Abbot translation which is the one recommended by AQA.

3   Ibid., p. 41.

4   Kant, *Groundwork of the Metaphysics of Morals*, trans. T.K. Abbott (1895), www.gutenberg.org, p. 8.

5   Ibid., p. 16.

6   Ibid., p. 19.

7   Ibid., p. 33.

8   Kant, *Grounding for the Metaphysics of Morals*, trans. Ellington, p. 30.

9   Kant, *Groundwork of the Metaphysics of Morals*, trans. Abbott, p. 20.

10 Kant, *Grounding for the Metaphysics of Morals*, trans. Ellington, p. 41.

11 Ibid., p. 46.

12 Kant, I. (1797), *Metaphysics of Morals*, trans. M. Gregor (1999), Cambridge University Press, section VI 405.

13 Carol Gilligan (1982), *In a Different Voice*, Harvard University Press.

14 Ibid.

15 B. Williams (1985), *Ethics and the Limits of Philosophy*, Fontana, pp. 66–9.

16 Kant, *Metaphysics of Morals*, section VI 224.

17 Jean-Paul Sartre (1987), *Existentialism and Humanism*, Methuen, pp. 35–8.

18 Kant, *Metaphysics of Morals*, section VI 333.

19 Ibid., section VI 332 (p. 473).

20 James Rachels (1995), *The Elements of Moral Philosophy*, 2nd edn, McGraw-Hill, p. 133.

21 Kant, *Metaphysics of Morals*, section VI 347 (p. 484).

22 Kant (1795), *Perpetual Peace: A Philosophical Sketch*, trans 1927, George Allen & Unwin, section 1.

23 Ibid.

24 Kant (1997), *Lectures on Ethics*, trans./ed. P. Heath and J. Scheewind, Cambridge University Press, p. 240.

25 Kant, *Metaphysics of Morals*, section VI 457 (p. 575).

26 Kant (1798), *Lectures on Anthropology*, trans 1979, Akademie-Textausgabe, 7, p. 127.

27 Jeremy Bentham (1789), *Introduction to the Principles of Morals and Legislation*, Clarendon Press (2nd edn 1823, reprint 1907), p. 311.

1.1.3

1   The opening lines from the labyrinthine gangster film *Miller's Crossing*, directed by Joel Coen, 1990.

2   Julia Annas (2004), 'Ancient ethics and modern morality', in James Sterba (ed.), *Ethics: The Big Questions*, Blackwell, pp. 311–12.

3   We follow the convention here of using the figures and numbers corresponding to the relevant pages, columns and lines of Bekker's Greek text.

4   See Jeremy Hayward, Gerald Jones and Daniel Cardinal (2014), *AQA AS Philosophy*, Hodder Education, pp. 167–9.

5   For example, Michael Pakaluk (2005), *Aristotle's Nicomachean Ethics: An introduction*, Cambridge University Press, pp. 48–51. If Aristotle were offering a proof that 'all acts are aimed at some good, therefore there is some good all acts are aimed at' it would be guilty of the 'Quantifier Shift Fallacy'.

6   There are daemons attached to all the characters in Philip Pullman's trilogy *His Dark Materials*, and in Plato's dialogue, *Phaedrus* 242b, Socrates reveals that his daemon reprimands him about the speech on Love he has just given and advises him to give another, more honest one.

7   Although we refer throughout this section to human beings, Aristotle in the *Ethics* talks only of men, and it is probably the case that he is not including women, or 'barbarians' or slaves when analysing the concept of *eudaimonia*.

8   Alasdair MacIntyre (1971), *A Short History of Ethics*, Routledge, pp. 7–9.

9   Although, for Aristotle, plants cannot really be *eudaimon* – only humans can truly flourish in this sense.

10 Kathleen Wilkes (1980), 'The Good Man and the Good for Man in Aristotle's Ethics', in Amelie Oksenberg Rorty (ed.), *Essays on Aristotle's Ethics*, University of California Press, pp. 341–56.

11 Hayward, Jones and Cardinal, *AQA AS Philosophy*, pp. 249–50.

12 Alasdair MacIntyre (1981), *After Virtue*, Duckworth, p. 174ff.

13 For example, see Daniel Goleman (1995), *Emotional Intelligence: Why it can matter more than IQ*, Bloomsbury, pp. IX–XIV.

14 MacIntyre (1971), *A Short History of Ethics*, Routledge, p. 80.

15 Jones, Cardinal and Hayward (2006), *Moral Philosophy: a guide to ethical theory*, Hodder Murray, pp. 111–14.

16 See Plato (1987), *The Republic*, 331c, Penguin, p. 66, and Kant's essay 'On a supposed right to lie from altruistic motives', extract in Christine Korsgaard (2004), 'Kant on dealing with evil', in James Sterba (ed.), *Ethics: The Big Questions*, Blackwell, p. 199.

17 Rosalind Hursthouse (1999), *On Virtue Ethics*, Open University Press, pp. 44–8.

18 We offer our own toolkit which can help develop ethical thinking skills in Jones, Cardinal, Hayward, *Moral Philosophy*, pp. 219–31.

19 Hursthouse, *On Virtue Ethics*, pp. 36–9.

20 James Rachels (2003), *The Elements of Moral Philosophy*, McGraw-Hill, pp. 184–5.

21 J.L. Mackie (1990), *Ethics: Inventing Right and Wrong*, Penguin, p. 186.

22 St Thomas Aquinas, *Commentary on the Nicomachean Ethics*, trans. C.I. Litzinger (1964), Chicago, pp. 546–7.

23 Hursthouse (1999), *Humans and Other Animals*, Open University Press, p. 173.

24 Rachels, *The Elements of Moral Philosophy*, pp. 186–7.

25 Alasdair MacIntyre (1981), *After Virtue*, Duckworth, p. 179.

26 Mark A. Costanzo and Ellen Gerrity (2009), 'The Effects and Effectiveness of Using Torture as an Interrogation Device: Using Research to Inform the Policy Debate', *Social Issues and Policy Review*, Vol. 3, No. 1, pp. 179–210.

27 See for example, Aristotle, *Politics*, 1333a30.

28 Matt McCormick (2001), 'Is it wrong to play violent video games', *Ethics and Information Technology*, Vol. 3, p. 277.

29 Christopher Vogler (2007), *The Writer's Journey: Mythic Structure for Storytellers and Screenwriters*, Michael Weise Productions.

30 Martha Nussbaum (1986), *The Fragility of Goodness: Luck and Ethics in Greek Tragedy and Philosophy*, University of Chicago, ch. 11.

31 Hursthouse (2006), 'Applying Virtue Ethics to our Treatment of the Other Animals', in J. Welchmen (ed.), *The Practice of Virtue*, Hackett, p. 137.

32 Tom Regan (2004), *The Case for Animal Rights*, University of California, p. 198.

33 Peter Geach (1979), *The Virtues*, Cambridge University Press, p. 114.

1.2

1 Primo Levi (1987), *If This Is A Man*, Abacus, p. 92.

2 Ibid., p. 177.

3 In philosophy the prefix 'meta' has come to mean something like 'beyond' or 'at a more abstract level'. This is quite odd because 'meta' in ancient Greek in fact means 'after'. The story goes that in the first century BC Andronicus of Rhodes was wondering what to name a work by Aristotle in his catalogue. This unnamed work dealt with certain theoretical issues about the fundamental nature of the universe, and it was placed in the catalogue after Aristotle's work on physics. Hence it was called *Metaphysics* (i.e. 'after physics').

4 Cardinal, Jones and Hayward (2014), *AQA AS Philosophy*, Hodder Education, pp. 317–19.

5 Ibid., pp. 318–19.

6 Jonathan Swift (1985), *Gulliver's Travels*, Penguin, pp. 230–1.

7 Another particularly brilliant invention is a huge machine, manually operated, which could write philosophy books by printing out every combination of word that there is. Ibid. pp. 227–9.

8 John Stuart Mill, *Utilitarianism*, ed. Mary Warnock, Fontana, p. 257.

9 Henry Sidgwick (1874, reprinted 2012), *Methods of Ethics*, Cambridge University Press, Book 3, ch. 3, section 5.

10 Hume, *Treatise of Human Nature*, III.1.1, p. 469.

11 J.R. Searle (1969), 'How to derive an ought from an is', in W.D. Hudson (ed.), *The Is/Ought Question*, Macmillan, pp. 120–34.

12 Moore, *Principia Ethica*, Preface, p. x.

13 Ibid. p. 15.

14 Well, maybe not that absurd. Some philosophers, possibly ones with a lot of time on their hands, have doubted whether all unmarried men are in fact bachelors. See Terry Winograd's article 'Moving the semantic fulcrum', *Linguistics and Philosophy*, Vol. 8, No. 1 (1985), pp. 91–104.

15 Moore, *Principia Ethica*, p. 67.

16 Mary Warnock in her introduction to Mill, *Utilitarianism*, p. 26.

17 Moore, *Principia Ethica*, p. 224.

18 These are the words of the economist J.M. Keynes, as quoted in MacIntyre, *After Virtue*, p. 15.

19 H.A. Prichard (1949), 'Does moral philosophy rest on a mistake?', in *Moral Obligation*, Oxford University Press, p. 8.

20 Prichard, like many of his fellow moral philosophers of that time, puts forward slightly more gentle examples, such as wondering whether we have a duty to slow down as we approach a main road! For Mary Warnock, it was examples such as these that revealed the impoverished and trivialising nature of much meta-ethical philosophy, and its failure to address the real moral issues that confronted humanity in the twentieth century: genocide, starvation, the exploitation of developing nations, the threat of nuclear war. See Warnock (1960), *Ethics since 1900*, Oxford University Press, pp. 132–3.

21 W.D. Hudson (1984), *Modern Moral Philosophy*, Palgrave Macmillan, p. 91.

22 G.J. Warnock (1970), *Contemporary Moral Philosophy*, Macmillan, p. 16.

23 Hayward, Jones and Cardinal, *AQA AS Philosophy*, pp. 296–7.

24 J.L. Mackie (1977), *Ethics: Inventing Right and Wrong*, Penguin, p. 35.

25 Ibid., p. 38.

26 Hayward, Jones and Cardinal, *AQA AS Philosophy*, pp. 167–9, 186.

27 For example, see Charles R. Pidgen (1997), 'Naturalism', in Peter Singer (ed.), *A Companion to Ethics*, Blackwell, p. 423.

28 Hume, *Treatise*, II.3.3, p. 416.

29 Ibid., III.1.1.

30 A.J. Ayer (1936), *Language, Truth and Logic*, Dover, p. 143.

31 Alasdair MacIntyre (1981), *After Virtue*, Duckworth, p. 16.

32 Ayer, *Language, Truth and Logic*, p. 142.

33 C.K. Ogden and I.A. Richards (1923), *The Meaning of Meaning*, Kegan Paul, p. 125.

34 MacIntyre, *After Virtue*, p. 17.

35 R.M. Hare (1952), *The Language of Morals*, Oxford University Press, p. 168.

36 Sample quote: '*Ethics, as I conceive it, is the logical study of the language of morals*', ibid, p. iii.

37 Although we haven't mentioned him, the shadow of Wittgenstein is present throughout this chapter, as it is throughout the twentieth century philosophy of language. It was Wittgenstein who urged philosophers to turn their attention to the meaning of terms in ordinary language usage. It is only by looking at how terms are used that we will understand their meaning, and Wittgenstein says terms are used in very many different ways. So any theory such as emotivism which claims to have found the 'single' meaning is bound to be oversimplifying the case.

38 R.M. Hare, *The Language of Morals*, p. 91.

39 G.J. Warnock *Contemporary Moral Philosophy*, p. 30.

40 Ibid., p. 35.

41 Jared Diamond (2002) lists dozens of twentieth-century genocides in *The Rise and Fall of the Third Chimpanzee*, Vintage, pp. 256–8.

2.1

1 Descartes, *Meditations on First Philosophy*, Meditation 2.

2 David Chalmers (2003), 'Consciousness and its place in nature', in S. Stich and T. Warfield (eds), *Blackwell Guide to Philosophy of Mind*, Blackwell, p. 3.

3 J. Levine (1983), 'Materialism and Qualia: The Explanatory Gap', *Pacific Philosophical Quarterly*, Vol. 64, pp. 354–61.

4 Other monists claim that the one ultimate reality is neither mental or physical and so is neutral about its nature; a view known as *neutral monism*.

5 *Meditation 6.*

6 *Meditation 2.*

7 Descartes in the *Synopsis of the Meditations*.

8 *Synopsis of the Meditations.*

9 For a further philosophical discussion of this topic see Thomas Nagel (1971), 'Brain Bisection and the Unity of Consciousness', *Synthese*, Vol. 22 (May), pp. 396–413.

10 Hume, *Treatise on Human Nature*, I.iv.6.

11 Ibid., I.iv.6.

12 *Meditation 2.*

13 Jonathan Bennett, 'Objections to the Meditations with Descartes' Replies', *The Fourth Objections*, available at: http://www.earlymoderntexts.com/pdfs/descartes1642_2.pdf, pp. 56–7.

14 *Meditation 6.*

15 Descartes (1644), *Principles of Philosophy*, section 169.

16 See also *Meditation 6* where Descartes discusses the role of the brain and the functions of the nervous system.

17 Charles Darwin (1859), *On the Origin of Species*, John Murray.

18 Because Descartes held that the essential nature of the mind is consciousness, he was committed to the idea that a person couldn't cease to be conscious without ceasing to have a mind. Sleep, therefore, would seem to involve the destruction of the mind and with it the person you are. Rather than accept this, he argued that we remain conscious throughout sleep, that is, we dream continually even if we don't afterwards remember all our dreams. Modern brain scanning techniques again, however, appear to show that much of sleep is dreamless and anaesthesia also shows that it is possible to deactivate consciousness and this also strongly suggests that the brain needs to be active for consciousness to appear.

19 Leibniz (1714), *Monadology*, section 17.

20 Anthology extract 2.1: Chalmers, 'Consciousness and its place in nature'.

21 Ibid.

22 Ibid.

23 Ludwig Wittgenstein (1953), *Philosophical Investigations*, Basil Blackwell, p. 126.

24 Dan Dennett (1995), 'The Unimagined Preposterousness of Zombies', *Journal of Consciousness Studies*, Vol. 2, pp. 322–6 (at p. 325).

25 Ibid., p. 325.

26 F. Jackson (1982), 'Epiphenomenal Qualia', *The Philosophical Quarterly*, Vol. 32, No. 127 (April), pp. 127–136 (at p. 127).

27 Ibid.

28 Ibid.

29 D. Lewis (1988), 'What Experience Teaches'. in J. Copley-Coltheart (ed.), *Proceedings of the Russellian Society*, Vol. 13, pp. 29–57. Reprinted in Ludlow et al., 2004. Jackson's response is given in 'What Mary didn't know'.

30 Patricia Churchland (1986), *Neurophilosophy: Toward a Unified Science of the Mind-Brain*, The MIT Press, p. 332.

31 Dennett (1991), *Consciousness Explained*, Allan Lane Penguin Press, p. 401.

32 Dennett (1988), 'Quining Qualia', in A. Marcel and E. Bisiach (eds), *Consciousness in Contemporary Science*, Oxford University Press, pp. 43–77 (at p. 43).

33 Paul Churchland (1981) 'Eliminative materialism and the propositional attitudes', *The Journal of Philosophy*, Vol. 78, No. 2 (February), pp. 67–90.

34 Examples from 'Quining Qualia', p. 383.

35 Wittgenstein, *Philosophical Investigations*, section 293.

36 Descartes, *Meditation 6.*

37 Letter from Princess Elisabeth of Bohemia to Descartes, 6 May 1643, available at: http://www.earlymoderntexts.com/pdfs/descartes1643_1.pdf, p. 2.

38 Ibid.

39 Ibid.

40 C.D. Broad (1925), *Mind and Its Place in Nature*, ch. 3, available at: http://www.ditext.com/broad/mpn3.html

41 Hume, *Enquiry Concerning Human Understanding*, Book 1, section 4, para. 25.

42 Ibid., para. 23.

43 Ibid., para. 25.

44 George Santayana (1930), *The Realm of Matter*, Scribner.

45 Thomas Henry Huxley (1874), 'On the Hypothesis that Animals are Automata, and its History,' available at: http://facultypages. morris.umn.edu/~mcollier/Philosophy%20 of%20Mind/huxley.pdf

46 Descartes, *Passions of the Soul*, Art. xiii.

47 Huxley, On the Hypothesis that Animals are Automata, and its history', p. 240.

48 Ibid., p. 244.

49 Ibid., p. 240.

50 Ibid., p. 244.

51 B. Libet (1985), 'Unconscious cerebral initiative and the role of conscious will in voluntary action', *Behavioral and Brain Sciences*, Vol. 8: pp. 529–66.

52 Huxley, 'On the Hypothesis that Animals are Automata, and its history', p. 241.

53 Jackson, 'Epiphenomenal Qualia', pp. 135–6.

54 Wittgenstein, *Philosophical Investigations*, section 293.

55 Gilbert Ryle (1949), *The Concept of Mind*, Routledge, p. 15.

56 Ibid., p. 15.

57 Mill, *Examination of Sir William Hamilton's Philosophy*, ch. 12, cf. Hospers *Introduction to Philosophical Analysis*, p. 252.

58 Ryle, *The Concept of Mind*, p. 51.

59 Wittgenstein, *Philosophical Investigations*, section 398.

60 Ibid., sections 243–315.

61 Descartes, *A Discourse on Method*, part v.

2.2

1 Also known as logical or philosophical behaviourism.

2 A.J. Ayer (1936) *Language, Truth, and Logic*, Victor Gollancz, ch. 7.

3 Carl Hempel (1998), 'The logical analysis of psychology', J. Heil (ed.), *Philosophy of Mind. A Guide and Anthology*, Oxford University Press, pp. 84–95 (at p. 89).

4 Gilbert Ryle, *The Concept of Mind*, first published 1949 by Hutchinson. This edition published 2009 by Routledge.

5 Ibid., p. 7.

6 'Descartes' Myth' is the title of the first Chapter of *The Concept of Mind* where Ryle attacks Cartesian dualism.

7 Ryle, *The Concept of Mind*, p. 14.

8 Ibid., p. 34.

9 Ibid., p. 94.

10 Ibid., p. 38.

11 Ibid., p. 101.

12 Ibid., p. 106.

13 Hilary Putnam (2004), 'Brains and behaviour', in J. Heil (ed.), *Philosophy of Mind. A Guide and Anthology*, p. 102.

14 Ibid., p. 104.

15 J.J.C. Smart (2004), 'Sensations and brain processes', in J. Heil (ed.), *Philosophy of Mind*, pp. 116–27, (at p. 119).

16 Ibid., pp. 117–18.

17 Putnam (2004), 'Psychological predicates', in J. Heil (ed.), *Philosophy of Mind*, pp. 158–67 (at p. 159).

18 C-fibres are nerve fibres responsible for pain.

19 The distinction is due to Gottlob Frege in his paper 'On sense and reference', *Über Sinn und Bedeutung*, 1892.

20 Putnam, 'Psychological predicates', p. 160.

21 Ned Block (1978), 'Troubles with Functionalism', in C.W. Savage (ed.), *Perception and Cognition*, University of Minnesota Press, pp. 261–325 (at p. 265).

22 See S. Kripke (1972), 'Naming and necessity', in D. Davidson and G. Harman (eds), *Semantics and natural language*, Reidel.

23 Putnam, 'Psychological predicates', p. 162.

24 Ibid., p. 164.

25 Ibid., p. 166.

26 Example from Block's 'flea-head' discussion in 'Troubles with functionalism', Section 1.4.

27 Block, 'Troubles with functionalism', section 1.6, p. 293.

28 His story is dramatised in a film, *The Imitation Game* (2014).

29 J. Searle (1980), 'Minds, Brains and Programs', *Behavioral and Brain Sciences*, Vol. 3, pp. 417–57.

30 Stephen Pinker (1997), *How the Mind Works*.

31 Dennett (1987), *The Intentional Stance*, The Massachusetts Institute of Technology.

32 Paul Churchland (1981), 'Eliminative materialism and the propositional attitudes', *Journal of Philosophy*, Vol. 78, No. 2 (February), pp. 67–90 (at p. 67).

33 There remains some controversy over this which we can ignore for our purposes.

34 Ibid.

35 Ibid., p. 68.

36 Ibid., p. 74.

37 Ibid., p. 74.

38 Ibid., p. 70.

39 Ibid., pp. 72–3.

40 A phrase Churchland borrows from the philosopher of science Imre Lakatos (1922–74), ibid. p. 75.

41 Ibid., p. 89.

42 Ibid., pp. 89–90.

Index